CONTAINS HUNDREDS OF
COST-CUTTING IDEAS!!!

SHRINKING
THE
CORPORATE
WAISTLINE

BRIAN P. WOOLF
Former CFO of Food Lion, Inc.

Don J. Beville, Publisher

FINE BOOKS DIVISION

CADMUS PUBLISHING GROUP

1934 E. Parham Road, Richmond, VA 23228

(800) 899-8833 · (804) 266-0140

Guarantee

If you don't save many times the cost of this book from applying its ideas please return it, with your sales receipt, for a refund.

Return to publisher:

Teal Books
P.O. Box 16405
Greenville, SC   29606

Tel: (803) 458-8277

Guarantee expires December 31, 1995.

Dedication

This book is dedicated to Ralph W. Ketner and
Tom E. Smith . . . two cost-conscious grand masters
from whom I learned so much.

To order additional copies of this book you may:

- contact your local bookstore, or
- call 1-800-345-0096 (VISA/MC), or
- use the order form on page 228, or
- for quantity discounts, call (803) 458-8277.

Printed in the United States of America.

Library of Congress Cataloging-in-Publication Data
91-091554

ISBN: 0–9632025–1-0

Woolf, Brian P. 1943-

Shrinking the Corporate Waistline

CONTENTS

INTRODUCTION

Being overweight is just as much a problem for corporations as it is for you and me. And just like for us, it's usually the last ten pounds of corporate fat that are the most difficult to shed. This book is written for those executives who really want to have a leaner organization, who are seeking additional insight into what corporate cost leaders are doing to maintain their very trim waistlines, as measured by their Expenses to Sales ratio. It is also written for the leaders of young businesses who want to grow up lean and stay lean, who wish to avoid adding unnecessary weight as they hit business adolescence and adulthood. Even executives in companies that do not plan to be low-cost operators will find it helpful as it explains the nature and mentality of their cost-conscious competitors.

A fascination with cost saving is not new. Yet it is becoming increasingly more important as companies are subjected to major challenges and changes in the marketplace. As CFO of Food Lion, Inc., I gave many presentations to the investment community. One of the questions I was most frequently asked was: "How does your company have the lowest costs in the industry?" Usually, I would respond: "In the same way as other low-cost operators such as Wal-Mart, Price Club, and Lincoln Electric (all low-cost leaders in their respective industries)— through a company-wide cost-conscious culture that starts at the very top!"

Most cost-saving ideas are common sense. Many are just "ounces" which, collectively, add up to pounds. Cost-saving opportunities are usually thinly layered throughout the whole corporate body with deeper layers in predictable places! There are no magic formulas or tricks when it comes to cost saving. Losing corporate, or personal, weight is not easy. It's a daily event. As an executive devoted to cost reduction, I found knowing what others were doing to keep their corporate waistlines trim extremely helpful. What follows are many of the practices that I noted over the years in the companies for which I have worked or consulted, in their competitors, in visits to companies on three continents, and from studying hundreds of corporate case histories. These practices will provide you with an ideas bank as you consider how to shrink your own corporate waistline.

Focusing on costs has been the benchmark of many great business leaders. Andrew Carnegie's driving dictum, "Watch the costs and the profits will look after themselves," has echoed through the offices and corridors of many outstanding companies. Michael Porter, in his book *Competitive Advantage*, describes a cost advantage as "one of the two types of competitive advantage a firm may possess." The other is differentiation. The beauty of eliminating non-critical costs is that such savings immediately increase your profits. It is no accident that cost leaders such as Wal-Mart, Food Lion, Home Depot, Hancock Fabrics, Price Club, Kelly Moore Paints, Dillard Department Stores, and Fastenal are also sales and profits leaders in their respective industries. With lower costs a company can have lower prices. Lower prices, in turn, lead to higher volume, which leads to lower costs, which, of course, lead to lower prices, thereby continuing the cycle. As Morris Jarvis, the CEO of Hancock Fabrics recently told me: "There will always be a place for the high end, high price operator—but the real battle will be everywhere else and it will be won by those companies who offer the best price based upon a low-cost platform."

The decade just ended has been described by some as the "Excessive Eighties." In contrast, based upon what has already happened in the early years of this decade, together with the "slimming" plans announced for coming years by many of our corporations, this decade will rightly be called the "Diet Decade."

When reading this book please keep in mind that the ideas are taken from many companies. No one company practices all the ideas mentioned. Also, some ideas may not be completely compatible with others. And some are based upon regulations and current practices of the government and external organizations, such as those for utility companies. These, obviously, may change over time, so please check the current regulations and practices before implementing those particular ideas.

The book has two parts. Part A describes the advantages and characteristics of cost leaders together with an implementation plan for companies wishing to improve their relative cost position. Part B is an alphabetical checklist of cost-saving practices, including those mentioned in Part A, which is intended to help you review and improve the cost-consciousness of your organization.

Not addressed in this book are the problems of the truly obese companies with their excess layers of management, corporate jets, and palatial hangers, grossly extravagant expense accounts, company-provided hairdressers, and luxurious lodges and apartments. The solution to these companies' problems is obvious... and patently so to the many professional corporate raiders who see overweight companies as great opportunities!

The list of practices described is obviously not complete. No list ever will be, for there will always be more ways to improve. What this book does provide is an idea of the mindset which gives cost leaders a strategic advantage over their competitors.

Finally, it is fair that you might ask: why get so excited about running a low-cost operation? Why is it important, for example, that Wal-Mart's expenses: sales ratio is 16.5% compared with Kmart's 23.4%? Or Food Lion's is 15.3% compared with Winn-Dixie's 21.0% and A&P's 27.1%? Or Hancock Fabric's is 35.9% compared with Fabri-Center's 41.7% and House of Fabrics' 44.3%?

The critical advantage of being the low-cost leader in your industry is that it allows you to have the lowest prices. Low costs and low prices usually result in a superior return on equity which, in turn, allows you to grow faster than your competitors. This strong growth, combined with high profitability ratios, usually then results in outstanding growth in shareholders' wealth. For example, if on December 1, 1987, you had bought $10,000 worth of shares—equally divided among six of the low-cost leaders frequently mentioned in this book, Dillard Department Stores, Fastenal, Food Lion, Hancock Fabrics, Home Depot and Wal-Mart, your investment would have been worth $49,498 four years later on December 1, 1991. That is an annual average compounded growth in value of 49.2%!!

PART A

The Advantages and Characteristics of the Cost Leaders.

CHAPTER 1

A QUICK LOOK IN THE MIRROR

Every CEO, when asked, professes that his company is cost-conscious. I have yet to find one who doesn't! Yet, there is usually a big gap between the average company and the cost leader in each industry. Why? In most cases, it is because the average company is internally focused and measures its progress against what the company has done historically, rather than looking outside the company and seeing what its competitors are doing.

When talking to chairmen and presidents of companies about cost-consciousness, I am asked by many, "What do you mean by a cost-conscious company? Can you give me some examples of what cost-conscious companies do that we don't?" I usually respond with some of the following signs, large and small, that any senior executive should be able to answer very quickly about his or her company.

1. *Support costs.* Have your company's overhead costs been falling as a percentage of sales over the past three years?

2. *Headquarters.* Is your headquarters building simple, rather than sumptuous, with a low-key, low-cost lobby area? Is the total space at headquarters less than 220 square feet per employee?

3

3. *Annual Report.* Did last year's annual report cost you less than $1.25 per copy?

4. *Stock Transfer Agent.* Have your sought competitive bids for your stock transfer work in the past three years?

5. *Budgets.* To the degree that format budgeting is done at all in the company, is it quick and simple? Is the major control focus on just a few key productivity ratios?

6. *Travel.* Is it true that no employee ever flies first class? Do all employees, without exception, stay at nothing more elaborate than a Fairfield Inn or Hampton Inn, or their equivalent, when outside major metropolitan areas?

7. *Benchmarking.* Has your company identified various areas and activities in which you are not the best in the industry? Are you currently taking specific steps to improve in these areas?

8. *Expense accounts.* Are these sent directly to the accounts payable department for reimbursement according to policy rather than always being sent to the employee's manager for approval and signature?

9. *EDLP.* Are you a true Every Day Low Price operator?

10. *Net Investment.* Has your net investment per store or unit been declining over the past three years?

The more yeses you have answered to the above questions, the more cost-conscious you are as a company. What is the ideal number of yes answers?

There are no absolutes. Everything is relative to the cost leader in your respective industry. Each industry has different degrees of cost-consciousness. For example, a Nordstrom's store is run with a much higher cost structure than your local T.J. Maxx. However, each company must also keep an eye on forces outside of its industry because if the cost structure becomes excessive, outsiders will find a way to sell your product significantly cheaper than you, thereby threatening your whole industry. The motel industry did this to the hotel industry. Currently, the wholesale club industry is doing this to supermarkets, and office warehouses are doing it to traditional stationery suppliers.

CHAPTER 2

REAL CEO's
DON'T EAT FAT

Each company is a reflection of the values of its CEO. The leaders of companies with cost structures lower than their competitors typically exhibit a higher personal degree of cost-consciousness. They fly coach. Their offices are modest. No expensive art work adorns their office walls — or if it does, it's paid for out of their own pockets. They avoid expensive hotel accommodations. And, because they don't eat "fat" themselves, they set the example for the whole corporation to think lean.

Two recent examples come to mind. One low-priced retailer had a CEO with high-priced habits. When he went to New York he always flew first class (and never booked in advance to receive any special price concession); upon arrival he took the helicopter to downtown; he stayed at one of the most expensive hotels and had a limo constantly waiting for him wherever he went. To compete against the likes of Wal-Mart and maintain such habits seemed incongruous. Certainly, the CEO's Board thought so, too, as he was eventually moved out, followed, not surprisingly, some months later by the company being sold. This contrasts vividly with the story I heard of the top two executives of another retail chain who were invited to speak at the annual Investment Seminar of a major southeastern investment company, held at the Ritz Carlton in

Atlanta. Rather than book rooms at this high-class hotel, as most other participants did, these two shared a room at a nearby motel, thereby saving several hundred dollars. Needless to say, their company is the cost leader in its industry.

Most CEO's I know have a tough enough job cutting their cost level to where it is today. To move one step further and deliberately plan to narrow the gap between your company and the cost leader will obviously require a lot of additional effort, as this will involve changing habits, those of both the CEO and the whole organization. As we all know, changing habits is intellectually easy but difficult in practice.

For those who are contemplating shrinking their corporate waistline, it's helpful to answer the following questions before starting:

1. How much "fat" do I want to trim from my organization?

2. What is my target date for the reduction? (Be realistic: remember that it won't be done overnight. It takes time to change a corporate culture).

3. How will I measure my progress?

4. How will I involve everyone in the process?

5. Am I prepared for the pain and protests as the trimming process takes place? (Remember that most service organizations have a high degree of labor costs. Inevitably, part of the trimming will involve having fewer people on the payroll).

6. Am I prepared to cut deeper where the fat is thicker rather than expect an equal reduction from every part of the corporate body?

7. Am I prepared for the inevitable setbacks that will occur during the process?

8. Am I dedicated to running a lean organization for the rest of my business days? Is my commitment long-term? Or do I consider this cost reduction just a "fad diet" in which all the company does is stop eating for a while and then return to its old habits in 6–12 months? (As Dr. Maria Simonson, Professor Emeritus at John Hopkins University Medical Institution and Hospital, says: "Weight loss is not success. It is an achievement. To maintain that loss for 18 months to 2 years is success.")

Successful cost leaders realize four things:

1. Costs are either critical or nice. The CEO's job is to ensure that the largest portion possible of the company's costs is critical.

2. CEO's lead by example. For the rest of the organization to be cost-conscious, the leader must be.

3. Cost leaders formularize their cost structure, so that the maximum amount of corporate effort can be focused on customers and sales.

4. Cost leaders constantly challenge everything. A CEO who stops challenging expenditures is often misread by subordinates as not being as con-

cerned about costs as before. Cost leaders do not let up in their challenging every element of cost throughout the business. "Is that the best we can do?" is a trademark of the cost-conscious CEO.

In some ways, of course, CEO's have little choice but to exert every effort to reduce the cost gap between his or her company and that of the industry leader. The alternative, as we have seen so often in the early 1990's, is that high-cost companies are either bought out or forced to declare bankruptcy. Narrowing the cost gap is a lot more challenging and emotionally satisfying than these two options!

Probably the biggest single hurdle to any company becoming a cost leader is the temperament of the CEO. Not infrequently, he is a neophiliac, a lover of new things; he's always changing things, he's always enamored of the latest management fad. He has difficulty with the discipline involved in a routine business. He prefers a glamorous life to a simple one. He prefers being involved in many things rather than being focused on just a few areas week in, week out. He enjoys external activities, such as golf and trade associations, as much as or even more than his own business. One outstanding cost leader has often reminded me how wonderful it was when the CEO of a competing chain became head of their industry's trade association. "That means he's spending less time competing against me!" he'd chuckle. He also loved competing against CEO's with low golf handicaps, for the same reason!

We should not overlook the fact that none of the cost leaders mentioned in this book are conglomerates. They are all focused operations. A good example is seen in the airline industry, which is notorious for its losses. Southwest Airlines Co., based in Dallas, Texas, is a disciplined, focused regional operator. The company runs short hops with very fast turnarounds, which means it doesn't have to serve meals. Its reservation system is simple and low cost. It avoids the expensive major airports in various cities and flies to lower-cost airports wherever such a choice is available. Southwest focuses on providing good basic service for a low cost. Southwest has not become involved in hotels, rental cars, or a host of other distracting businesses. All the company's efforts, from the CEO down, are focused on running a successful, low-cost, profitable airline.

CHAPTER 3

THE BATTLE
OF THE BULGE

The "battle of the bulge" for service companies revolves around people. People costs are the largest single expense item for most service companies, and this critical cost experiences constant upward pressure. This is nothing new. William Baumol, a Princeton economist who has spent a large part of his professional life studying productivity over the centuries, has observed that, as a general rule, the increase in total labor costs over time exceeded the increase in the consumer price index. To illustrate his point, he reminds us that in London, in the mid 19th century, mail was delivered twelve times each day. However, because labor costs outstripped general price increases over time, mail deliveries are now down to once daily. Therefore, he argues, the traditional ways of doing things are usually changed or replaced over time because labor becomes relatively overpriced.

Understanding "Baumol's Law" helps explain an enormous amount of change in society. It explains many of the revolutions that have occurred in retailing over the decades. For example, as total labor costs increased over time, the supermarket was developed to replace the corner grocer because, with lower labor costs, the supermarket could sell groceries at a significant discount to the corner grocer. Since then, supermarket labor costs have grown faster than the growth of the consumer price index, which has encouraged the development of wholesale clubs, such as Sam's, Price Club, and Costco, with their 3–4% labor costs compared with 9–12% for supermarkets.

A similar revolution has occurred in gas stations. Over the past twenty years, full service gas stations have been transformed into self-service stations. One person now collects cash for up to 24 pumps and sells convenience foods on the side! Movies have experienced similar changes. As kids, many of us saw movies in a single theater with a single projectionist. Now, it's 6–8 movie theaters bundled together and run by one projectionist. All these examples illustrate that over time, as total labor costs rise, alternative, less labor-intensive service formats will arise to sell goods to customers at a lower price, thereby pushing the previous traditional format into an economic backwater.

Baumol's Law also helps explain why governments, federal, state, and local, have been having so much difficulty in recent years. Because many government functions, such as education and trash collection, are very labor-intensive, the costs of these services are increasing at a faster rate than the consumer price index, which is an approximation for the general level of tax revenues. Because of the high labor intensity of these services, little, if any, increase in their productivity has taken place. This means that to maintain the same services as before, we must increase taxes at a faster rate than the consumer price index, change the way we deliver the service, or cut back on the services we have had previously! Any of these choices, as we have seen, is extremely difficult for our politicians to make. More heartache lies ahead for government services unless they can find more productive methods to accomplish their goals.

Part of the increasing cost of labor, of course, has come from indirect charges, such as payroll taxes and the cost of employee health benefits.

In any business activity, as long as increases in the total cost of labor outstrip increases in the productivity of the labor, then significant changes will occur on a regular basis whereby people will be laid off in traditional industries and less people-intensive companies with lower costs will take their places.

We are currently witnessing this in the banking industry. We have all seen estimates that suggest as many as 25% of the jobs in banking today will be eliminated by the end of this decade! With competition from large credit companies, such as the credit arm of the auto companies, and companies like General Electric and Westinghouse Financial Services, and with labor replacement devices such as automatic bank teller machines, the projections don't surprise me.

Our newspaper headlines almost daily remind us of Baumol's Law. Citicorp, Ford, IBM, Atlantic Richfield, General Motors, Digital Equipment, DuPont, Hewlett-Packard, and Shell, to name but a few, have all announced major cutbacks in their white collar labor force. So too have well known retailers such as Sears, Ames, Hills Department Stores, and U.S. Shoe. The 1990's will truly be dubbed the Diet Decade!

Part of the reason for these cutbacks is that the focus over the past two decades has been on increasing blue, rather than white, collar productivity. A recent *Business Week* article stated that while factory productivity has increased 51% over the past 18 years, office worker productivity has actually dropped 7%! This, in an age of computers, calculators, fax machines, photocopiers, and great advances in telecommunications! A significant investment in office technology has been made, with no noticeable productivity gain. White collar America has been coasting. This will change. The trimming of white collar America is still in its infancy!

Part of the historical reason for not trimming headquarters staff, in my observation, is that the closer people physically are to the CEO, the kinder and more generous he or she is toward them. It's easier to issue edicts to trim employees in distant locations who are just "numbers" or "digits" on the corporate landscape rather than flesh and blood faces to a CEO. Walking around an office, a CEO sees that everyone appears to be busy and seems to be doing good work, with the result that he is often more generous in allowing pay increases and departmental expansion at headquarters than in the stores. Very few companies have developed effective ways to manage the growth of headquarters' numbers and costs.

Two that have are Cypress Semiconductor Corporation and Food Lion. At Cypress, once the sales targets have been finalized for the upcoming quarter, all requests for additional people for the quarter are submitted and discussed at one meeting involving all department heads. Together with each request is the department's past history of people productivity, measured in sales per employee. Given the corporate-mandated goal of constant increases in productivity, all requests are reviewed and are granted on a priority basis but with the overall additional headcount low enough to ensure an increase in overall people productivity. After that meeting, no other approvals can be sought or granted for additional people during the quarter. Such must wait until the following quarter's meeting! People productivity increases like clockwork each quarter at Cypress!

At Food Lion, which in recent years has been adding more than 100 supermarkets annually to its store count, each headquarters department is measured in terms of hours per store per week. For example, the payroll department may have used 2.0 hours for each store week last year. This means that if the company had been operating 800 stores in one week, the payroll department used 1,600 employee hours. The objective of the payroll manager, as the company grows from 800 to, say, 900 stores, is to reduce the number of hours worked in the department from 2.0 hours per store, say, to 1.9 per store, a 5% productivity increase. Such real productivity gains are used to offset any increases in the average hourly rate of the employees in the department. It's a very simple, but highly effective, method of departmental self-policing without the need for a long, argumentative budgeting process!

Another common problem at headquarters is "salary grade creep." As a company becomes larger, everyone believes that his or her job becomes more important, with the result that everyone continually wants to increase their salary grades from their existing levels to one or two above. One simple way to minimize this grade inflation is to set a target for your Human Resources Vice President each year for the increase in the weighted average hourly rate in the pay scale. This is done by multiplying the midpoint of each salary range by the estimated (and later, actual) number of hours worked in each salary range and then dividing the total pay by the total number of hours.

In the example following, we can see that the target average hourly rate for the coming year is $8.82 compared with last year's figure of $8.40, an increase of 5.0%. Then it is up to the Human Resources Vice President to balance claims for grade inflation against the weighing of the number of hours worked by people within each salary range. The more people brought into the company at lower grades, the more he can allow upward job reclassification. But one must balance the other. I've seen some companies where grade inflation has been so rampant that no one is left in the bottom two salary scales!!

Minimizing Grade Inflation

Salary Grade	Midpoint Of Salary Range	Projected Hours Per Store Week	Projected Midpoint Pay
1	$ 6.50	200	$ 1,300
2	7.50	400	3,000
3	8.50	1,000	8,500
4	9.50	700	6,650
5	10.50	500	5,250
Total		2,800	$24,700
Target AHR		($24,700/2,800)	$8.82
Last Yr AHR (actual)			$8.40
Target Increase			5.0%

Another successful approach to this problem that I have seen is to have very wide salary scale bands, with an overlap of up to 90%. For example, the salary scale for grade 3, above, may be $6.50 to $10.50, and grade 4, $7.00 to $12.00. This avoids the need for grade hopping yet allows management to offer benefits appropriate to the grade without the need for frequent revision and changes.

The number of people at headquarters is part of the corporate mind-set. Dillard's, the department store chain based in Little Rock, Arkansas, runs with a very low headquarters head count to total employee count ratio. Sears, by contrast, has a dramatically higher ratio.

Without exception, every high-cost company with which I have worked or consulted has had a high people count at headquarters relative to the cost leader in their industry.

Companies are addressing this issue in different ways. Baby Superstores, a fast-growing chain based in Greenville, South Carolina, has halved its non-store staff over the past five years while more than doubling its sales! A few years ago, the company's founder, Jack Tate, realized that his district managers were really acting as message carriers, "policemen," and printout analysts. In abolishing their positions, he spelt out very clearly his expectations of store managers, taught them what they needed to know, and provided them with incentives to do the right things. At the same time, he increased the store managers' pay with the result that they now are financially better off, have more responsibility, and much greater job satisfaction. At Au Bon Pain, a bakery and restaurant chain in the Northeast, similar changes were made with similar results.

Given the technology available today, together with the ease of communication, a leaner, more focused headquarters can deal directly with a much larger number of stores, with many fewer intermediaries. Technology, intelligently applied, can replace a large number of the functions that field middle management used to perform. This substitution will increase in intensity over the coming decade.

The options available to run a leaner headquarters are limited only by management's imagination. Several years ago, one of Ireland's trade representatives in the United States told me of the increasing number of companies that are transferring their back office work to Ireland. He mentioned, for example, that five of the largest American insurance companies flew claims forms for processing to Ireland every night. Where else in the world, he asked, can you find well educated, English-speaking college graduates to do such work for $10–12 per hour ? This is not dissimilar to software companies based in America which have software written for them in India, with workers connected by satellite. Or the credit card companies which are moving to states like South Dakota that offer special cost advantages. In this age of technology, corporate executives are realizing that paperwork can be processed anywhere. It doesn't have to be processed in the same physical building where the top executives work. Nor for that matter does it have to be processed by people on your own payroll. It can be contracted out.

This, of course, is the rationale behind the great growth of Electronic Data Systems (EDS), founded by H. Ross Perot. You don't have to "own" your data processing department to achieve good results. Instead, companies such as EDS contract for defined services and then run the department function at a lower cost than the company had been itself! Such professional data processing companies gain their cost advantage through their enormous computer-buying power as well as their sophisticated technical knowledge. Kodak is one of many well known examples of companies that have contracted their MIS department to an outside processor. EDS has been so successful in managing and running the MIS function for companies that it is now expanding its role to running some of the accounting functions as well, such as accounts payable. Based upon the company's disciplined process-flow mentality, it is usually able to "re-engineer" the way the accounting departments do their work, thereby enabling the departments to run more effectively and efficiently than before.

Outsourcing, of course, is not new, but it is on the increase as companies search for the most cost-effective way to accomplish their various activities. Outsourcing MIS and accounting functions is no different in principle to outsourcing your trucking fleet, cleaning services, advertising, or even various parts of your employee health benefit programs.

Other companies, in an effort to reduce head-quarters costs, have set up individual departments as internal businesses that contract with the company to process their work for a specified annual fee. This fee is negotiated each year, with the "clients" having the freedom to go outside for competitive bids. Likewise, the internal business can contract for outside work. Such an agreement has worked successfully for departments ranging from print shops to legal to accounting.

A variation of this, which we are now seeing in the public sector, is departmental sharing whereby two adjoining cities may share a common service. There is no reason why non-competing companies could not do the same thing in such areas as accounting, training, and human resources.

Offshore manufacturing was a big cost saver over the past twenty years. Offshore, and off-site, paper processing will be one of the big cost savers during the next twenty! Baumol's Law will force us into it.

CHAPTER 4

THIN PEOPLE
LIVE SIMPLY

Cost leaders generally have simple tastes. We are more likely to find a cost leader based in a small, low-cost town such as Salisbury, North Carolina, Bentonville, Arkansas, or Tupelo, Mississippi, than we would in a high-cost city such as Boston, New York, or Washington. After all, it's a lot cheaper to expand your market into the high-cost Northeast from a low-cost headquarters and distribution base somewhere in the South, say, than to expand into the South from the high-cost Northeast.

Companies that are cost leaders operate their businesses in a more routinized and standardized manner than the cost followers in their industries. There are fewer crises, fewer exceptions, fewer layers of management, and less volatility in their business patterns from week to week. Everything seems to run smoothly. As Peter Drucker once observed: "A well run business is often a boring business!"

Even the way cost leaders go to market is simpler because they have realized that a simple marketing strategy leads to a less complicated and therefore less expensive operating cost structure, as well as providing them with better control of the business.

In the majority of cases, the cost leaders' simple marketing plan is based on Every Day Low Prices

(EDLP). Wal-Mart, Food Lion, and Home Depot are the acknowledged leaders in Every Day Low Price marketing. Price Club and Costco have also adopted this pricing strategy and in the department store industry, Dillard's is the closest to such a strategy. In book retailing, Crown Books is an outstanding example of EDLP, and Auto Zone, with over 600 outlets in the automotive do-it-yourself business, is dedicated to an EDLP philosophy. Charles Schwab and Quick & Reilly practice it in the stock brokerage business and Toys R Us in the toy business. EDLP is the pricing practice of Blockbuster Video and Old Country Style Buffet, in two very dissimilar industries. It has even emerged in the fast food industry in recent years at Taco Bell with its 39, 59, 79, and 99 cent Every Day Low Price strategy. Taco Bell's dramatic sales and profitability gains have caused competitors, including mighty McDonald's, to reduce prices to bolster their declining real unit sales.

In my mind, Every Day Low Pricing has been the single most important dynamic in retail marketing in the last 30 years. Consider some of its benefits:

- By lowering the price of everything in your store, you are appealing to a much wider group of customers than by deeply cutting prices on a few select items. Different people know the price of every item you carry. One customer may know the price of Grandma's Molasses, another the price of Old El Paso Taco Sauce, and yet another the price of Nescafe coffee. People know the prices of the products they buy, be they fast or slow movers! I shall never forget the dramatic increase in sales of the slower selling items when a supermarket with which I was associated converted to Every Day Low Prices from a weekly special/high shelf price strategy. Increases of these slow sellers were in the hundreds and thousands of percent!

- Customers no longer have to guess how many of each sale item they need to buy before it comes on "special" again. Indeed, the shopper doesn't have to stock up on items at all in an Every Day Low Price operation because products remain at the same low price from week to week. The store becomes the pantry of the customer!

- Every Day Low Price operators avoid frustrating customers with stockouts of advertised items. Estimating the correct quantity required for each advertised sale item for every store in a chain is extremely difficult. Either the store will run out of the product, which will upset customers, or it will have too many of the product, in which case the store has an overstock which becomes, in many cases, an operational problem.

- Advertising costs tumble because there is no need to hype the current week's "fix" in the form of deep and not-so-deep price cuts on selected items. It's not unusual for Every Day Low Price operators' advertising costs as a percentage of sales to be less than half that of their non-Every Day Low Price competitors!

- Sales are less volatile and easier to predict, which allows for better labor scheduling, and therefore, lower labor costs. Labor costs are also reduced because of the simpler work flow involved with Every Day Low Pricing.

- In manufacturing terms, an Every Day Low Price strategy is the equivalent of a level production strategy, the most efficient form of production. Therefore, Every Day Low Price allows a company to be both the price and process (cost) leader, an unbeatable combination.
- The physical volume of goods sold through each store will generally increase when a company converts to EDLP which, in turn, lowers the fixed cost per item sold. This helps the company's "productivity loop."
- Sales, margins, and costs all become much more predictable and controllable with this operating philosophy, thereby allowing everyone to focus on "tweaking the model" rather than constantly trying to guess how the customer might respond to every week's changing advertised offer!
- The company can still pass on special lower price deals to customers through temporary price reductions, bonus buys, and similar in-store features. This gives management much better control over its gross margin, one of the big problems with traditional "specials" retailing.
- It's an honest offering to the customer.

Companies such as Kmart, Winn-Dixie, and Albertson's have followed, in various degrees, in the footsteps of their industry's cost leaders. We even see it spreading to other industries. Recently, for example, several auto dealerships have introduced an Every Day Low Price program because they realize that customers were unhappy with constantly having to negotiate price and never knowing whether they were getting a good deal. One dealership went so far as to eliminate its sales force, put Every Day Low Prices on all the cars in its lot and increased its business significantly because its prices became the lowest in their city.

It is interesting to note that some of the manufacturers supplying the retail industry are now moving towards "every day purchase prices" in place of the traditional frequent promotions ("specials") of their products. Procter & Gamble is leading the charge. Because of its dominant status this move will be carefully monitored, and mimicked, by others.

Apart from its obvious cost advantages, we should never discount the tremendous price integrity of EDLP in the marketplace. Many department stores have lost their price integrity in customers' minds because of their constant sales and frequent markdowns. Customers who buy items at full price in department stores, and see them advertised at lower prices several weeks later feel cheated . . . and avoid being cheated again by gradually moving their business elsewhere. The same price integrity issue is being raised in the current pizza wars. Anyone who pays full price for a pizza from Domino's or Pizza Hut currently feels cheated, given the abundance of coupons and deals they offer. In time, I am sure we will see an EDLP pizza program initiated by one of the leaders in an effort to regain its price integrity in the marketplace.

There is no question about the cost and marketing superiority of an Every Day Low Price strategy. However, that does not mean that every company's attempt at EDLP will automatically translate into improved results overnight. The Sears experience with EDLP attests to that. When it unveiled its new EDLP program in 1989, customers found that many of the new prices were still not sufficiently competitive, so Sears had to re-introduce "specials." It was neither a pure EDLP or weekly specials operator, a very difficult competitive position in which to be. Further, the company did not move aggressively enough to streamline the organization so that its operating structure matched its marketing posture. The result was a disaster for its bottom line.

Switching to EDLP requires a great deal of detailed planning and preparation. Some make the transition overnight as Sears did. Most do it gradually as Home Depot did. Bernie Marcus, the CEO of Home Depot, said that it took him three years of intense scrutiny within each department to identify the right mix of merchandise to achieve an acceptable gross margin and still be a true EDLP leader. Dillard Department Stores are still in their transition. Each year they issue one less promotional flier as they wean their customers from traditional department store pricing.

Also keep in mind that all EDLP operators do not offer the same prices. EDLP operators may choose from three different pricing formulas: a standard markup percentage for different categories; a standard unit add-on to each item's direct product cost; or matching key market competitive prices and the adoption of one of the previous two formulas for all other items.

In addition, competing EDLP operators have different cost structures. Some are more cost-conscious than other EDLP operators.

Even allowing for the preceding variations, Every Day Low Pricing will, I believe, continue to be the dominant marketing strategy of the low-cost leaders during the rest of the Diet Decade.

However, two significant refinements will be made to the basic EDLP formula due to technology becoming simpler, more powerful, and less expensive. The two refinements are **modular pricing** and **stealth marketing.**

Sixty years ago, the corner grocer knew all of his customers by name as well as their individual preferences. Retailers' great customer knowledge was lost in the age of mass marketing. Customers became digits. Instead of focusing on individual customer needs, because we didn't have the appropriate technology, retailers focused upon the stock-keeping units (sku's) sold as their method of keeping up with the marketplace and changes in it. Now we have come full circle. With low-cost, point-of-sale technology, we are able to run our businesses based on knowing our individual customers once again. We are moving from **sku management** back to **cue (customer unique entries) management.** This has significant marketing implications for all retail and service companies.

Over the years, retailers and service companies have considered sales the most important driver. In reality, however, sales are an output rather than a driver. What drives sales are:

- The customer transaction count,
- The number of items sold to each customer, and
- The average selling price of each item sold.

It's the multiplication of these three drivers that results in sales. And the most important of these three is the customer transaction count. Now, with powerful, point-of-sale technology, we can delve into the components of this primary driver, our customer transaction count, and develop marketing plans for customers with different characteristics. We can market to small groups of special customers, rather than to the masses of the past sixty years.

Government statistics tell us that 17% of the American population moves every year. In addition to this mobility loss, companies lose customers for a variety of reasons ranging from poor service to poor quality merchandise. Various groups, such as the Forum Corporation, Bain and Company, and Professor Earl Sasser of the Harvard Business School, have studied customer profitability. Their findings typically indicate that the profitability of an existing, loyal customer is at least five times that of a new marginal customer. Given this dramatic profit differential, the Every Day Low Price formula will be refined to provide greater benefits for the loyal, more highly profitable customer. By introducing a **modular** pricing system with different prices for different customers, rather than the same price for all customers, a company can build protective barriers around its most profitable customers, thereby increasing the retention rate of those customers, and increasing the company's overall profitability.

The Waldenbooks Preferred Reader Program is an excellent illustration of this. Any shopper at Waldenbooks can, for $10.00, buy a Preferred Readers Membership for one year. This entitles the card holder to a 10% discount on all purchases during the year with additional $5.00 gift certificates sent from headquarters for every $100.00 of purchases. In effect, this means a 15% discount on all purchases. To pay for the program, Waldenbooks reduced the number of "specials" offered at the front of the store available to all shoppers, loyal and browser alike. Instead, the company has moved a significant portion of the amount previously given as markdowns towards price discounts for the regular, loyal (more profitable!) shopper. The company has been delighted with the results. Not only do they now know what each of their customers is buying, how frequently each shops, and the profitability of each individual customer, but they are also now able to target each of their customers directly according to what they buy. For example, Waldenbooks may do a special mailing to those Preferred Readers who buy a lot of mystery novels, or business books, or computer books, and so on. The company found that the Preferred Reader spends, on average, 70% more than other shoppers, so it knows it is now tracking all the purchasing activities of its "gold" customers. In addition, it is able to monitor when its Preferred Readers stop shopping with them on a regular basis and can take corrective action with various "encouragements" for the customer to return.

It is this ability to market directly to each individual customer, without competitors knowing what you are doing (as your actions are not seen in the newspapers or on television, or even in the stores) that we describe as **stealth marketing**. Like a stealth bombing raid, such actions go undetected by competitors until they see the damage in the form of lost customers!

Another retail chain, CD Superstore, based in Durham, NC, introduced a program similar to Walden Books and is delighted with the dramatic increase in profitability as a result of the change. This chain previously used weekly and monthly specials, most of which were advertised in newspapers and available to anyone who walked into the store. After careful study and analysis, the company introduced a "members card" for an annual $12 fee, which entitles members to an automatic 10% discount on all CD's purchased. Instead of "specials" in newspaper advertisements, it now markets directly to its best customers, its club members, with communication costs paid for by vendors. By recording all customer transaction activities in its data base, the company is able to make special offers to various groups of customers and refine its marketing model, all without its competitors knowing what it's doing or the results of its actions.

Without a doubt, to the cost-conscious company of the 1990's, its customer data base will be its most valuable asset, even though it will not be recorded on the balance sheet. Modular pricing and stealth marketing techniques will be perfected and routinized by the cost leaders which, in conjunction with Every Day Low Pricing, will arm them with an even more powerful competitive advantage in the marketplace.

CHAPTER 5

INVOLVING THE WHOLE FAMILY

A weight reduction program is always easiest when the whole family is involved. If everybody in the family stands to gain from losing some weight, a mutually reinforcing set of behaviors takes over. So, too, in any organization. The CEO alone cannot mandate a lean organization. He may, indeed he will, establish a goal. However, the greatest long-term corporate weight reduction occurs when employees completely "buy in" to the idea. Ideally, this is achieved by appealing to both their emotions and their economics.

Most people want to be associated with an organization of which they can be proud. Lean companies are usually the profit and sales growth leaders in their industries. Employees belonging to such companies rightfully feel proud when they see their company referred to admiringly by competitors, by analysts, and in the press. It's always great to be associated with a winner rather than a company that is trailing the field.

People also like to be rewarded for their accomplishments. Therefore, cost leaders usually provide conditional rewards for various levels of performance by their employees.

In addition, the salaries and bonuses of their top officers do not make the "Overpaid Executives" list in Fortune Magazine. They typically live their values and share the rewards with the employees.

Food Lion, for example, has had a Profit Sharing Program in place for all employees who work more than 1,000 hours a year almost from the day the company started. The Profit Sharing is conditional. Up to 15% of the employees' wages are put into a company Profit Sharing Plan, which is fully vested after 5 years. The proportion of wages set aside depends upon the company's return on equity. Because of the strong, reinforcing, low-cost culture of the organization, the maximum 15% has been paid every year. It's not unusual, as you walk through one of the stores or headquarters, to hear one employee say to another, "Don't waste that, that's my profit sharing!"

Wal-Mart has traditionally paid a lesser percentage of wages than Food Lion in profit sharing. Instead, it has offered other additional, conditional rewards. For example, each store has an annual profit target. In those stores that exceed their targets, a portion of the profit above the target is shared among all employees. Similarly, any improvement over the shrinkage target triggers a pay-out for all employees in the store.

Such conditional economic rewards reinforce the values for which management strives throughout the organization. It is simply a matter of "watering what you want to grow."

Cost-conscious companies are led by example. There is one culture, not two. It's a one-class airplane. There's no first class for the select few at the top of the organization and coach class for everybody else.

The communication of values is a constant activity for top management. To develop the culture he wants through the whole organization, Bernard

Marcus, the CEO of Home Depot, insists that all officers of the company spend time in the classroom each month teaching all new managers. Training is a critical element of the company. The company has at least 12 classes per year. Each officer has a class, typically of one day. It's top management's belief that if a person can't teach, then he can't be an officer.

Robert Kierlin, the founder and CEO of low-cost and highly successful Fastenal, Inc., based in Winona, Minnesota, used to phone the manager of every store every Friday, from the day the company began. Now, with over 170 stores, he is able to call only about 70 managers a week! These calls are triggered by data indicating stores doing well in sales, new accounts, gross margins, or maybe an unusual sale. These congratulatory calls allow more time to chat about what is going on in the individual store. In addition, Kierlin travels with a different region manager one week a month, visiting stores. During that week, they share the driving in a van that yields 25 miles to the gallon gas mileage. The two also share $32 motel rooms. Such actions send an unbelievably powerful message about the cost-conscious culture to every employee and make Fastenal a very tough company against which to compete!

Mark's and Spencer, one of Great Britain's most successful and most cost-conscious retailers, has used a series of simple, catchy phrases to communicate the idea that complicating a business adds costs, while simplification saves money. Two such phrases illustrate this wonderfully: "Always use sensible approximation," and "the price of perfection is prohibitive." Management instills in their employees that knowing an answer down to the last four decimal places is usually a waste of time and that you don't need to know the answer to everything before making a decision.

Values also need to be communicated to newcomers to the organization and to other outsiders. Cost leaders do not put prospective employees into first class hotels during the interviewing process, if employees usually stay in more modest motels. They let them experience the culture of the organization before joining it. In fact, it is crucial that the prospective employee understand the cost-conscious culture up front before signing on. The same values apply for the newcomer's induction and early training. It always fascinated me to watch the cultural transformation of store managers, joining from relatively cost-lax supermarket chains, as they went through their first weeks at highly cost-conscious Food Lion. After a month or so of the Food Lion cost-conscious regime, they often commented that they now understood why Food Lion was growing so fast and the chain from which they came was not.

The company must also constantly signal its values to product and service suppliers. At any of the headquarters of the cost leaders mentioned in this book, vendors know from the environment and the no-nonsense attitude of the buyers that to do business with these companies they need the sharpest pencil in town! They are tough, but fair.

The same also applies when dealing with public accounting and legal firms. Each year, agree in advance with your accounting firm what the basis of the audit fee will be, broken down by component. Ask them how you can do work internally to reduce that cost further. Ensure that their fee increases less than the sales growth of the company, because a significant portion of their fee is a fixed cost and not related to volume.

Similarly, your legal firm must clearly understand that you don't wish to waste money on unnecessary legal niceties. Joe Cristiano, the CEO of Kelly Moore Paints, Inc., San Carlos, California, the cost and profit leader in the paint industry, never lets his lawyer send him a letter. He hears his opinion by phone and saves the company's legal bill from dictation, secretarial, and overhead costs for simply telling him the same thing again in writing! Through such actions your outside service suppliers understand that you are in deadly earnest about running a lean organization. They in turn will think thrice before charging you for any questionable item!

Another key element in strengthening the culture of an organization is to share information openly. Recently, I was in Japan on a learning trip and was fascinated to see during my tour of an Izusu truck plant the amount of information on open display for all employees to see. A large bulletin board on the factory floor showed, for example, that they were averaging 1.2 suggestions per employee per week (which incidently is over 100 times the number of suggestions per employee received by American automotive plants) as well as showing the day's and week's productivity figures.

Among American retailers, Wal-Mart is one of the most open with information. Yet it has never ceased to amaze me that even with such openness its competitors never seem able to narrow the gap! Wal-Mart has an information flow loop centered on its Saturday morning weekly review meeting at headquarters. Ideas and suggestions flow in from the stores. They are reviewed. Responses flowed back. All within a few days. In addition, every store now has its own satellite dish which permits it to be in touch with headquarters at all times. CEO David Glass can deliver a message to the "troops" all at the same time, throughout the whole country.

Another fascinating element of the open communications of Wal-Mart is the micro-merchant philosophy. Each store is composed of a number of small departments. Yet the head of each of these departments is treated as a merchant in his or her own right. Each department head knows the sales, gross profit, costs, and profits of his or her department. Every week, every department knows its ranking, as a percentages of sales, throughout the whole company. Imagine the pride, for example, of having one of the highest percentages of sales in the whole chain for your department. This specific feedback, on a weekly basis, showing relative performance with one's peers, is one of the most powerful bottom-line enhancers there is. It's far superior to measuring against any budgets because budgets are static and out of date as soon as they are published. However, constantly trying week after week to outperform your peers in other parts of the chain is a dynamic and very rewarding challenge. It is, in a way, like playing professional football every week. You are always trying to improve your score (sales distribution percentage), thereby improving your ranking in the league (where you stand in the company).

Food Lion uses a different, but equally effective, approach. Instead of showing each store's performance against a budget, the company shows, every four weeks, each individual store's performance against all stores throughout the chain with a similar sales volume. Then, line by line, the individual store's performance is compared with the average performance of all those stores with a similar sales volume. In addition, the company prints out an exception report which lists only those items that are outside the pre-determined "tolerance levels" of each line item. In this way, a store manager and his or her district manager can very quickly identify areas that deserve a significant pat on the back or warrant investigative and remedial attention. Once again, the focus is on a dynamic ongoing peer comparison.

In like manner, cost leaders push costs down to the lowest common denominator. Costs are not allocated. Rather, the person who spends the money is accountable for the cost. Travel expenses are a classic example. Every person is charged for his or her own travel expenses and monitored on a monthly and rolling quarter basis. These expenses are compared with those of one's peers. Significant variations require explanation. Those within tolerance levels are ignored.

Once cost-consciousness begins to permeate the whole organization, savings begin to appear everywhere. One quick litmus test from both an insider's and an outsider's viewpoint to see how deeply cost-consciousness has pervaded an organization is to look at the company's communication with shareholders. Contact the shareholder relations department of several companies and ask for a copy of their latest annual report, quarterly releases, and any other relative information. (If you want to check out comparability with your own company, have a friend request the same of your company). The responses can be very instructive. For example, only two of six companies from which I recently requested information came in envelopes with hand-written addresses (presumably written at the time of my request). These were from Costco and Toys R Us. The others were nicely, and more expensively, typed. One even had a beautifully typed "thank you for your inquiry" personalized letter from the head of the shareholders relations department. He was obviously under-worked or over-staffed!

The quality of the quarterly releases varied significantly. The most cost-effective were printed on "cheap" paper, folded in such a manner that the shareholder's name and address is affixed by label, and sent by bulk mail, not first class mail. Press releases were typically on plain paper with the cost-conscious companies printing them front and back. Buffets Inc. is a good example of this.

Then there is the annual report itself. As a group, I find banks to be the least cost-conscious sector when it comes to annual reports. They provide lengthy, high-gloss annual reports with lots of "blurbs" and color photographs. Some banks are so proud of their annual "masterpiece" that they send it, along with a nicely typed individualized letter, to many of their depositors, who, in turn, throw both into the trash can. Remember, an annual report is a score card and not a glossy cover-up of poor performance. If your results are good, an expensive annual report is not needed. And, if your results are poor, you can't afford an expensive report! Looking at the annual reports that cross my desk, I have often wondered if a negative correlation exists between the results of a company and the glossiness of its annual report!

From a cost-conscious viewpoint, four annual reports that stand out in my mind are Costco, Price Club, Office Depot, and Patlex. The last two mentioned even incorporate their 10K Form with their annual report. Each of these annual reports spell out all the necessary information about both their year's performance and their future hopes. They provide graphs and maps. However, they don't have glossy pages, photos of the board of directors (these companies obviously consider earnings per share more important than ego per share!), or multi-color presentations. Just plain vanilla reporting of high class results, and all produced for a lot less than $1.25 per annual report.

CHAPTER 6

IF YOU EAT WHAT EVERYBODY ELSE DOES, DON'T EXPECT TO BE THIN

The average American company is overweight. Its management has a tendency to follow the crowd, almost lemming-like, which causes it to finish with average results. Yet, what is average? The worst of the best or the best of the worst? Neither definition is comforting.

Looking at the average performance of the Fortune 500 year after year is not comforting either. In 1990, according to Fortune Magazine, the average company in this elite list increased its sales just 6.4% over the preceding year, barely beating the inflation rate. At the same time, profits fell 11.7%. Indeed, less than half of the Fortune 500 increased their profits over the previous year. One company out of every eight on the list of these, our biggest, best, and brightest companies, actually lost money! It should be no surprise that the median return on equity was a modest 13%. If you wish to follow the average company in the crowd, don't expect stellar results!

However, a company wishing to achieve results consistently superior to the average must, as Michael Porter points out, have lower costs, a very clear differentiation in the marketplace, or both. Therefore, a company seeking cost superiority must prudently select those cost areas, small and large, where it's prepared to be different from the crowd and act accordingly. For example, how have F. Kenneth Iverson and his team made Nucor Corp., now America's 7th largest steel company, into one of its most profitable? By being different. A high focus on productivity throughout the whole organization. No corporate jet. Everyone, including Iverson, flies coach. No pampered princes preening around a corporate palace. Indeed, their cramped headquarters are adjacent to a Charlotte, North Carolina, shopping center. Theirs is a very egalitarian corporation. So much so that several years ago their annual report had the names of every employee listed on its cover in fine print.

Being different from your industry peers is unsettling for some. However, it is necessary if you desire a different cost structure. Here are some such different ideas from various cost leaders.

* * *

Some companies are finding that **captive insurance** is a very cost-effective way of handling their insurance risks. A number of years ago, companies set up to handle captive insurance had to be offshore. However, in recent years, a number of states have set up favorable legislation, such as minimum capitalization and premium tax requirements, to encourage such companies to be domiciled in their state. In essence, a captive insurance company permits money, historically tied up in advance premiums, to be more effectively utilized by the operating company.

Recently, I had a lengthy conversation with the CEO of a company which is the cost and profit leader of its industry. In the first two years with its own captive insurance company, the company has built up a three million dollar surplus! The company originally became involved with captive insurance for two reasons: insurance rates, it was felt, were increasing dramatically; and insurance rates were set partially on the individual company's performance but also partially upon the company's industry's results. The CEO felt that his company had a much better control of costs than the average company in his industry, and he was not enthused about subsidizing his competitors. He told me that his executives were more careful in settling claims than the big insurance companies because "their" money was at stake. Like everything else this company does, they carefully researched the issue, and found a state that does not require the full $500,000 base requirement in cash. (This state required a base of $250,000 with a $250,000 letter of credit.) The company then set up its own captive insurance company, paid premiums (essentially to itself), and re-insured itself for all claims for $500,000 or more. The result was that any claims against the company were handled, part-time, by an existing executive of the company. The CEO believes that this executive fights harder for the company than the insurance company did because his company's results, as well as his profit sharing, are at stake!

Obviously, this program is not for all companies. However, if you believe that your insurance experience is better than the industry average and that your people can handle claims more effectively than your insurance company, then this is certainly worth pursuing. Remember that surpluses built up in the captive insurance company are, essentially, profits belonging to your company.

* * *

Dividends can be viewed in two ways: 1) as an ongoing, usually increasing, expense of a company, or 2) as a liquidation of the company's equity capital. Either way, they should be discontinued. Few companies which pay dividends are debt free. Therefore, in addition to paying the dividends, most companies incur two additional costs: all the expenses associated with paying the dividend (share transfer agent processing costs, mailing costs, bank fees, etc.) and the interest on the monies borrowed to pay the dividend. This interest compounds every year thereafter, or until the company begins to reduce its debt load. If you are ever looking for something to do on a quiet, wet, Sunday afternoon as an alternative to watching football or golf, take the annual reports of any dividend-paying company of your choice and total the dividends paid over the past five years. Add to this your estimate of their interest charges, compounded annually, on the dividends for the same period. This is the total portion of the debt on the balance sheet which has been borrowed to liquidate capital. Then think ahead to how much this debt plus interest figure will compound in the next five to ten years just to pay for these dividends of the past five years. In a number of cases, it starts to look like the way the government runs its finances! Not surprisingly, Berkshire Hathaway Company, the chairman of which is Warren Buffet, one of the great corporate wealth creators of this century, does not pay dividends!

Dividends are essentially an admission of management failure. "We are running out of profitable projects in which to invest and therefore must liquidate some of our shareholders' capital" is the message underlying the rationale for dividends. But even if this is the case, a company's capital can be shrunk in a better way: by buying back shares. When a company pays a dividend, it is forcing its tax-paying shareholders to pay taxes on that dividend. To avoid this masochistic practice, a preferable method is a company stock buyback. With this method, shareholders can elect, based upon their situation at the time together with their view of the company, to liquidate some or all of their ownership in the company if they so desire. The other great advantage of stock buybacks is that they allow companies to decide from year to year how much cash to use in shrinking their corporate capital rather than being under the pressure of having a fixed dividend commitment to honor. The advantage of this approach has been highlighted over the past few years when we have witnessed many companies suffering the humiliating agony of advising their shareholders that they are cutting their dividends because they can't afford such a high pay-out. Obviously, a no-dividend program, with the company buying back stock only when it can afford it, would better serve both the company's and the shareholders' interests.

"Ah, ha," you say. "What about the widows and orphans and their need for dividends?" The answer is simple. How many widows and orphans do you know that have invested all their money in your stock for the sake of dividends? The recent dividend cuts by the big auto companies of America remind us that widows and orphans should not be investing in stocks as a guaranteed dividend stream. Rather, they should invest some of their funds in bonds to generate the required regular income stream and then invest the balance in stocks for capital appreciation.

* * *

Now, some companies have realized that cash is important to them and that cash dividends are not important to their shareholders. This has resulted in their introducing a **dividend re-investment program**. Through such an action they are moving closer to the ideal: keeping cash in the company. However, this compromise approach incurs a lot of unnecessary costs for the corporation. The share transfer agent is still charging for processing these cash-less dividends! Simply eliminate the dividends and you eliminate the processing costs! You would also satisfy your shareholders who want to leave their money in the company anyway!

One company that has always fascinated me with its dividend policy is Winn-Dixie, Inc. It has proudly increased its dividends every year for decades. But these dividends are not paid quarterly. They are paid monthly! On top of that, the company has a dividend re-investment program. Now, wouldn't you love to be receiving a fraction of the share transfer agent's processing fees for that company!

From a cost-conscious viewpoint, one of the great absurdities is to see a dividend-paying company going to market to raise more equity capital every few years. If the company didn't pay the dividends in the first place, thereby depleting shareholders' equity, it wouldn't need to sell more shares to refill the depletion. Of course, some people benefit from this program: the investment bankers who peddle the new stock and the share transfer agents who process the dividends. The losers are the existing shareholders whose company profits are unnecessarily reduced by these costs.

*   *   *

In the 1980s, **investment bankers** made a great deal of money from helping companies in various ways. A great number of investment bankers are very smart people, but, like everybody else, they are subject to the laws of supply and demand. In other words, their fees, too, are competitive. Therefore, if you want any work done by an investment banker, invite bids from several competing firms rather than just asking "your investment banker" to do the job at the best price. Not surprisingly, this will result in nearly every case in a lower fee than if you did not invite competitive bids.

*   *   *

It is not unusual to have investment bankers recommend that you raise capital by issuing **convertible debentures.** Investment bankers love them because they are generally easy to sell and very profitable to them. Translated, this means that the shareholders are coming out second best. A more cost-effective alternative to convertible debentures is to sell warrants.

*   *   *

For those companies considering a **preferred stock** offering, it is more cost effective to set the dividend rate to float with the market rate of interest (e.g., X% above prime or above 30-year treasury bonds) rather than having a fixed rate. This approach avoids management ever having an incentive to call the issue, which typically forces further unnecessary refinancing costs.

*   *   *

Besides rushing to pay dividends, another lemming-like characteristic of a number of growing companies is to become listed on the **New York Stock Exchange**. Many companies feel that they have "made it" when they are finally listed on the Big Board. However, before blindly following the crowd and enjoying the ego trip of being listed on the doyen of world stock exchanges, check the costs. A few years ago, I had to analyze the comparative costs for a highly cost-conscious company of remaining on NASDAQ or switching to the New York Stock Exchange. The cost differential was such that the company stayed on NASDAQ rather than switch to the New York Stock Exchange. A number of very cost-conscious companies such as Price Co., Fastenal Inc., Food Lion, Inc., and Costco, Inc., remain off the Big Board, primarily for cost-related reasons, we can assume. The bottom line is that if you are contemplating switching from NASDAQ to the New York Stock Exchange, ensure that you are doing it for economic reasons and not for egotistic, follow-the-crowd, reasons.

*   *   *

Over the years I have worked for companies whose **budgets** have ranged from the very elaborate to skimpy. The former company's annual budget process usually began six months before the beginning of each financial year. It entailed many high level meetings as participants tried to make it as easy as they could for themselves in the following year. Generally, they were accompanied with great fanfare. Sadly, the budget became out of date on the day it was printed because in most instances it was nothing but a best guess forecast of what might happen the following year. Consider, for example, the components of a sales budget for a retail chain. The sales budget must consider the size and number of new stores to be opened and closed the following year, the number of weeks such stores will be open, together with how many customers they expect to have (broken down into the number of customers retained, the number lost, and the number of new customers to be acquired), how many items each customer is expected to buy on each visit, and the average selling price per item sold. In reality, this is extremely difficult to do. I have seen stores perform unexpectedly well when a nearby competitor closed. I have seen others do poorly when there was unexpected nearby road construction or when a new competitor moved into the area. In addition, given the myriad items a store sells, I take my hat off to anyone who can confidently budget what the change in the average selling price per item sold will be for the year, taking into account both the change in the product mix and the inflation rate on the products actually sold.

A more cost-effective approach is to eliminate budgeting in the traditional sense. Assuming you have an appreciation of the economics of your company, simply request your operating management to work on their key productivity ratios, such as the number of items sold per employee hour. Do this on a daily and weekly basis for the critical operating costs, and you'll have your major costs under control. In addition, assuming you have salary scales and expense policy guidelines, period costs can be best kept down by comparing each operations' results not against a budget drawn up in the previous year, but against its peers' actual performance. In the case of a retail chain, for example, simply take the results of each store and compare its performance, line by line, with all stores in the chain with a similar sales volume as described in chapter 5 and as seen in the appendix. It's amazing how a manager will be driven harder to beat the line-by-line performance of his (or her) peers than to beat his budget. In a single manufacturing plant, where such a peer comparison is not possible, a comparison with last year's results is generally the best measure. Too often, unfortunately, we see actual results compared with budget, but then we still go back to last year's results to see what the budget is based on and how much we have really changed. After all, isn't our constant objective to improve upon last year's performance? If so, why muddy the waters with budgets? Why not see by how much we can beat last year's performance, pure and simple?

CHAPTER 7

SHED OUNCES, LOSE POUNDS

At Food Lion, we used to use the expression, borrowed from Tom Peters, "Do 1,000 things just 1% better and soon you'll be 1,000% better." The underlying philosophy of this simple approach is intuitively obvious. If you develop one dramatic way of significantly reducing costs, it will stand out like a sore thumb, and your competitors will quickly copy you, thereby neutralizing your competitive advantage. However, if you do many, many things just a little bit better than your competitors, all of these cost-conscious actions, insignificant in their own right, together yield a significant cost advantage. Competitors have difficulty identifying these gains, and will scratch their heads and wonder how you can have such low costs. On various occasions I heard expense-heavy competitors suggest that Food Lion was "juggling its numbers." I'm sure that similar comments are made of all cost leaders in every business. Frankly, that's the sort of comment a cost leader likes to hear—it means that one's competitors are looking for excuses for their own poor performance rather than understanding why the cost leader is the cost leader!

Weight is added to and shed from the body, be it corporate or human, ounce by ounce. The pounds follow. The essence of any low-cost company is seen in the minutiae, in the little things, in the ounces and quarter-inches lost.

50

This was really brought home to me in the 1970's when I was visiting the headquarters of a highly successful, and very cost-conscious, fast food chain. When talking of their low-cost structure, the executive mentioned that his company did not put lids on drinks sold in their restaurants as did their competitors. "That's a 1.4 cent cost advantage on every such drink we sell!" he explained. "That, and a number of other little things, give us a real cost advantage day in and day out." Comments and thinking like that are what identify a cost-conscious company. When visiting companies, I get my best feel for how cost-conscious they are by observing how they handle incidental costs. That reflects how far a cost-conscious attitude has really permeated an organization.

The second section of this book, Part B, identifies many of these small tell-tale signs. The degree of practice of these and similar items reflects the mindset of the company. It measures the depth and commitment of the whole organization to cost-consciousness. No CEO can mandate the practice of all the points mentioned. They usually come naturally from the cost-conscious mindset of individual employees. Management's challenge is to ensure a high degree of cost-consciousness throughout the whole company.

The more highly developed this interest in saving "little costs" is, the more variable the costs in the organization are as sales fluctuate. There is less chance of being beset, as many companies are, by Hlavacek's Law which states: "When sales rise all costs are variable. When sales fall all costs are fixed!"

Another critical reason to think in terms of

constantly losing "ounces" is that it keeps the organization trim, which is particularly important in good times. As the great Roman writer Juvenal reminds us, "Luxury is more deadly than war." In easy times companies develop a welfare mentality. They are generous with benefits, staffing levels, advertising, working conditions, expense control, etc., etc. Then, when tougher competitive times come, as they inexorably do, the management and employees have difficulty changing to a leaner mindset. A number of our big Fortune 500 companies are wrestling with this transition today. In hindsight, they obviously would have been better to have run lean, tight, flexible organizations from their earliest days.

The rise and fall of companies and the rise and fall of nations have many parallels. Lean, vibrant organizations have kept welfarism to a minimum. So, too, have long-lasting civilizations. As the Soviet Union and Eastern Europe have recently discovered, you can't continue giving handouts and expect to have a vibrant competitive body. Rome was no different. Its welfarism started on a small scale. In 50 B.C. Julius Caesar had only 200,000 people on the dole. Forty-five years later, that number was up 50%, and the numbers kept increasing, as did the benefits. The trend never stopped, so by the year 274 A.D., the emperor Aurelian was overseeing cradle-to-the-grave care for citizens. He even declared that the right to relief was hereditary! Welfarism had developed to the stage where recipients received salt, pork, olive oil, and tunics, and the government even baked bread for them, instead of the original practice of giving them wheat and letting them bake their own! As in corporations, this wonderfully humane program began very small, but the benefits kept growing every year. This is essentially the same battle corporations are fighting. Here is one quick test of your company's welfare mentality. For those employees (I hope, a limited number) who have company-provided cars, who pays for their car wash? Surely, the very least they could do is to pay for them out of their own pockets rather than turning car wash expenses in on their monthly expense accounts!

Actually, most corporate welfare programs benefit the top part of the organization, rather than the lower paid at the bottom. Does top management really need company-paid country club memberships? Aren't golden parachutes really a form of upper class corporate welfarism? Margaret Thatcher had the right idea, when Prime Minister of Great Britain. Her goal was "pocket-book democracy." Stop spending money on behalf of people. Let them decide for themselves. Applying this to companies means paying people more but cutting back on perks. Let the employees decide how money is best spent on their behalf. You'll be amazed (or perhaps you won't!) at how employees stop spending on perks when they are paying for them out of their own income.

Keep in mind that cost-consciousness is not the same as cost-cutting, although you may have to do the latter to achieve a solid base for a cost-conscious culture. Cost-cutting is usually associated with trimming away a lot of fat (and often some muscle) accumulated over time. Being cost-conscious is avoiding that buildup in the first place because everyone understands that cost containment is critical. It is usually associated with constantly review-

ing each part of the system to see how to make
marginal cost improvements. This is best illustrated
in a conversation that Ralph Ketner, the founder of
the highly successful Food Lion supermarket chain,
once had. An investor asked him, as the economy
was moving into a downturn, where was he going to
cut costs to improve profitability? Ketner's reply
was straightforward: "No where, I hope! I would be
very upset if I found costs in my organization that
were there just because times were good!!" That is
the mark of a cost-conscious organization.

CHAPTER 8

THE TOFU DIET

Different cultures develop different ways to tackle problems. Just as American management has contributed so much to business thinking, so too, in recent years, is Japan increasingly contributing. The Japanese approach to costs has been particularly fascinating. Japan's contribution to cost reduction has been labeled "the tofu diet."

Three of Japan's significant contributions which are now starting to be more widely accepted in the United States are:

- Kaizen
- Upstream relationships
- Attitude toward profits

Kaizen

According to Masaaki Imai, "Kaizen strategy is the single most important concept in Japanese management—the key to Japanese competitive success." It's a view that nothing in the world is static. Everything is capable of continuous incremental improvement. It's the cornerstone of Japanese management practices. It is the logic behind suggestions systems and quality circles. It's the mindset that always looks for small gains rather than the big innovative breakthrough. It's the essence of this book: "Do 1,000 things just 1% better and soon you will be 1,000% better." In retailing, particularly, a very heavy emphasis is placed upon price comparisons. Very little emphasis is placed on process comparisons. Yet this is where the great opportunity lies for beating your competitors. It is no accident that Wal-Mart, Home Depot, and Food Lion are all everyday low-priced operators. Not only does it give them an overall low price position in the marketplace, but also the process costs of everyday low price operators are significantly lower than those of conventional competitors who have weekly specials and high shelf prices.

Studying the process flow of a business means studying all capital and operating expenditures. For example, Loren Ansley, the founder and CEO of Microtel, a new chain of low-cost motels, has not only eliminated meeting rooms and restaurants but also offers a smaller sized room. Even the nightstand is attached to the wall to reduce the amount of cleaning and, therefore, cleaning supervision. Through analyzing all the capital and operating elements of a motel operation, and trimming or eliminating the less than crucial elements, this new chain has developed a successful low-cost accommodation offering without the usual connotations of "cheap & nasty."

Another motel chain, focusing on its process flow, redesigned its new motels, placing the laundry next to the manager's office. This allows the overnight manager to process the laundry and do the overnight billing, as well as be the manager on duty for any matters that occur during the night.

A further example, also from the motel industry, was an experience I had several years ago. I was staying at a Hampton Inn and then later switched to a nearby Fairfield Inn which was 25%

lower in price. Not only was it less expensive, but it had a larger living area, a larger work desk, better quality furniture, better lighting, was more sound-proof, offered four drawers instead of two, had a footstool on casters, the air conditioning was quieter and more modern, and it had a wider range of free cable channels on TV. "How do they do it?", I kept asking myself. So I sat down and did a process comparison. The Fairfield Inn had seven towels and face cloths vs. nine in the Hampton Inn, a 22% saving. They provided morning coffee, but no rolls or cereal. They had open clothes racks in the room vs. an enclosed closet, as well as open bedside units vs. drawers. Their smaller bathroom meant less construction costs and less exhaust equipment costs, and they also had a smaller hand basin and sink outside the bathroom. Their bathroom fan was connected to the light switch which meant that it went on only when the bathroom light was on. This contrasts with a separate exhaust fan switch in the Hampton Inn which could be left running indefinitely. It had one as opposed to two bedside tables, no coffee table, a reading chair instead of a more expensive couch, and a small, easier-to-use electric clock rather than a more difficult radio alarm. In essence, the Fairfield Inn gave more for less because they had focused heavily on analyzing the process, not just the price. Those companies who are both price leaders and process leaders have the world, and many happy shareholders, at their feet!

In manufacturing, some people call Kaizen re-engineering. Others call it de-specing. What it is called doesn't really matter. The issue is the mind-set that focuses on continually improving the process flow of the whole company in any way possible.

Many Japanese companies go one stage further and specify process flow improvements as part of their annual goal-setting program. For example, they may set a goal of a 5% improvement in costs not knowing exactly where the improvement will come from, realizing that by making it important, everyone's attention will be focused on accomplishing the goal. Several leading low-cost retailers with which I am familiar have as part of their corporate mandate the goal of lowering costs, as a percentage of sales, by 0.2% annually. With such a mindset, they are always finding new ways to do things better and for a lower cost.

Getting an organization always to think continuous improvement is not easy. As mentioned earlier, it starts at the top. No detail is too small. Robert Crandall, CEO of American Airlines, some years ago eliminated one olive from every salad served on flights. That one action saved tens of thousands of dollars. Recently, the CEO of the Intercontinental Hotel chain eliminated the two chocolates on guests' pillows at night. In both cases, non-essential cost items were identified and eliminated.

I have worked with a fast food chain where we analyzed every element of the building, equipment, and leasehold costs and were able to reduce the investment total of these items by 15% without the customer noticing anything was different. The great principle we must never forget is that we can improve our return on investment 15% either by reducing the investment costs approximately 15% or improving our profits 15%. In many cases, the former approach is easier. The key comparison is the cost of your process versus your competitors. Morris

Jarvis, for example, describes several examples of process advantages that his company, Hancock Fabrics, Inc., gains over his competitors. Hancock's store fixtures cost less than half of their competitors. How do they accomplish this? By making the fixtures with relatively cheap plywood and sending them to new stores for assembly on-site. Jarvis explains that the cheaper fixturing is covered by fabric, so no one knows its quality. Similarly, Hancock has always opened its stores in strip centers, where the rental costs are usually at least 30% lower than the malls where its competitors are located.

American manufacturers are years ahead of the American service industry when it comes to Kaizen. Part of the reason for the great success in manufacturing productivity improvements in the last decade has been the focus on improving the process and eliminating no-value work. Many manufacturing companies have reduced the number of parts required to make equipment. Some have rearranged equipment to minimize the number of steps required by employees. Others have standardized the thickness of steel in equipment. The list goes on. Even state governments are becoming interested. Some schools are now being built for less than half the cost of the traditional school by using simplified classrooms that can be relocated as the size of the school age population changes.

Another great benefit of a Kaizen mentality within a company is that it helps management understand the total process flow of the business and all the interrelationships existing within the business, both in physical and in dollar terms. This leads to the development of an economic model of the whole firm, tying all these relationships together. For example, some of the interrelations could include the amount of distribution space per thousand square feet of store selling area; the number of weekly customer transactions per square foot of store selling area; and the weekly number of kilowatt hours used per square foot of selling area. Costs can then be broken down into the elements which drive them, which in turn allows a business to formularize its costs, freeing management to focus primarily on customers. Such a model, once refined, becomes the "success model" of the company. Kaizen then becomes an ongoing function of continually tweaking the model.

Kaizen and the economic model are deeply intertwined. For as W. Edwards Deming has pointed out, the most efficient operations have a "profound process knowledge" of their business. The model is a mathematically based accounting representation of this detailed knowledge.

Upstream relationships

Upstream relationships started with what the Japanese call Kanban and the Americans call the Just In Time (JIT) system. Kanban is Japanese for "small card" which describes the tag attached to inventory indicating when more is needed. In America upstream relationships have also been described as "co-manufacturing" and "partnering." The philosophical drive behind developing close relationships "upstream" with one's suppliers is to eliminate cost duplication which occurs due to treating the product as if it is not moving through one boundary-less process from source to customer.

Electronic Data Interchange (EDI) is one example where such improved relationships have helped the costs of both supplier and retailer. Working from computer to computer, paper is eliminated; data doesn't need to be re-keyed; obviously, accuracy improves and information is more timely; all this results in reduced costs with the savings shared by the vendor and retailer.

The acknowledged leader in partnering today in the retail arena is Wal-Mart. Wal-Mart has always had good relationships with its vendors. The company began the "America First" program to promote American-made products. Years ago, Wal-Mart had computer tie-ups with various manufacturers so that orders could be filled quickly. In turn, the manufacturers had similar ties with their suppliers to receive their requirements more quickly to make the goods for Wal-Mart. Wal-Mart has provided space in some of its stores for suppliers to "do it their way" so that suppliers can set up "their" department selling "their" products and run it as they think it should. Then, several years ago, Wal-Mart and Procter & Gamble embarked on a very ambitious project which would help these two giants. Their objectives were simple: to reduce Wal-Mart's out-of-stock level; to reduce the inventory level; to reduce process costs from source to customer; and to increase sales. The methodology was simple: an open relationship between the two companies with over 30 Procter & Gamble employees having a permanent office at Wal-Mart's headquarters! Instead of the traditional semi-antagonistic relationships between vendors and retailers, the mind-set in this relationship was different: how can the vendor, having the full trust and inside knowledge of the retailer, help the retailer? The results? Total inventories dropped over 30%. Sales jumped dramatically, moving Wal-Mart from Procter & Gamble's third largest customer to its largest customer in a short time. Inventory turns almost doubled.

This program was so successful that in December 1990 Wal-Mart announced to 220 other vendors that "partnering is the new way of life." Kmart followed with a similar announcement in April 1991 with its major vendors. Supermarket chains such as H. E. Butt have announced their own variations of the concept. So too have other manufacturers such as Quaker Oats. The power of partnering is enormous. Even apart from eliminating costs duplicated by both the vendor and the retailer, the significant reduction in inventory levels has, in itself, enormous implications for competitive pricing. For many retailers, a reduction in net inventory levels of 10% will allow them to drop their prices up to 3% and still earn the same return on investment! This will have significant implications on the competitive strategy of retailers.

Attitude Towards Profits

As a general rule, American service companies tend to focus on results and the last person in line who produces them. In contrast, many Japanese companies focus on the process with the responsibility for profitability resting squarely on the shoulders of top management.

To illustrate this difference, let's consider the produce department of a supermarket. American supermarkets often pay the produce manager a percentage of the profitability of his department. Unfortunately, on too many occasions, I have seen bruised peaches and nectarines on the bottom of packs sold to customers, apples that should have been regraded and sold for a lower price left on display with top quality apples, and so on. The thought process of the produce manager is that "If you want the maximum of profits I will give it to you because that is what you're rewarding me for." It's a very short-sighted approach and really hurts sales, costs, and profits in the long term as customers over time stop buying their produce there because of the lower quality they receive.

By contrast, a Japanese produce manager's bonus is part of the total corporation's bonus awarded twice a year. Here the produce manager is rated upon the actions that will generate long-term profitability, such as the quality and presentation of the produce, the cleanliness of the produce area, and the interaction with the customers. In other words, the focus is on the process that leads to long-term sales and profit maximization and cost minimization.

Focusing on the process and the team is not a new concept to America. One outstanding example is the basketball team at the University of North Carolina under coach Dean Smith. The remarkable record of this team over the past decade is, in no small way, attributable to the development of the team as a team. When someone scores a goal, it is not just the scorer that is recognized but also the assist. Coach Dean Smith fully understands that the process does not begin with the scorer. John Wooden, another famous coach, summed up this concept extremely well when he said, "The main ingredient of stardom is the rest of the team!"

The focus on the team implies a longer-term view of profitability.

Another attitudinal difference that we can learn from the Japanese is that they often define profits as price minus cost. Too often, in American service industries our profits are defined as an add-on to cost. This is a significant difference. By focusing on the former definition, constant attention is paid to reducing both the selling price of the product and the cost price of the product. The understanding is that the standouts in the marketplace have the lowest prices as well as the lowest process costs. This attitudinal difference is what explains the heavy emphasis on Kaizen and on the upstream relationships.

CHAPTER 9

THE ROLE MODEL EFFECT

We all have heroes. We learn all we can about them and then try to copy them. One woman I know admires Raquel Welch. She has bought her exercise and beauty book. She reads all the articles she can about Raquel Welch. She even cuts out photographs in magazine articles of Raquel's various hairstyles and takes them to her hairdresser to develop similar ones for herself. In so many ways, my friend has emulated her hero (with excellent results, I must say!).

So too, can companies also emulate heroes. By identifying business leaders and companies we admire, we can learn a great deal. I have found it most helpful in my business life. One of my four business heroes for many years has been Sam Walton. I have read and studied everything possible about him and Wal-Mart. As a result, I have adapted many ideas and practices into my own business philosophy and into the companies with which I have worked.

Cost leaders constantly are looking for ideas to improve their own operations. Sam Walton teaches his people to gain at least one good idea from every other retail operation they visit, even if it's in poor shape. The pre-eminence of the Toyota Motor Company, the leader in quality and in "lean" manufacturing, has its roots in a three-month study tour of American auto plants by Eija Toyoda in 1950. After studying U.S. auto practices, he returned to Japan with the thought that his company could improve upon what he saw. It took a long time to accomplish

65

his dream, but the Toyota Production System today is synonymous with the highest quality and the most efficient operations in the auto industry throughout the world.

The buzz word for looking outside of one's company and comparing oneself with the best practices among competitors and others is benchmarking. Some companies, such as General Electric, simply call it Best Practices. The idea was first popularized in this country in the early 1980's after Xerox Corporation was unhappy about the in-roads Japanese manufacturers were making on the photocopy business. Xerox undertook a comprehensive study of its competitors' products and processes and was amazed to see how much more its competitors were accomplishing at significantly lower costs. Armed with this detailed "benchmark" of the most cost-effective methods of developing copiers, Xerox radically changed how it built its machines and how it marketed them, thereby reversing its declining fortunes. Today, Xerox is considered a world-class leader in the photocopy industry.

Without question, one of the most effective ways a company can significantly narrow the gap between itself and the cost leader of its industry is to carry out a benchmarking study of the leader in its industry. This has become quite common practice in manufacturing over the last decade, and is now creeping into the service and retail sectors. I have seen one retail chain systematically study every element of its industry leader and like Eiji Toyoda, make improvements upon what it saw, and now, after three years, this retail chain is outperforming the leader in certain key result areas. It can be done in any industry by any company!

Unfortunately, the major focus for too many companies is internal. Comparisons are made against last year's results or against budget. Everyone works hard to accomplish the results, and congratulations flow when the company beats them. But what if the company is performing at a significant disadvantage to the leader in its industry? For too many companies, an external focus is ignored until the company is in deep trouble, and sometimes even until filing for bankruptcy under Chapter 11. Often, only then do some companies become serious about the performance benchmarks of the leaders in their industry.

One simple set of benchmarks that airlines use is the Transportation Department's monthly report on customer complaints per 100,000 fliers and the percentage of flights that arrived on time. The scores for all airlines are reported. Obviously, an excellent ongoing benchmark comparison. But you don't have to wait for your industry association to benchmark your performance. You can do it yourself. The best such benchmarking I have seen is carried out, in-house, by Smith's Food and Drug Centers, a very successful chain based in Salt Lake City. The company has a team of employees who are constantly calling consumers, on a random basis, in the company's various markets and measuring how these people think about Smith's and its competitors on about 20 critical benchmark issues. The responses are summarized on a weekly basis with immediate corrective action initiated by CEO Jeff Smith wherever warranted. A full summary is presented to board members at every Board Meeting. The company has realized for a long time that the most important benchmarking of all is that of relative customer perceptions, not just process (cost) benchmarking, as the former drive the latter.

In business, results are relative, not absolute. Earning an 18% return on investment may be fine in the absence of any comparison. Earning an 18% return on investment is disappointing, however, if the industry leader is earning 27%. Assuming a similar dividend payout ratio, the industry leader can grow 50% faster than you with such returns. That does not augur well for the future.

A formalized systematic benchmarking program is one of the most valuable cost improvement programs that any company can introduce. Even for the cost leaders, such a program is important because while the cost followers are trying to narrow the gap, the cost leader needs to consider ways to widen the gap. Seldom will a company have the best practices in every phase of its process flow within its industry. Everyone can always learn something from one's competitors. But even a company which is the leader in all areas of its industry's process flow can look outside to other industries to find even better practices. One of the leading exponents of benchmarking in manufacturing today is General Electric. The company identifies non-competing companies anywhere in the world which are leaders in some particular function and asks if GE can study them. In return, General Electric shares its findings with the company and then invites it to study some element of GE, in exchange. GE has benchmarked practices in companies ranging from Honda to Hewlett Packard. This constant search for continuous improvement is what makes companies great.

Each retail industry usually has a peculiar strength. Other non-competing industries can usually learn from them. For example, Toys 'R' Us adopted the highly efficient supermarket method of labor scheduling which had a very positive effect not just on labor costs but on the total cost structure. Between 1985 and 1989, for example, their expenses to sales ratio fell more than 2% of sales, a dramatic figure in retailing.

The sources for ideas of what and who to benchmark are diverse, ranging from attending trade association meetings, to discussions with investment analysts and consultants, to weekly business magazines. Another excellent source of learning about some of the best practices is recently written Harvard Business School case studies. For less than $10.00, one can buy their annual catalog of all cases produced. Just pick and choose, by area of interest, the cases that interest you. And, of course, there are the low-cost successful companies in other industries. Understanding how companies such as Conner Peripherals, Cypress Semiconductor, J.B. Hunt, Amerada Hess, Lincoln Electric, Emerson Electric, Cooper Tire and Rubber, AMP, UPS, and Cabletron Systems run their businesses at cost levels significantly below their competitors can also give you extremely helpful ideas for your business.

It never ceases to amaze me that for many years now, the Japan Productivity Center, based in Washington, D.C., has done nothing but study the management practices of American companies with the simple objective of helping share good ideas with companies in Japan. Perhaps it's time we set up a similar center in Japan! And several other countries, too, for that matter! Certainly, within our own companies, we should have someone responsible for coordinating similar activities.

CHAPTER 10

MEASURING YOUR WAISTLINE

The most effective monthly management reports I have seen summarize all key aspects of the company's performance in four single pages. They are:

Table 1—Operating Results Statement (ORS)
Table 2—Operating Balance Sheet (OBS)
Table 3—Operating Profit Statement (OPS)
Table 4—Operating Cash Statement (OCS).

All of these reports are presented in a way to help operating management rather than the accountants. I find that too many monthly reports should really be called monthly accounting reports rather than monthly management reports!

These four reports, which are included in the appendix, cover all critical financial and non-financial data that management needs to monitor and improve its business. For example, the Operating Results Statement includes a number of key non-financial data such as the company's customer satisfaction index, its customer retention rate, the number of suggestions received per employee, advertising cost per customer transaction, and other key cost measures relevant to the organization.

The Operating Balance Sheet reformats the traditional balance sheet to show the company's net investment and then follows with a summary of the sources of funds for that net investment. These balance sheet numbers are shown both in total and as an average per store. The latter calculation is particularly important because management can much more readily comprehend a balance sheet when it is broken down into an average investment cost per store basis.

The third table, the Operating Profit Statement, focuses on sales, gross profits, and costs on an average per store, per week basis. However, it separates the operating costs and profits from the accounting paper entries such as LIFO, net capitalized lease credits, and any other adjustments which are really paper entries, such as the expensing of goodwill. The operating profit is simply the gross profit less direct "real" operating expenses, before the accounting paper entries. This shows operating management how well they are operating the business before the accountants fuzzy the results! Then, from this operating profit figure a charge for cost of capital on the company's net investment is deducted. The resultant figure is the Operating Profit After a Charge for Capital, or OPACC. This figure is the single best number to measure a company's performance because it ties the balance sheet with the profit statement. In my experience, poorly and average performing companies ignore this relationship. Their top management focuses all the time on the profit statement and generally ignores and therefore doesn't manage the balance sheet. By using the company's cost of capital and charging for it on the profit statement, the importance of the balance sheet is brought to everyone's attention. The value of money tied up in inventory, in idle assets, in supplies, etc., becomes much more meaningful.

The Operating Cash Statement, our fourth table, shows the changes in the key components of the company's cash position over each of the past four quarters, together with projections over the next four quarters and the resultant bank balances. It highlights, for both past and future quarters, the key ratios of the drivers of the business, such as the number of weeks' inventory and labor productivity, expressed in physical terms.

These four pages are really all that top management needs to review to manage the business. Obviously, each element of each table has various levels of detail according to whom the reports are issued. The value of this approach, defining top management needs and then fanning information downwards, is that everyone understands the way top management looks at the business, and they, in turn, will think in the same terms. For example, the monitoring of non-financial advance indicators such as your company's customer satisfaction index and customer retention rate means that all employees become much more aware of these critical measurements, even though they are not recorded in the company's accounting ledger. Similarly, the recording of physical measures, such as number of units sold per employee hour, the number of customer transactions per store per week, and the number of items sold per customer transaction, allows not only internal year-to-year comparisons, but also inter-company comparisons on a real basis. Such measurements allow you to benchmark not just within the U.S., but worldwide, because they ignore the distortion caused by different currency values and inflation rates.

The Operating Profit Statement shows the average weekly per store performance this year versus last year for the current period and the year to date. There is no budget comparison. To improve results this year over last, just focus on improving the average store's results one week at a time!

For individual store results, some cost leaders use a dynamic comparison. As described earlier, they compare each element of a store's performance to the average performance of all stores in the chain with a similar sales volume. Every four weeks such a Norm Form (see appendix for a simplified example) is issued to each store showing its performance against its peers for the latest four- and twelve-week periods. Variances from the average performance of the group are identified, and those exceptionally good and poor performances for any line item are appropriately highlighted. Some chains, as indicated in Chapter 5, go one stage further and develop an exception report for management showing only those items that are exceptionally good or bad. This saves an enormous amount of managerial time spent pouring over pages of reports. By identifying exceptions and printing them on a separate computer sheet, management then knows where to focus its attention for the next four weeks. Those stores operating within the pre-determined "normal" parameters can be left to keep on doing their good job.

Exception reports can be used in so many ways throughout an organization to improve operating results while at the same time significantly reducing the amount of time that management must spend on paperwork.

One variation of the exception report is the decile report. Simply rank your stores from top to bottom in sales volume, break them into tenths, or deciles, and then analyze relative performance within each decile group.

Measuring performance in both physical and financial terms gives a business a better understanding of its overall process and what drives the cost of that process. It helps avoid the "average costing cancer" which seems to be a real problem in many service industries today. Department stores, in particular, seem to be prone to this malady through their constant advertising of one- and two-day sales. Consider the department stores' costs involved in such things as the numerous meetings to decide what should be advertised, the time involved in preparation of the sales program, the cost of sign preparation, the cost of advertising, and on top of all that, the costs of the merchandise markdowns. Ask a department store executive what the true cost of such activities is, and most won't be able to answer accurately because these costs are averaged into their annual programs. Knowing the costs on an activity basis rather than an average basis would give department stores a foundation to address their inherent problems. Knowing the true costs of such promotions could even help department stores develop a new marketing plan, such as Every Day Low Prices toward which Dillards is moving, or stealth marketing techniques to give markdowns only to the best customers rather than signaling that the markdowns are available to the world at large.

The average costing cancer is not confined to department stores. Supermarkets also suffer from the same mindset. One example is the use of the express checkout lane. Many supermarkets have express checkout lanes for customers who buy ten items or less. Typically, the items purchased by such customers are bread, milk, beer, and cigarettes—all low-margin merchandise. After allowing for the processing costs of such orders, the supermarket often loses money on these transactions. Yet the supermarket gives priority to these small order customers, while customers who really contribute to the supermarket's profitability, those with shopping carts full of merchandise, wait three or four deep in line alongside these privileged few!! By contrast, the wholesale club industry has it right. They have check stands set aside exclusively for their business customers who typically spend three times the amount of the individual members. They are rewarding the right customers, whereas the supermarkets are rewarding the wrong customers. They understand their costs.

Measuring performance through numbers is obviously extremely helpful. Another way to measure progress in reducing the corporate waistline is to have an outside person or group come in, with a fresh perspective, and make recommendations for improvement. One cost-effective method of doing this is, instead of going to high-priced consultants, is to approach a business school you respect and invite it to send a team of students to review your performance. Many business schools, such as Harvard, Wharton, Chicago, and the University of South Carolina, all have such programs which give students course credit for such "consulting" work. It's low cost to the company, great experience for the students, and usually highly beneficial to both parties. Some schools, such as Babson College, have summer intern programs which have been very beneficial to participating companies.

Overall, cost-conscious companies have a better understanding of all the elements of their cost structure, yet, at the same time, focus on just the few driving activities which have the greatest influence on overall profitability. Wal-Mart, for example, which manages detailed information so well, just focuses on three numbers each week: sales, sales per square foot, and labor costs. The challenge for all of us is to develop within our companies a culture which focuses on the few critical numbers, knowing that everyone will be controlling the little numbers, too!

CHAPTER 11

GETTING STARTED

Quickly read Part B of this book, describing specific cost-conscious practices of lean organizations. Then ask yourself whether the waistline of your company is larger than it should be. Do you want to shrink it? Do you want to change the culture of your company into that of a lean team? If you do, on the following pages one possible approach is described to help you accomplish this. Obviously, there are many different ways of reaching the same end goal. The ideal approach for you will depend upon such things as your company's relative position in the industry, the urgency of the need for cost reduction, the existing corporate culture, and the recent history of the company. Therefore, use the program as an ideas check list to help you develop your own unique program suitable for your needs.

A. *Where are You?*

Ask yourself:

1. How do you compare with the industry leader and other significant players in the industry from the point of view of sales growth, cost structure, and profitability?

2. What are the long-term implications for your company if you continue on your present course, relative to your competitors? What are the long-

term implications for your company, relative to your competitors, if you develop a lean team culture?

3. Decide where you would like to be in three or four years' time, relative to the industry leader or an average of your significant competitors.

4. How will you measure your progress? (Using the Operating Profit After a Charge for Capital is recommended because it ties in both expense and asset management as well as ensuring that sales and gross profits are kept in focus.)

5. As a leader, what are you prepared to do yourself, both in symbolic and real terms, to lead by example? Remember that credibility is all-important if you want to change the culture of your organization. Here is what others have done by way of example:

- Sold the corporate jet.
- Started flying coach instead of first class.
- Moved out of a large office into a smaller modest office and converted the previous executive office into a group of offices.
- Converted the board room into a general meeting room to be used by anyone.
- Sold the art work in the building.
- Put a significantly larger portion of their pay at risk by reducing their salary and increasing their bonus portion (which is conditional upon performance).
- Eliminated their privileged parking spot to reduce the barrier between the top and bottom of the organization.

6. Do you see any changes in your marketing strategy, such as a switch to Every Day Low Prices,

that will help you trim costs? If so, do you plan to introduce this program now, before a cost reduction program begins, or at a later stage, as a refinement to the cost reduction program?

7. Decide what you will tell employees about job security as you introduce this program. Be completely honest with yourself, and with the employees. If you believe some employees will become redundant, ask yourself:

- Will you offer them job security and reassign them as jobs become open due to attrition, early retirement, and the elimination of temporary help?
- Or will you lay people off as positions become redundant?
- Will you guarantee alternative jobs for people who recommend that their own jobs be consolidated or eliminated?

The answers to the above questions are extremely critical because people costs are your largest costs and probably the greatest area for improvement as you streamline your operations. However, employees will not recommend job consolidation and elimination if they see themselves or their friends dismissed as a result. The critical issue here is to think through how you can realistically reassure employees that some employees will probably lose their jobs, but you'll do everything possible to ensure fairness and equity. You may even consider the appointment of an ombudsman to be an arbitrator should any cases of perceived inequity arise. The ombudsman should be someone you respect and whom you believe the employees will trust. This person could possibly be an outside board member, the VP of Human Resources, or an outside facilitator.

8. Do you see any excess layers of management that need elimination, any weak executives who need to be demoted or dismissed, or any necessary departmental consolidation? If so, think through whether it would be best to announce such changes prior to the introduction of your cost program, concurrently with the program introduction, or as part of the program. If you elect the last option, be aware that this may be the most difficult path as employees will see themselves as vulnerable to layoffs.

9. Decide how prepared you are to be open with all relevant information, both good and bad, with employees. It's preferable to be more open. Rest assured, employees generally will respect the need for confidentiality of information.

10. Decide how you will share the rewards of improvement with your employees. One approach is to share a percentage of the increase in your Operating Profit after a Charge for Capital over the base 12 months to all employees working over 1000 hours during the coming year and who are on the payroll at the end of the 12-month period. The bonus pool could be allocated to all employees, from top to bottom, on the basis of salary earned. If an employee's pay is 0.35% of the total salary base for the year, then that employee receives 0.35% of the bonus pool. If you wish, you could adjust for outstanding performers (up to 10% of employees) by paying them twice their salary weighting. In the second year of the program, and thereafter, the bonus pool could switch to a flat percentage of the

Operating Profit after a Charge for Capital, shared in the same manner as above.

11. Decide whether you want to organize this whole program yourself or have a facilitator assist you. If you decide upon the latter course, an outside, rather than inside, facilitator is often selected because employees generally feel more comfortable disclosing their thoughts on cost reductions to an impartial outsider than to an insider. This is particularly the case in the early stages of such a program because many employees are still trying to assess how serious you are about the whole program.

12. Decide the time, the place, and who should attend your first management meeting to discuss this whole program. How will you gain their acceptance and active involvement?

13. Discuss, formally or informally, with Board members your plan and receive approval, where appropriate, for any significant changes you plan to make.

B. *Preparation for the Meeting with Management*

1. Working with your facilitator, draft a letter to those who will be invited to the meeting, broadly discussing the purpose of the meeting. Advise that a questionnaire will follow your letter to help them prepare for the meeting and also to gather feedback prior to the meeting.

2. Develop a questionnaire for the attendees. Ask for their specific suggestions for cost reduction ideas in the company. Ask them to pull no punches. To ensure the best and most open response, have

the completed questionnaires sent back to the facilitator, rather than yourself.

3. Respect the confidential nature of these responses by asking the facilitator to rearrange the wording of some responses, if necessary, to protect the source of the suggestions, and to collate all answers.

4. Review the cost-saving suggestions received and use them as a basis for finalizing your meeting plan.

C. *The Management Meeting*

In planning this meeting, keep in mind some of the thoughts that many attendees will have:

a. How will this cost-saving program affect me and my job? Will I have a job?

b. If I make cuts in my department, will all other departments be equally tough on themselves?

c. How serious is top management about cost-cutting? Is this a flash in the pan or are they really serious about this on a long-term basis?

d. Will they really listen to my cost-cutting ideas?

The above concerns should be addressed in planning the meeting. Below is a possible agenda for the meeting.

I *Address by CEO*

- Welcome.
- Purpose of meeting.

- Company position in industry.
- Implications for the future.
- The solution: price and process improvements.
- The focus today is on process improvements.
- Spell out the amount of savings, in total, you believe possible in the following 12 months.
- Stress how serious you are about this program.
- Stress that it is a long-term process rather than a quick, one-shot deal.
- Outline your decisions from Section A above, including your thoughts on any marketing plan changes, job security, appointment of an ombudsman, and sharing the gains with employees.
- Ask for everyone's help for the meeting today and the challenges in the future.

II *Presentation by Facilitator and/or CEO*

- The purpose of any business is to maintain the marketing mission with the least amount of non-critical costs.
- The advantages of a cost-conscious company.
- Stress how complexity costs and simplicity saves.
- Show the need to scrape the barnacles off the bottom of the boat regularly, the need to eliminate non-essentials.
- Thank participants for responding to the questionnaire and share with them a summary of all their responses.
- Seek their input and help through discussion

groups and open discussion on such matters as:

Involving everyone in the company in the program.

Identifying likely roadblocks to success at all levels of the company, and how to remove them.

Identifying what information is needed to measure progress.

Finding ways to reward, reinforce, and communicate progress of the program.

Developing a consensus as to the four or five most important goals to focus on during the coming 12 months.

Developing a method of handling cost-saving ideas, communicating back to the originators, and implementing the ideas.

Selecting a name for the project (one company called their program, PLUS, standing for Prevent Loss and Unnecessary Spending!)

Identifying how to introduce and make effective a process of continuous improvement throughout the whole company on a long-term basis.

Agreeing on how to introduce the whole program to everyone else in the company.

III *CEO Wrap-up*

Summarize the major points of the day.

Announce dates of follow-up meetings for this group, if any, over the following two years.

Pledge your long-term commitment to the program.

Thank everyone for their contribution.

D. *Implementation*

1. Follow through on the ideas and decisions from the management meeting.

2. Meet with all levels of the organization. All top management should be involved in these meetings on a regular basis during the following 24 months.

3. Measure, monitor, and reinforce progress.

4. Top management must lead by example. They must constantly reinforce the cultural changes required to implement the program. They must recognize cost reduction ideas and their originators. They must help remove roadblocks placed in front of some cost-saving ideas. They must stress that this is a long-term process and encourage every incremental gain made.

A Few Words of Caution.

Unless you are in desperate straits, don't go overboard! There will be an urge to purge. Remember that crash diets seldom lead to a change in lifestyle. Far better to plan for the long term. Losing half a pound a week for 60 weeks is more likely to lead to a completely new way of life in the long term than dropping 30 pounds in three weeks. However, there are usually some obvious cost-reduction targets. Act on them quickly. Get some successes under your belt!

Analyze tasks, functions, and process. Eliminate the unnecessary ones before reassigning or releasing people. Many cost-reduction programs have failed because employees were let go without management eliminating, streamlining, or consolidating their functions first.

Let employees come up with as many cost-saving ideas as possible rather than having top management force them down upon the company (unless you are in an urgent crisis situation).

Be patient, but persistent. You will trim your corporate waistline. Good luck!

PART B

Cost-Saving Practices.

COST-SAVING PRACTICES

Use this list of cost-saving practices to help you review and challenge your organization's current cost habits.

Some of the ideas should save you thousands of dollars as soon as they are implemented. Most will save smaller amounts. However, collectively, the practice of these ideas will add a great deal to your profitability . . . and to the cost-conscious mentality of your whole organization. This heightened cost awareness will, over the years, save you untold amounts of money.

Remember that no one company practices all the items on the list, but the more cost-conscious a company is, the more it practices.

The list includes the ideas mentioned in Part A as well as many, many others.

AAA.

Check to see whether your real estate or operations departments regularly purchase maps of cities and states. If they do, why not replace this practice by having designated employees become members of the American Automobile Association. Some employees are probably members already, so you may not even have to pay for the memberships from corporate funds. With this membership AAA will provide free maps of anywhere in the United States. In addition, members of AAA are entitled to a rate reduction at many hotels and motels as well as special low-cost help in the case of vehicle breakdowns, etc. Members are also eligible to receive free membership in a VISA credit card program. This obviously would be more cost effective than if these employees are on a company-sponsored credit card program.

Accounting, Centralized.

A centralized accounting system is usually the most cost-efficient method of processing your information. Having one person who really understands, say, property taxes, is more economical than many part-time specialists scattered throughout the organization.

Accounting, Physical Measures.

Wherever possible, record all significant physical measures in your accounting system. Include such things as hours worked by department, miles driven, cartons of merchandise handled, and items sold per department. This information is critical in measuring productivity among similar departments as well as over time. Using physical measures is inflation (or deflation!) proof and eliminates the need for budgeting. Simply aim to beat last year's actual productivity results. Another excellent by-product of physical measures is that it can help control headquarters costs. For example, you can measure the productivity of, say, the Payroll Department by monitoring the number of hours worked in Payroll, either per number of stores or per number of employees processed. Your report would look like this:

Payroll Productivity (Dept. hours per 100 employees processed)

Cur. Per.		YTD		Better (Worse) %	
TY	*LY*	*TY*	*LY*	*CP*	*YTD*
1.86	1.98	1.93	1.91	6.1%	(1.0%)

The above tells us that for the latest 4 week accounting period, the Payroll Department used 1.86 employee hours to process each 100 employee payroll records, a 6.1% improvement over the same period last year. However, on a year-to-date basis, the department's productivity of 1.93 hours for every 100 employees is 1.0% worse than for the same year-to-date period last year.

Accounting, Responsibility Based.

Wherever practicable, identify all costs on a responsibility-based system. In this way, expenses can be identified by activity, person, or department on a regular basis. For example, a telephone bill should be broken into the basic service charge with a separate account for long distance phone calls. It's the latter account which varies from month to month and needs the greatest amount of control and attention. Also, at headquarters, each telephone extension should have the cost of each call identified with a weekly or monthly report issued for each extension.

Accounting, Utility Bills.

Have one person dedicated to monitoring utility bills. This can save a great deal of money. In addition, every year or two, have an external specialist company review your utility bills to see if you are missing anything in your internal process. You typically pay them 50% of any additional savings they make for you.

Advertising Agencies.

As soon as size justifies, set up your own in-house advertising agency. Paying the 15% advertising commissions to yourself is always preferable to paying them to an outside agency!

Advertising, Bumper Stickers, Customers.

To maximize advertising effectiveness, have a bumper sticker campaign which encourages customers to put your company's bumper sticker on their cars. Have a sweepstake for all customers who take a bumper sticker. The bumper sticker with your advertising message usually stays on your customers' cars a lot longer than the life of the program!

Advertising, Bumper Stickers, Employees.

Have your employees advertise for the company by displaying the company's bumper sticker with its appropriate message. To encourage widespread usage by employees, you may wish to have a drawing each month of, say, ten employee names (use your payroll employee numbers). To those employees drawn who have the bumper sticker on their cars, give a $100 savings bond (the cost per bond obviously is a lot less!) from the company.

Advertising, Charitable.

Don't! Avoid advertising in such things as school annuals, opera programs, etc., unless a real benefit is obvious. Such advertising is usually in the realm of charitable donations and their cost effectiveness is highly questionable. It usually warms the advertiser's heart but not his cash register drawers!

Advertising, Cooperative.

Take full advantage of any cooperative advertising allowances. Monitor them to ensure that you utilize all of this "free" advertising allowance.

In addition, ask for your advertising allowance monies to be received at the beginning of the year or quarter. Agree to send the vendors appropriate tear sheets at the end of each quarter with a promise to refund any allowance not used. Cash is always nicer in your hands than in your vendors'!

Advertising, Corporate Annual Results.

Avoid. Save your money! As we are reminded, by good authority, "by their fruits ye shall know them." Good results always seem to be found by the investment community. So, too, are poor results. Placing a paid advertisement describing your latest year in *Barrons*, *Forbes*, or the *OTC Review* may make you feel good, but it doesn't help your bottom line or stock price.

Advertising, Delivery Trucks.

Each delivery truck is a moving billboard for the company. Use it accordingly. The message you carry on the rear of your trailer is critically important as it is read by the driver of every following vehicle. Similarly, the rear mud flaps of your delivery trucks can carry a message for you. Drive behind a Wal-Mart truck sometime and you'll read: "Low Prices Every Day ... Wal-Mart" and, on their mud flaps, "Wal-Mart ... Every Day Low Prices." Even their license plates read EDLP! For some companies, the cost of the company message on their delivery trucks is less than five cents per thousand people "impressions," which is very cheap advertising! The courtesy and speed of the drivers of these trucks are also part of the advertising package, so ensure that your drivers constantly exhibit road courtesy. Similarly, the cleanliness and appearance of the truck is an important part of your message to the outside world.

Advertising, Freelancers.

A number of companies have found freelancing advertising executives not only cost less than agencies but also provide the utmost attention.

Advertising, Internal.

Sell your employees company-related products at cost—such things as tee shirts, company hats, etc. They will wear these items with pride while exposing the company name to potential customers. You can sell the same items to customers . . . happily, for a profit! It's a twist on an old expression: "They pay to advertise!"

Advertising, License Plate Frames.

Most employees are proud to work for your company. Allow them to buy (at cost, or less) license plate frames with your company logo on it. Another option is to give such frames to long-service employees as part of their recognition package for long service. They'll advertise your company with pride! Certainly, all company vehicles should have such a frame.

Advertising, Newspapers.

Follow the old adage of "four columns wide and go over the fold." This means that no one can have a bigger advertisement than you on the page. It also allows for written material to be placed alongside your ad, which encourages readers to stop and read the page rather than flip it, a frequent occurrence when a page is completely covered by an advertisement. This ensures that you receive similar readership, if not more readership, than a full page, at a lower cost!

Advertising, Television.

Once you have identified your target market, arrange with your agency (if you use one) to buy that television target market at a certain cost per thousand. Allow your agent to approach various television stations and negotiate that price accordingly. Make no stipulation as to when the commercials should be shown, provided they reach the required number of target viewers per week. It's also cost effective to buy your television advertising for one year at a time, even though you may not advertise on certain weeks.

Advertising, Television.

Whenever you run a television commercial with any product in it, ask the manufacturer of that product to pay for at least the cost of the production of that commercial. Usually they will! They love the exposure!

Advertising, Total.

Over time, the company's total advertising as a percentage of sales should be reduced as volume grows. This is taking advantage of the economies of scale. The reduction should be steeper where the company grows in the same and/or contiguous geographic areas with overlapping media coverage.

Advertising, Word-of-Mouth.

This is the most powerful form of advertising because of the believability of the advertiser. Customers will do it for you without prompting if you treat them well. Employees will, too. But you can also encourage employees to tell a certain number of people each week about your company, as one prominent restaurant chain does.

Air Conditioning.

Use water-cooled refrigeration units, rather than air-cooled units, to reduce costs. Also, avoid having air conditioning in your back rooms. Large area fans do the trick a lot cheaper! Place timers on your airconditioning switches to turn them off and on automatically at the right time. Use programmed thermostats which cannot be adjusted without a special security code.

Airplanes, Corporate.

Sell them! Find a travel agency that will guarantee you the lowest available rates on all booked flights. Request a monthly report showing the regular fare, what you paid, and the savings. In those rare (we hope!) cases where a private plane is necessary, charter one from the local or a nearby airfield or from another company with a corporate jet. Let them have the ego . . . let you have the savings!

Air Travel.

No one should fly first class at company expense. After all, can anyone show you how the quality of their thinking is better in first class? Should any employee wish to fly first class, that person can use his or her Frequent Flyer mileage bonus points received from previous traveling on your company business for an upgrade to first class.

Air Travel Discounts.

In this age of unbelievable special deals for "senior citizens," are you taking advantage of them? For example, many airlines offer discounts to travelers who are at least 62 years old. These airline travel discounts usually come in the form of a book of coupons. Some, however, give you a straight 10% discount just by showing proof that you have reached that golden age. Are all of your "senior" employees who travel for you on company business taking advantage of these deals? Not only airlines give these generous concessions. Many hotels and motels do also. In fact, it would probably be worthwhile to have all of your senior employees join AARP because of all the discounts that organization generates for its members. There is just no reason in the world why businesses should not take advantage of all of the deals available in the marketplace!

Air Travel, Expenses.

Have someone internally monitor all air travel expenses for errors and incorrect billings. It's amazing how many personal trips seem to end up billed to the company.

Amnesty.

It never ceases to amaze me as I wander around offices to see the great accumulation of pens, pencils, pads, etc., on employees desks. One simple way to trim this "excess inventory" is to have an annual amnesty day whereby cartons are placed in each major office area and employees put in all their surplus stationery that has accumulated at their desks. What is reclaimed can be recycled through the stationery and supplies department. It's also a very simple message to remind everybody in the organization that every penny is important.

Analytical Department.

Establish an analytical department that does nothing but research questions on costs anywhere within the company for any manager requiring this information. This is a lot cheaper than having managers spend their time researching cost variances.

Anniversary Cards.

Cards acknowledging the anniversary of being hired are preferable to birthday cards because: (1) they are unexpected; (2) you don't have to send them every year..you can send them in years 3, 5, 7, 10, 15, etc.; and (3) preparing them reminds you how lucky you are to have such long-service employees, many of whom are probably the unsung heroes of the organization.

Annual Reports, Cost.

Review the cost per copy of your annual report. If you're spending more than $1.25 per copy, you are probably spending too much. (To those in the whole-sale club industry, if you are spending over twenty five cents per copy you are spending too much! Their annual reports have sometimes been in a simple newspaper format!) It is not the glitter in an annual report that moves the stock price. It is the results and message in it. Therefore, reduce the number of pages, the amount of photography, and evaluate whether you really need those color photos.

Annual Reports, One per Address.

Include in your annual report a request to shareholders asking them to authorize the company to mail only one annual report to their address. This eliminates a number of annual reports going to a whole family at one address. For example, in a recent annual report of Food Lion, Inc. shareholders were invited to return a card, if appropriate, which read:

"Since I have access to a copy of Food Lion's Annual Report at this address, I hereby authorize Food Lion not to mail another copy to my account. I understand that dividend checks, proxy material, quarterly reports and other publications will be mailed to me as usual. Should circumstances change, I shall advise you so that Annual Reports will again be sent to this account." (Underneath this statement, the shareholder gave his or her name, address, account number, and signature.)

Annual Reports, Bi-pak.

Use bi-pak envelopes for mailing your annual report and proxy to shareholders. These two pieces of mail have different mailing rates and can be charged accordingly, even though mailed together.

Annual Reports, Mailing.

If your annual report is ready at least ten days prior to the statutory mailing date, then it can be sent at bulk rates through the mail and meet the statutory requirements.

Annual Reports, Requests.

Annual reports sent in response to requests during the year should be sent as "Bound Printed Matter, Fourth Class." After all, many annual reports finish up, unread, in someone's filing cabinet.

Anti-union.

If your company is non-union, and you believe it's cost advantageous to keep it that way, then regularly communicate with all your employees why it's in their interests to have a non-union company. On a regular basis, have a labor lawyer speak to your key employees about how to keep your company union-free. Such a regular small investment could save a large cost in the years ahead.

Art Work.

Any executive who wishes to hang pieces of art in his office should be allowed to do so . . . but at his own expense. Allow your executives to express their own individuality through their paintings and art in their office, but not at corporate expense.

Attorneys.

Keep calls from your people to attorneys to an absolute minimum. Legal fees seem to be escalating like medical costs! A few select people within the organization should be appointed as the only ones who may call your attorney. As one wit once said, describing a lawyer: "As your attorney, it is my duty to inform you that it is not important that you understand why you're paying me so much money. What's important is that you continue to do so!"

Attorneys, Calls.

One CEO of a highly profitable company never lets his lawyer send him a letter. He receives his opinion by phone and saves the company's legal firm's bill from dictation, secretarial, and overhead costs for telling him the same thing again in writing!

Audit.

Plan your internal audit program so that the worst performing areas, based upon predetermined criteria, are audited most frequently. In this way, you get the maximum return on your audit time.

Audit Fees.

Sit down with your external auditors once a year and go over the audit fee for the following year. Stress the critical importance of cost consciousness and challenge every element of their fee. Typically, your audit fee should increase at a rate less than your sales increase because a significant amount of fixed, repetitive work is included in an audit. For example, if sales are expected to increase 20% in the coming year, it is unlikely that fees should increase by more than one-third of this figure or approximately 7%. If you are still unhappy with the value for money from your auditors, hire a legal-auditing firm to analyze your audit billings.

Audit Fees, Bids.

Every 5–10 years, seeking competitive bids for your audit work is wonderful, both for your audit fee structure and for keeping your auditors on their toes. How many companies stay lean and cost-conscious when their contracts are automatically renewed each year without competitive bids? Auditors are no different. As an old Arab proverb goes: "All sunshine makes the desert."

Audit Reports.

Provide a section on all your internal audit reports for any cost-reduction ideas the auditor may have while auditing (simplification, elimination, etc.). Internal auditors have a wonderful perspective on the company . . . utilize it.

Audit Scope.

Insist that your external auditors, when determining their fees, plan on performing only the work necessary for statutory purposes. Remind them also that you have no need for beautifully (i.e., expensive) bound presentation folders and similar frills.

Audit, Year End.

External auditors, not surprisingly, have the habit of utilizing internal auditors and internal accounting staff as much as possible during their year-end audit. To keep this hidden cost under control, spell out, in your annual audit fee agreement, how many hours of internal time can be used, and what you will charge them for all hours used in excess of this limit. After all, they have budgeted their hours when setting their fee. Why shouldn't you?

Auto Fleet.

Each year, put out for bids to various auto dealers the number of vehicles you plan to buy for the company. This is much more cost effective than buying them one at a time.

Auto Fleet, Vans.

Where appropriate, provide vans or station wagons for your District Managers so they can readily move merchandise on an as-needed basis.

Auto Repairs.

General Motors and other auto manufacturers have special fleet repair agreement programs. Ensure that you are taking advantage of this if one is available from the manufacturer of your fleet.

Auto Replacement.

Replace company cars in the 60,000–100,000 mile range, assuming employees with company cars follow the appropriate maintenance program for their cars. A long mileage life is usually more cost effective than replacing cars on a more frequent basis.

Auto Trade-ins.

As an incentive for employees to maintain their company cars, have them sell their old vehicle before they receive their new replacement. Very simply, when the 60,000 or 100,000 mile trade-in time arrives, consult the "Blue Book" for that vehicle's trade-in value, deduct $300-$500 for advertising, etc., and then let the driver sell his vehicle for no less than this figure. The better the vehicle has been maintained, the quicker it will sell (at that price), and the sooner the driver will have a new vehicle to drive!!

Average Costing.

Avoid the cancer of average costing. Know the true cost of each product, item, and service. Always remember that to the degree that any items are being subsidized by your significantly more profitable lines, those profitable lines are vulnerable to attack from competitors. Constantly review which, if any, of your lowest profit lines, or customer groups, you wish to continue.

Back Hauls.

Negotiate freight credits from your suppliers where you use your own trucks to back haul. In some cases, these credits are more than the allowance they may allow via common carriers.

Bad Checks.

Set a tolerance standard, usually in the form of a percentage to sales, for bad checks. Remember, if your bad check losses are too low, then your bad check policy may be too tight, causing you to lose sales and profitability accordingly! That may be as damaging as a very high bad check loss figure.

Bad Checks, Returned to Customers.

If customers wish to have their bad checks returned to them after reimbursing you, charge them, say, a $2 fee for postage and handling. You can mention this at the bottom of your bad check advice letter by indicating that they can "check here" if they want the check returned by including the $2 with the payment of their bad check and service charge. Also, after finally catching up with a bad check customer, you can "invite" them (where state laws permit) to pay an additional, say, $5 "reinstatement fee" to have their name reinstated in your computer so they can cash checks again in your store. Many will!

Bad Check Collection.

It's usually more cost effective to process all bad checks internally. Then, only those that you cannot collect after 90–120 days should be sent to an outside agency for collection.

Bad Check Status.

Occasionally, ask for a bad check status report. Ensure that the bad check balance in your accounting records can be supported by a listing showing each person's name, the amount of the returned (bad) check, and the date it was sustained. In particular, review who is responsible for collecting all bad checks which are over two months old and what specific actions have been taken to date to collect them. This is important because your bad check cost is usually an expense that's overlooked as everyone goes about their work, and the longer bad checks are left the fewer you collect.

Balance Sheet.

In my observation, too many companies focus too much on the income statement and too little on the balance sheet. As the cost of capital for many companies is in the 15–25% range before tax, anything that can be done to tighten the use of capital has significant impact on profitability. One effective way of coupling the asset utilization of a company with its income statement is to add a separate line to the income statement for the cost of capital. Then, each accounting period, multiply the cost of capital by the amount of capital deployed and charge this against the income statement. Then, if the net assets of a business are rising faster than its sales, this adverse trend quickly becomes apparent on the adjusted income statement. Using this approach shows everyone the real cost of such asset- intensive benefits such as cafeterias and gyms!

Bank Bags.

Use disposable bags. They are usually cheaper than cloth bags.

Bank Fees.

If you have a number of stores, have a survey done every month of the bank fees for 5–10% of your stores. Compare these with fees with those of nearby competitive banks. Switch banks where the cost differential justifies a change.

Bank Accounts, Consolidated.

Some banks will negotiate with a geographically dispersed company to have, say, 100 stores deposit their cash and checks into one consolidated bank account as opposed to a hundred different bank accounts. This results in a significant discount on the cost of processing the checks to those accounts. In addition, you receive one bank statement for those 100 stores which you can have automatically reconciled using the bank tapes of their transaction records.

Bank Rates.

Whether investing or borrowing, avoid a cozy relationship with one bank. Daily, call 4–6 banks to get the best investing or borrowing rates. Make decisions accordingly.

Benchmarking.

Compare your detailed cost structure with the industry average and the industry best (which are usually available in various publications and from industry associations). Also, compare your cost structure with similar companies in another part of the country. Assess how you can improve your cost structure based upon these comparisons. Make it a high priority. Do it before you are forced into action due to lagging results, potential takeover, or bankruptcy.

Bill Paying.

Take your payables checks to the post office on the last day possible, at the latest time possible, usually after 5 P.M., to ensure that you maximize your cash flow. Also, have your checks date-stamped on due date.

Birthday Cards.

These are great if they are individualized to an employee. However, if the person sending the card does not know personally the person whose birthday is being celebrated, it is best that the card not be sent. Avoid standardized birthday card mailings.

Better still, don't send birthday cards at all. Instead, call those people you know and care about on their birthday. It will mean a lot more to them.

Blanket Purchase Orders.

Using a blanket purchase order avoids the cost of issuing a new purchase order for purchasing similar items over a period of time. For example, you may agree to purchase from a vendor 100,000 items, at X dollars per item, over the subsequent six months. Then, each time you order that item quote the one blanket purchase order number. This can be done for merchandise, equipment, supplies, etc. Another cost-conscious angle on this, when negotiating price, is to ask: "What price could you give us if we increased our order 10% (or 20%, or 40%, etc.)?" After receiving the new, lower price, respond by giving a blanket order for the larger quantity, together with a specific first order of, for example, 30 days supply, against the blanket order.

Board Members.

As a rule of thumb, fewer board members are preferable to more!

Books.

When searching for a gift, reward, or prize for an employee, books serve a double purpose. Not only do they fill the need, but assuming the recipients read the books given, the company can benefit from the digested contents—especially if the books include such titles as *The Effective Executive* or *Managing for Results* by Peter F. Drucker, *A Passion for Excellence* by Tom Peters & Nancy Austin, and *Kaizen* by Masaaki Imai.

Budgets.

Eliminate! Achieve the same end result, or better, by focusing on the key productivity ratios of the company. This, in addition to expense (both operating and capital) guidelines and a good reporting system, generally overcomes the need for budgeting. Norm forms (see later) are preferable to budgets. A detailed economic model of the firm also helps overcome the need for budgeting. In some firms which have budgets, they are considered a license to spend, or an exercise in "padding," or both!

Bulk Mailing Rates.

Once a year, review the post office's bulk mailing rates. Challenge your mail department to come up with ways to take even more advantage of these rates on such things as your mailers, statements, vendor checks, etc.

Business Cards.

Review who has them, who is entitled to them, and why. Check the number of cards printed on each run and their cost. Check the number of colors used and whether embossed printing is used. You will probably find that: (a) more people than really necessary have them, (b) too many are being printed on each run, and (c) a simpler, cheaper business card is available. Another cost-effective approach I have seen at store level is to use blank business cards on which the employee writes his or her name as needed.

Business Licenses.

Annual business license fees are usually based upon a store's sales. So estimate your annual sales for business license purposes very conservatively. Then, if sales are higher than the estimate, you typically pay the difference the following year, without penalty.

Buying Terms.

To ensure that you are receiving the best buying terms available from your vendors, have them sign a statement that no other company is accorded any better terms than you are and will not during the coming 12 months. Repeat annually.

Cafeterias.

Avoid them wherever possible. I have yet to see one that is not subsidized by the company. Instead, provide a break room with vending machines, microwave ovens, and refrigerators, and let employees look after themselves.

CAM Charges.

Given constantly rising common area maintenance (CAM) charges, negotiate an annual cap to the CAM charge portion of any lease.

Capital Expenditures.

Outside of any planned, preapproved capital expenditure for the year, have any other capital expenditure involving more than, say, $1,000 be approved by the CEO or someone he designates.

Captive Insurance.

For a number of companies, a captive insurance company is a very cost-effective way of risk insurance. Historically, such companies had to be offshore. However, a number of states now have enacted favorable legislation, such as no absolute minimum capitalization or no premium tax requirements, to encourage such companies to domicile in their states. A captive insurance company permits money, historically tied up in advance premiums, to be more effectively utilized using the captive's payment plan. One company using this program, with less than $250 million in annual sales, has already built up a $3 million surplus in just two years on the program!

Cardboard.

Empty cardboard cartons should be baled and sold. Why pay to have it sent to the dump when others will pay you to take it away?

Car Wash.

If you provide certain employees with company cars, the least they can do is pay for the car to be washed out of their own pockets, rather than turning in car wash expenses on their expense accounts. Stamp out any element of the corporate welfarism mentality.

Cash Balancing, Weekly.

Rather than having each store balance its cash completely on a daily basis, have them do it on a weekly basis.

Centralization.

Typically, cost-conscious companies are extremely centralized. Centralization minimizes the layers of management and reinforces the unity of strategy and the high degree of cost consciousness throughout the total organization. Wal-Mart even has its Region Managers live in their headquarters town. They are in the field Monday-Thursday and at headquarters Friday and Saturday.

Centralized Buying.

Regardless of the number of distribution centers a cost-conscious company might have, all buying is usually done centrally. In this age of computerization with daily polling, inventory management is relatively simple. By doing all buying centrally, buyers can be more specialized in individual products, thus yielding better deals.

CEO Challenge.

For an organization to be truly cost-conscious, the CEO must constantly be challenging every part of the organization regarding costs. He challenges the buyers to ensure that they are receiving the very best buying terms. He challenges operations to simplify procedures to improve productivity. He challenges the insurance department to find better rates. He challenges accounting to locate better rental car discount rates than at present, etc., etc. After all, an axle that squeaks is eventually oiled! If the CEO squeaks about costs constantly, the organization becomes very cost conscious.

Chamber of Commerce.

Although this is a very good organization, avoid automatically joining the Chamber in any town you move to. Join only if there is a demonstrated economic advantage.

Checklist.

Use simplified, standardized checklists wherever possible, ranging from a detailed preparation checklist for your annual shareholders meeting to a day-by-day checklist of things to do for each week of your current business period.

Christmas Decorations.

Don't throw them away after Christmas. Have them boxed and stored for the following year. Then just spend a few dollars extra each year "refreshing" your decoration package.

Christmas Party.

If your organization has a Christmas party at the end of the year, send a memo to all appropriate department heads reminding them of the Christmas party. In addition, remind them that as the party is expensive, the organization does not want any other expenditure at departmental level, such as Christmas luncheons. Such should be paid for by the department head, should he wish to do anything additional for his employees.

Cleaning Supplies.

Avoid the automatic habit of buying standard cleaning supplies from a supermarket or store. There are cheaper, effective alternatives. For example, here's a recipe for a simple, low-cost method of making a cleaner which is great for windows and other similar surfaces: mix 1 pint of isopropyl alcohol with 1 teaspoon of dishwashing detergent, add 1/2 cup of sudsy ammonia, and then add 7 pints of water. This will give you one gallon of cleaner.

COBRA.

Charge the full service fee allowed by law to COBRA users, rather than a nominal fee. Review annually the maximum allowed by law, and adjust your charges accordingly. COBRA is a very expensive program. The least you can do for your organization is to receive back from COBRA users the maximum permitted by law.

COLA.

Assuming your company is not unionized, avoid like the plague the mindset of an automatic cost of living salary adjustment (COLA) each year for employees. Some employees think that because inflation has occurred in the economy they should automatically have their wages adjusted, regardless of how the company is faring or how they are performing! Instead, stress that each year wage reviews will be made. However, any increases given will be strictly on merit. There will be no automatic cost of living adjustment. After all, if you have automatic cost of living adjustments, how much do you have left for merit increases?

Color Blocked Forms.

If a form is complicated, even after all your simplication efforts, determine whether different parts of the form can be printed in different colors to allow easier to understand form completion. Printing will cost more, but it may save many, many employee hours spent trying to complete the form correctly. Our objective should always be to have all corporate forms self-explanatory. No one should have to go to another document to read how to complete a form.

Company Cars.

The only employees who have company cars should be those who really need them for company work. Typically, officers do not need a car. District managers and construction coordinators do. Company cars should be basic rather than fancy.

Company Magazine.

Many outsiders, such as vendors, are interested in receiving a copy of your internal company magazine. Rather than providing it free to them, charge them for it. Also, ask them whether they are interested in placing paid advertisements in it, too! Many will!

Compensation.

As much as possible of the total compensation package for all levels of employees should be variable. The base salary should be as low as is reasonable for the area, with incentive bonuses paid for meeting/beating performance standards.

Compensating Balances.

If you have a bank loan which requires a compensating balance, re-negotiate the loan to eliminate it. Typically the cost of a compensating balance is more expensive than the cost of capital of your company. Paying a higher interest rate with no compensating balances is usually preferable.

Competitive Bids.

Always seek three or more. When only two bids are requested, the chances of winks and nods between the bidders increase significantly at your expense. Keep requesting competitive bids on what you buy. You'll be surprised how even your regular supplier is able to cut prices when he knows you are really serious about cost.

Computer Czar.

Appoint a computer report "czar" who has authority to approve, reject, or amend, all new computer reports. This will force everyone to justify the critical need, and cost, of each new report. Some reports are critical, but many are just nice to have.

Computer Equipment.

When considering purchasing new computer equipment, ask for bids from the authorized representatives of computer companies in addition to the computer companies themselves. Receiving a lower bid from the authorized reps (IR's) is not unusual as they often operate on lower margins than the computer company salesmen!

Computer Paper.

Companies produce reams of computer paper. When a printout is more than one hundred pages, use the reverse side of the printout for another run. Also, accumulate the first and last pages of each printout, which are blank, together with any other blank pages, and make them into scrap pads for internal use. After computer paper has been printed on both sides, shred it, and have it recycled.

Computer Report Requests.

Computerization is changing the way companies do business. There is a great demand for such people as systems analysts and computer programmers with the result that they are highly paid. Therefore, it makes sense to minimize the amount of time spent by these people on computer report requests. To do this, requesters wanting a new computer report should show the exact report they want, prepared on a personal computer, in the exact format required. Also, wherever possible, the requester should show that the report has been prepared on a PC for at least three consecutive periods to ensure that it has been largely "de-bugged." Changing a PC report is much cheaper than having highly paid computer programmers continually change reports because the requester didn't think through carefully enough what he or she wanted in the first place.

Consultant Accommodation.

On the odd occasion when you hire a consultant and he has to stay overnight in your hometown, you should book his motel room in your standard accommodation, using your corporate rate. If it's a lower grade than he is used to, this is a wonderful way to make him realize you are serious about being cost conscious.

Contiguous Expansion.

Expansion into adjacent territories is typically much more cost efficient than expanding into a different part of the country. For example, you can distribute from the same warehouse, you receive advertising economies of scale, you gain from an intense knowledge of the market area, and supervisory costs are less when you move "next door" rather than to a geographically distant market.

Contingency Planning.

This is an excellent way to test how cost conscious each part of your organization really is. Once a year, or every second year, ask each departmental head for their action program should sales in the following year fall, say, to 5% below this year, or to 10% below this year. Ask for their specific action program that will minimize the impact on the overall corporate results should either scenario occur. One positive by-product of this exercise is that the department heads will typically realize there are still areas of their department where they can cut costs. Usually, they go ahead and effect the cost saving immediately rather than wait for the possible sales decline! Some companies have labeled the different levels of their contingency plan with names such as:

WNP   ...   Worst Nightmare Plan
HOEP   ...   Hell on Earth Plan
CAP   ...   Competitive Action Plan

There's nothing like having fun, even in the worst of times!

Contracts.

Request a list of all contracts that each department has entered into and that are still current. Ask someone to review them with a view to making any changes, if necessary. Ask also that, in the future, a copy of any potential contract be sent to that same person for review and recording prior to finalization. This will minimize the cost exposure you have with contracts. In addition, ensure that contracts are audited annually by your internal audit staff.

Convertible Debentures.

Investment bankers love them, as they are profitable and relatively easy to sell. However, in most cases, the company never comes out on top with convertible debentures. A preferable deferred funding mechanism is to sell warrants.

Corporate Limos.

Dispense with your corporate limos, and you will automatically eliminate the need for corporate drivers! Besides discovering that taxi cabs are cheaper, you may also have the problems of the world solved for you, gratis, by the cab driver as you drive from point A to point B!

Corporate Message.

Reproduce your corporate message or slogan on all internal memos and external correspondence. It's a very cost-effective way of reinforcing what you stand for. Done consistently and effectively, your message becomes part of the vernacular. So much so, that you "wouldn't leave home without it"!

Corporate Offices.

Typically, they are simple, relatively spartan, and modest in size. Extras for the office are paid for out of the pocket of the executive.

Correspondence Response.

Wherever possible, respond to outside correspondence by jotting a reply on the face of the letter received and return it. If necessary, make a photocopy for your own files. Some calculate a typewritten reply costs $4–7 per letter.

Costs.

Costs can be divided into two classes: critical and nice. Ensure as large a proportion as possible of your costs are in the former category!

Country Clubs.

Unless a critical business need exists for an executive to be a member of a country club (e.g., meeting other clients at the club), they should be avoided. Given the cost of country club memberships, it seems that you could take your clients to dinner at some very fancy restaurants, many, many times, before you approach the break-even point with your country club membership and dues. Here's a test. Eliminate corporate-sponsored country club memberships. Give your executives the dues paid as added salary. See how many maintain their membership!!

Credit Card Fees.

Shop around to see which bank should have the privilege of handling your VISA and Master Card processing. The fees charged range from approximately 1.0% to 4.0% of sales. Ensure that your company is receiving the most competitive rates. At least every three years put your credit card processing business out for bids.

Credit Cards, Corporate.

Avoid having corporate credit cards for your employees. Not only does it waste time because the accounting department must reconcile them, but why pay the annual fees on such credit cards when personal no-fee credit cards are available? Lists of banks offering no-fee cards are published every so often in magazines such as *Money*, *Forbes* and *Business Week* (e.g., *Money*, November 1991, page 26 and *Business Week*, August 6, 1990, page 85). Your employees should apply directly for these no-fee cards and let them bill you monthly for reimbursable expenses.

Current Projects.

As these change regularly, empty a drop-file drawer in your desk of all its files and put in its place an expansion file. Using detachable yellow sticky labels, identify each pocket. Then, as information on each project comes to your desk drop it in the appropriate pocket. When ready to work on a project, simply take everything out of the appropriate pocket. When a project is completed, detach the yellow label and put a new one in its place. This is a great time and space saver!

Customer Retention.

Monitor your customer retention rate. Focusing on maintaining a very high customer retention rate minimizes your operating costs, as it is less expensive to service existing customers than to seek replacement customers. Most studies show that the cost of keeping existing customers is only 20% of the cost to acquire new ones.

Daily Bankings.

All monies received at headquarters, for whatever reason, should be deposited on a daily basis to maximize cash flow.

Daily Polling.

Many companies poll their stores or units every night for the information on that day's trading. Ask yourself: Is it critically necessary to know each day what sales were on the previous day? What changes do I make in our business as a result of this knowledge? (If it's so important, do you get Saturday's results called to your home on Sunday?) Consider having polling done every few days, or once a week (possibly on a staggered basis with one seventh of the units polled nightly).

Data-Based Marketing.

Many cost-conscious companies are moving towards direct marketing to customers and away from mass advertising. With the amazing detail available on households in America (read *The Clustering of America* by Michael J. Weiss if you want more insight on this) and the great advances in data-based marketing, aiming your advertising at your specific customers and their clones has become a very cost-effective way to advertise and promote. It also allows you to measure the effectiveness (cost and profitability) of each communication as well as your profitability by customer.

Deal Terms.

On a regular basis, hire an invoice checking firm to check your purchase records for the past 3–6 months. The outside firm will collect 50% of the difference between what you paid and any deals that were offered to the trade but for some reason you didn't take. You get the other 50%. It is also an excellent, cost-effective way to have a free audit of your buying and payables department.

Deals.

If you plan to make a large purchase of a trade deal, buy modest amounts during the deal period and place a large order on the last day of the deal period. This will allow you to have lower costs on this product for a number of weeks, possibly even until the next deal is offered.

Decals.

Some companies, rightly, have decals on their trailers which act as a moving advertisement. If you do this, it's cost advantageous to have metal decals because they can be easily attached and removed. This makes repainting your trailers every 18–24 months easy and avoids the need to buy or paint on new decals every time this is done.

Decile Analysis.

A simple way to analyze where costs are out of line is to sort your stores, departments, or units into decile groupings (e.g., your top 10% stores are decile 1, the next 10%, decile 2, etc.). Then compare the performance of each store only with its peers in the same decile. In this way, you are comparing apples with apples.

Deferred Compensation, Short-Term.

Reduce your planned salary scale increase for next year by 1.92%. Announce what you are doing, then advise that in the first full pay period of the following December, each employee will receive a special payment of 1.92% of their year-to-date pay. For an employee who has been there the whole year, this is the equivalent of one additional week's pay. Repeat this each year in December. The employees love having an extra week's pay prior to Christmas. Example: if you are planning a salary scale increase of 5.0% next year, reduce this to 3.08%, knowing that employees will get 1.92% of their year-to-date earnings at year end. This program also acts as an incentive for employees to stay with you through the year as they forfeit the right to this payment if they leave the company during the year. The company gains by not having to pay this deferred amount to those employees who join and leave the company during the year and by having the benefit of the cash flow through the year.

Deliveries.

Eliminate the checking in at store level of deliveries from your own distribution center. If there is a variance from what was ordered or charged, the variance is, hopefully, still within the company. Ensure, of course, that the delivery trucks are appropriately sealed between the distribution centers and your stores. If necessary, you can have a team at the distribution center randomly check deliveries before they are sent. Usually, only 1–3% of all orders shipped need be checked. Because of the cost of labor, this practice can significantly help your profitability.

Deposits, Utility.

Often included in the "Other Assets" of a balance sheet are deposits paid to utility companies. In most cases you can have these deposits returned to you (get that cash working for you!) by having your insurance company bonded for the amount of the deposits.

Desk Procedures.

Have all secretaries and assistants prepare a set of daily desk procedures covering what they do on a daily basis, how their boss likes things done, etc., etc., so that if they are away someone else can take over with the least amount of disruption and cost.

Desk Sharing.

Wherever possible, replace personal desks with desk sharing. One successful, low-cost operation has its accounting office working on this basis. Equipment and space are shared openly. Employees don't feel the need to say "This is my desk, my PC," etc.

De-spec.

Every 3–4 years review the total cost of your units. See how you can "de-spec" your operation by simplifying the specifications, replacing higher-cost components with equally effective lower-cost components, etc.

Directions.

If your company is geographically dispersed, and directions to each unit are frequently needed, have such directions typed out in one small bulletin. Have it updated regularly and available to all employees in the company. For your sales people, you can have a map, with directions, printed on the back of their business cards ... for their clients, of course.

Directories.

Often companies send out a whole new directory each month for such things as telephone extensions, store names and addresses, etc., etc. Avoid this. Instead, send out only a change list at the end of each month, and then every 3, 6, or 12 months, send out a whole new directory.

Disbursement Studies.

Every 3–4 years, request a disbursement study to see which bank you should be paying your checks from to maximize your cash flow. Saving just half a day in float can be significant!

Discounts.

Seek discounts on practically everything you buy, from merchandise to overnight mail rates to advertising rates. Keep pressing: "Is that the best you can do?"

Discount Taking.

Not all discounts are worth taking as an alternative to paying at the later alternative deadline date. Compare the trade-off using not your bank borrowing rate, but your cost of capital which for many companies is 15–25% before tax. Make the best decision for your company. Incidentally, cash discount is really a credit for the use of money and should not be deducted from the purchase price of the goods being bought, but rather treated as interest income.

Discount Taking, Late.

When in doubt, take the discount, even if a few days past due date. You will be surprised how many times vendors will not bill you back for the late discount taken. In addition, have prepared each month a "discount lost" exception report, with a reason written alongside each entry explaining why you did not receive the discount.

Discrimination Surveys.

Some companies have incurred enormous costs regarding discrimination issues. One cost-conscious company has developed an excellent way to avoid the possibility of discrimination claims against the company. Twice a year, it issues a questionnaire to every employee starting with the question, "Have you experienced discrimination in our company in the past six months? If yes, please describe the details." The questionnaire continues with other questions. If any response is a "yes," the company can address the matter immediately and minimize any potential cost down the road. If, as is usual, the answers are "no," then employees cannot come back at a later time and say they were subject to discrimination prior to their last discrimination questionnaire. Obviously, such a questionnaire has to be very carefully prepared in conjunction with your labor lawyer.

Dividends.

Don't pay them! Not only do they draw cash from your business, but they also incur fees with your share transfer agent for processing and disbursing the dividends. In addition, many companies that pay dividends are also in debt. Therefore, to pay the dividends, such companies must incur more debt. (The companies are, in effect, borrowing to pay the dividends!) Then they have to pay interest on monies borrowed for the dividend, not just that year, but on a compounding basis forever! (This changes only if the company reduces its debt). Another reason for not paying dividends is that it is, in effect, a compulsory liquidation of capital imposed upon the shareholders. This forces a compulsory tax on the dividend received on any tax-paying shareholder. It is preferable, from a shareholder and from a corporate cost viewpoint, for the company to buy back stock rather than pay dividends. Then the individual shareholders can decide what is in their best interests: whether they wish to liquidate part of their equity in the company and thereby pay taxes on the capital gains related to that liquidation, or delay liquidation until some later date more suitable. It also provides the company flexibility as to how much cash each year it wishes to use for this purpose.

Dividend Reinvestment Program.

Some companies have a dividend reinvestment program. They are illogical. If a high number of shareholders sign up for them it tells you that they don't want cash dividends. If a low number sign up, then it tells you it's not a good program. Either way the company loses. Further, the administrative costs of these programs are extremely high, especially when you consider that many companies pay dividends of less than $0.15 per share per quarter. So even if you pay dividends, at least avoid having a dividend reinvestment plan.

Donations.

Eliminate! Don't make them, unless it is clear that there is an economic benefit in making the specific donation. Donations are essentially a tax on your customers. Donations are generally given in response to requests rather than on any overall rational basis. They do not please everybody, and can cause some customers to stop shopping with you, as one large company recently discovered when it stopped its annual donation to one side of the abortion issue! One example of positively responding to requests for donations is to thank the requester for his letter but indicate that your company's philosophy is, say, to provide the lowest prices in the community, for the whole community, and singling out one group for preference is unfair to the rest. A second approach is to make a modest donation to, for example, the United Way at headquarters, and whenever requests are made for donations, advise the requester that your company has already contributed to the United Way and has no other budget allowance for contributions. Suggest that the requester approach the United Way for help! Yet another approach, if you really want to give donations, is to follow the lead of Berkshire Hathaway, Inc. which over the past few years has made donations to charities named by the individual shareholders. They have allowed each shareholder holding shares in his own name a certain amount per share to be sent directly to the shareholder's favorite charity from Berkshire Hathaway. True shareholder democracy! But, after all, it's their money!

Economic Discipline.

Build into your incentive programs an economic discipline for employees to minimize costs. For example, your incentive system could have deductions from the bonus pool for any bad check that was accepted outside of company policy, the overtime portion of any overtime labor, shrinkage costs beyond a certain threshold, directory assistance calls and long distance calls above a certain threshold, etc., etc.

Economic Model.

To gain a true appreciation of your cost structure, develop an economic model of your organization. This is a detailed breakout of all the interrelating cost inputs within your business. For example, it includes such things as the items sold per square foot, the number of square feet of distribution center space per thousand items sold, the number and cost of kilowatt hours used for each hour your stores are open, your required physical inventory levels at different sales volumes, etc., etc. Build your history of all these relationships going back over the past five years. Then you can project, with a high degree of confidence, what will happen over the next five years at different sales and growth levels. It is also an excellent tool with which to play "what if" games. The relationships within the model also become targets to beat each year from a productivity viewpoint. Once again, this is much better than the traditional budgeting system.

Elimination.

This is the greatest cost saver of all. Rather than cutting costs 10% across the board, it's preferable to identify those functions and departments that are no longer critical to the long-term success of the organization and eliminate them. Across the board cuts are unfair to those departments which are cost conscious. After a while, they'll give up and say, "There's no reason to be cost conscious if we are penalized equally with other departments."

Employee Leasing.

As companies grow (including the cost-conscious ones) salary scales and benefits creep above their smaller competitors. To allow for this, many companies are now "leasing" employees from employment agencies to keep total labor costs (particularly benefits) down. Some companies also use this practice as a screening device before hiring employees. They assess how the "leased" employee performs and fits in with their regular employees before deciding whether to bring them onto their staff. This is a variation of the two-tier salary scale in which all employees hired before a certain date are "grandfathered" into one set of salary scales, while all after that date are paid according to a lower set of salary scales. The same approach can be used with executives. Why not "hire" executives for a certain period to do certain specific functions before deciding to hire them permanently?

Employee Pay.

Where practicable, pay employees every two weeks instead of once a week and pay salaried employees monthly. This saves not only processing costs but also your cash flow.

Employment Advertising.

Use a standardized advertisement, outlining the benefits of the company, etc. Have a space for the specific job you are advertising. This will avoid preparing a new advertisement every time you wish to place one.

Employment Application.

Have a trusted senior company member review it annually to ensure that it complies with all current laws. An annual "ounce of prevention" may save a ton of attorney fees later! Then review it yourself: is it short, simple, and comprehensible? (Ask your child to complete it ... that's always a good test of clarity!) Ensure that the "at-will" paragraph is clearly stated. My favorite ending of a company's application form reads as follows:

APPLICANT'S CERTIFICATION
AND AGREEMENT

"(Please read carefully) I voluntarily give the company or any of its subsidiaries the right to make a thorough investigation of my past employment and activities. I also agree to cooperate in such investigation, waiving any rights or privileges I may now or in the future have pertaining thereto, and hereby release from any liability or responsibility, this company, its subsidiaries, and their officers and employees, and all persons, companies, or corporations listed above as reference who supply facts in the course of such investigation.

"I further agree that any false statements, omissions or misrepresentations on this application or any supplement thereto, or any false statements made by me in any investigation conducted by the company, may result in the refusal of or discharge from employment.

"I understand and agree that the position for which I am applying is an "at-will" position, meaning that if I am employed by the company, my compensation can be changed at the option of the company and/or my employment can be terminated, with or without cause, and with or without notice at any time, at the option of either the company or myself. I understand and agree that only the chairman or president, and then only if the agreement is in writing, has the authority to enter into any agreement for employment for any specified period of time.

"I understand that all offers of employment are conditional, and are subject to successfully completing a physical examination and the receipt of satisfactory reference and background investigations.

"If employed, I agree to abide by and observe all rules and regulations of the company. I will assist upon request in the company's program (1) to employ, train and promote people of diverse races, religions, and national origins in positions throughout the employer's entire organization without discrimination, and (2) to avoid and prevent accidents,

personal injuries, and loss or damage to customers',
employers', my own, or fellow employees' property
occurring in or about my place of work or becoming
known to me in any manner, and (3) to cooperate
with loss prevention activities conducted by authorized personnel at unannounced and random
times.''

Employment Contracts.

Avoid them. As long as you reward your good
people well, both economically and emotionally,
there is little need for employment contracts. Seldom are employment contracts completely fair to
both parties. Sometimes, where the contract is too
lopsided, the employee must arrange to be fired
rather than resign to take advantage of the contract
benefits! This, obviously, is not good for the company. Rather than having employment contracts,
sit down at least once a year, and ask your key
people: "What else can we do for you to make you
happy?" Then have your people ask the same question of you.

Envelopes, Reuse.

Reuse large envelopes received from outside the
company for interdepartmental mail within the
company.

Envelopes, Size.

For external mail, use envelopes of the appropriate size. Too often, 8-1/2" by 11" envelopes are
used to carry a one page letter. A cheaper 4-1/4" by

9-1/2″ envelope would suffice. Also, it's cheaper if the name and address is printed directly onto the envelope rather than on a label which is then adhered to the envelope.

Equipment.

Ask employees to turn off and cover all equipment such as calculators and typewriters at the end of each day. This saves power and extends the life of the equipment.

Equipment Location.

Have equipment located in such a position to minimize the time involved to use it. Equipment which is shared, such as microfiche viewers, should be located close to the main users.

Equipment Purchases.

Renegotiate your equipment purchase terms once a year to cover the potential equipment purchases during the following year. It's amazing how vendors sharpen their pricing pencils when they see big orders, even if spread out over a year. Requesting bids from three companies is preferable than from two as it minimizes the possibility of collusion.

Equipment Sales Tax.

Where you are geographically dispersed and are buying equipment for various parts of the country, ensure that equipment purchased is shipped directly to the state involved if that state has a lower sales tax on the equipment. Also, ensure that installation or other labor costs on an equipment invoice are stated separately from materials because in most states labor and installation are not taxable if separated from material costs.

ESDOC.

Use this formula in evaluating headquarters' tasks. Each task or function can be challenged with the following questions: Eliminate? Shift (within the office to someone who can do the job better)? Decentralize? Outsource? (Can the function be sub-contracted rather than done internally?) Computerize? (Can the function be computerized?) One company that uses this formula has seen its sales grow fourfold in the last five years while their corporate staff head count dropped 50%!

Every Day Low Prices.

As a general rule, cost-conscious companies employ an every day low price strategy. The cost savings to retail and service companies with such a strategy are numerous, including: no advertisements with weekly specials; no rain checks for "stock outs"; no weekly "specials" window signs; no excess inventory at the end of a week of an advertised item that didn't sell; no need to check off items in an advertisement against the displays in the store; and less labor involved in planning and implementing all these weekly changes. It's honest. It's simple. It's a lower cost of operating than having specials and promotions.

Example.

The most effective cost-conscious action is the example from the very top of the organization. Top executives are constantly being evaluated by employees to assess whether their actions match their words. Cost-conscious actions, rather than instructions, are what really count.

Exception Reporting.

Save enormous amounts of computer reports and executive time by establishing parameters for the key information for which you are responsible. Then have exception reports generated with only those items outside (either positive or negative) of those parameters. The ideal report a manager should receive is a computer printout with only 3–6 numbers on the whole page, these being the exceptions to predetermined norms. The full reports need not be issued. They can remain filed in your computer. Exception reports can be for such things as:

- labor variances
- overtime usage
- inventory levels
- capital expenditures
- long distance telephone expenses
- sales, gross profit, and supplies
- repairs and maintenance costs

Exception Reporting, Corrective Action Plan.

Once the exception reporting system is in place, it is not necessary to follow up with questions on the items shown on the exception reports. Instead, in advance, agree with your subordinates that they will give you within, say, three days of the issuance of the report, an explanation of each item listed with an appropriate corrective action plan, with deadlines. Suspense your copy of the report for the deadline date given. Then, on that date, check the results with the corrective action plan that you have on file.

Excess Departments.

Usually, you will not find in cost conscious companies such departments as strategic planning, economics, or even public relations departments. Legal departments, if they exist at all, are staffed at absolute minimum levels. One of the major reasons against internal legal departments is that it is not unusual for them to seek advice from external legal firms on matters referred to them. So why have high paid duplicate intermediaries?

Executives.

Count the executives of any cost-conscious company and compare the count with that of their competitors. You will find a lower count. The fewer the executives, the more focussed the company is and the less politics and empire building there is. Besides, you can pay your fewer executives more. For example, if you had 10 executives earning an average of $80,000 each and you trimmed back to 8 executives and gave them the salaries of the disappearing two, the average salary would be $100,000 each, a 25% salary jump. Think your key people would welcome that idea?

Executive Time.

Usually, a company has more projects than it has time available to accomplish them. This suggests that the return on executive time is one of the critical measures that should be considered, along with the return on investment, when reviewing any new projects. Executive time involvement should not be overlooked as a real cost in any project.

Expense Allowances.

In cases where certain employees spend money on discretionary items and you wish to keep some control over this, simply set up discretionary spending accounts for each of those employees, with a quarterly or rolling quarterly cap on them. Once the cap is met for the quarter, no more expense reimbursements are made to that employee. This overcomes the need to check off every item spent by an employee as well as giving that person responsibility to make decisions without someone constantly looking over his shoulder.

Expense Limits.

Have each departmental head identify all expenditure categories approved by his department. Then place a dollar limit on each type of expenditure and designate who can approve such expenditure up to that limit. Identify who is required to approve expenditure on such items over that limit. For example, supplies up to $2,000 may be able to be approved by one person. Up to $20,000 by another, and up to $100,000 by the vice president. The accounts payable department should have a company-wide list covering such limits to be used in verifying invoices for payment.

Expense Policy.

Develop an expense policy which covers the bulk of all expenditures by executives. Then, when expenses come in to the accounts payable department, a clerk simply checks the expense versus the policy. Only deviances from policy need be approved by an appropriate executive. This avoids the frequent practice of having all expenses going to a person's superior for approval, often on a subjective basis, prior to payment. Such is usually a waste of the superior's valuable time, as seldom do supervisors challenge expenses of subordinates. Instead, they usually find all the reasons in the world why exceptions should be made for "their" people.

Expense Policy, Capital Items.

Expense all capital items purchased under $1,000 per item to gain immediate tax benefits. Every couple of years review this limit with your independent auditors with the objective of increasing it.

Expense Policy, "Tight."

Have a widely-publicized, "tight" reimbursable expense policy. Then have expense reports sent in for payment according to policy. Any excesses over the policy amount will be automatically deducted unless specifically approved by a senior executive.

Expense Reimbursement.

Introduce a policy, after an appropriate grace period, that specifies a 25% cut in reimbursement for expenses submitted more than 60 days after they were incurred. You will be amazed how the laggards suddenly find the motivation to submit their expenses on time. This eliminates a lot of time wasted by office employees repeatedly tracking down the laggards.

Express Mail.

Have a special expense account for express overnight mail. Break it out by department. Have departmental or individual expenditures over certain target figures explained on a weekly or monthly basis. (Whatever did we do before the days of Federal Express?!) Many employees are very liberal with overnight mail. The author knows of one company which received a thank you letter from an investment funds manager by express overnight mail. It cost the sender $18. It also cost the sender's company the opportunity to invest the receiver's company's profit sharing funds, as the recipient company thought that if the investment fund managers were not careful on expenses such as mailing a thank you note, they would not be extremely careful when investing the profit sharing funds of their clients, either! In a recent series of advertisements, UPS reminds us that the "impulse" to 'overnight it' needlessly cost American businesses over three billion dollars!!" Once again, how urgent is that letter. . . ??!

External Boards.

Unless there is a very clear economic benefit to the organization (and there seldom is!), external board memberships by executives should be off limits. (Your people ought to have enough to do in their current positions!)

Fax.

FAX transmissions should take advantage of telephone calling rates. Transmit all non-critical messages between the hours of 5:00 PM and 8:00 AM, the cheapest transmitting times permitted by your telephone company. Also, regularly review what is being faxed. Despite postal rate increases, it's still usually cheaper to mail information that is not critically urgent!

Fax, Cover Sheet.

Each fax transmission must have an initial "address sheet." Rather than use a full 8″ × 11″ address sheet, use a 3″ × 11″ adhesive sheet (like a large Post-It(TM) sheet) which states your company's name, the date, time, number of pages, who it's to and from, and space for comments. This sheet is simply attached to the top of the first page of your material being transmitted. You save a page! The saving comes from the fact that the cost of the fax transmission is based upon the amount to be read by the fax machine. The less to read, the lower the charge. You can also save by "bunching" printed matter on a sheet to save fax time and, therefore, transmission cost. It's these little things in life that count. You can sit on a mountain but not a tack!

Filing Cabinets.

Despite the encroachment of computers into our offices, we still seem to have numerous filing cabinets in every location. To the degree that we must use them, why not vary the grades of filing cabinets from fireproof to cardboard? The last mentioned is very low cost and satisfactory for non-critical information, which usually describes the bulk of the information we store.

Filing System.

If your business comprises a number of similar outlets, have a standardized office filing system. A list of each drop file, in alphabetical sequence, for each drawer of your filing system can be updated and issued annually.

First Aid Kits.

Don't buy them. It's cheaper to buy the individual supplies at a drug store. Then have an employee keep it stocked rather than a medical supply service.

Flagship.

Many companies have a flagship store to show off to visitors. Unfortunately, some companies over-invest in such stores with the result that they lose money. Remember, flagship stores should be primarily flagships of profitability rather than flagships of profitless presentation.

Flex-Time.

This is particularly appropriate at any large office complex. Allow your employees to come in as early as they wish and to end as late as they wish. Overtime, of course, is not paid unless any employee works in excess of 40 hours for the week. Flex time yields enormous productivity and morale advantages.

Flowers.

It's always nice to see flowers around the office. They always add a nice touch. However, should anyone wish to buy flowers for the office, allow them the privilege of paying for them out of their own, rather than out of the corporate, pocket!

Focus.

Do one thing and do it exceedingly well. Lowest costs come by knowing your business the best. A few years ago an analyst asked the president of McDonalds if he would consider diversification. His answer, reflecting his concentrated focus on his basic business, was apt: "Not until we have 16,000 clean bathrooms every day of the year!"

Focus, Critical Numbers.

The company should focus on no more than two or three critical numbers every week. Typically these two numbers are sales and wages. Sales drive the business, and wages are usually the largest cost in a service organization.

Forms, Printing.

With desk-top publishing, most forms can be produced more cheaply in-house these days than by an outside printer. After all, internal forms do not have to be rated as works of art!

Forms Review.

Once a year, conduct a company-wide forms review. New forms are always being introduced. Old forms are seldom eliminated. This review should challenge the use of each form, the simplicity of it, the number of carbonized sheets involved, and its distribution. Review also whether several forms can be merged into one form. Recently, I was horrified to see in one company internal stationery supply request forms in quadruplicate! Even headquarters people had to complete such forms to receive supplies from another part of the building! A single one-page request form would have been perfectly adequate!

Foyer.

The foyer of cost-conscious companies is usually simple and spartan. Plain, simple seating. Modest walls. No fancy decor. This reminds all visitors that costs are important in this business and that vendors should have brought with them a really sharp pencil to discuss their offers!

Freight Rates.

Constantly get price comparisons for truck load and less than truck load freight rates from your vendors. Often you will find that you will be able to arrange for a common carrier to haul the load for less than the freight allowance the vendor is offering.

Fuel Tax Services.

Many cost-conscious organizations have an external specialist company take care of all aspects of the organization's fuel tax services relating to the company's vehicle fleet. These services include securing initial registration, fuel permits, emergency fuel permits, filing monthly or quarterly fuel tax returns, axle reports, etc., etc. Their expertise often saves a lot of money.

Garnishments.

Charge a fee for each check garnished. Yes, this is permitted by law. (See the fine print!) The charges are against the person paying the amount. The income received will help offset some of the administration costs of this procedure.

Gift Policy.

The company should make it very clear, both internally and externally, that it has a "no gift" policy. Some companies have statements on their walls reminding visitors that no gifts can be given to anyone in the company and that they can't even take anyone out to lunch! Some companies insist that even samples cannot be kept by the buyers. They are turned over to an employee store to be sold at a low price to any employee.

Headquarters Costs.

As a percentage of sales, headquarters costs should fall from year to year. This is based on the premise that building shareholders' wealth is more important than building empires at headquarters.

Headquarters Location.

Typically, you will find cost-conscious companies with headquarters in lower-cost small towns rather than large cities, or in lower-cost states rather than higher-cost states. Wal-Mart (Bentonville, Arkansas) and Food Lion (Salisbury, North Carolina) have their headquarters in low-cost towns in low-cost states. Thus, they both win twice over against some of their competitors.

Headquarters Space.

As a rough rule of thumb, if you have more than 200 square feet per employee in your headquarters building, you have excess space. This figure is calculated by dividing the total floor space of the building by the total head count of people who have desks in the building. The space includes all headquarters space: break rooms, hallways, conference rooms, and bathrooms. Often modular furniture will help you in accomplishing this goal.

Health Pay.

Rather than having one week's sick pay available to employees each year, reverse the concept and make it one week's "health pay." This means that when an employee has a minor sickness during the year, he does not receive any payment for time off. However, during the first pay period of December, each employee receives 1.92% of their year's income for health pay. This encourages employees not to take time off to use up accumulated sick days. Further, it rewards your healthy employees. It also acts as an incentive for employees to stay with the company through the end of each year, as anyone who leaves during the year loses their health pay for that year.

Heat Sealed Checks.

Once you have a certain number of employees on your payroll, it becomes cost justifiable to issue payroll data, including the payroll check, using a heat-seal system. You also have the ability to include messages to individual employees in this system (e.g., a welcome on their first payroll check or a note of congratulations on their anniversary), or you may have a general message for everyone. The same system can process W-2 information, annual retirement or profit sharing statements, etc. Some banks are now using this system for clients' monthly statements. The savings includes time, labor, and envelopes.

Idea Groups.

On a regular basis, have groups of employees come together on a voluntary basis, to suggest ways to reduce costs and improve ways of doing things within the company. Every business is a process flow. The process can always be refined and improved.

Ideas.

Seek out cost-saving ideas from other industries and other countries. For example, catalog companies learned from retailers. Now retailers are learning from catalog companies. Similarly, the Japanese learned from the Americans. Now Americans are learning from the Japanese. Ideas know no industry or geographic boundaries. Remember, superiority in business comes only in two ways: doing it better, or doing it differently, than your competitors.

Idle Assets.

Twice a year, request a list of all assets considered "idle." This would include such things as closed stores, new and old equipment, inventories and supplies sitting in back rooms and warehouses. Then take the appropriate steps to turn the assets into cash.

Incentives.

Provide incentives to employees to reduce costs. For example, one cost-conscious company shared its shrinkage improvement in each store during one whole year on a 50:50 basis. 50 percent of the reduction went to the employees; the other 50 percent went to the company.

Information Comparison.

On a regular basis meet with similar, but non-competing, companies to exchange ideas on how to reduce costs and improve profits. Participants don't need an I.Q. above room temperature to be able to gain valuable cost-saving ideas from one another.

Initials.

Many effective executives just put their initials on correspondence indicating to whom they wish to send it. If clarification is necessary, their secretaries fill out the person's name and department. If saves seconds and thus, over time, hours of very expensive time.

Insurance.

Review your insurance deductibles in all parts of your insurance program. Increase the deductible limit wherever economically feasible.

Insurance Materials.

Most insurance companies set aside a certain amount of money in their budgets for promotional materials for their clients. Find out the amount they have and then spend it on such things as safety coloring books for children, safety pennants, etc.

Internal Mail.

Rather than having all employees running around the building with mail, have a mail collection and delivery system whereby the mail is collected and delivered two or three times a day to employes at their individual desks. This eliminates the need for a large amount of unnecessary non-productive people movement around the building.

Intra-Company Correspondence.

Either buy, or have printed, large envelopes with many blocks on the front (and back) which state: "Deliver to last person named. Cross out previous address. Use until all spaces are filled." This is yet another reminder to employees that you don't like wasting anything.

Inventories.

Keep them lean. Set up internal reporting systems of sales and inventories in terms of physical units. Calculate the number of inventory weeks, in physical units, based on the projected sales during the coming 8–10 weeks, rather than the past 8–10 weeks. In this way you are allowing for the true seasonality of the business. Also, each buyer should be responsible for his net inventories (inventories less payables). Multiply this figure by your before-tax cost of capital and deduct this from his gross profit to measure his true contribution to the company.

Inventory Reduction.

At least annually, have your marketing people meet with your manufacturing people. Tell your marketing group they should not drop any item that will adversely affect profitable sales. Tell the manufacturing group that their objective is to reduce the number of stock keeping units (SKU's) by analyzing their movement data. Those that do not meet minimum movement figures are "drop" candidates. Then tell both groups they should agree on as much as possible. Any disputed items can be presented to a higher level for resolution.

Investment Bankers.

A great number of investment bankers are very smart people. But remember that their fees, too, are competitive. Therefore, if you want any work done by an investment banker, invite bids from several competing firms. It should come as no surprise that this will usually result in a lower fee than if you didn't invite competitive bids.

Investor Presentation, Meals.

Avoid accepting invitations to speak to any investor group where you have to pick up the meal tab or pay for the privilege of speaking to the group. Some societies charge up to $4,000 for such a luncheon! Politely advise that you will speak to any investor group where there is no charge to your company. After all, attendees are getting their money's worth by listening to your success story!

Investor Presentations, Slides.

If your company does presentations each year involving a large number of slides, instead of having the slides professionally prepared outside the company, buy and use one of the many PC software programs that are now available, and make the slides internally. Your training department will be able to use this as well.

Investor Responses.

The majority of responses to potential investors can be accompanied with a standard form letter (see following). There is no need to write a letter to someone who asks for a copy of the latest Annual Report. Yet many companies do! As an investor, when I receive such an individualized letter, it's a red flag to me that the company is not as cost conscious as it could be. All that is usually needed to accompany investment information is a standardized note similar to what Berkshire Hathaway, Inc. sends out. It reads:

"The accompanying copy of the most recent annual Report to the Stockholders of Berkshire Hathaway, Inc. (and/or interim report(s), if requested) is sent in response to your recent request. Copies of reports to Stockholders are sent to anyone who makes a request therefor, subject only to availability of a supply for such purpose. A copy of the most recent form 10-K of the Company will be mailed to shareholders at their request when such request includes a good-faith representation that the requester was a beneficial owner of common stock of the Company as of the record date most recently fixed for an Annual meeting of Stockholders. Otherwise, copies of documents which the company may file with the Securities Exchange Commission are available through the SEC. The company does not maintain a permanent mailing list." This preprinted note says it all!

Job Descriptions, Flexible.

Some companies are keen on having job descriptions. Others are not. To the degree that your company has job descriptions, keep them very brief, very broad, and very flexible. After all, you are running a business in a changing world, rather than running a big bureaucratic government department.

Job Descriptions, Cost Clause.

Cost-conscious companies often include a cost clause in their job description. Somewhere in the job description they will insert the following phrase: "To find more efficient ways to do the job and to seek to reduce costs and improve labor productivity." Is a phrase similar to that in every job description in your company?

Kaizen.

This is the Japanese word meaning continuous improvement. This attitude is typical in cost-conscious companies and is reflected in such practices as quality improvement, suggestions, procedure manual reviews, etc. It's a mindset that underscores that no matter how well you are doing, you can always do better. It also reflects the mindset that, in a world of constant change, parts of your business are constantly becoming outmoded and are in need of change simply to stand still, let alone progress.

Labor Scheduling.

Labor hours should be scheduled based upon standards for the core functions that must be performed every day and week, with an additional variable allowance for physically handling and selling the merchandise. Labor standards should be based upon the physical needs of the business and not in terms of a target wage percentage. They are expressed in physical terms related to physical items (e.g., items per hour) for year-to-year productivity comparability. Once fair labor scheduling standards have been introduced, simply monitor and manage major exceptions each week.

Lease Agreement, Update.

Update your standard lease agreement each year, incorporating new ideas, experiences, and trends.

Lease Agreements, Overnight Collect.

When negotiating, if the potential landlord wants the agreement back in a hurry, send it to him by overnight mail—collect, of course!

Lease Agreements, Standardized.

Develop your own standardized lease. Spell out the fine details in the lease and print it on bond, watermarked paper. Therefore, as the tentative agreement moves back and forth between yourself and an outsider, there is no need to check for any alteration on the contract apart from those written in, provided it is still on the bond, watermarked paper. Standard addendums should also be on un-numbered bond, watermarked paper, to be used as appropriate.

Legal Fees.

Scrutinize your legal bills each month. Challenge times and costs on a regular basis. Ensure that your legal representatives understand your obsession with cost consciousness. As a result, they will think three times before charging you for anything unnecessary or extravagant! In addition, if your legal bills are a large expense item, hire a specialist legal bill audit firm to check for excessive, inappropriate, and duplicate billing charges.

Letter Formats.

If you have a word processing department, have all letter and report formats standardized. If there is no word processing department, have the same formats standardized among all secretaries. This will save both time and money.

Letterheads.

Here's a nice sensitive one for people at higher levels in an organization. Cost-conscious organizations typically do not have personalized stationery for anyone in the organization whether paid for by the company or the individual. No exceptions. From the CEO down. The standard corporate letterheads should be used by everyone. Remember, it's earnings per share, not ego per share, that we are trying to maximize. A few years ago I received a letter from a friend in a competing company. The company claimed to be low-cost, but when I saw his personalized letterhead, showing that he was a Vice President, I knew of at least one ounce of fat they were carrying. I suspect a number of other ounces surrounded that one!

Library.

Provide a range of books, magazines, and audio and video tapes related to your business and business generally. Allow employees to borrow individual items for a certain period to study in their own time. You may even have a self-quiz to accompany each item borrowed. This program will increase employees' knowledge and morale, at minimal cost to the company.

LIFO.

Inventory should be valued on a LIFO (Last In First Out) rather than a FIFO (First In First Out) basis. Even though it reduces your reported "paper" profits, it increases the lifeblood of your company, your cash flow, through lower taxes. Not only that, your shareholders love it. Financial researchers have established that a company's share price goes up in proportion to the amount of taxes saved when the company announces a switch from FIFO to LIFO.

Lighting.

If you have an automatic relamp program whereby all the lights are replaced on a regular basis, keep the best 10% of the old lamps and use them in case of need prior to the next relamping cycle. In addition, some companies take their lamps from the retail area and recycle them in back rooms and warehouse areas.

Lighting, Back Room.

Have lighting in your back rooms at a lower intensity than in your selling and office areas. You can do this simply by removing various lamps and/or taping over the appropriate light switches.

Lights, Sensors.

In large office areas and in some hallways, install a lighting system which is activated by movement sensors. If there is no movement under a certain group of lights in any 5-minute period, those lights automatically go off. This is particularly cost-effective in a large office area where just a few people are working. This system allows, automatically, only a few lights to be on in those areas where employees are working.

Lines of Credit.

Always have them. However, avoid paying any committment fee for these lines of credit because there is usually, in the fine print, an escape clause for the bank if conditions become extremely bad for you which is, of course, the time you actually need the line of credit!

Loans, Low-Interest.

If you have the negotiating muscle, follow the example of some companies and request below-market rate loans from your vendors. If your business is important to them, they may help you!

Lobby Area.

If a number of salesmen regularly visit your company, provide in the lobby area pay telephones, a pay photocopy machine, and a pay coffee machine. This avoids lots of interruptions as well as saves your company money.

Location Cards.

Provide each person in your office with 10–20 location cards (bathroom, conference room B, break room, etc.). Then, when an employee leaves his desk, he simply leaves the appropriate card on his desk signifying where he is. This saves a great deal of time when trying to track people down.

Magazines.

To save time sifting through the mountain of magazines you receive, have your secretary tear out or photocopy the table of contents of the magazines that come to you. You then simply circle the articles you want to read. She can either cut them out or photocopy them for you to read at a later more appropriate time.

Magnetic Tape Billing.

Work with vendors to receive their billing on a computer-to-computer basis to eliminate the cost of having your employees key their statements into your system.

Magnetic Tapes.

Have your computer department reuse magnetic tapes ("scratch tapes") for storing back-up information. New tapes just aren't necessary for all computer work.

Management Statistics Book.

A simple way to avoid wasting of executive time looking for management reports is to develop a standardized management folder for each executive. Have separate tabs for week, month, quarter, year, and multi-year. At the start of each section, identify the reports that will be in that section, together with who prepares the report and the page number of the report. Also, the page numbering system should be identified on the management report, for standardized easy filing. For example, your monthly tab might include the following:

- Monthly sales per store per week..page M1
- Monthly comparative sales data..page M2
- Store sales ranking report..page M3
- Year-to-date shrinkage, by month..page M4
- Store 3-month rolling shrinkage..page M5
- Store telephone exception report..page M6.

Your secretary can update your statistics book as soon as each new management report is received.

Mailbags.

Where a large amount of mail is transmitted from the field to headquarters, use different colored mail bags for each department at headquarters to avoid a bottleneck in the mail department and allow the mail to go directly to its intended destination.

Mailing Lists.

If you must have one, keep it to the absolute minimum. Depending on the size of the company, this could be as low as 10–12 names, typically those of investment analysts. Mailing lists are almost unnecessary in this modern age where all publicly issued statements released by a company are usually transmitted over the various news wires. It is amazing to me, but some companies still send out their monthly sales release to every requester, using first class postage!

Mail Scales.

Check their accuracy on a regular basis. A lot of money can be wasted with inaccurate scales.

Maintenance Agreements.

In many cases, these cost you more money than if you hire repair services on an as-needed basis. If in doubt, spin off part of your operation which has a maintenance agreement and pay for repairs as required. Compare the costs with your maintenance agreement costs. Incidentally, if you find that equipment is breaking down frequently, why not replace it rather than repeatedly repairing it?

Management.

A thin middle and a very thin top layer of management is all that is needed to run a successful business. If you do not have a thin middle/top group you may need to re-examine the way you organize your business. The observation, "The more you know about your business, the fewer the people you need to run it," generally holds true.

Manila Folders.

Once the tab on one side has become outdated, reverse the folder and use the other side of the tab. Once that is used, put a label over the top and write on that. Remember, every hundred pennies saved is another dollar of profit.

Manual Checks.

Not only does cutting checks manually for employees disrupt work and waste a lot of time, but it also adds extra work to your monthly bank reconciliation program. You'll avoid a lot of unnecessary time wastage if everyone is asked to plan ahead and avoid requesting manual checks.

Manufacturing.

The service industry is often tempted to manufacture some of the products it sells. As manufacturing skills are different from service skills, self-manufacturing is usually best to avoid. However, one way to receive the same low price advantages without owning a manufacturing plant is to draw up a 3–5 year contract with a manufacturer to buy a certain quantity from him each year, assuming certain quality standards are met, using a certain price formula. The manufacturer can then take this guaranteed purchase agreement to his bank and leverage himself very highly, thereby reducing his cost of capital below your level, allowing him to produce goods for you at a very low price.

Marginal Business.

Eliminate any marginal product lines or departments. Sol Price calls this the "the intelligent loss of business."

Measure.

Whatever it is you wish to improve, measure it. You can't manage anything unless you measure it. So don't set any goals or spell out lofty ideals in a mission statement unless you intend to measure progress regularly against such goals.

Meetings.

One highly effective CEO did a survey of his time a few years ago. He found that he received most telephone calls from the field during the periods of 8:30–10:30 a.m. and 1:00–2:30 p.m. As a result, he scheduled meetings with his headquarters staff for 11:30–12:30. This not only allowed for direct field access but he also found that often his staff would skip lunch, make the meetings short, and/or make quicker decisions!

Memos.

Regular, operational-type memos to a large number of readers should be:

a. action oriented. Have all the "to do" items in one section of the memo with space along side for the reader to check each item as it is done, with a separate section for "information only" items;
b. double sided;
c. on white paper (that's the cheapest); and
d. three-hole punched (in case anyone wants to put them in a binder).

Memos, Distribution.

Establish a distribution code, and keep it updated, for internal mail as an alternative to listing those people on internal memos who should be receiving copies. For example, the code D could mean all department managers and up; the code H could mean all headquarters employees; the code E could mean all designated executives above a certain level; etc.

Memos, General.

Rather than send each employee a copy of a general memo, either have the memo circulated among employees or post a copy of it on the notice board. Another approach, for both memos and reports, is to have one central copy for the department, filed in one location for all to read at their convenience.

Memos, Handwritten.

Brief memos to another person should be handwritten where practicable. Also, respond to memos by writing answers on them and then returning them.

Memos, Internal.

Internal memos should all be on the same size stationery, usually 8–1/2″ x 11.″ This is advantageous for both filing and photocopying. In addition, letterhead stationery is not necessary for internal memos. Save the cost of the letterhead paper as well as the space where your letterhead goes!

Memos, Necessary.

Before sending your next memo, ask yourself two questions:

(a) how much of this is really necessary?
(b) would a phone call be better?

Memos, One Page.

The CEO of Procter & Gamble is reputed to have enforced a rule that all memos to him could be no more than one page. This certainly saved a lot of paper as well as a lot of executive reading time!

Memos, One Person.

Address any memo for which you want a response to only one person. You may provide copies to other people if necessary. When you address a memo to more than one person, each addressee usually leaves the response to the others on the list!

Memos, Partial Page.

Where a multi-page memo includes part of an additional page, have your secretary automatically review it to see what can be condensed, or whether the memo can be shrunk, so that you avoid using the additional page. This is particularly important when multiple copies of the memo are to be distributed.

Memos, Problems.

If problems are occurring in certain stores or parts of the company, don't send a memo to everyone in the company about it. Just contact the problem areas. Example: If a handful of stores have excessive long distance telephone charges, don't send a memo to all stores about controlling their long distance charges. Just contact the stores in question.

Memos, Same Floor.

Have our inter-company communications become so bureaucratic that we must send memos to fellow employees on the same floor of the building? Not only would personal communications be a better way to communicate, it would also build team inter-play, a priceless asset in any organization.

Merchant's Association.

Avoid automatically joining the merchant's association in any mall area in which you locate. Join only if there is a clear economic benefit or if you are obliged to because of your lease agreement.

Minimum Thresholds.

Set minimum tolerances on activities below which you will take no action. For example, avoid researching accounting errors of less than $10 or $20. Don't send statements to customers on a monthly basis if their balance is less than, say, $10. Such statements could probably be sent once a quarter.

Miscellaneous Purchases.

Check with various discount department stores in your area to see if they will give a discount to your company for miscellaneous purchases. It's not uncommon for such companies to give a 10% discount to other businesses.

Motels.

Have all employees, from the CEO down, stay at the same motels which are, of course, budget or economy motels. There's seldom any need to stay at a motel more expensive than a Fairfield Inn or a Hampton Inn, if they are available. After all, you are only looking for a nice clean room, aren't you? To achieve the same objective, provide a daily allowance for accommodation (which may vary according to the size of the city), and let employees decide where they want to stay. If they wish to stay anywhere fancy, they can pay the excess over the daily allowance.

Motel Rates.

Negotiate corporate rates with individual motels. This can be done by your local people, where appropriate. Track expenditures with each motel, and when they exceed a certain threshold figure, go back and renegotiate even better rates. Typically, for really favorable preferential rates, you need to be averaging in excess of 50 room nights per month. Issue the list of approved motels to all appropriate employees. Show, in town sequence, the recommended motel and approximate rate. For example:

Town	Motel Recommended	Approx. Rate
Stockton, CA 8827 James Road (209) 838–7767	Value Inn	$40.00

Name Registration.

If you plan to grow beyond your current geographical area, register your company name in a number of surrounding states. You will need to pay the appropriate registration fees in those states, but that is usually cheaper than buying the right to your name from some other person who has registered your name there, when, later, you wish to operate in those states.

Negotiating.

Two negotiating phrases that, in a number of cases, reduce your costs are:

- Is that the best you can do?
- That's an interesting first offer!

New York Stock Exchange.

Many companies feel that they have "made it" when they are finally listed on the New York Stock Exchange. The fee structure to be listed on the New York Stock Exchange is quite different from that for listing on the NASDAQ National Market System, where many companies start their lives as publicly traded companies. Therefore, if you are contemplating switching from NASDAQ to NYSE, ensure that it is for economic reasons and not ego reasons!

Norm Forms.

An effective alternative to budgeting is to compare one store's results against the average of all stores with a similar sales volume. For example, a company with individual stores sales ranging from $5,000 a week to $100,000 a week may break them into sales volume classes of

	Weekly Sales
Class A:	less than $10,000
Class B:	$10,000-$19,999
Class C:	$20,000-$29,999, etc.

As expenses usually vary in direct proportion to volume, comparing each store against its peers' actual results and not against a budget provides a real comparison and incentive to improve. Every manager wants to perform better than his peers.

Further, as managers improve their individual performances against the average, that, in turn, improves the overall average for their sales volume class. This norm form reporting system provides the company with a method of constantly improving results and provides a target which floats with the real conditions of that particular week, month, or quarter, as opposed to some static budget figure determined at the start of the year. It is a far more effective self-management tool than a fixed annual budget. A simple example of a Norm Form is included in the appendix.

Notice Board.

Want your company bulletins to be read? Place a company notice board in each restroom. This generally guarantees the highest readership!

Office Furniture.

Identify a simple office furniture package and standardize it for your general offices. Have a better package for your executive offices if necessary. Then buy in bulk as you grow.

Office Hours.

The corporate headquarters of one very cost-conscious and highly profitable company has its hours posted outside its main door. Hours: 8–12 and 1–5. Between 12 and 1 pm the front door is locked, the telephone system is switched to a recorded message system ("our office hours are . . ."), and the receptionist goes to lunch. This cost-saver is more appropriate to smaller rather than larger companies.

Office Lighting.

Should your employees turn off their office lights when they go out for a coffee or lunch break? Ask for an assessment from your electrician. One company that had fluorescent lights was advised that they would not save any power unless the lights were off for 30 minutes or longer. In other words, if you leave your office for only ten minutes, leave the lights on. But get an assessment for your particular lighting situation.

Office Lighting, Evenings.

If your cleaners (or any employee) works in the evening, ensure that they turn off all but the security lights when they leave the building at night. Similarly, they should turn off any designated electrical equipment, such as coffee and copy machines.

One Person Rule.

When making a presentation, or trying to sell something, send only one person. When two or more people turn up for a presentation, a cost-conscious executive thinks that the visiting company has money to burn (and therefore the product is too expensive), or else that neither presenter is competent to give the full story!

Operating Balance Sheet.

Too much time is spent on the Income Statement and too little on the Balance Sheet. This is because the typical balance sheet is not user-friendly. Make it so by dividing each total by the number of stores both for this year and last year. Then identify, by line item, where investment costs are increasing and decreasing for the average store. This is a very simple and effective measuring tool which will help you reduce your net investment per store thereby freeing cash for other purposes. A typical operating balance sheet for a chain retail or service company is included in the appendix.

Overtime, After 40 Hours.

Avoid paying overtime unless an employee has put in 40 hours for the week, regardless of the number of hours the employee worked on any one day or the time of the day the employee worked. If you wish to pay a premium for Sunday work, it is preferable to pay an additional amount per hour (e.g. $2 per hour) rather than a certain percentage of their base pay. This is simpler to calculate and to manage. It is also less inflationary over time.

Overtime, Approved.

Overtime should always be approved in advance by a supervisor. Where overtime would exceed more than, say, two hours a week, have the supervisor receive prior approval for this from his manager.

Paperwork.

Keep it to an absolute minimum. For example, sending either complete wage or general ledger details to individual stores or departments usually has no corporate advantage. If a store needs to know more details about its wages, costs, or any expense account, the manager can call the accounting department for details. Do not bog your people down with paperwork!

Partnering.

It's amazing how many vendors are prepared to help you with free labor, particularly when it involves selling more of their products. At least one leading cost-conscious company has brought a team of vendor employees into their corporate offices on a permanent basis to minimize out-of-stocks and to effect just-in-time inventory replacement. The company's inventory turn on that vendor's products has increased dramatically. The company is so happy with the results that it has extended this concept to include its other vendors.

Payables.

Pay on time. Not before time. Negotiate longer payable terms if the discount conceded is less than your cost of capital.

Payables Department.

Request from your accounts payables department, on a weekly or four weekly basis, details of any payment that seems extravagant or out of the ordinary in either capital or operating expenditures.

Payroll Taxes.

Under current regulations, a company can arrange for a delay of 5% of the payroll withheld income and social security taxes. In accordance with Regulation 31.6302 (c)-1 (b) and the instructions for form 941, companies are required to make their payroll deposits within 3 banking days after the close of each appropriate period during the month. However, in part 1 of this regulation, an exception is made to depositing 100% of the amount where 95% is deposited within 3 banking days and the remainder is deposited in a specified following period. By taking advantage of this exception, a company can gain a permanent lag of 5% of their withheld income and social security taxes. This can be a big savings!

Performance Appraisals.

Many human resource departments spend a great deal of time, unnecessarily, affixing computer-generated name labels onto performance appraisal forms and sending them to the manager of each employee who is due for a performance appraisal. A more cost-effective method is to have a set of blank appraisal forms at each company location and have human resources generate a computer printout for each location on the first of each month, indicating those people who are due for performance appraisals during the following 30 days. Then the human resource department need simply collect the completed forms.

Performance Appraisals, Annual.

Rather than prepare performance appraisals on each employee's anniversary date with the company, a more effective system is to have performance appraisals for each department of the company done at the same time each year, regardless of the anniversary date of the individual employees. For example, the performance appraisals of store employees could be done in January-February (their quiet time of the year), and April-May for the accounting department (their quiet time), etc. By doing a number of employees at the same time, the appraisals are easier to prepare and fairer because they are relative to other employees at the same moment in time.

Personal Computers.

Set a standard for the minimum number of hours a personal computer must be used each week for a department or employee to retain that personal computer. A minimum figure of 15–18 hours is commonly used. The MIS department can track and log the weekly usage of each computer.

Personal Computers, Network.

Where you have a network of personal computers (more than four PCs), set up one database to avoid the unnecessary duplication of data.

Phone Calls, Personal.

Apart from emergencies, have a policy that personal phone calls should be made only during break and meal hours.

Photocopier Lines.

Limit the number of people standing in line to use a photocopier to the person copying plus one in line.

Photocopying, Personal.

Any employee photocopying personal items should reimburse the company, on an honesty system, at 4 or 5 cents per page. Simply have an "honesty" box at or alongside each photocopier. If this doesn't work satisfactorily, you can install insertable counters on your copy machines and charge the employees later.

Photocopy Equipment.

Rather than having many different types of copiers and copy paper throughout the company, seek bids for one type of copier to be placed in all locations. Seek, also, a service commitment from the various photocopy companies submitting bids. Not only will you save by having the same copy paper, but it will be easier for employees to have only one set of operating instructions for any copier throughout the company. You will also need only one photocopy serviceman who can check other copiers on the same visit that he is repairing a broken one.

Photos.

Have your regular photos developed at the cheapest place available. Seldom is there a need for expensive one-hour photo developing. Very few businesses have a need to have all their film processed expensively with a beautiful finish.

Plants.

If plants are necessary in company facilities, ensure that they are artificial rather than fresh. Not only are they cheaper but this eliminates the cost of a hired gardening service wandering around watering them! If, by any chance, you persist in having live plants, at least cancel the hired garden service and have various employees "adopt a plant" and water and nurture them.

Policies and Procedures Manuals.

As these comprise, usually, many, many pages, have them typed on 8″ x 14″ paper and shrink it on your copier to 8″ x 11″ to minimize the number of pages processed. Because they are regularly updated, produce them on cheaper rather than expensive paper. Also remember to have on each sheet the Revision Date and the name of the issuer, in case of questions.

Postage Paid Envelopes.

When you have a packet to send another company which has sent you a postage paid envelope and your packet won't fit in the envelope, simply tape the postage paid envelope to the outside of your packet and mail. The postage will be paid by the recipient.

Postage, Personal.

Employees, not the company, should pay for their personal postage from the very top of the organization to the very bottom. After all, if the top brass don't pay for their personal postage, why should anyone in the organization be honest about anything?

Preferred Stock.

Set the dividend rate to float with the market rate of interest (e.g., x% above Prime or 30-year Treasury Bonds). This will mean that management will never have an incentive to call the issue, which usually forces unnecessary refinancing costs.

Pre-Opening Expenses.

Expense all costs possible that are incurred prior to opening a new store, rather than capitalizing them. This allows you to gain your tax deduction immediately rather than over the following years. Cash now is always better than cash later!

Printing.

With the advent of laser printers and desk-top publishing, many companies can now produce their own in-store signage, product literature, promotional flyers, price lists, etc., cheaper than the traditional printing methods. A high speed, high resolution copier in your mail center for running off such materials is also usually cost effective.

Procedures Manual, Examples.

Procedures manuals are usually filled with all sorts of examples. To simplify the learning process (and, therefore, cost) have examples relating to different steps of one master example. To illustrate: your examples relating to ordering, receiving, selling, and handling customer returns should all be drawn from the same master example.

Process Flow.

Essentially, every retail and service business is a process flow with the customer the most important part of the flow-line. Constantly challenge your people to find ways to simplify and reduce the cost of the process. Your accounting system should also measure the costs of each part of the process to show improvements (or otherwise!) from period to period and year to year.

Productivity Measures.

Use physical productivity measures, such as items sold per square foot, rather than dollar-based productivity measures, such as sales per square foot. Only in this way will you know whether you are improving your real productivity from period to period and year to year.

Profit Sharing.

A profit sharing plan is usually preferable to a defined pension plan because the latter is constrained by so many laws and frequent change of regulations. Profit sharing plans, by contrast, are usually simpler, easier, and cheaper to administer.

Property Taxes, Distribution Centers.

If you have a number of distribution centers with varying property tax rates, balance your inventory levels amongst the distribution centers at year end to minimize your overall property tax bill.

Property Taxes, External Specialist.

If you have many properties spread over a large geographic area, it is usually cost effective to have a specialist external company handle all your property tax listings. Because they specialize in this one function, they typically have a better overall knowledge of each jurisdiction's listing requirements as well as a keen insight into the mindset of the various taxing authorities. If handling this function internally, have an external specialist company audit your work every 2–4 years.

Property Taxes, Minimization.

To minimize property taxes, reduce the value of your inventory by deducting discounts earned, freight allowances, expense allowances, promotional allowances, and other special allowances from the value of the inventory. Similarly, in those states that do not specifically exclude LIFO as a deduction from inventory valuation, deduct your LIFO figure to reduce your inventory valuation and therefore, your property tax assessment.

Proprietary Charge Cards.

In these days of American Express, VISA, Master Card, Discover, and the AT&T Universal card, why have your own proprietary company charge card for customers? It's just another card to fill customers' wallets besides adding receivables to your books. However, if you feel your own proprietary credit card is a critical part of your business, evaluate factoring your receivables to an outside party to remove them from your books. The factoring discount is usually less than your cost of capital, making it economically feasible.

Public Holidays.

Pay every employee for each public holiday in the week that the holiday occurs, even though they may be working on the holiday (in which case they are paid twice). This is more cost effective than allowing employees to accrue such holidays and take them later, as it avoids the administrative costs of keeping up with all these exceptions as well as the cost of processing these entries as a special entry at a later date. Simplicity saves. Complexity costs!

Publicity.

Mae West had it right when she once said, "I'd rather be looked over, than overlooked!" The same approach should be taken with publicity. Generate it, whenever you can, when you see the opportunity for doing so at zero or minimal cost. Now this does not mean setting up a Publicity Department or Public Relations Vice President. I've yet to see either that were really a cost-effective contributor to the corporate bottom line.

Purchase Terms.

Two terms in purchase agreements that have saved companies lots of money are "most favored customer" and "won't exceed." Include in your purchase agreement a clause stating that you won't be charged more than the vendor's most favored customer. If your vendor won't agree to this, then get a commitment that your price won't exceed $X during the next 4 months.

Quality Improvement Systems.

Define quality, set up a quality improvement system, and then work towards continuous improvement. Savings in this area alone can be dramatic.

Quarterly Reports, Shareholders.

Simply attach a shareholder's mailing address label to his or her actual quarterly report and mail using bulk mail rates. Save the cost of the envelope and first class postage!

Real Estate.

As a general rule, cost-effective companies lease, rather than own, their properties for two major reasons: having cash tied up in properties which are, usually, yielding a return less than the cost of capital is harmful to the shareholders; and liquidating these properties as they, or their neighborhoods, deteriorate over time is often difficult and costly.

Receptionists.

Receptionists and switchboard operators should always have a pile of work to process during any down time. Some have a computer terminal into which they can key information. They should not be permitted to read a newspaper, books, or magazines during company time. Not only is that wasteful but it sends a very bad signal to visitors and fellow employees alike.

Recognition.

Wherever possible, recognize people in some tangible way for cost-saving ideas. For example, in addition to anything else you do, you could give a coffee mug to every employee who comes up with a cost-reducing idea. The mug could have something appropriately inscribed on it such as "I saved the company money," or "I'm helping make the company great!" Not only does this recognize the contribution but it also reinforces the cost-conscious culture to all who see the mug.

Recycled Paper.

Another use for your discarded paper is to have it recycled and converted into paper towels for your office. One cost-conscious company has recycling bins strategically placed around the office. A portion of the recycling proceeds is used to buy pizzas for the employees to recognize and reward their recycling efforts.

Regression Analysis.

This is one of the most useful tools available to determine equitable operating standards throughout your company. Using this simple calculation process allows you to identify any significant exceptions and variances in your operation quickly. It also allows you to set standards for your company based upon your actual operating performance. Regression formats are now common on PC software. Ask someone in your accounting department to demonstrate how it works and how it could help you. A simple regression analysis relating hours worked to units sold is included in the appendix.

Reimbursement, Moving Costs.

In the agreement involving moving costs for employees, the employee should be required to pay back a certain portion of the moving cost if that employee should resign within a year of the transfer. A similar approach can be taken with seminars employees attend at company expense.

Rent, Percentage.

For many retail and service organizations, rental costs are structured as the greater of X dollars per year or Y percent of sales. If your business is subject to sales volatility, negotiate your lease, if at all possible, with a lower fixed rental cost plus a higher percentage of sales than normal. In this way, the landlord has a greater vested interest in your sales success and is "encouraged" to help promote your center's business. It means that you pay a lower rent than normal when sales are slow and more when you're doing well and can afford it.

Rent, Walk Away Clauses.

As rent is usually the second largest expense for a retail or service chain, introduce "walk-away" clauses into your rental contract so that you can walk away if sales fall below a certain figure or if a predetermined percentage of your shopping center is vacant for more than three months, or if the major tenant moves.

Rental Car Insurance.

Check that your insurance covers any employee while driving a rental car while on company business. Most do. If such coverage exists, advise your employees never to take any of the additional insurance offered by the rental companies when renting cars. Alternatively, a number of credit card companies, such as the AT&T Universal Card, automatically cover the renter for collision damage if their credit card is used when renting the car.

Reports, Elimination.

Don't send out certain reports for one, two, or three weeks. See who notices and who doesn't notice. You will usually be able to trim your distribution list and eliminate some reports after measuring the reaction (or lack of reaction)!

Reports, Requirements.

All reports should have on them:

- the distribution (who it is to)
- who it was prepared by
- the date of preparation

In this way you can quickly trace who issued a report if you want further elaboration on any point, check any number, and keep up to date with any changes in the distribution.

Reports, Results.

Some employees love producing new reports and/or adding extra lines of information to existing reports. One single challenge to such report proliferators is: "How are you going to improve results as a result of this change?" Suspense the answer on your tickler system for 90 days, and see if the expected results are being achieved.

Research, Invoices.

When vendors ask you to research invoices that are over one year old, charge them $50 per hour.

They should be ashamed that their paperwork is so out of date.

Safety.

Placing a heavy emphasis on safety usually results in lower insurance costs. The safety record of your truck drivers is an excellent area to focus on to reduce insurance costs. Your distribution center is the next most important area. A safety committee and accident review process serves as a way to concentrate on safety and accidents within the company with the ultimate direct aim of reducing insurance costs.

Salary Changes.

To simplify salary administration costs, all salary changes below a certain level should be made effective on the first pay period of each calendar quarter. Employees above that level could have their salary reviews made effective in the first pay period of either January or April (or some other month) each year. This will allow for a fairer review of relative performance done at the same time. Obviously, exceptions, where really necessary and with the appropriate approval, can be made to the above guidelines.

Savings Bonds.

Savings bonds are a good prize for corporate incentive programs. They can have a high face value yet the cost to the organization is typically only 50–75% of the face value of the bond.

Say "No."

Just say no to bad business ideas. Teach your people to do the same thing. If you want to find out what happens if you don't, read Jerry B. Harvey's *The Abiline Paradox.*

Scratch Pads.

Unused paper, with at least one clear side, should be reprocessed into scratch pads for employee use.

Search Firms.

Avoid using them except in extreme circumstances. They are expensive. Usually, a short list of good people to fill key positions can be obtained by talking to vendors, suppliers, investment analysts, and executives in other companies.

Secretaries.

If an office has more than 10 secretaries (or administrative assistants), each of them should report to a secretarial supervisor with a dotted line relationship to "their" executive. In this way, you gain by having someone who is able to help develop each secretary as well as monitor their relative performance [and provide equity at salary review time] as well as cover their responsibilities when any secretary is away. Also, review who really needs a full-time secretary. The simpler you make your business the less need anyone will have for a full-time secretary.

Seminars.

Rather than sending a large number of people to the same external seminar, send only one or two people. After the seminar, have them run an internal seminar covering the essence of what they learned. One cost-conscious company considers many seminars to be vacation days! The only seminars that employees in that company are allowed to attend must cost no more than $100. The CEO says he'd rather the employee take the day off, go to the public library, get a book on the seminar subject, study it and come back with recommendations. He believes such gives greater value for money!

Seminar Payments.

Often one has to reserve a place in a seminar months in advance. However, rather than paying for the seminar this long in advance, have your company issue a purchase order to be paid one week prior to the seminar. The seminar people will have proof of your intention to attend and pay and you have the advantage of the cash in the meantime.

Sensible Approximation.

"The price of perfection is prohibitive," Marks & Spencer's, one of Great Britain's leading low-cost retailers, reminds us. Review your procedures to see where approximating results will not materially affect your results—for example, in taking inventory or in allocating costs between periods. This philosophy of sensible approximation saves paperwork, labor, a lot of frustration, and significantly speeds up your monthly and year-end reporting.

Shareholders' Letter.

The letter to shareholders in the annual and quarterly reports from the chairman and president should be written for them, possibly by someone in the accounting department. They can make any refinements to the proposed drafts prior to publication, should they wish. This saves a great deal of expensive executive time.

Share Transfer Agent.

Seek bids for this work every two to four years. Ask your current agent to bid as well as those who act on behalf of your competitors. It's another way to ensure your costs are lower than theirs.

Shrinkage Hotline.

Set up an 800 number that any employee can call with suggestions for improving shrinkage. Place a poster on the inside of every bathroom cubicle in the company advising employees of this 800 number and reminding them that theft kills jobs. Offer a reward for any information which leads to the prosecution of any employee for theft. In a bathroom cubicle, employees can copy down the number without fear of anyone seeing them. Thus, their subsequent call can be completely anonymous, if that is desired.

Simplify.

Constantly simplify. Simplify everything possible. You will make great savings not only in training time and costs but you will also not need to hire the highly skilled [and expensive] people who are usually necessary to handle complexity. A simple, standardized operation is easier to grow and usually makes more money. Sure, it may be boring, but as Peter Drucker once said: "A well run business is a boring business."

Small Towns.

Where your organization is geographically dispersed, and you have a choice of locating distribution centers in either small towns or large cities, small towns have a number of cost advantages, such as lower accommodation costs, lower rents, lower meal costs, lower labor costs, and, usually, a good work ethic with less labor turnover.

Source Filing.

Adding to the problem of filing cabinets is the desire of everyone to keep copies of the same documents. This can be avoided by using a system of source filing whereby the originator of any internal document keeps a copy of it for, say, two years. Then there is no need for everyone to keep copies of the same document in their filing systems. They can discard them and always feel assured that they can go to the source for a copy if they ever need it again. This eliminates a large number of filing cabinets around your office. Of course, the originator need not keep it in paper form if it can be retrieved from a computer.

Span of Control.

With the unbelievable computing power and information now available, much of the paperwork of middle management is being eliminated. As this occurs, use the time saved to expand management's span of control. If you don't, what payback are you getting on your computer investment?

Standardization.

Standardize everything possible. It is easier, quicker, and less expensive to train people in standardized procedures. Similarly, it is cheaper to build a standardized store rather than develop a new design for every store you open. A standardized operation has enormous economies in fixturing, signage, and pricing, and facilitates rapid expansion. A standardized layout results in a predictable gross profit and labor productivity results. A standardized operation also means significantly fewer committee meetings than a non-standardized operation.

Statement Reconciliation.

Do not reconcile vendor statements with your internal records, if you're comfortable with your internal accounting and control system. Rather, always pay the lesser of what you are billed or what you understood you received, and leave it to the vendor to come back to you with any disputes on this. Then, every 6 or 12 months, send a letter to each vendor requesting notification of any variances in their records from yours. Otherwise tell them that, in the absence of such notification, you will assume that your records are in balance. You can even request the vendor to confirm in writing that your accounts are in balance.

State Support.

If opening a significant operation in a new geographic area, check to see whether any local or state support is available in the form of tax breaks, utility concessions, or free training of potential employees.

Store Number 999.

Many companies charge and credit their whole list of stores for small amounts. The result is a lot of processing costs with inconsequential impact on each store's results. To avoid this, set up a special dummy store number, such as 999, and charge to that store those items that don't directly relate to an individual store but are a store cost. Then, if necessary, at the end of each accounting period, the amounts in Store 999 can either remain there or can be charged out to all stores on a predetermined basis in one lump sum. This is another example of sensible approximation.

Subscriptions.

Ask the accounting department to provide you with a list of all magazine and other subscriptions and memberships incurred during the previous twelve months, sorted by department. Send this list to each department head challenging him to examine it closely and evaluate which items are critical and which are nice or no longer necessary, and return this list to you. After any further appropriate probing and challenging, send the final list to the payables department appropriately noted as to what subscriptions and memberships are approved for the following year. Note that many of trade publications are free to members of the trade. Ensure your employees receive these. Repeat this practice annually.

Suggestion Program.

Either set aside one month a year for cost-reduction suggestions throughout the whole company or have an ongoing cost reduction suggestion program. Or do both. Recognize all who make implementable suggestions. One company had a one month cost-reduction suggestion program. The president announced he would pay $5 for every implementable idea received. He requested a minimum of 200 ideas from the distribution center personnel and 100 ideas from each of his stores. In addition, he announced he would pay $300 for the best idea and $200 for the second best idea. There were also prizes of $300 for the most ideas from one person and $200 for the second most ideas from one person. Whether an idea was practical was decided by the distribution center manager and the store operations manager. The company received a tremendous payback on the program. As a result, the program is now an annual month-long event.

Sunset Dates.

We can learn from everyone, even the government! One good thing some government regulators have done is to introduce sunset dates into their policies and regulations. If the issuer wants the policy or regulation to continue after that date, a new one must be issued. Otherwise, it lapses on the sunset date indicated on the original instruction. The same should apply, wherever possible, to all policies, procedures, instructions, rules, and memos on notice boards.

Supplies.

Value your supplies on hand at each location at a standardized liquidation, not cost, valuation. This may be, say, $1000 per store. Then as each new store opens, capitalize $1000 of supplies automatically and expense all other supply purchases from then on. This avoids the time wasted in taking inventories of supplies, and the games your accountants may play switching supplies between inventories and expenses to adjust earnings, as well as ensuring that you get the maximum tax credit available from the IRS.

Supplies, Backup.

In your supplies room, keep back-up calculators, typewriters, small copy machines, etc., purchased (of course) at your bulk purchase price. Send these out to replace equipment that has broken down. This is a lot cheaper than buying such small equipment items on a one-by-one basis, unless you have such items covered by a low-cost blanket purchase order.

Supplies, Recycling.

Recycle internally such supplies as rubber bands received in incoming mail. Delta Airlines is reputed to have zero paper clip purchases using this principle.

Supplies, Shipments.

Two or three times a year automatically ship a base quantity of supplies to all stores (the base can vary according to the volume of the store). Then allow re-orders at other times. This should cut down on the constant order filling of small item supplies. A variation of this is to have your stores tell you what they have on hand and let your computer calculate their supply needs over the coming quarter.

Surveys.

Companies are regularly requested by external organizations to complete surveys. Don't waste your time completing them unless mandated by law or there is a clear economic benefit to the organization in doing so. Similarly, don't buy survey information unless knowing what the "average" company is doing is critical to your future success.

Tasks.

Allocate tasks and functions to the area most skilled to do it. For example, the human resource department is more skilled in giving advice, etc., than in processing paperwork. Therefore, keep human resources to a small core of competent specialists working in their field. Pass on the processing of payroll, insurance, even the handling of a great deal of their paperwork, to the process-oriented accounting department.

Tax Review Meeting.

Hold a tax review meeting with your outside public accountants at the start of the fourth quarter each year. Discuss opportunities still available for the current year to minimize taxes as well as tax reduction opportunities for the following year. Given the penchant of Congress to fiddle with taxes, there are always new tax wrinkles to consider, evaluate, and take advantage of every year.

Telephones, Automatic Answering.

If you are a small company and wish to filter out a lot of unnecesary, unsolicited external calls to your organization, you may have all incoming calls to your headquarters activate an automatic answering system which asks the caller to leave a message for whom they wish to speak. If they need accounts payable, that specific extension is given. In this way, not only is a receptionist eliminated, but it allows the selective returning of calls as deemed appropriate internally. Obviously, a seperate unlisted phone number for the headquarters is given to the individual stores to call in on.

Telephones, Call Coding.

At headquarters, have a call coding analysis done in which all calls, their duration, and cost are identified by telephone extension. Follow up on exceptions outside of preset norms.

Telephones, Centralized Switchboard.

Avoid direct external lines for individual executives. Each such direct line typically costs hundreds of dollars extra per year compared to a centralized switchboard.

Telephones, Consoles.

Review your telephone console policy. Typically, you will find too many telephone consoles with too many knobs and buttons on them, relative to need. Most extensions need only a basic extension console. They do not need a panel of direct lines to call, automatic dialing, a speaker phone or some of the other wonderful features available.

Telephones, 800 Numbers.

For those companies that your company calls on a regular basis, ask for their 800 number and circulate them internally.

Telephones, Intra-State Calls.

Check with your local telephone company. Some permit intra-state long distance calls to be at a lower rate during the lunch hour (12:00–1:00 PM). This is a good time to make such calls as well as transmit intra-state fax messages if they must be processed during the business day.

Telephones, Long Distance Calls.

Have all non-critical long distance calls placed after 5:00 PM (your time), to take advantage of the cheaper calling rates. If you are located on the West Coast, place them before 8:00 AM.

Telephones, Speed Dial.

At headquarters, have all stores programmed for speed dialing. Use the store number as the speed dial number.

Telephones, Unused.

Have a regular review of all telephones. With personnel changes, it's not unusual to find unused, or little used, extensions. Eliminate them.

Telephones, WATS.

Except where your business solicits external phone calls, do not issue your WATS number to anyone other than internal employees. You can reinforce this message by having a little sticker placed on each telephone to remind employees of this. Also, some companies change their WATS number occasionally to eliminate unauthorized users.

Telephone Calls, Vendors.

Use vendors' WATS lines wherever possible. Otherwise place collect calls to vendors.

Telephone Directory Assistance.

At your headquarters, your telephone system can block off all calls for directory assistance. This will save you paying the query cost for such calls. Obviously, your operator could place a directory call in case of need. It's amazing how many employees call directory assistance for a phone number rather than look it up in a phone book. For phones not blocked off, have an exception report issued for all directory assistance calls for appropriate follow-through.

Telephone Extensions.

At headquarters, allocate easy-to-remember extension numbers, such as 1111, 2222, 3333, to the most frequently dialed numbers. In this way, people in the field will find it easy to remember such extensions and therefore save the time needed to look them up each time they have to call those numbers.

Telephone Lines.

On a regular basis, have tests done on the "blockage" of your headquarter phones to make sure you don't have too many or too few lines coming into your telephone system.

Telephone Listings.

Have a clear company standard on the type size for your company listing in the white pages of the telephone directory. Also spell out your annual yellow page listing plans together with who will place such listings. This will save a great deal of time and cost each year when so many people in the organization are approached about this issue.

Telephone Messages.

If your organization is not using a voice mailbox system, one cost-effective way of passing messages to all stores in a hurry is to have a calling sequence for the message. For example, headquarters calls store A, store A calls store B, etc., within each district.

Telephone Music.

Don't have music played over the telephone when external calls are placed on hold, unless this feature comes absolutely free with your telephone package. This is another nice but non-critical cost.

Telephone Numbers.

Where possible, have your store telephone numbers end with an easy-to-remember array. For example, Baby Superstores, Inc., a chain of specialty stores in the Southeast, has the telephone number of each store end with the digits 2229 (i.e., BABY).

Telephone Sharing.

Where there is not a high intensity of telephone usage, a number of people should share one phone extension.

Telephones, Automated.

An automated attendant and voice mail system usually reduces the operator costs as well as speeding up communication from the outside to frequently called insiders.

Testing.

Prior to committing the company to a large amount of expenditure on some new technological advance, test it in a limited number of areas before making a final decision. For example, prior to introducing scanning devices in your stores, test them thoroughly in several stores to assess the economic benefits that you might gain. If you are not getting the benefits in a few stores under test, you are not likely to benefit chainwide.

Tickler System.

Have your secretary keep a tickler system for you. On the day you want a piece of paper that you've scribbled some notes on, or a memo, or report, etc., she will give it to you. The system is simple: Write a large T on the note you want returned to you on a later date. On the left hand side of the T write the month and on the right hand side of the T write the date you want it. If you want something on a regular basis, such as the third day of each quarter, write Q on the left hand side of the T and 3 on the right hand side of the T.

Time Cards.

Where plasticized time cards are used, combine their function with both employee identification and security, rather than having separate cards. The card can have the employee's photo on it, and the unique employee coding on the time card can be used to allow the employee in and out of the building within prescribed limits.

Time Clocks, Recording Minutes.

Record beginning and ending times worked to the hundredth of an hour. Then, at the end of the week, round the total to the nearest upwards quarter hour. This is more cost effective than rounding everything to the nearest quarter hour on a daily basis. If using manual time recording systems, use military time. It's much easier to calculate, and your employees make fewer errors.

Time Clocks, Work Area.

If time clocks are used, have employees check in and out on the time clock nearest their work area so that you do not pay them for time spent removing coats, stopping by break rooms, bathrooms, and coffee rooms before and after work.

Tires.

As you purchase new trailers for your fleet, take the tires off these trailers and replace them with recaps. The new tires should be placed on your tractors when they need tire replacements. This is both a safety and a cost saving move. A blow-out of a tire on a tractor is much more dangerous than on a trailer.

Tire Tracking.

Some companies attach bar codes to each tire and track them individually. For expensive tires, this can be very helpful.

Trade Shows.

Unless your organization is one that sells products or services to attendees at trade shows, avoid making presentations at them. Not only do they waste a lot of your executives' time preparing for the presentations, they also usually involve passing along to your competitors information about your company which is best kept within your organization.

Trailers, New.

When you add new trailers to your fleet, have them loaded with merchandise at one of your suppliers, on the way from the factory to your warehouse, to insure that you get maximum utilization of them from their first day of operations!

Training, Free.

Some companies around America provide one-day training sessions free to employees of other companies. They are excellent, as attendees gain insight as to how good companies operate. Such companies include Lincoln Electric, Ben & Jerry, and winners of the Malcolm Baldridge Award, such as Federal Express.

Transfer Forms.

Have pre-numbered transfer forms, but avoid store-specific pre-numbered forms. Do not keep records of the transfers that go to each individual store. Rather, process the documentation you receive back at headquarters. Such practices save a great deal in printing, control, and administrative costs.

Travel Advances.

Avoid wherever possible. Most employees have credit cards and really don't need them. If you must give an advance, treat it as a salary advance rather than a travel advance, and have the employee sign an authorization to have the amount deducted from his next paycheck. This is an incentive to get travel costs in quickly to accounts payable, and ensures that the accounting for travel remains simple.

Travel Expenses, Daily Limits.

Place a ceiling on daily travel expenses for all employees, e.g., $45 per day for accommodation, $25 for meals.

Travel Expenses, Specific Limits.

Alternately, set specific limits as to what can be spent on travel, accommodations, meals, long distance calls, etc. when employees are traveling on your behalf. Eliminate frills such as spas and in-house movies. Reimburse only what is approved in these policy guidelines. Limits on meals, particularly, rather than full reimbursement, seems to make sense because the employee would be spending his or her own money on meals if at home, anyway.

Trip-Masters.

Have installed in all your delivery trucks a trip monitor which records all mileages, stops, etc. to ensure that you receive maximum productivity and that your drivers are doing what they are supposed to be doing. In addition, it will discourage drivers from exceeding the speed limit and therefore minimize your accident exposure.

Truck Loads.

Do everything possible to ensure that each truck leaving your distribution center leaves full. One way to do this is always to have standby basic merchandise that can be added to a shipment at a moment's notice. Shipping empty space is very expensive!

Unemployment Taxes.

Towards the end of each year, evaluate your unemployment tax status by state. In some states, it is possible to achieve a reduction in the unemployment tax rate for the following year by making a voluntary contribution in the current year. One company, for example, found that making a voluntary contribution of $12,000 early one December in one state reduced its unemployment tax rate to yield a savings of $131,000 in unemployment taxes the following year!

Utilities, Costs.

Lower the temperature setting on your thermostats during the winter, and raise them during the summer. Have your thermostats placed in tamper-proof units to avoid the temperature setting being changed all the time by different employees. Also consider zone controls throughout your building.

Utilities, Hot Water.

Set your hot water generating and storage temperature level to the minimum required for washing hands, usually about 110°F. Increase the hot water temperature locally only where required (e.g., for kitchens).

Utilities, Lighting.

Light switches for closets and interior areas can be colored and equipped with a light when the light in these enclosed areas is on. Similarly, you can use color-coded light switches to designate which should be on and off during non-operating or non-office hours. Alternately, you can put 5-minute shut-off timers on such lights. In back rooms and storage areas, remove some of the fluorescent tubes to reduce the lighting intensity to a level appropriate for such areas.

Utility Payments.

Some utility companies have fine print tolerances for paying their monthly utility bills. The fine print indicates that even though payment is due net 20 days, no 1% penalty is charged until after 25 days. Therefore, a company can gain a permanent payment lag of 5 additional days from those utility companies that have these tolerances. It's recommended that you discuss your 5-day delayed payment plan with the utility company before starting, however, to avoid any misunderstandings.

Vacations.

Have a policy of "use them or lose them." One cost-conscious approach is to have vacations fall due for all employees on the same date each year. Then allow employees 12 months from that date to use the vacation time earned in the previous period. In setting the date, it's best to choose a date which is preceded by a quiet period as some employees will, each year, delay taking their vacations until the last moment.

Variable Costs.

Structure your costs as much as possible so that they are variable rather than fixed. This eases the pain in down times and allows you to pay more in good times. The ideal business would be to have every employee on straight commission, sell merchandise on consignment, have a pure percentage rental agreement, and have all other costs a percentage of sales. Then all costs would be variable and your total focus would be on maximizing sales!

Variable Cost, Vacations.

One example of variable costs used to reduce employee turnover is to have one week's vacation a year but allow, in addition, an extra half-day's vacation for every month of perfect attendance (which could be defined to include arranging a substitute, if absent). This approach, obviously, has some advantage over giving everyone a flat two-week vacation each year. It is particularly helpful in companies with high absenteeism and employee turnover.

VEBA Trust.

Section 501 (c) (9) of the Internal Revenue Service allows you to set up a VEBA Trust. This allows you to deduct expenses for your Group Benefit Plan (and therefore receive a reduction in your tax bill in advance of spending the money) as well as to have the tax-free interest earned on the plan.

Vendors.

Often vendors have "freebies" available (usually with their corporate logos). For example, rather than buy clocks for your offices, etc., see if any of your vendors are giving these away . . . free!

W-2 Forms.

At the end of each year, rather than mailing employees W-2 forms to their homes, save the cost and send them to stores in your regular company mail system.

Wage and Salary Scales.

Over time, these tend to be increased. However, when doing so, just increase the top of the scale. Leave the bottom where it is. This will give you more pay flexibility within each scale.

What If.

Ask yourself: What if a real, no-nonsense cost-cutter came in to run this business? What would he eliminate? How much would someone like "Ming the Merciless" really cut and eliminate from the way your business is currently run? What would happen if you did those same things?

Wages.

Wherever it is possible, pay employees based upon productivity using physical productivity standards appropriate to their area of work. Paying for results seems more logical than paying just for turning up for work!

Wind Deflectors.

Install wind deflector shields on your delivery fleet. It lowers wind resistance and increases your miles per gallon results.

Worker's Compensation.

Any employee off work because of a worker's compensation disability should be encouraged to come back and perform some light work so that you can get at least some benefit from your cost.

Zip Presorting.

Wherever possible, presort your mail by zip and get a reduced rate from the Post Office. For those companies which don't have a large quantity of mail, mail-sorting companies will include your mail with their total and share the presorting price break with you.

	NORM FORM	dept.	current period		norm	better (worse)	
			norm class G avg. wkly. sales $220,000 - 230,000				
	SAMPLE CORP.	dept.	averages per week		norm	than norm	
	weeks ending	#	$	%	%	%	$
1	SALES	1	110,610	49.18	47.32	1.86	2,055
2		2	45,066	20.04	19.06	0.98	440
3		3	28,439	12.64	13.79	(1.15)	(326)
4		4	29,960	13.32	13.02	0.30	90
5		5	10,843	4.82	6.81	(1.99)	(216)
6	TOTAL SALES		224,918	100.00	100.00	0.00	N.M.
7	sales incr. (decr.) over LY			4.56	2.81	1.75	
8	SHRINKAGE	1	1,665	1.51	1.05	(0.46)	(504)
9		4	247	0.82	0.96	0.14	41
10		5	452	4.17	3:82	(0.35)	(38)
11	GROSS PROFIT	1	24,533	22.18	20.62	1.56	1,726
12		2	8,463	18.78	19.88	(1.10)	(496)
13		3	7,204	25.33	27.89	(2.56)	(728)
14		4	10,180	33.98	31.65	2.33	698
15		5	5,304	48.92	51.34	(2.42)	(262)
16	TOTAL G.P. after shrink		55,685	24.76		0.42	937
17	SALARIES	1	3,296	2.98	3.12	0.14	155
18		2	906	2.01	2.03	0.02	9
19		3	1,701	5.98	5.38	(0.60)	(171)
20		4	2,858	9.54	9.87	0.33	99
21		5	4,205	38.78	35.97	(2.81)	(305)
22		c/out	4,971	2.21	2.14	(0.07)	(157)
23		mgt	2,182	0.97	1.04	0.07	157
24	TOTAL SALARIES		20,118	8.94		(0.09)	(213)
25	SUPPLIES	3	694	2.44	2.57	0.13	37
26		4	267	0.89	0.97	0.08	24
27		5	536	4.94	4.26	(0.68)	(74)
28		c/out	832	0.37	0.33	(0.04)	(90)
29	TOTAL SUPPLIES		2,328	1.04		(0.05)	(103)
30	CASH SHORT (OVER)		202	0.09	0.03	(0.06)	(135)
31	LAUNDRY		337	0.15	0.18	0.03	67
32	REPAIRS		1,057	0.47	0.38	(0.09)	(202)
33	TELE. BASIC		67	0.03	0.03	0.00	0
34	LONG DISTANCE		247	0.11	0.07	(0.04)	(90)
35	CR. CARD / BANK FEES		2,744	1.22	1.33	0.11	247
36	UTILITIES		2,384	1.06	1.12	0.06	135
37	CONTROL. COSTS (17..36)		29,486	13.32			(293)
38	STORE CONTRIB. (16 - 37)		26,199	11.65			1,230

appendix 2 the four key management reports							
TABLE 1		**OPERATING RESULTS SUMMARY (ORS)**					
SAMPLE CORP.		current period		year-to-date		Inc(Dec) % over LY	
weeks ending		TY	LY	TY	LY	cur. per.	ytd
	ADVANCE INDICATORS						
1	CUST. SATISFACTION INDEX	#					
2	CUST. RETENTION INDEX	%					
3	SHOPPING BASKET INDEX	#					
4	EMEE. SATISFACTION INDEX	%					
5	SAME STORES SALES GAIN	%					
	SALES DRIVERS						
6	CUST. TRANS. COUNT PSW	#					
7	x ITEMS PER TRANSACTION	#					
8	= ITEMS PER ST. WEEK	#					
9	x AVG. SELLING PR. PER ITEM	$					
10	= SALES PER STORE WEEK	$					
11	x AVG. NO. STORES OPEN	#					
12	x NO. OF WEEKS IN PERIOD	#					
13	= SALES	$k					
	COST DRIVERS						
14	ITEMS PER EMEE HOUR (ST.)	#					
15	ITEMS PER EMEE HR (DC/SC)	#					
16	AVG. HRLY. RATE (ST.)	$					
17	AVG. HRLY. RATE (DC/SC)	$					
	INVESTMENT						
18	STORE INVENTORY PSF	$					
19	STORE INVENTORY PSF	#					
20	NON-ST. INVTY. wks. on hand	#					
21	NET INVESTMENT PER ST.	$					
	OTHER KEY RESULTS						
22	OPACC	$k					
23	EARNINGS PER SHARE	$					
24	AVG. CUST. TRANSACTION	$					
25	ADVERT. PER CUST. TRANS.	$					
26	SPSF (annualized)	$					
27	IPSF (annualized)	#					
28	EMEE. SUGGESTIONS PSW	#					
29	AVG. STORE SELLING AREA	sf					
30	STORES OPENED/ OPEN	#					

		OPERATING BALANCE SHEET (OBS)					
TABLE 2							
	SAMPLE CORP.	TOTAL $000		PER STORE ($)		Increase (Decr.)	
	as at	TY	LY	TY	LY	$	%
	NUMBER OF STORES (#)						
1	INVENTORIES: Stores						
2	+ :DC						
3	+ :Other						
4	=INVENTORIES (FIFO) : TOTAL						
5	- TRADE PAYABLES						
6	= NET INVENTORIES						
7	+ OPERATING CASH						
8	+ RECEIVABLES						
9	+ PREPAID EXPENSES						
10	- ACCRUED EXPENSES						
11	- INC. TAXES PAYABLE						
12	= NON CASH NWC						
13	LAND & BUILDINGS						
14	+ FURN. & EQPT.						
15	+ VEHICLES						
16	+ LEASEHOLD IMPVMTS.						
17	+ OTHER ASSETS						
18	+ CAP. LEASES						
19	= FIXED ASSETS at cost						
20	- ACCUM. DEPREC.						
21	= NET FIXED ASSETS						
22	+ NON CASH NWC (L. 12)						
23	= NON-CASH NET INVESTMENT						
24	+ INTEREST-EARNING CASH						
25	= NET INVESTMENT						
26	NOTES PAYABLE						
27	+ DEBT: ST & LT						
28	+ : CAP. LEASES(ST&LT)						
29	+ DEFERRED TAXES (net)						
30	+ OTHER DEFERRALS						
31	+ LIFO RESERVE						
32	+ SH. EQUITY : CAPITAL						
33	+ : RET.EARNINGS						
34	= NET INVESTMENT						
35	OPBIT (latest 12 months)						
36	SALES (latest 12 months)						
37	NET INVESTMENT (BEG.)						
38	NET INVESTMENT (AVG.)						
39	ROI (BEG.) (L35/L37)						
40	ASSET PRODUCTIVITY(36/37)						

TABLE 3

OPERATING PROFIT STATEMENT(OPS)

SAMPLE CORP.
weeks ending

		Per Store Week, except Rows 31-33				Incr(Decr)% over LY		Entries as a % of Sales			
		current period		year-to-date		cur. per.	ytd	current period		year-to-date	
	$ except where indicated	TY	LY	TY	LY	%	%	TY	LY	TY	LY
1	SALES per store week										
2	GROSS PROFIT : STORES										
3	: DC/SC										
4	: MEM. FEES										
5	GROSS PROFIT : TOTAL										
6	DC OPER. COSTS										
7	STORE SAL/BEN. STD										
8	(B)W THAN STD										
9	SUPPLIES										
10	CR. CARD/BANK FEES										
11	OTHER DIR. COSTS										
12	ADVERTISING										
13	UTILITIES										
14	RENT										
15	PRE/POST-OPENING EXES										
16	SC SAL/BEN.										
17	OTHER O/HEAD										
18	OTHER OPS. (P)/L										
19	DEPRECIATION										
20	INTEREST(INC.)										
21	= OPBIT (L5 - L6..20)										
22	- COST OF CAPITAL (bef. taxes)										
23	= OPACC										
24	LIFO EXPENSE										
25	CAP. LEASE (CREDIT)										
26	INTEREST EXP.										
27	OTHER ADJMTS.										
28	= PBT (L21-24..27)										
29	-TAX PROVISION										
30	= Profit After Taxes (PAT)										
31	store weeks (#)										
32	TOTAL SALES ($000)										
33	TOTAL PAT ($000)										

note :   DC = Distribution Center   SC = Support Center(HQ)

OPBIT = Operating Profit before Interest Expense & Taxes

OPACC = Operating Profit After a Charge for Capital

220

TABLE 4	OPERATING CASH STATEMENT (OCS)				Prepared by:			
SAMPLE CORP.	HIST	HIST	HIST	HIST	PROJ	PROJ	PROJ	PROJ
as at	Q	Q	Q	Q	Q	Q	Q	Q
1 PAT - DIVIDENDS								
2 + INC(DEC) IN RET. EARN .(B.O.Y.)								
3 + INC(DEC) IN CAPITAL								
4 = INCREASE IN SH. EQUITY								
5 + DEC(INC) IN INVENTORIES								
6 + INC(DEC) IN PAYABLES								
7 + DEC(INC) IN RECEIVABLES								
8 + DEC(INC) IN PREPAID EXES								
9 + INC(DEC) IN ACCRUED EXES								
10 + INC(DEC) IN TAXES PAYABLE								
11 + DEC(INC) IN LAND & BLDGS								
12 + DEC(INC) IN FURN. & EQPT.								
13 + DEC(INC) IN VEHICLES								
14 + DEC(INC) IN L/HOLD IMPVTS.								
15 + DEC(INC) IN OTHER ASSETS								
16 + DEC(INC) IN CAP. LEASES								
17 + INC(DEC) IN ACCUM. DEPRN.								
18 + INC(DEC) IN CAP. LS. OBLIG.								
19 + INC(DEC) IN DEF. TAXES								
20 + INC(DEC) IN OR. DEFERRALS								
21 + INC(DEC) IN LIFO RESERVE								
22 = INC(DEC) IN CASH PRODUCED								
23 + INC(DEC) IN DEBT(ST/LT)								
24 = INC(DEC) IN NET CP/DEBT								
25 + DEC(INC) IN OPER. CASH								
26 + DEC(INC) IN INT. EARN. CASH								
27 = INC(DEC) IN NOTES PAYABLE								
28 ENDING BAL: NOTES PAYABLE								
29 + ENDING BAL: DEBT(ST/LT)								
30 + ENDING BAL: INT. EARN. CASH								
31 = ENDING BAL: NET DEBT								
32 - ENDING BAL: OPER CASH								
33 = ENDING BAL:NET NET DEBT								
34 ENDING BAL: SH. EQUITY								
35 DEBT:EQUITY (L.31 /L.34) x								
36 DEBT:EQUITY (L.33 /L.34) x								

221

appendix 3   example of a simple regression analysis

A common use for regression analysis is in setting up and checking the amount of labor relative to the number of units sold. Here we assume we have the units sold and the number of hours paid for our 30 stores last week.

Steps:

1) In Sec. 1, record the units sold and hours worked in columns A and B, respectively.
2) Calculate multiplications in columns C, D, and E.
3) Total columns A...E on line 31.
4) Divide these totals by the number of store readings (line 32) to get the average number of units sold and hours paid on line 33.
5) In Sec. 2, note the notation representing lines 31-33 of Sec. 1.
6) In Sec. 3, solve the formula $y = a + bx$, using data from lines 31-33.
7) Test your formula's accuracy by using the data for the average store on line 33.
8) In Sec. 4, calculate the standard number of hours for each store based on its actual units sold, in column N. We use the results from the formula to do this, e.g., line 1... std. hours (col. N) = 130.4 + (.004489 x 17,300) = 208 hours
9) Record the actual hours used in column O, and calculate columns P and Q.
10) Identify the largest variances (stores 1, 5, 14, and 29) and investigate reasons.

Note: Applying this equation gives us is the closest approximation of the average number of hours we use at any sales level between 12,760 and 22,760 units (the lowest and highest points in our sample in Sec. 1).

		units sold	hours paid	calculations for regression analysis		
		A	B	C=A x B	D=A x A	E=B x B
store #	1	17,300	220	3,806,000	299,290,000	48,400
	2	15,520	198	3,072,960	240,870,400	39,204
	3	16,650	200	3,330,000	277,222,500	40,000
	4	15,670	200	3,134,000	245,548,900	40,000
	5	15,630	189	2,954,070	244,296,900	35,721
	6	16,250	193	3,136,250	264,062,500	37,249
	7	20,980	230	4,825,400	440,160,400	52,900
	8	16,550	211	3,492,050	273,902,500	44,521
	9	15,810	209	3,304,290	249,956,100	43,681
	10	15,160	194	2,941,040	229,825,600	37,636
	11	13,200	189	2,494,800	174,240,000	35,721
	12	13,670	198	2,706,660	186,868,900	39,204
	13	14,700	190	2,793,000	216,090,000	36,100
	14	13,470	181	2,438,070	181,440,900	32,761
	15	17,560	219	3,845,640	308,353,600	47,961
	16	18,380	217	3,988,460	337,824,400	47,089
	17	20,520	228	4,678,560	421,070,400	51,984
	18	16,660	198	3,298,680	277,555,600	39,204
	19	19,110	207	3,955,770	365,192,100	42,849
	20	19,030	216	4,110,480	362,140,900	46,656
	21	18,420	213	3,923,460	339,296,400	45,369
	22	14,380	197	2,832,860	206,784,400	38,809
	23	17,030	200	3,406,000	290,020,900	40,000
	24	20,180	228	4,601,040	407,232,400	51,984
	25	13,970	199	2,780,030	195,160,900	39,601
	26	13,240	192	2,542,080	175,297,600	36,864
	27	15,280	191	2,918,480	233,478,400	36,481
	28	15,680	210	3,292,800	245,862,400	44,100
	29	12,760	197	2,513,720	162,817,600	38,809
	30	22,760	224	5,098,240	518,017,600	50,176
totals	31	495,520	6,138	102,214,890	8,369,881,200	1,261,034
/no.stores	32	30	30			
=average	33	16,517.3	204.6			

use these symbols to represent the preceding totals

totals	31	A	B	C	D	E
/no.stores	32	N	N			
=average	33	F	G			

Sec. 3

then, solving the formula y = a + bx

where y is the number of hours paid, and x is the number of units sold

b = $\dfrac{C - (A \times G)}{D - (A \times F)}$ = $\dfrac{102.214.890 - (495.520 \times 204.6)}{8,369,881,200-(495,520\times16,517.3)}$ = 0.004489

a = G - (b x F) = 204.6 - (.004489 x 16,517.3) = 130.4465

therefore, in the preceding example we may say

y = 130.4465 + .004489 x

or, the no. of paid hours = 130.4465 hours + (.004489 x no. of units sold) hours

prove the formula using the average (Sec. 1, line 33)

paid hours   = a +(b x no. units sold) = 130.4465 + (.004489 x 16,517.3)   =   204.6 hrs

Sec. 4

#	units sold	standard hours	actual hours	standard - actual hours	standard - actual %
	M	N	O	P=N-O	Q=P/N
1	17,300	208	220	(12)	(5.7)
2	15,520	200	198	2	1.1
3	16,650	205	200	5	2.5
4	15,670	201	200	1	0.4
5	15,630	201	189	12	5.8
6	16,250	203	193	10	5.1
7	20,980	225	230	(5)	(2.4)
8	16,550	205	211	(6)	(3.1)
9	15,810	201	209	(8)	(3.8)
10	15,160	199	194	5	2.3
11	13,200	190	189	1	0.4
12	13,670	192	198	(6)	(3.2)
13	14,700	196	190	6	3.3
14	13,470	191	181	10	5.2
15	17,560	209	219	(10)	(4.6)
16	18,380	213	217	(4)	(1.9)
17	20,520	223	228	(5)	(2.4)
18	16,660	205	198	7	3.5
19	19,110	216	207	9	4.3
20	19,030	216	216	0	0.0
21	18,420	213	213	0	0.0
22	14,380	195	197	(2)	(1.0)
23	17,030	207	200	7	3.3
24	20,180	221	228	(7)	(3.1)
25	13,970	193	199	(6)	(3.0)
26	13,240	190	192	(2)	(1.1)
27	15,280	199	191	8	4.0
28	15,680	201	210	(9)	(4.6)
29	12,760	188	197	(9)	(4.9)
30	22,760	233	224	9	3.7

224

SUGGESTED
FURTHER READING

Abegglen, James C. and George Stalk, Jr., *Kaisha*, (ISBN 4–8053–0504–5)

Aguayo, Rafael, *Dr. Deming: The American Who Taught The Japanese About Quality*, (ISBN 0–671–74621–9)

Camp, Robert C., *Benchmarking*, (ISBN 0–87389–058–2)

Cialdini, Robert B., *Influence*, (ISBN 0–688–04107–8)

Davis, Stan and Bill Davidson, *2020 Vision*, (ISBN 0–671–73237–4)

Drucker, Peter F., *The Effective Executive*, (ISBN 0–06–091209-X)

Drucker, Peter F., *Managing for Results*, (ISBN 0–06–091339–8)

Figgie, Harry E., JR., *The Harry Figgie Guide to Cost Reduction and Profit Improvement*, (ISBN 0–917253–83–3)

Henderson, Bruce D., *The Logic of Business Strategy*, (ISBN 0–88410–983–6)

Imai, Masaaki, *Kaizen*, (ISBN 0–07–554332-X)

Lincoln, James F., *Incentive Management*, (Published by the Lincoln Electric Co., Cleveland, Ohio)

Peters, Tom and Nancy Austin, *A Passion for Excellence*, (ISBN 0–394–54484)

Porter, Michael E., *Competitive Advantage*, (ISBN 0–02–925090–0)

Rapp, Stan and Tom Collins, *The Great Marketing Turnaround*, (ISBN 0–13–365560–1)

Richardson, Peter R., *Cost Containment*, (ISBN 0–02–926432–4)

Schaffer, Robert H. *The Breakthrough Strategy*, (ISBN 0–88730–404–4)

Sloma, Richard S., *No-Nonsense Management*, (ISBN 0–02–929220–4)

Stewart, G. Bennett, III., *The Quest for Value*, (ISBN 0–88730–418–4)

Walsh, William I., *The Rise & Decline of The Great Atlantic & Pacific Tea Company*, (ISBN 0–8184–0382–9)

Womack, James P, Daniel T. Jones and Daniel Roos, *The Machine That Changed The World*, (ISBN 0–06–097417–6)

To The Reader:

The list of cost-conscious practices is endless. If you have any cost-saving ideas that you think should be considered for the next edition of this book, please photocopy this page, write the idea on it and mail it to me. Add extra pages if necessary. Include your name, address, and phone number. All ideas used will be acknowledged and the suggester will receive a free copy of the edition in which the practice first appears.

. . . .

To: Brian Woolf
      Teal Books
      P.O. Box 16405
      Greenville, SC   29606

Here's a cost saving idea you may want to include in your next edition:

ORDERING INFORMATION

Additional copies of *Shrinking the Corporate Waistline* may be obtained from the publisher:

Please send me _____ copies at $14.95 ea.*_____

plus shipping/handling   3.55

      Total $ _____

*For order of 24 or more copies, there is a 25% discount.

Ship to: _____
      Name

      _____
      Address

      _____
      City   State   Zip

      (_____)_____
      Daytime Phone

Mail your order to:
      Teal Books
      P.O. Box 16405
      Greenville, SC   29606

Please include your check or money order, in U.S. funds.

* * * * * * * *

About The Author

Brian Woolf is a retail strategy consultant. Formerly the Chief Financial Officer of Food Lion, Inc., the low-cost fast growing supermarket chain, Mr. Woolf now assists retail and service chains worldwide in strategy development, information simplification, stealth marketing, and cost improvement. He also gives seminars on these and related subjects.

Besides his experience at Food Lion, Inc., he has been a Board member of three publicly traded retail companies, the Executive Vice President of an overseas-based retail chain, and President of a high-growth apparel chain. He has degrees in Economics and Accounting from the University of Auckland, New Zealand, as well as an MBA degree from the Harvard Business School.

If you are interested in more information on the concepts in this book, you can contact the author at the Retail Strategy Center, Inc., 6 Parkins Lake Court, Greenville, South Carolina 29607–3628, tel: (803) 458–8277.

PRAISE FOR JANE GREEN

"[*Jemima J*] conveys with sass and humor both the invisibility of the overweight and the shallow perks that accrue to the thin and beautiful. Green has entertainingly updated the Cinderella story . . . Bottom Line: Sweet and Tasty."
—*People* magazine

"Cleverly probes the world of a very smart, very funny, very fat reporter . . . Americans will enjoy this confection and appreciate how Green renders a certain humor-impaired California earnestness about health, happiness, and love."
—*USA Today*

"The perfect summer confection . . . absolutely delicious."
—*New Orleans Times-Picayune*

"The kind of novel you'll gobble up at a single sitting." —*Cosmopolitan*

"A brilliantly funny novel about something close to every woman's heart—her stomach."
—*Woman's Own*

"*Jemima J* is a fun, fast-paced novel about a woman who hates her body and decides to do something about it . . . Skinny or fat, Jemima is always endearing. Her lessons about life and love are sweet and at times ironic . . . Green's ability to evoke laughter from a serious subject makes *Jemima J* a charming, worthwhile read."
—Lauren K. Nathan, Associated Press

"Kick up your feet, relax, pour yourself a lemonade. You're in for 400 pages of ups and downs and a trip halfway around the world."
—*South Florida Sun-Sentinel*

"A hit in the U.K., Green's Jemima is a charmer." —*New York Daily News*

"Jane Green proves common ingredients—weight-loss problems, dating, and Internet romance—can be used in fresh ways to cook up some delicious comedy."
—*Boston Heral*

Also by Jane Green

Jemima J

Jane Green

Broadway Books, New York

Mr. Maybe

BROADWAY

Mr. Maybe was originally published in the United Kingdom in 1999 by Penguin Books.

A hardcover edition of this book was published in 2001 by Broadway Books.

Broadway Books titles may be purchased for business or promotional use or for special sales. For information, please write to: Special Markets Department, Random House, Inc., 1540 Broadway, New York, NY 10036.

PRINTED IN THE UNITED STATES OF AMERICA

BROADWAY BOOKS and its logo, a letter B bisected on the diagonal, are trademarks of Broadway Books, a division of Random House, Inc.

Visit our website at www.broadwaybooks.com

First trade paperback edition published 2002

Designed by Ralph L. Fowler

The Library of Congress has cataloged the Broadway Books hardcover edition as follows:

Green, Jane, 1968–
Mr. Maybe / Jane Green—1st ed.
p. cm.
1. London (England)—Fiction. 2. Young women—Fiction. I. Title.
PR6057.R3443 M7   2001
823'.914—dc21

00-045481

ISBN 0-7679-0520-2

10   9   8

To David

Acknowledgments

Once again there are a million people who ought to be thanked profusely, only a handful of whom can be mentioned here.

Thanks again go to the entire team at Broadway Books: Lauren Marino, Cate Tynan, and everyone else who made the whole experience of being published in America such a delight.

A special thanks to Heather Flaherty, who, with sweetness and perseverance, achieved publicity I never dared expect.

To my U.S. agent, Deborah Schneider, and my U.K. agent, Anthony Goff. Both of you are the best of the best.

To everyone at Penguin back in the U.K., especially Louise, Tom, and Harrie. I wouldn't be here if it weren't for you.

And finally to Harrison Burke and David Burke. The former for lighting up my life, and the latter for everything.

Thank you.

Nick was never supposed to be The One, for God's sake. Even I knew that. And yes, I know those that are happily married often say you can't know, not immediately, but of course I knew. Not that he sounded wrong—Nick spoke the Queen's English slightly better than myself, but nothing else was right, nothing else fitted.

There was the money thing, for a start. My job as a PR might not be the highest-paying job in the universe, but it pays the bills, pays the mortgage, and leaves me just enough for the odd bit of retail therapy. Nick, on the other hand, didn't earn a penny. Well, perhaps that's a bit of an exaggeration, but he wasn't like all the other boyfriends I'd had, wasn't rolling in it, and, although that's not my main motivation, what I always say is I don't mind if he can't pay for me, but I do bloody well mind if he can't pay for himself.

And though Nick occasionally offered to go dutch, it was with such bad grace and I used to feel so guilty, I'd just push his hand away, tell him not to be so silly and drag out my credit card.

And then there was politics. Or lack thereof, in my case, might be more appropriate. Nick was never happier than when he was with his left-wing cronies, arguing the toss about the pros and cons of New Labour, while I sat there bored out of my mind, not contributing just in case anyone asked me what I voted and I had to grudgingly admit I voted Conservative because, well, because my parents had.

Speaking of pros and cons, it might be easier if I showed you the list I drew up soon after I met Nick. I mean, if I sit here telling you about all the reasons why he wasn't right for me, it would take all day, and I've still got the list, so you may as well read it. It might help you to see why I was so adamant that he was just a fling.

Pros

I fancy the pants off him.
He's got the biggest, softest, bluest eyes I've ever seen.
He's very affectionate.
He's fantastically selfless in bed. (Make that just fantastic.)
He makes me laugh.

Cons

He's got no money.
He lives in a grotty bedsit in Highgate.
He's left-wing/political.
He likes pubs and pints of beer.
I hate his friends.
He's a complete womanizer.
He's allergic to commitment.
He says he's not ready for a relationship. (Although neither am I.)

So there you have it—far more cons than pros, and, if I'm completely honest, the cons are much more important, I mean, how could I have even thought of getting involved with someone whose friends I hated? I have always, always thought you could judge a person by their friends, and I really should have known better.

But then again, I suppose you can't help who you fancy, can you? And that was the bottom line. I fancied Nick. Fancied him more than I'd fancied anyone in years, and somehow, when someone gives you that tingly feeling in the pit of your stomach, you stop thinking about the rights and wrongs, the shoulds and should nots, and you just go with it.

You're probably wondering how I met Nick, because, let's

face it, our paths were hardly destined to cross. I'd known him for a while, actually. He was one of those people I used to see at the odd party when I went out with my friend Sally, Sal, and I never took much notice of him, I didn't see him enough to take much notice of him because I didn't see Sal all that much.

I used to work with Sal, indirectly. Years ago, when I first started as a lowly PR assistant, Sal was a journalist on one of the magazines, and she was about the only person who didn't treat me like shit, so we formed a friendship on the basis of that.

Not that I dislike her. She's a great girl. She's just different. To me, that is. She's more like Nick, and I vaguely remember her having a crush on him. That's probably the only reason I did remember him, she'd ask me to watch him to see if he stared at her, all that sort of stuff, and I did, because she was my friend and it gave me something to do, which was better than standing around bored, wishing I were somewhere else.

She used to drag me along to these parties, student parties I'd think snootily, except no one had been a student for years, but they were always in dilapidated houses, held by the four, or six, people who lived there, and they were never my scene.

Not that I could have afforded the lifestyle I wanted. Not then. Champagne tastes and beer pockets, my mother always used to sniff, if I made the fatal mistake of wearing a new outfit when I went round to see my parents.

"What's that?" she'd say, in a disapproving tone of voice.

"What? This old thing?" I'd learn to say, dismissing my fabulous designer outfit that I loved so much I was wearing it for about the sixth day on the trot. "I've had this for ages." Or, "It was lying around the fashion cupboard at work, so they gave it to me. Do you like it?" It took me a while, but eventually I learned that, as long as I didn't admit to it being new, my mother would like it. If I ever told her I had actually bought something, she'd raise her eyebrows and say, "How much was that?" And I'd mumble a price, usually knocking off around a hundred pounds, and she'd roll her eyes again and shake her head, making me feel like an errant child.

I used to have these dreams about being a career woman. I wanted shoulder pads, briefcases and mobile phones. I wanted designer clothes and a fuck-off flat which had wooden floors and white sofas and enormous bowls of lilies on every polished fruitwood table. I wanted a Mercedes sports car and chunky gold jewelry.

Unfortunately, life in PR is probably not the best way of going about it, because PR seems to be one of the worst-paid professions in the world. I know what I should have done, I should have gone into the City, because I graduated at the tail end of the eighties boom, and I could have made a mint, but I never had a very good brain for money, or numbers, and I would have been hopeless. And PR seemed like the easiest option. It sounded glamorous, exciting, and I wouldn't have to start as a secretary, which I was loath to do, because I would have hated people asking me what I did for a living. In PR I was able to start as a Public Relations Assistant, which, at the ripe old age of twenty-one, made me feel like I'd won the lottery.

I answered an ad in the *Guardian,* and when I went along for the interview I decided that if I didn't get this job I would die. The offices of Joe Cooper PR were in a backstreet in Kilburn, not the most salubrious of areas, I know, and from the outside it looked just like a big warehouse, but inside it was magnificent. A huge loft, wooden floors, brightly colored chairs and velvet cushions, and a constant buzz of phone conversations from some of the most beautiful people I'd ever seen in my life.

And I looked completely wrong. There they were, everyone in jeans, super-trendy T-shirts and big motorbike boots (which was the look at the time), and there I was in my little Jigsaw two-piece cream suit, with matching high heels and a briefcase clutched in my hand to look more professional.

Shit, I remember thinking when I walked in. Why oh why didn't I research this before I came, but then Joe Cooper came to shake my hand. "You must be Libby," he said, and as soon as I met him I knew I'd like him, and, more important, I knew he'd like me. And he did. And I started the following week on a pittance, but I loved it. God, how I loved it.

Within a month all my friends were green with envy, because I was already on first-name terms with some of the hottest celebrities on TV, and I spent my days helping the actual executives, typing press releases, occasionally baby-sitting those celebrities on their excursions to radio and television shows where they plugged their latest book, or program, or film. And it was so exciting, and I met so many people, and my Jigsaw suit was placed firmly at the back of my wardrobe as I dressed like all the others and I fitted in.

My budding champagne tastes were brought to full fruition at Joe Cooper PR. Admittedly, not in quite the way I'd planned. Instead of Yves Saint Laurent I wanted Rifat Ozbek. Instead of Annabel's I wanted Quiet Storm. Instead of Mortons I wanted the Atlantic Bar, or whatever the hell was in at the time, I can't actually remember. A lot of the time I was "entertaining" clients, so it was on expenses, but when you throw a girl into that sort of lifestyle at work, you can't expect her to be happy with takeaways in the evenings, can you?

And now, finally, I can just about afford to fund my lifestyle, with the help of a very understanding bank manager who agreed to give me an overdraft facility "just in case." Just in case of what? Just in case I should ever not need it? Because I fill my overdraft facility pretty much all the time, but hell, it's only money, and as far as I'm concerned we're only here for about eighty years if we're lucky, so in the grand scheme of things nothing really matters very much, and certainly not money. Or even men, when it comes to it.

Friends are what matter, that's what I've decided. My social life is swings and roundabouts. Sometimes I'm on a social whirl, out every night, grateful for the odd night in watching television and catching up on my sleep. But then everything will slow down for a while, and I'll be in every night, flicking through my address book, wondering why I can't really be bothered to talk to anyone.

Well, not quite anyone. I talk to Jules every day, about five times, even if we don't really have anything to say to each other, which we don't usually, because what news can you possibly tell someone you last spoke to an hour ago? We usually end up talking shit. She'll phone me up and say, "I've just eaten half a packet of biscuits and a cheese and pickle sandwich. I feel sick."

And I'll say, "I had a toasted bagel with smoked salmon, no butter, and one stick of Twix," and that will be it.

Or I'll phone her and say, "I'm just calling to say hi."

And she'll sigh and say, "Hi. Any news?"

"No. You?"

"No."

"Okay, talk to you later."

"Okay."

We never, ever, say goodbye, or talk to you at the weekend, or even tomorrow, because, unless we're speaking to each other late at night when we're in bed (which we do practically every night), we know we are going to talk to each other later, even when we've got nothing to say.

What's really surprising about this is not how close we are, but the fact that Jules is married. She married James, or Jamie as he's more commonly known (good isn't it, Jules et Jim), last year, and I was terrified I'd never see her anymore, but if anything the reverse has happened. It's almost as if she isn't married, because we hardly ever talk about Jamie. He never seems to be there, or if he is he's shut away in his study, working, and for a while I was worried, concerned that perhaps she'd made a mistake, perhaps their marriage wasn't all it should be, but, on the rare occasions I see the two of them together, I can see that it works, that she's happy, that marriage has given her the security she never had, the security I long for.

And meanwhile, I've still got my friend, my touchstone, my sister. Not that she is, of course, she just feels like it, and Jules is the wisest woman I know. I'll sit and bore her with my latest adventure and she'll listen very quietly, wait for a few seconds when I've finished before speaking, which really used to bother me because I thought she was bored, but actually what she's doing is thinking about what I've said, formulating an opinion, and when she does give me advice it's always spot-on, even if it might not be exactly what I want to hear.

She's what my mother would call a true friend, and I know that no matter what happens we'll always be there for each other, so even on those nights when I'm cocooning, when I decide that I'm not quite ready to face the world, Jules is the one person I always phone. Always.

And at least my flat's comfortable for those solitary periods of takeouts and videos. Not quite the flat I've always dreamed of, but I've made it pretty damn nice considering most of my furniture has either been inherited from my parents or bought secondhand from junk shops.

But if it hadn't been for my parents, bless them, I'd never have been able to afford to buy somewhere. I'd probably be sharing some dilapidated house with four, or six, other girls and spending every evening arguing about the washing-up or just resenting them even breathing. I may not have ever had to do it, but I've got enough friends who have, and quite frankly I got sick of them ringing me to ask if they could crash on my sofa because they needed some space.

My flat is tiny. Tiny. The tiniest flat you could ever imagine that's actually a flat and not a studio. It's in a basement in Ladbroke Grove, and you walk in the front door and straight into the living room. But, surprisingly, for a basement it's quite bright, and I've tried to emphasize this by keeping it as neutral as possible. Except I can't help the clutter, the shelves of books, and photographs, and cards, because I never throw anything away, you never know when you might need something.

There's an L-shaped kitchen off the living room, a galley kitchen, open plan, and opposite the large window there are french doors leading into a bedroom. It's so small there's a bed that folds up into the wall, except I never bother putting it up unless I have a party, and then off the bedroom is a minute bathroom, and that's it. Perfect for me, although I haven't lost sight of my dream of huge spaces and high ceilings—I've just about accepted that working in PR is most unlikely to buy me what I want, and I'll just have to marry a rich man for the lifestyle to which I want to become accustomed.

So. Men. Probably the one area of my life that's a complete disaster. Not that I don't meet them, God, it seems as if they're crawling out of the woodwork, except the ones who crawl out to meet me are always worms. Typical, isn't it. Jules can't understand it. I can't understand it. Every time I think that this time it might be different, this time they might treat me well, look after me, but every time it ends in tears.

I thought Jon was the one. Yeah, yeah, yeah, I know I say that every time. But I really did. He was everything I'd ever been looking for. He was a property developer, which is a bit boring, I know, but he wasn't boring. He was handsome, well dressed, had a beautiful flat in Maida Vale, a Mazda MX-5, knew brilliant people, was great in bed. . . . Well, the list goes on and on, really. The only problem was he didn't like me very much. I mean, sure, he fancied me, but he didn't like me, he didn't want to spend time with me, and I kept thinking that if I were perfect, if I acted like the perfect girlfriend, he'd fall in love with me. But he didn't. The more I tried to be the perfect girlfriend, the more awful he was to me.

In the beginning he used to call me, but the phone calls practically dwindled away to nothing, and then eventually people used to call me up and ask why I wasn't at that party last night that Jon went to. And he used to go away for weekends without telling me, he'd simply disappear, and I'd spend all weekend in floods of tears, ringing his answering machine and banging the phone down before the end of his message.

My parents met him. Big mistake. Huge. They loved him. They loved the fact that I had finally met someone who could

take me off their hands, look after me, and, amazingly and un-
usually, the more they loved him the more I did. But eventually
I couldn't do it anymore. I couldn't deal with the stress of being treated like shit, and, I'm quite proud of myself for this, I
ended it.

The bastard didn't even seem to care. He sort of shrugged
and said he was happy with the way things were, and, when I
said I needed more, he just shrugged again and said he was
sorry that he couldn't give me more. Bastard. BASTARD.

But no, that was a long time ago. I was apoplectic with grief
for about a week. I kept bursting into tears at work, and everyone was massively sympathetic without actually saying anything. Every time I cried at my desk I'd feel a hand on my
shoulder, and a cup of tea would be placed in front of me, word-
lessly, which was so sweet. My colleagues' way of showing me
that they cared.

Then after a week Jules said I had to get my act together and
she knew from the beginning that he wasn't for me and that he
was far too arrogant and I deserved better and that there were
plenty more fish in the sea and blah blah blah. But I began to
see her point.

I started putting myself "out there" again. Going to bars,
parties, launches. And even though I felt like shit I pretended
to have a good time, and after a couple of months I realized that
I actually was having a good time, and that was when I decided
that I'd had enough of men. At least for a while.

Yup, I thought. No more bastards for me. But then about six
months on I started getting withdrawal symptoms. Not from
Jon, but from cuddles, affection and, all right, I'll admit it, from
sex. Now I know there's a cutoff point. I know that when you've
been used to having regular sex with someone you miss it for
about six months, and that after that you don't really think
about it anymore because it's just not a part of your life, and
then when you finally do it again you're astounded that you
went without it for so long because it's so damn nice. I know this
because I've had two BIG dry periods in my life. One for ten

months and one for . . . God, I don't even know whether I want to tell you. Okay. One for two years.

I know. Twenty-seven bloody years old and I went without sex for two years. Sad, isn't it?

I was probably just about to reach the cutoff point where sex stopped being important, when, instead of waiting for those horny moods to disappear, I decided I'd have a fling. I don't want a relationship, I thought. I just want sex. That's all.

I was in that rare state of mind that women always tell you to aspire to, but which you usually find impossible to reach. That state of mind that is completely happy without a man, isn't looking for anyone, is completely fulfilled by work and friends.

And I really was. I realized, post-Jon-trauma, that I definitely didn't want to be in a relationship with someone unless they were absolutely right, and, let's face it, how often do you meet someone who you really fancy and really like? Exactly.

I do what most women do. I meet someone and some of it's right, maybe he looks right, or has the right job, or the right background, and, instead of sitting back and waiting for him to reveal his other bits, I make them up. I decide how he thinks, how he's going to treat me, and, sure enough, every time I conclude that this time he's definitely my perfect man, and all of a sudden, well, not so suddenly perhaps, usually around six months after we've split up, I see that he wasn't the person I thought he was at all.

So that's where I'm at when Sal phones, and I haven't seen her for ages, and she invites me out, breathless with excitement about her new boyfriend, and when I arrive at the bar Nick is there and he remembers me, and that's that.

Well, not quite, but more of that later. So you would have thought I'd have learned my lesson after Jon, but have I? Have I? Have I hell. Except with Nick I know from the beginning that I'll never be able to fill in the blanks and reach a conclusion I'll be happy with. And so that night, that night in the bar when there suddenly seems to be this amazing chemistry, I decide that Nick will be my fling, that he'll be perfect for a few weeks of brilliant sex, that I won't get involved, and that we'll probably stay friends.

And I feel really strong. I feel, for the first time in my life, that I can actually do this. That I can have sex with someone and not get emotionally involved, not suddenly start dreaming of marriage and babies and a happy ever after. I feel like a woman. I feel like a grown-up.

Chapter 2

"Libby!" cries Sal, flinging her arms around me in a huge bear hug. "God, it's been ages. Look at you! You look fantastic!" This, incidentally, is the way Sally speaks. In exclamation marks.

"Thanks," I say, believing her because who, after all, wouldn't look fantastic in their brand-new, superexpensive, long, pale gray, cotton-ribbed cardigan, teamed with gray flannel trousers and sexy high-heeled black boots. "So do you," I add, although Sal always looks the same to me. With her natural auburn hair in a sort of fluffy medium-length layered bob, she always looks good in a timeless sort of way because Sal doesn't believe in following fashion, she believes in finding the look that suits you and wearing it until you die.

So, as I said, she always looks pretty much the same. Long, flowing skirts, occasionally jodhpurs, riding boots, fitted jackets and a silk scarf knotted casually around her throat. Tonight it's the turn of the jodhpurs, and I see why.

"Jesus, Sal," I say, stepping back, because there is something different about her tonight. "You've lost so much weight."

"Have I!" she says, with a cheesy grin, because of course she knows she has. She'd never dare wear those camel-colored skintight jodhpurs if she hadn't. "Must be love!" she whispers loudly, taking my hand and leading me to a table in the corner. "You must come and meet the others."

What an, er, eclectic, bunch. This is something that I've always admired about Sal: her choice in friends, her willingness to mix and match, just to throw people together and not worry about the consequences. I, on the other hand, spend my life in a constant panic about whether people will get on with one another, desperately trying to keep my groups of friends separate. There are my trendy media friends, mostly people I've met through work; my university friends; my oldest friends from school; and my art class friends, except I haven't been for ages so I haven't really seen them recently. And then there's Jules, who's my take-anywhere friend, because she's the one person who fits in with everyone.

But Sal doesn't discriminate, and I can see that there are a few familiar faces.

"Hi," I say with a smile to Kathy, Sal's oldest friend, a tall stunning blonde who oozes style and sophistication and seems to have a constant stream of equally gorgeous men at her side.

"Libby," she says, stretching out a smooth tanned cheek to kiss the air next to mine. "How are you? It's been so long. You must meet Phil," and she gestures to the drop-dead gorgeous hunk at her side.

"Delighted to meet you," he says, in possibly one of the poshest voices I've ever heard, and holds out his hand to shake mine, which floors me for a few moments because outside the office nobody I know shakes hands, but then I realize why he's holding out his hand, so, surreptitiously trying to wipe my damp palms on my cardigan, I shake his hand firmly and say a businesslike "How do you do," because I can't be too friendly to someone this gorgeous in case Kathy thinks I'm flirting with him, which I'd never do, and as soon as I say it I turn away to see who else I know.

"You remember Paul," says Sal, putting a stool down next to a baby-faced scruffy young man sipping from a pint who I know is her latest boyfriend, but I'm not sure why I should remember him.

"Umm." I'm not sure I do, actually.

"Of course you do," she says. "Paul worked with me on the *Sunday Mail*."

"Oh, Paul!" I say. "That Paul. Sorry. God, finally I can put a face to the name."

He grins at me. "I know what you mean. You must spend all

day talking to journalists and never knowing what they look like."

"Unless," I say, grinning cheekily, suddenly remembering that I have seen him before, "unless, the journalist in question has been out for the day wearing a miniskirt to test the latest men's fashion."

"Shit," he groans. "I thought I'd lived that one down." And we both laugh.

"And Nick," says Sal, making big eyes at me which I don't quite understand, but then I turn to Nick and realize that he's the one she used to fancy and that she's trying to warn me telepathically not to say anything. "You must remember Nick."

Nick turns to look at me, and nods. "Hi, Libby," he says, and somehow the way he says my name makes it sound really intimate, and I feel a tiny shiver at the base of my spine.

Hello? What's this all about, then? And I look closely at Nick and it's as if I'm seeing him for the first time. God, I think. I never realized his eyes were that blue. And he's had his hair cut. It's not in a straggly ponytail any more, it's a short buzz cut that brings out these incredible sculpted cheekbones, and Jesus, he's handsome, and in an instant I remember what that shiver is. Lust. Pure and simple.

This could be my fling, I think, settling back into my chair and switching into flirt mode. Nick. Perfect.

"So what have you been up to?" he says, giving me what is definitely an appreciative glance.

"Working hard as usual," I say, instantly regretting how dull it sounds, and racking my brain for an amusing story.

"I like your hair," he says, and another shiver goes through me. "You've changed it."

And I have. I'd had long hair, dead straight, and a fringe the last time I saw Nick. Now it's shoulder-length, no fringe, and flicking up at the bottom.

"You're not supposed to remember hair," I laugh. "You're a bloke."

"You'd be surprised at what I remember," he says with a smile.

"What do you mean?"

"The last time I saw you was at Sal's party two years ago," he says.

"Nope." I shake my head. "Not impressed. Any bloke would remember that."

"You had your hair up," he continues, still smiling. "And you were wearing black leather trousers, sneakers and a bright orange T-shirt which said 'Bizarre' on it."

"Jesus Christ." My mouth is hanging open. "Now I am impressed. How the hell do you remember what I was wearing?"

He shrugs. "I told you you'd be surprised."

"No, but seriously," I push, "how did you remember that?"

"Let's just say I have a very good memory for things I want to remember."

"Oh," I say in a small voice, as it dawns on me that maybe he wasn't being standoffish all those times I had met him. Maybe he fancied me? Maybe?

"So the exciting world of PR is still as exciting as ever, then?" he says.

"I know you think PR's a complete waste of time," I start, even though I don't know, I just suspect, "but it suits me. I like it."

"I don't think it's a waste of time." He sounds surprised. "And when my novel becomes a best-seller you'll probably be the first people I come to."

"You've got a deal?" My voice is high with excitement. This is getting better and better. If Nick's signed a deal, then he's got money, and if he's got money that instantly makes him eligible, and if he's eligible, then, and only then, can I imagine us together.

"Nah," he sighs. "Still trying."

"Oh. What's the book about?" I'm being polite, okay? I think he'll just give me a two-minute synopsis, but ten minutes later he stops, seeing my eyes glaze over.

"Shit, I'm sorry. I've bored you."

"No, no," I say quickly, shaking my mind awake. "I just don't know all that much about politics, so it doesn't mean a great deal to me.

"But it sounds excellent," I add enthusiastically. "I can't believe it hasn't been published."

"I know," he says sadly. "Neither can I.

"What are you drinking?" He stands up, and I tell him a sea breeze if they've got it, and if they haven't got any cranberry juice then a vodka and soda with a dash of lime.

"Well," says Sal in a knowing voice when he's gone off to get the drinks. "You and Nick seem to be getting on rather well."

I shrug. "He seems nice, that's all. I never realized."

"You should go for it," she says. "I could see you two together."

"You don't fancy him anymore then?" I whisper.

"Don't be daft," she laughs. "I've got Paul now. I don't know what I ever saw in Nick—" She stops, realizing what she's just said. "I didn't mean that, he's gorgeous, it's simply that I see now we would never have been right together. You, on the other hand—"

I laugh. "Sal! You're crazy. I can't see us together at all."

"Why not?" She looks startled, and I remember how she doesn't think about the important things, about our lifestyles, how different we are.

"Just look at us," I say, feebly gesturing at my designer clothes, and then pointing at Nick, at his dirty jeans, his scruffy loose sweater with holes in the sleeves, his scuffed Doc Martens.

"What?" she says again, brow furrowed because she isn't getting it. "What am I looking at?"

"Oh, never mind," I laugh. "He's definitely not the one for me, but he is nice. He's really quite sexy."

"Maybe you should just get together and see what happens," she says, smiling, leaning back to make way for Nick, who's returning with a fresh round of drinks.

"Maybe I should," I say, thinking that the getting together bit would suit me just perfectly right now, but I know what would happen. We wouldn't fit, is what would happen. But that's okay, I remind myself. I don't want a potential husband or even a boyfriend. I just want some fun. No strings attached.

"What are you two gossiping about?" says Nick, and I can tell from his smile his ears were burning.

"Er, just work," says Sal, who is completely crap at lying.

"I see," he says, sitting down and sliding my vodka over to me. "Not discussing men, then, were you?"

"No!" says Sal, giving me a hugely indiscreet thumbs-up and turning to snuggle into Paul's shoulder.

Nick and I talk all evening, and, once the book is out of the way, it turns out that he really is interesting, and funny, and different.

"If you won the lottery what would you do?" he asks at one point, and I practically squeal with pleasure because I love questions like this.

"How much?"

"Whatever," he says.

"No, no. You have to do it properly. You have to name a figure."

"Okay," he says, grinning. "Five million pounds."

I sit back, thinking about all the lovely things I could buy with five million pounds.

"Well," I start. "I'd buy a house."

"What kind of house and where?"

"One of those huge white ones in Holland Park."

"You do realize that would set you back about three million quid."

"Oh. Okay. A small white one in Maida Vale."

"For how much?"

"Five hundred thousand?"

He nods. "And how would you decorate it?"

I describe my dream house, except I get a bit lost after I've done the living room, the bathroom, the kitchen and the bed-room, because I've never had to think about any other rooms.

"What about the dining room?" Nick asks. "What about bed-room number four? What about your second bathroom? What about the study?"

"Oh, God," I finally groan. "Too many rooms. Maybe I'll just settle for an amazing two-bedroom flat with huge rooms and a split-level galleried bit to work in."

"So. You've got four and a half million left."

"No, a bit less. I'd probably spend about a hundred thou-sand doing it up."

He looks at me as if I'm crazy, then shakes his head and laughs. "Okay, 4.4 million pounds to go. What else?"

"I'd buy a holiday home in the Caribbean."

"You're big on homes, aren't you?"

"What do you expect? I'm a child of Thatcher's generation."

"Hmm," he sniffs. "Don't tell me you voted for her?"

"No," I lie expertly, saying what I always say. "I voted for the Green Party."

"Did you?" He looks, well, if not impressed, at least not completely pissed off, and for a moment I think of telling him the truth, that I don't give a stuff about politics and the only rea-son I voted Tory was because my parents had, that it could have been anyone leading my country. I just didn't care.

I decide to keep lying.

"Yes," I say, nodding. "None of the other parties seemed to offer anything, and you know what politicians are like. They're all untrustworthy bastards." This last line I'd heard at a party, and I thought it sounded rather good, like I knew what I was talking about and it works. Nick nods in agreement, as if I've just said something very sensible.

"Anyway," I continue, bringing the conversation back to more familiar footing. "My house in the Caribbean."

"Ah, yes," he says, smiling. "That's far more important than politics."

"Absolutely." I go on to describe the house I would build on the tiny island of Anguilla.

"So we're about a million down," he says. "What else?"

"I'd probably take about a hundred thousand and go on a mad shopping spree," I admit.

"A hundred thousand? Jesus Christ. What would you be shopping for? Diamonds and pearls?"

"Nope." I shake my head. "Far too old for my youthful years. I'd go to Armani, Prada, Gucci . . ."

"Top Shop?" asks Nick. "Oasis?"

"Are you crazy?" I say. "I'd never demean myself by stepping foot in anywhere like that."

"Oh, right." He grins. "Of course. How stupid of me." And he holds out his hand, which I slap very gently.

"Anyway," I say, "how come you know about Oasis?"

"I know a lot of things," he laughs.

"You're not really a bloke, are you?" I say, narrowing my eyes and squinting at him. "You're a girl."

"Damn," he says, shaking his head and laughing. "And I hoped you hadn't noticed."

At about three million pounds I run out of ideas. I have, by this point, two homes, a wardrobe that would make Oprah Winfrey jealous, a convertible Porsche 911, a live-in cleaning woman who doesn't actually live with me, but in the granny flat I stick on to the basement of my house and numerous investments in property. I don't know what to do with the rest.

"I'd, er, give the rest to charity," I say magnanimously, hoping he won't ask which ones, because I couldn't name a charity if my life depended on it, and anyway I might give a bit to charity, but I honestly can't see me donating two million quid. No matter how worthy.

"Which charity?" he asks. He would.

"I'd give to a few. That breast cancer one. The . . ."—I think hard—"NSPCC." I remember those little blue plastic collection boxes they used to give you at school. "AIDS research, lots to them. And animal charities! Yes, I'd give loads to animal charities so no more little ponies and horses in my cat food.

"What about you?" I look at Nick. "What would you do?"

He sits and thinks about it for a bit. "I don't think I'd move," he says. "There's no real point because I'm quite happy."

"Where do you live?"

"In Highgate."

"Do you live by yourself?" But that isn't what I'm asking. I'm asking whether he owns his own flat, whether he is responsible, whether he can support a wife. But no, I stop myself, I'm not going to be his wife. He's not going to be my husband. It doesn't matter.

"Mmm." He nods. "I've got a bedsit, and I suppose I could get a one-bedroom flat, but I'm happy where I am."

"You'd have to buy somewhere," I say sternly. "You've got to get your foot on the ladder." Another phrase I've picked up somewhere that I always use when talking about property.

"Do I? Why?"

"Because . . ." I suddenly don't know why, other than that I've been brought up to believe that everyone should own their own house if they possibly can.

"Because you're one of Thatcher's children, right?"

"Well, so are you," I say in my defense.

"Ish," he says.

"Ish?"

"I may be only a couple of years older than you, but my parents were dyed-in-the-wool Labour supporters."

"But you grew up during Thatcher's time."

"So does that mean I was supposed to believe in her?"

"No, it's just sometimes hard to go against what you've been brought up to believe in."

"It wasn't what I was brought up to believe in."

I'm getting out of my depth. I stand up. "Another pint?" and he laughs.

"So okay, you won't buy a mansion," I say when I come back.

"No, no," he says. "I've been thinking about it and you're probably right. I should buy somewhere, but it wouldn't be anything amazing. I might even buy the flat I'm living in."

I look at him in horror. "A bedsit?"

"Okay," he laughs. "I'll buy a one-bedroom flat."

"What else, what else?"

He sits deep in thought. "I know!" he suddenly exclaims, his eyes lighting up. "I'd buy a proper computer."

"You mean you're writing a novel and you haven't got a computer?" I say slowly.

"I've got one of these typewriter things that has a tiny screen and you can see about three lines of what you've written on it."

"You must be spending a fortune on Wite-Out," I say.

"There we go." He grins. "I'd buy a lifetime's supply of Wite-Out."

"But you wouldn't need Wite-Out if you had a computer."

"I might get nostalgic."

"For your battered old typewriter that takes forever and can't go back and correct?"

"How do you know it's battered?"

"It is, isn't it?"

"Yes, slightly. But it has character. Computers seem a bit clinical."

"Okay," I sigh. "We've probably spent less than a hundred thousand so far. You're not doing very well."

"I could donate a sizable amount to the Labour Party," he says sheepishly.

"How much?"

"A million?"

"You can't give a million quid to bloody politicians!" I say in horror. "You're hopeless."

"Sorry," he says, looking it. "I'm just not very money-oriented."

"Evidently." And luckily he laughs, and when he does I can't help but notice how white his teeth are, how his face softens, how goddamned gorgeous he looks.

"So," says Sal, leaning over and interrupting us. "Have you got any good stories for me, then, Libby?"

I sit and think. "Not really stories, but maybe you'd be interested in an interview with Sean Moore?"

"Sean Moore!" Her eyes light up. "Are you doing him?"

I nod. "We're doing the PR for his new TV series, and I'm setting up a round of interviews in a couple of weeks. You should have got the press release, I sent it to you last week."

"Oh," says Sal, looking guilty. "I probably did get it, but I get so many press releases, half the time I don't even look at them."

"What?" I say in mock dismay. "You mean I go to all that trouble to think up something witty and clever, and it goes in the bin?"

"No," she says. "It joins the towering pile on my desk that's threatening to topple over and knock someone out."

"You're forgiven. . . ." I pause. "As long as you give Sean a good show."

"Double-page spread?"

"That would be brilliant."

"One condition."

I know what's coming.

"Can we have it exclusively?"

"I hate it when journalists say that," I groan.

"But you know why we do," she says. "There's no point in running an interview with Sean Moore after it's appeared everywhere else."

"Tell you what," I say. "I can't promise you an exclusive because we have to try and get as much coverage as possible, but what I can do is give it to you first, but, and I mean this, Sal, you have to run it when you say you will." I'm sick to the back teeth of giving newspapers exclusive interviews, running out to buy the paper in the morning and finding it isn't there because another story was deemed to be more important. I then have to chase the journalist for days, and they usually keep telling me it's going in, they just don't know when, and before you know it the whole thing has been forgotten about.

"I will." She nods. "Promise."

"Okay," I say. "Ring me in the office tomorrow."

At eleven o'clock everyone starts getting up to leave.

"You know how it is," says Kathy. "School night." And we put on our coats and wander outside, standing around in a big huddle to say goodbye.

"Where do you live?" asks Nick, just as I'm wondering how to say good night to him, and if, in fact, I want to say good night to him at all.

"Ladbroke Grove." The regret is obvious in my voice. I mean, there's no way I can offer him a lift back to Highgate, it's just too damn unsubtle. "Are you driving?" I say.

He shakes his head. "No. I don't drive."

"How do you get around?"

"I cycle."

"So where's your bike?"

"I got the tube."

"Oh."

And then I have a brain wave. "Do you want a lift to the tube?"

His face glows. "I'd love one."

And as we walk off I can see Sal grinning at me, and I can't help it. I start grinning too.

We walk to my car in silence. I stride along next to him, wondering why my heart is pounding, why I suddenly feel slightly sick, but once the engine is on and the music comes blaring out of the stereo, I start to relax a bit. I mean surely this is the perfect fling?

Not that I want a one-night stand with Nick, just maybe a few weeks of delicious sex before saying goodbye with no broken hearts. One-night stands aren't my style. I don't think they're anyone's style, are they? Sure, we've all done it, but even when you can't stand them, even when it's just a drunken mistake after a party, you still want them to call, don't you, even if it's just so you can turn round and tell them you never want to see them again. It's an ego thing. Definitely. I don't want you, but I want you to want me anyway. So, I don't want a one-night stand with Nick, but then there's always the worry that it'll be taken out of your control. You think there's going to be a repeat experience and you sit by your phone and wait for weeks for them to call and they don't, and unwittingly you've added another bloody one-night stand to your list.

But as far as I'm concerned true one-nighters only really happen with strangers. When it's someone you know, particularly someone who's connected to you by friends, they usually do call again, and I sort of know, even while driving in the car that night, that no matter what happens Nick will call me again.

And you see, in normal circumstances, I would never dream of sleeping with him on the first night, as it were. If I had looked at Nick and thought, yes, you could be The One, I would have given him my number and let him take me out a few times before even considering going to bed with him. I don't put a time limit on it, though. As far as I'm concerned you just know when it feels right, but according to Jules you have to spend thirty-six hours in their company before you sleep with them. God knows where she got that from. Probably some trashy magazine, but I suppose that's about seven dates, which sounds about right.

Oh, all right, then, maybe after four dates.

But if I stop being clinical about it, I suppose the time I decide I'm going to jump into bed with them is the time when I know, as an absolute certainty, that they are crazy about me and they aren't going to disappear.

Although I have got it wrong. But only once. That was Michael. We fell in love for two weeks, spent as much time together as we possibly could, and, although I knew I probably should have waited, it felt so right I just thought, fuck it, let's have sex. Immediately afterward he was fine. It was only when he hadn't called me for four days—and this was the man who had called me three times a day, every day, for two weeks—that I realized something was wrong. Sure enough. He'd changed his mind. I can't even remember what shit he came out with. Something about not being ready for a relationship, blah blah blah. Usual crap. I was devastated. Devastated.

But it taught me a lesson, and the only reason I'm choosing to unlearn the lesson with Nick is because Nick is never going to be my boyfriend, and when it's just sex, the rules change.

When it's just sex, you're allowed to be predatory, to make the first move, to entice them into bed, because it's not necessary to make them fall in love with you.

When it's just sex you're allowed to put your hand on their thigh while driving your car and say huskily, "Will you come back to mine for coffee?"

When it's just sex you're allowed to lead them into your living room and kiss them passionately before they've even had a chance to take their coat off.

And then you're allowed to . . .

Sorry, I'm jumping ahead of myself here. Where were we?

Ah, yes, in the car, listening to music, and neither of us is actually saying anything because I don't want to start just in case he tells me which tube station to drop him off at, so I keep driving, and eventually we turn into Ladbroke Grove and I have to say something, so I do.

"The tube's just down the road," I say. Unimaginatively.

"Oh," he says. And I smile inside.

"Do you want to come in for a coffee?" I say.

"I'd love one," he says. And he grins.

So I park the car and I can't look at Nick because I'm very aware of his presence, of the chemistry, of this unspoken agreement we are entering into, and I just unlock my front door and we both walk in.

And you know what I love? Even though Nick isn't boyfriend material, I love the fact that he seems to feel instantly at home.

"Do you mind if I take my shoes off?" he says, and naturally I say no, although as I say it I pray he doesn't have nasty socks with holes, or smelly feet, or something that will put me off him forever. And I take a quick glance, and his feet, or rather his socks, look really quite nice, and I can't smell anything other than the smell of home, so I go into the kitchen to put the kettle on.

"You have incredible taste," he says, wandering around, picking up things and putting them down. "Really," he reiterates. "Such style."

"Thank you," I say, going through the motions of putting the kettle on, and watching curiously to see where he'll sit. If he sits on the chair, I think, I'm in trouble, because how can I maneuver myself into a position where he'll kiss me? Maybe I can perch on the arm of the chair, I think, watching as he seems to hover ominously by the armchair.

Phew. He seems to think twice about the chair and settles into the sofa. I kick my own shoes off, ready to curl up like a cat, bring the mugs to the coffee table, then panic about my makeup and quickly disappear into the bathroom.

I blot the shine off my nose and forehead, and think about a fresh coat of lipstick, but no, too obvious, so I just shake my hair around a bit to give it a wild, wanton look, then sashay back into the living room to put on some music.

Seduction music, I think. I need something soft, jazzy, sexy. Something that will put us both in the mood. I flick through the CDs until I find my fail-safe Sinatra CD. Perfect. It always worked in the past, and I put it on and turn the volume down so it's barely throbbing in the background, then I walk over to the sofa where Nick is sipping his coffee and watching me.

"I need a woman's touch," he says, as I curl up at the other end of the sofa, not wanting to sit too close, but knowing that I'm only a hop, skip and a touch away from the passion I'm so desperate for.

I raise an eyebrow and he laughs.

"I meant in the home," he says, and I laugh too, then we both make big shows of drinking our coffee, although you can't really drink it, it's far too hot.

"What's your flat like, then?" I ask.

"A hovel," he says, and he laughs.

"No, really," I push.

"Yes, really," he says.

"Why?" I ask, although quite frankly I'm not that surprised. Bachelor pads seem to fall into two categories. If the bachelor in question has money, it's all black leather and chrome, with nasty airbrushed pictures of sports cars on the wall and huge, fuck-off TVs and stereos. And if he, like Nick, hasn't got a pot to piss in, it will be overflowing with books and papers, and dirty clothes, and rubbish. Trust me. I know these things.

"Well," I say, raising my mug. "Here's to winning the lottery."

After this we seem to relax. We talk about Sal, about her boyfriend, about us. I tell him I'm not into relationships, I've had enough of getting my heart broken and I'm not ready for anything serious.

He nods intently while I say this, and says he knows how I

feel. He grins and tells me he hasn't had a serious relationship in two years, but that after his last—a miserable five-year relationship with Mary, who loved him but didn't seem to like him very much—he definitely isn't ready for commitment.

And then he looks up at me with those incredible blue eyes and says, "But I'm very attracted to you," and even though I'm the one who's supposed to be in control, the one who's made the decision to have a fling with him, my stomach turns over and does a little somersault and I start to feel ever so slightly sick.

There's a long silence, and then I say, "Thank you," because I don't know what else to say, and I can't say that I'm very attracted to him too because it sounds really naff, and anyway he must know that because why else would I have invited him back.

So we sit there in silence for a bit and then I offer him another coffee, even though I've hardly touched mine, and he shakes his head and my heart plummets.

Shit, I think. Shit, shit, shit. He's going to go home. Oh fuck. But he doesn't. He grins and says, "You know what I'd really like?"

"No." I shake my head.

"I'd really like a bath."

"A bath? Are you mad?"

"I know it sounds bizarre, but I've only got a shower in my flat and I miss baths. Would you mind?"

I shake my head, wondering what the hell this is about, because this is a completely new one on me. Am I supposed to sit here and file my nails while he has a bath, or am I supposed to talk to him? What on earth am I supposed to do?

I don't have to think about it for very long because just then the phone rings.

"Hi, babe," says Jules. "It's me."

"Hi," I say guardedly, in the tone of voice that tells her this is perhaps not the best time to be calling.

"Uh-oh," she says. "Something tells me you're not alone."

"Mmmhmm," I say, as Nick gets up off the sofa and turns the music down slightly.

"Who's there?" she says. "It's a bloke, isn't it?"

"Mmmhmm," I say again, eyes widening slightly as Nick starts grinning manically at me, unbuttoning his shirt.

"What's going on?" she pleads, as I start giggling.

"You really want to know what's going on?" I say.

"Yes!"

"Okay," I say, as Nick starts dancing around the room doing a bloody good imitation of a stripper, except it isn't sexy, it's very, very funny.

"Okay," I repeat. "There's an extremely gorgeous man jumping around my living room and taking off his clothes."

Nick wiggles his hips in appreciation of my description of him.

"Oh ha bloody ha," says Jules. "Seriously. What's going on?"

"Seriously," I say. "He's about to take his shirt off."

Nick takes his shirt off.

"And," I continue, as lust starts to rise up from my groin, "he's got a perfect washboard stomach."

"I don't believe you," she says, as I hold the phone out to Nick.

"Hello," he says, as I practically salivate over the sight of his lean, muscular, naked torso. "Who's this?"

There is a pause. "Nick," I hear him say, as he unbuttons the fly of his jeans, giving me minor heart failure. "Having a bath," he says next, and then he starts laughing as I grab the phone off him.

"What did you say, what did you say?" I beg.

"Bloody hell!" says Jules. "Now I believe you. But who the hell is Nick?"

"It's a long story," I say, thanking God that Nick wears boxer shorts and not something disgusting like purple Y-fronts or those revolting briefs. "Can I call you tomorrow?"

"Just tell me, is he naked?"

"Not yet," I say, eyes glued to Nick, who is trying to balance on one leg as he pulls off his socks, "but I think he will be soon."

Nick wiggles off into the bathroom.

"Fucking hell," I whisper quickly. "He's gorgeous!"

"As long as you know what you're doing," she laughs.

"Having fun," I say. "Something I haven't had for a while."

"Okay," she says. "I'll let you go. Call me first thing, and for God's sake use a condom."

"Right," I say, and laugh, because Jules is the only person in the world who knows about the condom drawer—a drawer in my bedside table that's filled to bursting with condoms of all different shapes, sizes and colors, most of them, it has to be said, supplied by her.

I can hear the bathwater running, so I get up, walk through the bedroom, thanking God I had the presence of mind to make the bed this morning, and gingerly push the door open before creasing up with laughter.

Nick is sitting in the bath as the water pours in, and he's put in practically a whole bottle of bubble bath. This doesn't bother me because it means I can't see anything, which I've been dreading because I don't know him well enough to take it in my stride—and he's put a plastic shower cap on his head.

If he wasn't so damn gorgeous he'd look ridiculous. As it happens, he looks cute as hell, and I pull the loo seat down and sit on it, shaking my head.

"You really are crazy," I say, as he rubs his face.

"No I'm not," he says, lying back. "This is lovely. Why don't you join me?"

"I had a bath earlier," I say.

"So? I need someone to scrub my back."

Oh fuck it, I think, standing up and untying my cardigan. This isn't exactly the way I'd planned it, but what have I got to lose?

Thankfully Nick doesn't watch me getting undressed. He lies back in the bath and closes his eyes, and I keep a close watch on him to check he isn't peeking. I'm not quite ready to take off all my clothes in front of him, so when I'm down to my underwear I grab a towel and go back into the bedroom.

"Libby?" he shouts as I go. "Have you got any candles?"

I find three, and, after I've taken my bra and knickers off in the relative privacy of my bedroom, I wrap a towel around my-self, light the candles, and switch the light off in the bathroom, putting the candles around the room.

Nick sits up, facing away from me, and I let the towel drop and climb in behind him in the bath.

"Here," he says, handing me the soap over his shoulder. "Back scrub time."

"You just did this because you wanted a massage," I say, soaping his back and wondering how on earth I've managed to get so intimate with someone I hardly know in such a short space of time.

"Mmm," he murmurs. "A bit lower. Yup, that's perfect."

I look at my hands circling his back with soap, at the flicker-ing candlelight picking up the definition of his spine, his shoul-der blades, and when his back is covered I put the soap on the side of the bath and slowly, smoothly rub his back.

I have my legs on either side of him, and, as I rub his back, Nick picks up the soap and starts soaping my calves. I catch my breath as I feel his big, strong hands gently soap my legs, over the knee, down to the ankles, holding my feet as he rubs them in silence.

And as we half sit, half lie in the bath, the music coming from the living room seems to take on a distinctly sexual feel, and before I even know what I'm doing I lean forward and kiss his neck. I hear him groan as my lips touch his skin, and I open my lips and taste him, sucking softly as my lips travel up to his earlobe. His hand stops circling on my leg. He's stopped mov-ing, and everything seems to be happening very slowly.

He turns as the water sloshes around him in the bath, then looks at me through eyes glazed with lust, before kissing me softly, open lips teasing mine for what seems like hours, before finally licking my upper lip as I moan and slide my tongue into his mouth.

I'm vaguely aware that as he's kissing me he's half standing up, twisting his body round, and when he sits down again in the warm water he's facing me, his legs over my legs, his lips never leaving mine.

And as we carry on kissing, I pull the bath cap off his head and drop it over the edge of the bath, and slink my hands around his neck, pulling him closer as he drops his head and kisses my collarbone.

I shiver.

He sits back and picks up the soap again, still looking at me as if to check this is okay, which by this time it most definitely is, and very gently starts soaping my arms, my elbows, my hands, and sweet Jesus, I never knew how sensual hands could be, or how turned on I could be by someone gently slipping and sliding soap over my fingers.

And he moves the soap up my arms, on to my shoulders, then slowly circles my breasts, moving closer and closer to my nipples, which are rock hard, but not quite touching them, not yet.

Then he slides the bar of soap over my left nipple and I gasp, and look down into the water because by this time the soap has made all the bubbles disappear, and I can see his cock, thick and hard, and I slide the soap out of his hand and down the side of his cock, and it's his turn to gasp as I slide it up and down the shaft, around his balls, up around the head.

The soap slips out of my hand, and he picks it up and traces a line down my body, over my nipples, down my stomach, and across my clitoris as I close my eyes to feel these incredible feelings, and all I can think of as I reach again for his cock is that I want to feel him inside me.

I hear a slurping noise and I jerk my eyes open and Nick laughs as he holds up the plug, and it breaks the spell for a second, but just a second, because as the water slips out of the bath

Nick pushes me on to my back, and, as my legs rest on either edge of the bath, he kisses his way down my body until I feel him pause between my legs, and I open my eyes and look at him, and he's looking at me as if to ask, is this okay, and I close my eyes and sigh to show him that it is.

And I feel his tongue slip in between my legs, and, as he licks, sucks, laps at my clitoris, I feel a wave of orgasm building up inside me, and after I've come, my body jerking like crazy in the confines of the bath, Nick looks at me and smiles, and I kiss him, tasting myself in his mouth, and I lead him out of the bathroom and into bed.

I slip a condom on his cock that is jerking with anticipation, and I push him on to his back and straddle him, positioning myself so I can ease him inside me, and when he's about an inch in, I gasp because I really had forgotten how good this feels.

And it's perfect. The perfect fuck. Not too short, and not too long, because nothing, nothing is worse than men who think all it takes to satisfy a woman is hours and hours of deep, hard pounding. Please. I'd rather watch paint dry.

But Nick is perfect, and I love that feeling of power, being on top, being in control, and I love watching his face as he finally gives in to an orgasm.

When it's over I think he'll probably be the type to roll over and fall fast asleep, but he doesn't. He puts his arm around me and cuddles me for ages.

"That," he says, after squeezing me very tightly, "was lovely."

"Good," I say. "I thought so too."

"And you," he says, kissing my nose, "are one hell of a sexy lady."

"I aim to please," I laugh.

"You certainly did," he says. "And now I want a story."

"A what?" I raise myself up on one arm and look at him.

"A story. I want you to tell me a bedtime story."

"What about?"

"Anything you like."

"But I can't think of anything."

"Oh, for God's sake," he sighs dramatically. "I suppose I'll have to tell you one, then."

"Yes, please!" I say, in a little girl voice, feeling strangely like a little girl, all safe and warm and protected, encircled in his arms.

"Once upon a time," he starts, in a soft, low voice, "there lived a little girl called Libby. Libby lived all by herself in a huge yellow sunflower at the bottom of a beautiful garden."

I sigh and snuggle up closer.

"At the back of the garden," he continues, "was a great big house, and in the house lived Mr. and Mrs. Pinchnose. They were called Mr. and Mrs. Pinchnose because every time they went into the garden they pinched their noses because Mr. and Mrs. Pinchnose hated the smell of anything fresh and beautiful, but what they never knew was that it wasn't the smell of the flowers, or the trees, or the river, it was the smell of Libby."

"Are you saying that Libby smelled?" I say indignantly, although I'm smiling.

"I'm saying that Libby smelled fresh and beautiful," he says.

"Oh," I say. "That's okay, then," and I pick up his hand and kiss it as he carries on talking, and before I know it I'm fast asleep.

I hate the morning after the night before, because you never know how you stand, and even though we wake up and have sex again, I'm still not sure what will happen once we both break the spell by getting out of bed, and, in my case, going to work, so I try to put the moment off for as long as possible by snuggling up to Nick, because let's face it, it's not as if he has anywhere to go.

But after the fifth time the alarm goes off I have to get up or I'll be severely late for work, so I go into the kitchen to make some coffee, and Nick rolls over groaning about the sunlight.

I wrap myself up in the silk dressing gown that was a present from Jules last year, which I only ever wear if a man stays the night, so needless to say it still looks brand new, and try to fluff up my hair and wipe away the mascara from under my eyes in my powder-compact mirror in the living room.

I carry a mug of coffee back into the bedroom for Nick, and stand for a while watching him. He isn't asleep, but he has his eyes closed and he's lying there, the duvet covering his legs, the rest of his body bare, with one arm slung across his eyes, and I stand there thinking, fucking hell, he may not be what I'm looking for but Jesus is he gorgeous.

And as I stand there he opens his eyes and when he sees me he holds his arms out and says, "Come and give me a cuddle," and as I'm lying in his arms and he's making me laugh by giving me big, punchy kisses, I'm thinking, God, I could get used to this.

No, Libby. No, you could not. He's not what you want. You really think you could spend your life in a grotty bedsit in Highgate? You think you could spend your social life in pubs drinking warm beer? You think you could forget all about your dreams of being a rich man's wife and a lady who lunches? I don't think so. No. I am not going to fall in love with this man. I'm going to be a woman of the nineties and just enjoy the sex, and so what if he happens to be affectionate and quite funny? That's just a bonus.

Nick sits up in bed and drinks his coffee while I get ready for work. He makes me laugh when I open my wardrobe, and he says, "What on earth are those?" pointing to a load of hangers covered in tissue paper and cellophane.

"That's my dry cleaning," I say, as he shakes his head in amazement.

"Dry cleaning? Jesus, we really do come from different worlds."

"I suppose you don't even do ironing," I laugh.

"Not if I can possibly help it," he says, and then, when I'm putting my makeup on in the bathroom mirror, he comes in and sits on the edge of the bath to talk to me and, as he puts it, "see what I'm doing."

"What's that for?" he keeps saying, as I root around in my makeup bag and pull out yet another suspiciously alien thing—at least to his eyes.

"I dunno," he says eventually, shaking his head as I pout at my perfect reflection. "If you ask me you look far better without anything."

"Now I know you're joking," I say, because I'd never dare leave my house without the full appliance of science.

"No, I'm serious," he says. "You don't need to wear all that makeup. I know there are some women who do need it because without it they look like complete dogs, but you're really pretty naturally, and you honestly do look better without."

I don't know about you, but flattery, for me, will get anyone just about anywhere they want to go, and I could kiss him for saying that. In fact, I do. I completely forget about the makeup bit and just concentrate on the pretty bit. He says I'm pretty! He thinks I'm pretty!

By the time we leave the house and walk up to the tube station, I'm flying as high as a kite. Not that I've fallen in love, not even close, but it's just so nice to have had a night of snuggling up to someone, to have someone to talk to in the morning, to have compliments again.

But as we separate in the tube station, him to go north, me to go to Kilburn, I do feel a tiny twinge, because even though I know this isn't going to go anywhere, I don't think I can stand it if he just says, "Bye." I think Nick must see this in my face, because he puts his arms around me and gives me a huge hug.

"That was the nicest night I've had in ages," he says, while my heart sinks, because surely this is the lead-in to, "Take care."

But no. I'm wrong.

"When can I see you again?" he says next, and, despite myself, I feel like doing a little jig on the spot.

"Umm," I say, pulling away and digging my diary out from my bag. I flick the pages open and have a quick look. "I'm a bit busy this week," I say. "So either the weekend or next week?"

Please say weekend, I think.

"Saturday?" he says.

"Great," I say, beaming.

"Okay," he says. "Why don't you come to me?"

"What, and set foot in your hovel?"

Nick laughs. "We could go out for something to eat. I'll give you a call at work to arrange a time. How's that?"

It's fine. It would have been better if he'd arranged a time there and then, because once a man says he's going to call you, even if you know you're going to see him again, you still sit and wait for his call, but hell, at least I have a firm date, if not a time, and I'm suddenly feeling a lot happier than I've felt in months.

"You look like the cat that got the cream," says Jo, our super-trendy receptionist at the office.

"Do I?" I say innocently, but I can't help it, a huge Cheshire cat grin plasters itself to my face.

"You're in love, aren't you?" she says.

"Nope." I shake my head. "Definitely not. But"—and I skip

away at this point, just turning back before I disappear through the doorway—"I may well be in lust." And I wink at her before making my way to my desk.

Do I get any work done? Do I hell. I sit and moon at my desk, looking out the window and shivering with lust at the occasional flashbacks of my passion-filled night.

And the flashbacks seem to come at the most ridiculous times. I'll be talking on the phone to a journalist, and suddenly, mid-sentence, a picture of Nick licking my neck slides into my head and I'll pause, grin and lose the plot completely.

It really isn't that I'm falling for him, it's just so damned nice to have had a gorgeous man in my bed, to have been reminded that I am attractive, sexy, that I can still pull.

Because, to be perfectly honest, I've been starting to doubt myself these last six months. Not hugely, because there haven't been that many men I've been interested in, but I do have a tendency to fall for the ones who will never be interested in me, and the ones that fall for me are generally pretty revolting.

I can't figure out why I fall for the wrong ones. Jules can't figure it out either. I meet these men, fall desperately in love, and become friends with them in the mistaken hope that one day they'll see the error of their ways and realize they're madly attracted to me. But of course that doesn't happen. I just go out with them as friends and misinterpret every look, every sigh, every touch, and try to convince myself they're about to make a move, and each time I end up feeling like shit, because yet another man I fancy isn't interested.

The last time it happened was Simeon. I made a beeline for him at a press launch, and, because I fancied him, was the brightest, funniest, sparkiest person I could be, and naturally Simeon thought I was great.

But thinking I'm great doesn't mean he fancied me, and I set off on a mission to make Simeon feel the same way. I started by phoning him a couple of times a week, and he didn't seem to mind, he always sounded really pleased to hear from me, which is hardly surprising since I did all the talking, digging up my wittiest stories to make him laugh.

And eventually I invited him to a party, and spent the whole evening glued to his side, and he didn't seem to mind that either. In fact, he rather seemed to like it.

And gradually I forced my friendship upon him until he had no choice but to be friends with me, and soon he was phoning me as often as I was phoning him, and each time my heart would lift and I'd convince myself he was slowly starting to feel the same way.

Eventually we ended up at a party, where Simeon made a beeline for a short brunette with crappy dress sense and an American accent, and I stood on the sidelines watching this and feeling like shit.

And a week later when he phoned, full of excitement at his date with the American the evening before, I put down the phone and burst into tears, and that was when I decided I'd had enough of falling in love with men who didn't want me. I was going to let someone fall in love with me, and they'd have to treat me like a princess for me to be even the slightest bit interested.

But that's love. Lust is something completely different, and it feels like ages since I've been attracted to someone who feels the same way about me, and okay, that doesn't mean anything, it certainly doesn't mean Nick's The One, but it just makes me feel good about myself, which is good. Isn't it?

In fact, I'm feeling so good that I'm not the slightest bit stressed about my job, which is a bloody miracle, because lately I've been given more and more accounts and I have to confess that there are times when I really don't know how I'm going to cope.

My accounts? Okay, I'm currently working on Sean Moore, which you already know about. A performance artist called Rita Roberts, which is a bit peculiar because I don't tend to do the theatrical stuff as I know nothing about it; a film called *The*

Mystery Cup, which you won't have heard of yet but, if I do my job properly, you'll be reading about in every paper soon; the comedian Tony Baloney; and an aspiring television presenter called Amanda Baker. I say aspiring, which isn't really fair, because she is on television, although not nearly as often as she'd like. She presents a showbiz slot on one of the daytime shows, and the minute she got her face on-screen she decided she was a star. Unfortunately, nobody seems to know who she is, and it's a bit of a catch-22. The papers won't write about her because she's a no one, but without the coverage she can't raise her profile, and it's the hardest account I've got, not just because of that, but because she's such a complete bitch.

I managed to get her into a celeb round-up where one of the nationals wanted celebs to talk about their date from hell, and you'd think she'd be over the moon, but all she did was moan about being the smallest quote in there. For God's sake, did she really expect to take precedence over Germaine Greer, Vanessa Feltz, Emma Noble and Ulrika? Well, evidently yes. The stupid cow did.

But even the fact that Amanda's coming in today for a meeting doesn't ruin my good mood, and when the receptionist buzzes me to tell me she's here, I float down to meet her, and even manage to compliment her, which seems to throw her a bit. "I love your suit," I lie, taking in her tele-friendly pastel trouser suit, which looks vaguely Armani-ish except I know it's not because Amanda isn't nearly successful enough to afford Armani.

"This old thing?" she says, but I can tell she's pleased.

"Come through." I hold the door open for her, and say in my best PR voice, "So how are you?"

"Oh, you know," she says, running a hand through her mane of streaky blond hair. "Busy as ever."

"I caught the slot last week, the one where you interviewed Tony Blackburn. It was excellent, you really are good on TV."

"D'you think?" she says. "I didn't look fat?"

I laugh, because, stroppy cow that she may be, she still, like every woman I know, is convinced she's fat, and yes, admittedly, television does add around ten pounds, but nevertheless she does look the part of the perfect blond, fluffy, bimbo television presenter.

"Fat?" I say. "You? Are you mad? You're skinny."

"I wish," she says, but I've done it, I've actually put her in a good mood, which may make things easier because normally we start off on the wrong foot and end up with her moaning about the lack of press coverage. Hopefully now she'll be a bit more understanding. If I weren't so keen on my job, I'd tell her she's just another bloody wanna-be and I really can't be bothered, but obviously I can't do that, so I shuffle some papers around and ask what she wants to see me about.

"I really feel," she starts, "that now is the time we should be blitzing the papers and getting some more coverage."

"Umm, yes," I say, digging out the list to show her exactly who has been approached. "Was there anything specific you had in mind?"

"Well, yes, actually," she says. "I noticed in *Hello!* that they've done a profile of Lorraine Kelly with her new baby, and I've just moved house and done it up, and I thought it would make a very good feature."

"Okay," I say, groaning inside. "I'll ring them." Which I will and they will sit on the other end of the phone, doubtless raising their eyes to the ceiling while I start my PR spiel about how brilliant Amanda is, and then they'll say, sorry, we've never heard of her.

"And," she says, "I wondered exactly who you had spoken to recently about me?"

Aha! Here's my perfect chance for revenge. I slide the contact sheet over to her and start speaking in my most sympathetic tone of voice. "Last week I spoke to Femail in the *Daily Mail,* Sun Woman, the lifestyle supplement of the *Express, Bella, Best, Woman's Realm* and *Woman.* This week I spoke to *OK!, Here!* magazine, *TV Quick* and *Cosmopolitan.*"

"Oh." Amanda's voice is very small, and, for the first time

ever, and I swear, this must be down to the good mood I'm in, suddenly I feel sorry for her.

"Look," I say. "I know it's hard," and I give her my speech about catch-22. "We need to come up with an angle, really."

"What sort of thing?" she says, and for a moment I forget I'm with a client whom I don't really like and who doesn't really like me and before I can help it I say, "Couldn't you shag a celebrity?"

She looks horrified.

I'm horrified.

"That was a joke," I say, trying to laugh, except I can't quite manage it and it comes out like a little strangled groan. "Seriously, though," I continue, "have there been any life-changing events that we might be able to use, something that would make a good story?"

"Not like moving house, then?" she asks hopefully.

"Er, no. Not like moving house." Like stealing, pillaging, nervous breakdowns, I'm thinking.

"Umm." She sits there and I can almost see her brain try to kick into gear. Oops, nearly, nearly. Nope, she can't quite manage it.

"Okay," I say. "As a child, did you ever steal anything?"

"Are you serious?" she asks.

"Absolutely." I nod my head very seriously.

"No. Not really. Well . . ."

"Yes?" I encourage eagerly.

"Well, I did once take an eyeliner from Boots by mistake. I meant to pay for it but I completely forgot."

"Perfect!" I say. "My thieving hell from top TV presenter! I can see it now."

"Are you sure that will make a story?" she says doubtfully. "I mean, it was only an eyeliner and I was about fourteen years old, and I wouldn't say it was hell, exactly, except I did feel terribly guilty."

"We won't say it was an eyeliner, we'll say it was a complete set of makeup, and you won't have been fourteen, it will have happened last year, and the outcome of it was you felt so terri-ble, you didn't know what came over you, you went back and owned up."

"But that's lying!" she says.

"That's PR," I say. "Hang on," and I pull the phone over and dial a number. "Keith? It's Libby from Joe Cooper PR. Fine, fine, you? Great. Listen, you know Amanda Baker from *Break-fast Break*? No, no, the showbiz slot. No, no, she does the weather. No, no, the blonde. Oh well, anyway, she's doing more and more and she's getting really big and she's just confessed the most amazing story which would be perfect for your maga-zine. It turns out she had the shoplifting experience from hell last year, and she feels the time is right to confess all. Yup." I nod, listening to what he's saying. "Yup. Perfect. Full page? Brilliant. Okay." I scribble down the direct line of the journalist he wants to do it, and put the phone down.

"Well, Amanda," I say. "You've just got yourself a full page in *Female Fancies*, with photographs and everything."

"That's fantastic!" she says, almost breathless with excite-ment. "Photos! That's brilliant! Will it be a studio shot with a professional hair and makeup person?"

"We'll sort out the details later," I say noncommittally, think-ing now would not be the time to tell her they want to take pic-tures of her in a chemist's, furtively slipping a makeup bag into her large, voluminous raincoat.

"And," I say, dialing another number, "how about some radio?"

Amanda is so impressed she can't speak. She nods.

"Mark? It's Libby from Joe Cooper PR. Listen, you know that slot about Londoners and their favorite restaurants? How about Amanda Baker from *Breakfast Break*? I'll fill you in later, yup, yup. Brilliant." I can't be bothered to tell someone else who she is, and I knew he'd say yes because local radio will give just about anyone airtime, and it does the job because Amanda's thrilled.

"Libby," she says, standing up and dusting imaginary dirt from her jacket. "You are doing the most incredible job."

I smile.

"How about making a quick call to Femail and seeing if they'll do a feature on me?"

"Er," I stall. "I just spoke to the commissioning editor before you arrived and I know she's in conference so I'll call her later."

"Oh." Her face drops slightly. "Okay. Well, I'd better be off." She checks her watch. "Thank you." And with that she gives me two air kisses on either side of my face, which throws me somewhat because she's never before offered me anything other than a limp handshake.

"Ciao," she says, as I wince. "I'll speak to you later," and I know she will, because the smaller the star the bigger the pain in the arse they are.

"Libby?" says Jo, as I show Amanda to the door. "Jules is on the line. It's about the eighth time she's called. D'you want to take it or call her back?"

I'm already running back to my desk as she finishes the sentence. "I'll take it, I'll take it," I scream, diving into my chair and breathlessly picking up the phone.

"Libby!" shouts Jules. "I've been dying to speak to you, I can't believe you had a bloody meeting, I can't get any work done, who's Nick and what happened, you had sex didn't you, I know you bloody had sex, how was it, what's he like, tell me everything. . . ."

"Calm down," I laugh, lighting a cigarette and settling back in my chair for a good long chat. "First of all you can stop planning the wedding because he's definitely not for me, but yes, we did have sex, and fucking hell, Jules, he is gorgeous."

"Why isn't he for you? How do you know he's not for you?"

"Okay. For starters he's got no money. . . ."

There's a silence on the other end of the phone.

"Next he lives in a disgusting bedsit in Highgate."

"How do you know it's disgusting?"

"He told me. He's not looking for a relationship. He's very into politics. His idea of a good night out is down the pub with ten pints of beer."

"Okay, okay," sighs Jules. "I get the picture. But Libby, just because he doesn't have money doesn't mean he's not for you. Maybe you should start lowering your expectations."

"Jules! You know I couldn't seriously go out with someone like that. Anyway," I say, feeling slightly guilty at admitting all this, "it's not just the money. It's everything. We're like chalk and cheese."

"So what happened last night, then?"

And I tell her.

Chapter 5

The high as a kite feeling lasts precisely two days. Two days of floating around beaming with love. Sorry, lust. Two days of getting very little done other than daydreaming about the events of my night with Nick. Two days of leaping every time the phone rings.

And then, when he hasn't called, I start to feel sick. Now I know I'm being ridiculous because yes, yes, I know he's not The bloody One, but that doesn't mean I don't want him to want me. I mean, Jesus, he's supposed to be madly in love with me by now, and he's definitely supposed to be phoning me.

I call Jules.

"Jules," I moan, "he hasn't called."

"So?" she says pragmatically. "He will."

"But why hasn't he called? He said he'd call."

"Libby, for God's sake. You sound like you're madly in love, but you keep saying this is just a fling. Flings don't call every day."

"But just because I don't want him in that way doesn't mean I don't want him to want me."

"Now, that," says Jules, "is ridiculous. Stop being so childish. Anyway, you know you're seeing him, so of course he'll call, but it will probably be on Saturday, just to confirm the time, as he said he would."

"Okay," I grumble.

"And," she continues, "you don't want him to fall in love with you because that will only make the whole thing far more complicated."

"Okay," I grumble again.

"So just relax," she finishes.

"You're right, you're right. I know you're right."

"Naturally," she laughs. "I always am."

It's a bastard isn't it, how everything changes once you've slept with someone. How, even though you know you're not going to fall for them, you still have expectations, and you'll still be disappointed in the end.

Except no, not this time. I won't be disappointed. There's no commitment, just enjoyment, and I will enjoy Nick. Really, I will.

• • •

The phone rings at one o'clock on Saturday.

"Hello?" I'm already breathless.

"Hi, babe." It's Jules.

"Oh," I say, the disappointment more than clear in my voice. "Hi."

"What are you doing now?" she asks, and I decide not to tell her that I'm sitting next to the phone willing it to ring.

"Nothing much. You?"

"Nothing. Jamie's working and I'm bored. Do you want to go shopping?"

Now that sounds more like it. A bit of retail therapy never did anyone any harm, and besides, having looked through my huge wardrobe of super-trendy clothes, I see I haven't got anything to wear for tonight. Well, it's not exactly that I haven't got anything to wear, just nothing suitable, and Nick isn't the type to appreciate my John Rocha dresses or Dolce & Gabbana trousers.

"Do you want to come and pick me up?" I say.

"No," she says. "You come over here and we'll hit Hampstead. How does that sound?"

"Perfect," I say. "See you in an hour."

I check my bag as I leave the house. Yup. Got money, credit cards, checkbook, makeup. Shit! Nearly forgot my mobile phone, so I grab it and head down to my gorgeous car, Guzzle the Beetle, aptly named as he (and yes, I know that most cars are female but mine, with his gorgeous metallic blue coating, is most definitely male) guzzles petrol like there's no tomorrow.

And off we trundle to Jules's flat, and once again I sigh with envy as I walk in, because, thanks to being part of a couple, both with nice fat incomes—Jules is an interior designer and Jamie is a barrister—Jules lives in the flat I wish I had. A maisonette in a side road off Haverstock Hill. You walk into a huge, bright, airy living room with maple floors and floaty muslin curtains drifting on either side of french windows that lead to a large balcony. All the furniture is camel and cream, modern classics mixed with beautiful old antiques, and the canvases on the wall are huge, colorful, abstract, and beautiful.

The kitchen's in the basement, and Jules spends most of her time down there. As large as the living room, the kitchen is dominated by a massive scrubbed old French pine table, with enough room left for checked yellow comfy sofas at one end. More french windows lead straight on to the garden, and the units are the ones I dream about—slightly Shaker-ish but with a modern twist. It's my favorite room in the house, and the one we always end up in, drinking huge mugs of tea at the kitchen table, or curled up on the sofa with the sun streaming in.

It does look interior-designed, but it also looks like a home, like a place where you immediately feel comfortable. I adore it, and when I arrive I do what I always do and put the kettle on, and Jules doesn't mind, I know she loves the fact that I feel almost as at home there as she does, possibly more so.

"Hi, Libby," Jamie calls out from his study next to the kitchen.

"Hi, workie," I call back, the shortened version of workaholic, which is what I've been calling him for years. He appears in the doorway and comes over to kiss me hello, and, even though I know I couldn't stand to be with someone who works all the time, it has to be said that I can see exactly what Jules sees in him because he is, truly, gorgeous. The only man I know who looks handsome in a wig. No, not that sort of wig, the legal barrister sort of wig.

And before I met Jamie I always thought that all barristers were pompous assholes. They were all, from my limited experience, into ballet, opera and theater. They all spoke like they had a bagful of plums in their mouth and were as patronizing as hell.

But Jamie isn't like that. Jamie, when he isn't working, is actually a laugh. And Jamie doesn't wear pompous classically English clothes. Jamie wears faded jeans and caterpillar boots. Jamie wears midnight blue velvet trousers and Patrick Cox loafers. Jamie smokes like a chimney and drinks like a fish. Jamie, in fact, is cool, and one night, when we were all very drunk, he confessed that if he hadn't been a barrister he would have been a pop star, which made us all choke with laughter at the time, but actually I could see that. I could see Jamie being the lead singer in a seriously hip band and giving interviews with an insouciant toss of his head.

Jamie and I have an odd relationship, in the way that you always have slightly odd relationships with the men your girlfriends subsequently marry. Jules was my friend for years, and then Jamie came along, and yes, we hit it off immediately, but there's always that tiny bit of resentment because they took your best friend away.

But I forgave him. How could I not? And now, even though I don't see him that often, we have this lovely, teasing, almost brother-sister relationship, where he sits me down and asks about my love life and then tries to give me advice, which I almost always ignore because at the end of the day he's a bloke.

And I know what you're thinking. You're thinking that men are far better equipped to give advice when you're having man problems because they know how men think, but Jamie is a bit crap at all of that, because despite being gorgeously gorgeous, he wasn't exactly Mr. Experience before Jules came along and swept him off his feet. He was far too busy building up his career, and yes, he had hundreds of admirers, but never the time to notice them.

Jules was different from all the women setting themselves

up to be the perfect barrister's wife. Jules didn't wear designer clothes. Jules didn't go to the hairdresser's or have a manicure once a week. Jules didn't care about going to the best restaurants or the ballet. And, more to the point, Jules never tried to pretend she was anyone different to try to trap her man.

No, Jules has always been one of those women that men go crazy about because she has enough self-confidence to say this is me, take it or leave it. And, invariably, they take it. Or at least try to. They love the fact that she doesn't wear makeup. That her clothes, on her tiny, petite frame, are a mishmash of whatever she happens to pull out of the wardrobe that morning. That her laugh is huge and infectious, and, most of all, that she listens. She loves life, and people, and makes time for them, and even before Jamie came along men were forever falling in love with her.

I've tried to be more like Jules, but, even though there are rare occasions when I feel I'm getting close, at the end of the day I just haven't got enough self-confidence to pull it off, and they bloody know it. So they start by falling madly in love with me—with the exception, it would seem, of Nick—and they end, about three weeks later, by disappearing when they realize that I'm actually a bundle of insecurities and not the woman they thought I was at all.

But anyway, enough about me, back to Jules and Jamie. Despite Jamie spending all his time tucked away in his study, their relationship does seem to work, and what I love about going out with the two of them is that we have fun. They have fun, and it's catching.

So Jamie comes out of his study and gives me a huge kiss as I stand by the kettle and then says, "Tea? Excellent. I need a break. So," he says, pulling a chair out from the kitchen table, "how's the love life?"

He always asks me this because he knows I'll have a story to tell, and, if I do say so myself, I tell my stories brilliantly. I tell them so they're sparkling, witty, amusing. I tell them so they capture people's attention and make them clutch their sides with laughter, shaking their heads and saying, "God, Libby, you are extraordinary." I tell them so people think I lead the most glamorous, exciting life in the world. Except, when I'm telling them one-on-one to Jules, I can be honest. I can tell her how lonely I am. How I spend my life wondering why I never seem to have healthy, happy relationships. How I probably wouldn't know a healthy, happy relationship if it jumped on my head and knocked me sideways.

And she listens to me quietly, and then thinks about it, and finally tells me why these men aren't right for me, and that one day someone will come along who will fall in love with me, and that the trick is to stop looking and that it will happen when I least expect it.

Which is all very well for her to say, and it's probably true, but how am I supposed to stop looking when it's the one thing I want more than anything else in the world? Well, other than winning the lottery, I suppose, but only because it would increase my pulling power a thousandfold. But seriously, I've never understood all that rubbish that married women tell you about not looking, because how can you not look when you're looking, and how can you really be happy on your own when you're not?

Sitting here in the kitchen with Jules and Jamie, I tell them my funny story about Nick, and about him performing a striptease in the living room, and about him sitting in my bath with a shower cap on, and they laugh, and I laugh with them, and Jamie shakes his head and says, "God, Libby, what would we do without you?" and I don't take offense, I just shrug my shoulders.

"So where are you two off to today?" he ventures, standing behind Jules and rubbing her shoulders in a gesture that's so affectionate I practically sigh with craving.

"Just up the high street," she says breezily, as he rolls his eyes to the ceiling.

"Oh, God. I know what that means. I'd better warn the bank manager."

"No, darling," she says, "we're not going for me, we're going for Libby. Except I might see something I like, in which case—"

"I know, I know," he laughs. "So, d'you want a lift up there or are you walking?"

Jules looks at me, the disgust already written on her face because she knows exactly how I feel about walking—if God had meant us to walk he wouldn't have invented cars—and I don't have to say anything, I just give her a pleading look and she sighs an exasperated sigh and says, "You're giving us a lift."

We jump into Jamie's BMW, and I do what I always do and insist on sitting in the front seat so I can pretend to be married to Jamie, and Jules does what she always does and prizes off her engagement ring for me to wear, and we drive up the road with my arm hanging out the window in case anyone I know should be passing, which naturally never seems to happen, and he drops us off by the station.

"Jules," he calls out the window, just before driving off, "can you get me some socks?"

She nods and turns to me with a sigh. "And who said it was glamorous being married to a barrister?"

We go to Whistles, Kookai and agnes b. We mooch round Waterstone's, Our Price and David Wainwright. We ooh and aah for hours in Nicole Farhi, and finally, in a tiny little sports shop tucked away at the top of the high street, I find exactly what I'm looking for.

"You're not seriously buying those," says Jules in horror, as I stand in the mirror with supertrendy Adidas sneakers on my feet.

"Why not?" I look innocent as hell, even though I know exactly what she's going to say.

"But they're not you!" she manages in dismay. "You're Miss aspiring Prada, Miss Gucci. You're not Miss Adidas."

"Look," I say to her slowly and seriously, trying to make her understand, "let me put it this way. I'm getting tired of being Patsy, so now I want to see what it's like to be Liam for a change."

"What are you talking about?"

"Patsy's always in Prada and Gucci, and Liam's in Adidas, so now I fancy a more casual look and these are exactly what I've been looking for."

"But what are you going to wear them with?"

"T-shirts and jeans."

"T-shirts and jeans!"

"Yes. T-shirts and jeans."

"But you haven't got any T-shirts and jeans."

"Yes I do, Jules. Don't be ridiculous. Thank you," I say, turning to the shop assistant with my most professional tone. "I'll take them."

Actually that whole Patsy, Liam stuff is a load of shit, and, although Jules probably would understand, probably in fact does understand, I can't be bothered to explain it to her right now. You see, it's not that I'm trying to change myself for Nick, God no. I mean, I hardly know the guy, it's just that these somehow seem more his style, and I can hardly go to his local Highgate pub in my designer togs, can I? These are much more appropriate, and anyway I've wanted a pair for ages. Honest. So, armed with my wonderful new sneakers (and what a bargain, 54.99!), we go for a cappuccino, and as we sit down I pull my mobile phone out of my bag and ring the answering service just in case it rang and I didn't hear it, but no, the recorded voice on the end says, "You have [pause] no [pause] new messages," and now I'm starting to get seriously pissed off, but Jules sees what I'm feeling before I've even started really feeling it and she says, "No. Stop it. He's going to phone," so I relax a bit, and it's fine.

Over coffee, Jules says, "Are you sure you're not going to get too involved?"

And I sweep her comment aside with a toss of my hair and laugh in a very grown-up, in-control sort of way and tell her she's being ridiculous, but meanwhile why the bloody hell hasn't he called? My mobile number's on my answering machine at home, and I could ring in to pick up my messages, except that if I do that I won't be able to press 1471 to find out who last called me, which is what I do automatically every time I walk in my flat, and he might be the sort of person who hates mobiles and hates leaving messages, so he might have phoned but not left a message, but Jesus Christ, Libby, SHUT UP. I'm doing my own head in.

"What makes you think I can't have a fling?" I say eventually. "You know, sex with no strings attached?"

"Because you can't," she says firmly.

"Now that's where you're wrong," I say. "I haven't done it for a while, but I've had loads of flings with men when I haven't been emotionally involved. It's just been sex. I've fancied them but I haven't liked them, or I've realized they're not for me."

Jules sits and thinks for a minute. "And when was the last time you did that?"

"About five years ago, but I could have done it loads of times since then."

"So why haven't you?"

"I just haven't."

"You don't think that perhaps we change between the ages of twenty-three and twenty-eight or -nine and that what was so easy for us when we're in our early twenties becomes almost impossible when we're nearing thirty, which is why we don't do it anymore?"

"What do you mean?"

"The reason women generally stop having flings, or sleeping around, or whatever you want to call it, is because they realize they can't do it, because the older they get the more they see you can't sleep with someone on a regular basis and not want more, not when you've reached an age where society, unfortunately, still tells you that you should be married and having babies."

"No." I shake my head. "I think you're either the sort of person who can or the sort of person who can't, and I'm the sort of person who can."

Jules doesn't say anything. She just looks at me.

"I am, you know," I insist.

And she keeps looking at me. And eventually I say, "For Christ's sake, stop looking at me," and she shrugs and changes the subject.

And eventually at five o'clock we wander back down the high street, which I don't mind in the slightest because it's downhill and even my disgustingly unfit body can cope with practically falling down a hill, and I jump in the car and drive home, and when I walk in there have been three messages, and, as I press PLAY, I'm praying, I'm seriously praying that Nick has phoned.

The first is from my mother. "Hello, Libby, it's me. Mum." As if I didn't bloody know.

"C'mon, c'mon," I urge her.

"Just calling up for a chat," she says, "and wondering whether you're coming for tea tomorrow. Call me later if you can, or otherwise in the morning, and if you're going out tonight have a nice time. If not, there's a really interesting documentary about magazines at nine o'clock tonight which I'll be watching with your father and—"

"Oh, shut up," I shout at the answering machine as she finishes. Anyway, what kind of sad git does she think I am, staying in on a Saturday night? Even if there's absolutely nothing to do I'll try to go out just so that I can tell people I went out. And yes, drinking coffee at Jules's kitchen table and watching *Blind Date* and *Stars in Their Eyes* does count as going out because I've left my house, and all I need to tell people is I went to some friends for dinner.

Message number two is from Joe Cooper, which always sends me into panic mode. Not that I don't like him, I adore Joe as much as, if not more, than when we first met, but every time I get a work-related phone call on the weekend I start having anxiety attacks, convinced that something has gone terribly and irrevocably wrong, but luckily this is just Joe asking for a phone number, and he ends the message by saying he'll try to get it from someone else.

Message number three is a silence. Then the phone's put down. Shit. I pick up and dial 1471.

"Telephone number 0.1.8.1.3.4.0.2.3 . . ." Yes! I don't bother listening to the end of the number because it's a Highgate number, and I don't know anyone else who lives in Highgate! Yes! He rang! And it gives me the burst of energy I need to run the bath so that I'll be ready whenever he calls again. Yes, I know I could call him, and I'm not playing hard to get, it's just that, having spent so many years chasing men, I now realize it's better not to call them. Ever. If you can possibly help it. And that includes calling them back. Except I'm not so good at that one.

And to make completely sure I don't give in to the urge to call him back I jump in the bath, and then, just as I've submerged my head under water, the phone rings and I jump up as if I've had an electric shock and go running into the living room, leaving a trail of sopping wet footprints. I pick it up and, trying to sound calm and collected and sexy as anything, say huskily, "Hello?"

"Libby?"

"Yes?"

"It's Nick."

Oh my God, I'm having a serious clothes crisis. The sneakers are great, better than great, perfect, but what the hell can I wear with them? I've tried the jeans and T-shirt, and it doesn't look quite right, and no, it's not that I'm that excited, but hell, I still want to look nice.

The bed is strewn with clothes, and eventually, right at the bottom of the wardrobe, I find a crumpled-up black T-shirt that I haven't seen for at least a year. I smell it tentatively, and okay, it's a bit musty, but I can spray perfume on it and iron it and yes! It's perfect. It hugs my body and sits perfectly around my waist, and with my black trousers it's just right. But hang on, even though I'm wearing sneakers all this black looks a bit imposing. Not fresh enough, not young enough. Shit.

An hour later I settle on a white T-shirt with a babe-type logo emblazoned across the chest, my oldest, most faded, most favorite 501s, and the beloved sneakers. I dig out some chunky silver earrings from the bottom of the papier-mâché box I use as a jewelry box and, what the hell, stick on some chunky silver rings as well. Perfect.

I'm meeting Nick at the Flask in Highgate, a pub I vaguely remember from my teenage years, and I know I'm going to be drinking so I leave the car at home and order a minicab, and just as I'm about to leave the phone rings.

"Hello, love, it's Mum."

As if I didn't know.

"What is it, Mum? I'm late and I'm going out."

"Oh, that's nice. Anywhere special?"

"I've got a date." Damn. I didn't mean to tell her. Now I'm going to get an onslaught of questions.

"How lovely!" she says, and I can almost hear her brain clicking into gear at the other end of the phone. "Anyone nice?"

Which I know will lead to what does he do, what car does he drive, where does he live, and, basically, is he good enough for our daughter.

This is the problem with having The Suburban Parents from Hell. Not that I don't love them, I do, it's just that they've got this thing about me marrying way, way above my station, and I try not to tell them anything about my life, except sometimes things have a habit of slipping out. "Yes, he's very nice," I sigh, "but I really have to go."

"Well," she stalls. "You young things. I don't know, always rushing around. Dad and I were wondering if you were coming round for tea tomorrow."

"Oh." I'd forgotten. "Okay," I sigh.

"Oh, lovely dear. I've got some of your favorite chocolate marzipan cake."

My mother thinks that my tastes are exactly the same as when I was six years old, and I don't bother telling her that these days I try to avoid chocolate marzipan cake like the plague, because it doesn't end up in my stomach, it ends up on my thighs.

"Okay, Mum. I'll see you about four?" I'm already mentally planning my day. A lazy breakfast in bed with Nick, perhaps a walk in Kenwood, and then a long kiss goodbye. Yup, if I time it perfectly I'll be able to make it to my parents in Finchley by four o'clock.

"All right, darling. What does your date do?"

"Look, Mum, I've got to go, the cab's here."

"He's not picking you up?" There's horror in her voice.

"No, Mum. I'll see you tomorrow. Bye," and I gently put the phone down with an exasperated sigh as the doorbell rings and the cab really does arrive.

Okay. Got everything? Clean knickers, toothbrush, makeup, moisturizer? Yup. My Prada bag's so full it's practically bursting, and I grab a jacket and run down the stairs.

And the closer we get to Highgate the more nervous I become. At Queen's Park I check my lipstick. At West End Lane I check I'm not shining. At Hampstead I flick my hair around a bit. At Kenwood I start tapping my feet and trying to ignore the driver staring at me in his rearview mirror.

"You are going somewhere nice?" he eventually says, in a thick Eastern European accent.

"Umm, yes," I say, because quite frankly I don't need to get into a conversation with my minicab driver and I don't like the way he's staring at me.

"You look nice," he says.

"Thank you," I say, in a tone of voice aimed to discourage him. It works. And then I feel guilty so when we pull up I give him a two pound tip and then I stand on the pavement for a bit, wondering what it's going to be like, and wondering where he is.

"Libby!" I look up, and there, sitting at a table outside in the large courtyard, is Nick, and as I walk over to him I feel all the tension disappear, because, after all, it's only Nick, and he looks gorgeous, he is gorgeous, and suddenly I'm beaming because everyone turned round to look at him when he shouted, and most of the women are still looking, and hey! He's with me! And then I'm standing in front of him, not sure what to do. Should I kiss him? Should I hug him? Should I just say hello? And then he leans forward and kisses me, aiming for my lips, and fool that I am I turn my head out of nervousness, so he just grazes the corner of my mouth, and he looks slightly surprised but then smiles and asks what I'd like to drink.

I can see that he's already halfway through a pint, and vodka and cranberry juice—my usual—would seem completely out of place, so I ask for half a lager and he seems pleased, and then he disappears inside to get it as I sit down and congratulate myself on such a good pull.

And he comes back grinning and puts the lager down in front of me, saying, "I'm surprised at you, Libby. I would have thought you were a spirits sort of girl."

And I pick up my lager and sip daintily, trying not to grimace, and say, "When in Rome . . ."

"Ah." He nods. "So you'd much rather be having a gin and tonic."

"Vodka and cranberry juice!" I say. "Please!" Because gin and tonics, delicious as they may be, always remind me of my parents, and it's the one drink that I never order because I absolutely know that that, more than anything else, will give away my background.

Nick laughs.

"So how has your week been?" he says, and I wonder whether to tell him about Amanda and the pictures she doesn't know she's going to be doing, and I do tell him because it's a good story, and he laughs and laughs, and I'm having a good time. In fact, I'm having a much better time than I thought I would be.

You see, the thing is that since the other night, the night I spent with Nick, every time I thought about him I thought about the sex. I never really thought about him as a person because sex objects don't need to have personalities, do they? But sitting here, in the early evening warmth, I'm surprised that Nick's so nice, so easy to be with, so laid-back.

And then Nick tells me about his week. He tells me that once again he did a mailshot, this time to eight publishers, sending them the first three chapters of his masterpiece, and that already he'd had one rejection letter saying interesting concept but "not for us."

"Would you ever consider going into another field?" I venture, wondering why he's bothering if he's no good at it.

"Nah." He shakes his head. "Well, maybe. If something interesting came along I suppose so, but this has always been my dream."

"But how do you live?"

"What d'you mean?"

"Where do you get money from?"

"Her Majesty's Government," he says proudly, and I blanch.

"You mean you're on the dole?"

"Yup."

"Oh." I'm speechless, and as I sit there wondering what to say next I think of how Jules would laugh. From Jon with his Mazda MX-5 to this. Oh dear. What the hell am I doing here?

"I don't mind," he says, laughing at my face. "Even though you, apparently, do."

"It's not that I mind," I say, and I decide not to tell him that I've never met anyone before who's on the dole. "It's just that it seems a shame to waste your talents."

"But I'm not wasting them. I'm waiting for them to be recognized."

"Oh," I say. "Well, that's okay, then."

"So," he says, after our fourth drink (I got two rounds, I'm not that stingy, particularly given that he's on the dole), "are you hungry?"

And I realize that I am. Starving.

"There's a really nice pizza place around the corner. I thought we could walk up there and have some dinner."

"Mmm." I nod my head vigorously. A little too vigorously, perhaps, because those lagers have gone straight to my head. "That sounds perfect." And we get up and start walking, and it's not round the corner, it's practically the other side of bloody London, and after about twenty minutes I say, "Nick, where is this place?"

"Nearly there," he says. "God, you're hopeless."

"I'm not," I say, and playfully slap him, and he turns to me and grabs me, saying, "Don't you slap me, young lady," and I giggle as he tells me my punishment is to kiss him, and I reach up and give him a quick peck on the lips, and he stands back and smacks his lips.

"Nope," he says. "That wasn't enough."

I give him another kiss, just slightly longer, and he stands there again and shakes his head, so I move over again, and this time he opens his eyes and looks at me as I'm kissing him, and before I know it, it's turned into a huge, delicious, yummy snog, and my stomach turns upside-down.

And it breaks the ice—the little there was left. I don't notice the last twenty minutes of the walk because we're holding hands and stopping every few minutes to kiss each other passionately, and we're giggling like teenagers and I've forgotten all about my hunger and my aching legs, and suddenly Nick turns to me and asks how my legs are.

"They're fine," I say, having stopped moaning about the walk the minute he kissed me.

"You don't want a piggyback?"

"You're crazy!" I laugh. "No, I don't want a piggyback," but before I know it he flings me over his shoulder in a fireman's lift and runs down the road, while I scream delightedly and bang his back to let me down, which is sort of what I want but only because I'm worrying that I'm too heavy, and then we're there, and you know what? I wish this walk could go on forever because I can't remember having had this much fun in ages.

And we have a tiny cozy table in one corner with a candle in a wax-covered bottle in the center, and everyone else in there looks exactly like Nick: young, trendy, struggling, but they're all smiling, and I wonder whether perhaps I could get used to this, this world away from the smart, posey bars and restaurants I'm used to, where the people seem to be more relaxed, unconcerned about dressing to impress, and whether Nick's way of life isn't so bad after all.

The waiter comes over to take our order, and he obviously knows Nick and there's much shaking of hands and "good to see you's," and then Nick tells him what he wants while I sit there thinking, you should have asked me first, and then I think it really doesn't matter, and I say that I'll have a pizza fiorentina and a side salad, and Nick orders a bottle of house red.

As soon as the waiter goes, Nick gets a slightly serious look on his face and sighs.

"What's wrong?" I ask.

There's a silence.

"Okay," he says finally. "Do you think it's time we should have that talk?"

Oh shit. Shit. Shit. Shit. I knew this was too good to be true. This is the time he tells me he doesn't want to see me again.

"Well," I say hesitantly. "I didn't think we had anything to talk about, but if there's something on your mind perhaps you'd better get it off your chest."

"Okay." He nods. And then he sighs. And then he doesn't say anything and I start feeling sick.

"Look," he says. "The thing is," and he stops and looks at me and then takes my hand over the table, but after about two seconds I pull away because I know I'm not going to like what he's about to say and I don't want to have my hand in his while he's saying it.

"Jesus," he says. "This is so difficult."

"For Christ's sake," I say, my nervousness giving my voice a loud, sharp edge, "will you just say it?"

"Okay." He nods. "The thing is, I'm not ready for a relationship."

I don't say anything. I don't need to. I've heard it all before.

"But"—and he looks up—"I really like being with you."

"So what are you saying?"

"I don't know." He sighs and shakes his head. "I think what I'm saying is that I need you to know that I'm not ready for commitment. I'm not really ready for a relationship. I've been single for a while, and I'm really enjoying it and I'm not ready to give that up."

"So is this it?"

"Well, no," he says. "Because I really like you and I want to keep seeing you, but I just don't want you to get the wrong idea."

"But, Nick, I'm not ready for a relationship either," I say, which is true. "I've been single for a while and I'm in exactly the same position." He looks relieved. "And I know that you're not The One, and I know I'm not The One for you, but that doesn't mean we shouldn't enjoy each other."

The relief on his face is spreading. I swear, I can practically see his shoulders relax.

"So you're okay with that?" he says.

"Absolutely." I nod firmly. "We like being with each other, we have lovely sex, so let's just relax and enjoy it for as long as it lasts."

"Libby," he says, reaching over the table and kissing me, "you're fantastic!"

And I blush and I think to myself, there. That wasn't so bad. And at least it will stop me from falling for him. Not that I would, you understand. It's just that now I definitely won't. There'd be no point.

And we have a lovely dinner. No, that's not actually quite true, because although I can't speak for Nick I know that I hardly noticed the food, I was far too busy kissing him over the table and holding his hand under the table, but it was lovely. The evening was lovely. He was lovely.

And you know the nicest thing about it? The nicest thing was to be with a man on a Saturday night. To pretend that we were a couple. To pretend that I'm as good as the rest of the women in here, that I've got a man too, that I'm not some sad, single, lonely woman out with the girls again on a Saturday night.

You probably think I'm mad. I know Jules thinks I'm mad, because there are advantages to being single. When you're busy and sociable and meeting men and going on dates, it's the best thing in the world and you wouldn't want it any other way. But, when all your single girlfriends suddenly seem to have boyfriends and you're the only one who's on your own, it's as miserable as sin. You phone your partners in crime and ask them if they'll go to a bar with you on a Saturday night, and they apologize profusely and say they're with Steve, or Pete, or Jake, but they can meet you for a coffee in the afternoon. If you're lucky they'll glide in on their own with huge smiles on their faces and sit and regale you with tales of how wonderful He is; and if you're unlucky they'll drag Him along so you're forced to make small talk with someone you don't know, as your friend gazes into His eyes, enraptured by every boring thing He comes out with, and you make a move as quickly as is decently possible.

And you spend Saturday nights on your own or, worse, at dinner parties they've organized when more often than not they've been let down by the creepy spare man they've invited for you, so it's three couples and you on your own and you spend the whole evening feeling like shit.

But tonight I'm one of them. I belong! And you know what? I love it.

We finish dinner and walk back to Nick's flat, because it's presumed that I'll be staying, even though neither of us has mentioned it, because what, after all, does "enjoy each other" mean, if not sex? And Nick leads me up a path to a tall, redbrick Victorian building, and there are slatted blinds on the window at the front. I can just about see through, and it doesn't look horrible, it looks lovely.

A light's been left on, and okay, it's not quite my taste, but I can see that it's nice, not the hellhole I expected at all. And I walk through the front door and, as Nick riffles through the envelopes on a table in the hall, I put my bag down by his front door and wait.

Nick looks up and starts laughing. "That's not mine," he says. "I'm upstairs."

"Oh," I say, flushing and picking up my bag. "Sorry."

And we go upstairs and he unlocks the door that really is his front door, and I walk straight into what I presume is the entire flat, and it's horrible.

Not that it's dirty, at least not on first sight, it's just that it's so messy, and untidy, and uncoordinated. There's an unmade futon at one end, which I presume doubles as a sofa when Nick can be bothered to make it, which he evidently didn't do this morning because the duvet's still crumpled up at the bottom, and there are piles of papers and magazines everywhere. And I mean everywhere. You can hardly walk and, as I pick my way across the room, I think that the piles of papers are probably preferable to the floor, because the few bits I can see are swirly orange and brown pub carpet, and I sit gingerly on an armchair that's obviously seen better days. Far, far better days. A long time ago.

The furniture all looks as if it's been picked up at junk shops, which it undoubtedly has, and it's falling apart, and shelves have been put up haphazardly everywhere, and there are so many books that they're stacked up instead of neatly lined up like in my flat, and it's a dump.

A bloody dump.

"Would you like some tea?" Nick says, disappearing into what must be the kitchen, and I get up to follow him in there but he comes back out and says, "Stay here. The kitchen's a mess. I'll bring it out to you," and I wonder what the hell the kitchen can be like, and decide that as long as I'm here I'm never setting foot in it.

"Sorry it's a mess," he says, bringing out the tea in two chipped mugs. "I meant to tidy it today but didn't have time."

"It's fine," I say, racking my brain to try to come up with a compliment. "It's exactly what a writer's flat should look like."

"You think?" he says, obviously chuffed.

"Definitely." I nod.

"It suits me," he says. "But I do need to clean it up a bit more often."

I keep quiet and sip my tea.

And then he comes and sits next to me and starts stroking my back, and I put my tea down and lean into him and after a few minutes forget about the flat, forget about the mess, forget about everything except the feeling of his hand on my back, and I turn around to kiss him, and, I suppose, one advantage of this place is that it only takes a second to move to the futon, and I don't even notice the state of the sheets because Nick's pulled my T-shirt up and he's undoing my bra and mmm. This is lovely.

And I unbutton my own jeans, furiously tugging them off, not wanting to waste a second, and then I watch as Nick unbuttons his, and I watch, mesmerized, as his cock stands straight out of his boxer shorts, and Nick watches me watching him stroke his cock, and then I lean forward and kiss the tip, and he groans, and I push him back so he's on his knees, and I open my lips and take the tip in my mouth, then the whole of the shaft, and he exhales very quickly.

After a while he whispers for me to stop or he'll come, and he pulls me up and our tongues mesh together with passion, and he strokes my breasts before moving one hand down, over my underpants, and it's my turn to exhale loudly, and he teases me for a while, and then he pulls the fabric aside and yes, that's it, his fingers stroking my clitoris, reaching inside me to make them wet, to help them slide, and with the other hand he circles my breasts until he reaches the nipples, and he pinches them and I moan and sink back on the bed.

And then all our clothes come off, and I can't take this anymore, I insist he put a condom on and enter me NOW, and he does and it's better, God, so much better than I remember, and as he moves in and out I suck his neck, and I wonder why it's never felt so good before, and then I stop wondering because Nick pulls me up to change position, and I look confused because why move when this feels so good, but he whispers, "You'll see," and he turns me around and enters me from behind, and as he does he moves one hand down to rub my clitoris at the same time, and suddenly I'm moaning in rhythm with him, and I feel the build-up and then I'm making these incredibly animalistic sounds as the most intense orgasm of my life sweeps over me.

And afterward I'm exhausted, and I do something I've never ever done before. I fall asleep in his arms.

Chapter 7

"So Libby dear," says my mother, pouring the tea out of her best china teapot. "How was last night?"

You know, it's an extraordinary thing but here I am, twenty-seven, independent, mature, sophisticated, yet the minute I step through my parents' front door I regress to being a surly teenager, and I feel the same exasperation at my parents' questions now as I did ten years ago.

"It was fine," I say, determined to be nice, not to let them get to me.

"And?" my mother says with a smile.

"And what?" I grunt, picking up the delicate teacup.

"And is he nice?"

"He's okay."

"If he's just okay why are you going out with him?" She trills with laughter, and pushes her hair behind her ears—a nervous habit I've unfortunately inherited.

"I'm not going out with him," I grunt. "We just went out last night."

God, I think, mentally raising my eyes to the ceiling. What would she say if I told her the truth? If I told her that yes, I went out with someone, and then we went back to his place and shagged each other senseless until we both fell asleep, and then in the morning had tea in bed (sorry, my romantic notions of breakfast in bed were slightly ambitious, given that the only things in Nick's fridge, he grudgingly admitted, were a six-pack of beer, a tub of butter and half a pack of bacon that was meant to have been eaten three months previously), then had sex again, and that I came straight here (again, we never managed that walk because Nick wanted to watch the football, so I amused myself reading back copies of *Loaded*).

"And what does he do?"

"He's a writer."

"Ooh, a writer. How exciting. What does he write?"

She may be irritating, but I can't tell her the truth. "He writes, er, he writes articles."

"What sort of articles?"

"For men's magazines."

"That's nice. He must be successful."

"Yes. Mum?" I've just thought of something to change the subject. "I thought you had chocolate marzipan cake."

"Oh, silly me," she says, standing up as I breathe a sigh of relief. "I completely forgot. It's in the kitchen." And she disappears while I catch Dad's eye and smile as he rolls his eyes to the ceiling.

And then Mum comes back out and says, "Does your young man have a name?"

"He's not my young man, and yes. His name's Nick."

"Nick," she repeats, thinking about it. "Nicholas. Oh, I do like the name Nicholas. Where does he live?"

"Highgate."

"Very posh," she says, and I think how she'd have heart failure if she saw his flat. "He must be doing well if he can afford to live in Highgate. Has he got one of those lovely big houses, then?"

"No, Mum," I sigh. "No one I know lives in big houses, you know that. We all have flats."

"Of course you do," she says. "So have you been there? Is it a nice flat?"

"Give her a break," says my dad, putting down the paper. "It's early days, isn't it, Libby?" and I nod, smiling at him with relief.

"I just worry about you," says Mum, smoothing down her

apron and sitting down. "When I was your age I was happily married and you were three years old. I don't understand all you girls. So independent."

"Yup. We're women of the nineties," I say. "And anyway I'm not bothered about getting married, I'm far too interested in my career."

God, if only that were true.

"So how is work?" says Dad, and, as usual, I dredge up all the work stories which fascinate them both, and I tell them about Amanda, expecting them to laugh, which my dad does, except he suppresses it pretty damn quickly when he sees my mother's expression.

"That's not very nice of you, Libby. Don't you think you ought to tell her?"

"Oh, Mum," I groan. "It'll be fine. She'd pose naked if she thought it would get her publicity."

"Well. You know best." She says it with raised eyebrows, meaning I don't know best and she disapproves.

"So how's Olly?" I ask finally, knowing that the only way to put her in a truly good mood is to ask about my beloved brother, the apple of her eye.

"Being a rascal as usual," she says. "Loving his job, and breaking all the girls' hearts, I shouldn't wonder."

Much as I hate to admit it, I adore my brother. Twenty-six years old, drop-dead gorgeous, he has me in fits of laughter whenever I see him, which isn't nearly as often as I'd like. He's the kind of person that everyone instantly adores, and although I sometimes feel I ought to be jealous of that, of his easygoing nature, I'm not, and the only time I get slightly pissed off with him is when he tells me to lay off Mum.

When we were children, though, I hated him. I hated him for always being clever, and sporty, and popular. For never putting a foot wrong, for so obviously being Mum's favorite. And then, when I left home to go to university, things suddenly changed, and on my first holiday at home he stopped being an annoying little brother and started being an equal.

It helped that he began smoking as well, and we'd both lock ourselves in my room and puff furiously out the window, spraying huge amounts of sickly sweet air freshener around when we finished. He was the first person to introduce me to spliff, showing me how to take a large Rizla and sprinkle it first with tobacco, then slightly burnt bits of hash, and roll it into a joint, suspiciously similar to a super-plus Tampax.

But naturally Mum never knew. She'd shout and scream at me for drinking or smoking or coming back late at night, but Olly could do no wrong, and the older I got the more we laughed about it together, and suddenly Olly was sticking up for me and telling Mum that I hadn't been drinking, or shagging, or whatever.

And she'd listen to Olly. She'd start off on a rant, and Olly would come in and say he'd bumped into me earlier and I'd been with Susie, and she must have got the wrong end of the stick, and she'd believe him!

We even talked about sharing a flat together for a while, but then I decided that, love him as I do, I couldn't put up with his mess, so I got the flat and he got the job in Manchester.

And he's happy. He loves it there. He rents a huge flat in Didsbury, works for a large TV company as a producer and hits all the clubs on the weekend. He doesn't have a serious girl-friend—relationship trouble must run in the family—but he has more than his fair share of flings. I call him every weekend, usually waking him from the depths of yet another killer hangover, and more often than not he has to call me back when the result of last night's session has put her makeup on and gone.

And he's the best person to sort out my love life, other than Jules. He's not as wise as Jules, but he's bloody good at giving the male perspective on things, and I've spent many hours on the phone to him working out strategies for catching the man of my dreams.

"How's his job?" I ask, because I've been a bit too caught up with my own life to call him recently.

"He's got a new program about food," she says proudly,

puffing out her chest with pride, because television producing is something she knows about. At least she should do, the amount of TV she watches. PR, as far as she's concerned, doesn't count. She can't boast about her daughter working in PR because she's never really understood what it's all about, even though I've tried to explain it a million times, and anyway she doesn't think I should be working. She thinks I should be at home cooking delicious meals for my husband, who's out making lots of money to keep me and my ten children in the style to which she'd like me to become accustomed. Anyone would think she was living in the bloody Dark Ages. But a television producer? That's something she understands, something she has tangible evidence of, and "my son the television producer"? It's become her catchphrase.

"Food?" I laugh. "But Olly doesn't know the first thing about food, unless it's about takeaway curries and hamburgers."

"It's called *The Gourmet Vegetarian*." Evidently she's decided to ignore my last comment.

"The Gourmet what?" Now this I really can't believe. "But Olly's your classic meat and two veg man."

"I know," she says, "and quite frankly I don't understand all this vegetarian nonsense, I'm convinced you all do it because it's fashionable, but there it is." And she looks at me pointedly while I glance away because any chance to get a dig in and she'll be there with a shovel.

Yes, okay, so? I was vegetarian once, for about eighteen months, and I could say that it was because of cruelty to animals, but actually it was because all my friends were doing it so I decided to do it too. And it was fine. I didn't even miss meat. But all that stuff about vegetarians being healthy is crap. Sure, it's true if you eat salads and nuts all the time, but me? I lived on bread, cheese, eggs and pastry, and I ballooned. I remember the first time I ate meat again, I was out with some friends, different ones, carnivores—and we'd gone to get Chinese takeaway and I stood in the shop, smelling all these delicious smells, and everyone was ordering sweet-and-sour pork and lemon chicken, and I stood there and thought, fuck it. If I have to eat stir-fried vegetables again I'm going to scream, so I didn't. I had barbecued pork spareribs. And it was delicious. And I never looked back.

But Olly making a program about gourmet anything is ridiculous. And I say so.

"He's already reading cookery books," says Mum proudly, "and you know Olly, he'll be an expert before you know it. I can't think why neither of you has inherited my cooking skills."

"I can cook!" I practically shout.

"Libby, dear, spag bol is hardly cooking."

"Excuse me, Mum, but, bearing in mind you've never eaten at my flat, how would you know whether I can cook or not?

"As it happens," I continue, on a bit of a roll now, "I'm an excellent cook."

"Are you?" she says, sounding bored. "So what's your best dish?"

Shit. I sit there trying to think of something and nope, the mind's gone blank.

"I can cook anything," I bluster.

"Yes, dear," she says, and that's it. I've had enough.

"I've got to go," I say, standing up and going over to my dad to kiss him goodbye.

"Off so soon?" he says, lowering the newspaper again.

"Yup. You know how it is. Things to do, people to see."

"But Libby," says Mum, "you've only been here five minutes."

More like a bloody hour, and whatever it is it's about an hour too long.

"Sorry, Mum. I'll speak to you in the week." And I dash out before she can start making me feel guilty.

I get in the minicab I called earlier and switch my mobile on immediately. Damn. No messages. But what was I expecting? That Nick would call and say he was missing me? Hardly. But then it starts to ring and Jules's number appears on the little screen and I pick up the phone.

"Where've you been?" she moans. "Your mobile's been off. I hate it when you do that."

"Sorry," I say, settling back into the car seat and lighting a fag before I look up and see my mum twitching at the curtains. "Shit. Hold on." I haven't even told the bloody driver where we're going. "Ladbroke Grove," I say to him, and I wave at my mum as we crawl down the street until I'm out of view, and then I put the phone back to my ear. Mobile phones, naturally, are yet another "modern appliance" my mother can't quite get to grips with.

"So?" she says.

"So?" I laugh.

"So how was it?"

"Amazing," I say. "It was so nice, he's so nice."

"And did you stay at his?"

"Yup. And we had fantastic sex again." I drop my voice to a whisper so the driver can't hear.

"And is his flat as disgusting as you thought?"

"Oh God, Jules," I groan. "Worse. Much, much worse."

"How so?"

"Just such a bloody mess. Honestly, Jules, it's a good job this is just a fling because I couldn't live like that. I don't know how he manages."

"Was it dirty?"

"No, although the sheets didn't exactly smell of Persil, but it was just grotty."

"Okay. The real test is the bathroom. Doesn't matter what the rest of the flat's like as long as they've got a decent bathroom."

Hmm. Interesting. "Actually, the bathroom was fine. Nice, in fact. And he lied about not having a bath!"

"No stains to be seen?"

"No. Sparkling clean."

"Thank God for that. I don't care if a man lives in a pit as long as he's clean."

"He's definitely clean," I say, remembering his lovely, clean, masculine smell.

"You're not in love, then?"

"God no! We ended up having a chat about things last night." I relay the conversation, word for word, touch for touch, to Jules, who listens carefully and then says the same bloody thing as yesterday.

"You're sure you can handle it?"

"Of course! Jules, listen, if I thought he was going to be serious I'd tell you, wouldn't I?"

"Hmm."

"But anyway, after that talk we both know exactly where we stand and it's fine."

"As long as you don't get hurt."

"Shut up, Jules, you know I hate that expression."

And it's true. I do. Why do people bother saying it, I mean what's the choice? You lock yourself away in an attic and never go out because you're frightened of getting hurt? Bollocks. As far as I'm concerned you have to give every relationship your all because if you're going to get hurt, you're going to get hurt, but at least at the end of it you'll know you gave it your best shot.

Although I'm not planning to give this relationship, or fling, or whatever this is, my all, at least not when we're out of the bedroom. No, this feels good. Healthy. I'm in control, and that's something I have very little experience of. Hell, I haven't even thought of Nick since I left him. Not much. Oh, okay, not as much as I've thought about boyfriends in the past, then. Happy now?

You probably think I'm lying, but it's true, because in the past I've thought about new boyfriends every second of every day. Well, almost. This is what I've never understood about men. No matter how crazy they are about you, they can get on with their lives, their work, their friends, and not give you a second thought. When they do think of you, which is generally when they're not thinking of anything else, they'll pick up the phone and call you, completely oblivious to the fact that you've been sitting there crying for a week because they haven't called.

Personally I think it's because men are crap at juggling. I'm not talking about juggling work and children and all that rubbish, but just doing more than one thing at once. Women can iron, watch TV, chat on the phone and answer the doorbell all at the same time, but men? Men can only do one thing at one time. Ever try chatting to a man when he's trying to park the car? Exactly. He'll ignore you because he can only concentrate on one thing at a time. So we get on with our lives while they take up space in our heads, rent-free, and they get on with their lives without giving us another thought.

And I'm not saying that our way is right. Jesus. The number of times I've wished I could stop thinking about someone and get on with work, but I can't. Once they're in your head, they're there for keeps until they either dump you or you manage to get over them. To be honest I find the whole process completely exhausting, and that's why, sitting in the car on the phone to Jules, I decide that I'm not going to do it this time. In fact, I'm fed up with talking about him, remembering him, analyzing him.

"Jules, I've got to go," I say.

"Why? Where are you going?"

"Home, but I've got to get into a bath and I'm in a minicab and I really can't talk."

"Okay. Will you call me later?"

"Yup. Are you in?"

"Yup."

And when I get home I jump in the bath, and as I lie there, soaking in lavender-scented bubbles, I remind myself that I'm not going to think about Nick, but then I think, a few thoughts wouldn't hurt, so I decide to allow myself three minutes of thinking about Nick and that's it, at least for today.

So once his three minutes are up I pick up a book and start reading, and every time Nick threatens to creep back into my head (which is about once every two pages) I push him out again until I'm so immersed in the book I genuinely don't think about him, and when Jules calls me later I'm in the middle of a good Sunday night film, which, I think you'll agree, is a perfectly valid reason not to talk to your best friend given that TV's normally shit on a Sunday night, and by the time I climb into bed I'm so tired I haven't got the energy to think about Nick even if I wanted to. Which I don't. Just in case you're wondering.

Chapter 8

Sal calls the next day about the interview, and because I'm still basking in that old postcoital glow and feeling more than a little magnanimous, I try Amanda Baker out on Sal.

"Amanda who?" she says, and I groan.

"You know, Sal," I say. "The showbiz reporter on *Breakfast Break*."

"As if I'm ever up early enough to watch *Breakfast Break*."

"She's the blond one, very stunning." I know already I'm on to a losing battle.

"Nope. Don't know."

"Oh. Well, I suppose you wouldn't be interested in doing a feature on her, then?"

"Come on, Libby, you know I can't write about someone nobody knows."

"Yeah," I sigh. "I know. Anyway, how's the big love of your life?"

And sure enough, her voice goes all dreamy. "He's wonderful," she says. "Really, Libby, this is completely different to all of the others."

"Which others?" I say, because truth to be told I've never heard Sal really talk about men before.

"Just all of them."

"How long is it since you had a relationship?" I ask curiously.

"Bloody years," she says. "Up until now I haven't really done relationships, I just seem to do flings. And generally with married men. Bastards."

And we both laugh.

"What are you doing after work?" she then says, and I can

tell from her voice that she's desperate to talk about Paul, to tell me every little detail about him, and even though I know I'll be bored, you never know, I might find something out about Nick, and I don't really have any plans unless you count watching *Brookside*.

We arrange to meet at the Paradise Bar, equidistant to work and home, and I say I'll see her there at 7 P.M.

And I get a hell of a lot of work done that afternoon. I sit there phone-bashing, and I manage to persuade two journalists to write about Rita Roberts, as well as organizing the launch for Sean Moore's series. All in all, a good day's work, and the best thing about it is I hardly think about Nick at all, except to congratulate myself that I've hardly thought about him at all, if you know what I mean.

And I'm looking forward to seeing Sal. She may not be someone I see that much, but I always have a good time when I'm with her, there seems to be so much to talk about—maybe that's because we lead such separate lives, there's an awful lot to fill each other in on.

I'm really happy that she's found Paul. I've always thought that Sal would make a perfect wife and mother, because, even though she's only a year older than me, there's something incredibly warm and maternal about her, and I've never understood why she's been single for so long. She never seems to have problems attracting men, but they always run off soon afterward, perhaps that whole maternal stuff scares them a bit. But Sal, more than anyone else, needs to be in a relationship. She makes her own bloody marmalade, for God's sake, how could anyone resist that?

She's there when I arrive at the Paradise, sitting in a corner table at one side of the bar, and she gives me a huge hug and kiss on the cheek when I walk over.

"I'm completely starving," she says. "Shall we reserve a table for later in the restaurant?"

"Fine," I say, "I'll do it," because I'm already standing up, and as I walk off she calls me back.

"Ask for a table for three," she says. "Nick's going to join us later, is that okay?"

"Oh," I say, slightly flummoxed, because I don't know whether Sal knows about us, and why didn't he call me, and am I excited about seeing him or am I nervous and should I tell Sal and how should I act when he arrives, but fuck it, Nick's coming!

I get a drink on the way back to the table and sit down, one eye on the door to see Nick when he comes, and Sal starts telling me all about Paul.

"He's just so thoughtful," she says. "He keeps buying me these little presents." And she holds out her arm to show off a beautiful silver charm bracelet. I make the appropriate oohing and aahing noises, and though I'm listening to her, I'm suddenly desperate to talk about Nick, to tell her about him, but somehow I don't quite know how to do it.

"So do you think he's The One?" I say, which is a question I always ask my girlfriends when they start going out with someone, not so much because I want to know the answer, but more because I want to know how they know, and whether I'll know too. Jules says I'm an idealist, that I have this ridiculously romantic notion of being swept off my feet and knowing instantly when I meet the man I'm going to marry, and I suppose she's right. Maybe because I've never really had long relationships, I've always thought that it would happen really quickly, that I'd meet someone, we'd fall in love, and we'd probably both know by the end of our first evening that this was It. I'm not sure how I'd know, but I'm convinced I would. The only problem with that is, as Jules keeps pointing out, I think I know with all of them.

Every time I meet someone new I ring Jules and tell her that this time it's different, this time they're different, and though I still think it I try not to tell her anymore because she just starts laughing and says that she's got a very strong sense of déjà vu.

And as far as Jules is concerned, you don't necessarily know when you meet the man you're going to marry. She's the only person I know who says this. Everyone else I've spoken to—and believe me, I've done my research here—says they knew. Jules hated Jamie on their first date. I remember it clearly. She met him at a party and in her drunken stupor gave him her number and promptly forgot all about him. He phoned two weeks later (two weeks! Can you imagine if she'd fancied him and had to wait two weeks!), and she didn't have a clue who he was. When he told her where they'd met, she still couldn't remember him, but she agreed to go out for dinner with him just to see whether she had met him before.

And even then she didn't remember him, which she was bloody surprised about because he was so gorgeous she was convinced she wouldn't forget a face like that. But being gorgeous does not necessarily mean you're nice, and Jamie (I've heard his side of the story now, so I've got the whole picture) was so nervous he behaved like a total idiot. He spent the whole evening talking about himself, and drank so much he ended up with his face in a plate of passion fruit sorbet. Jules was disgusted. She walked out, and refused to take his calls or accept an apology.

It was only when he turned up at her office with a huge bouquet of flowers and a very sheepish look on his face that she decided to give him a second chance, but she never, for a second, thought she'd marry him.

And that's why this whole thing with Nick is so refreshing, because I know, beyond a shadow of a doubt, that he isn't It, and normally I wouldn't bother getting involved with someone unless there was potential there, but I just need some fun right now.

"I really think he might be." Sal answers my question. "And I've never felt that about anyone before."

"Really?" This is so alien to my own experience, I'm fascinated. "You've never thought that you'd marry someone before?"

"God, no!" she laughs. "And if you'd met them you'd see

why. Nah, even the short relationships I had in my early twenties were with self-obsessed assholes. That's the difference, I've never been treated well before, and before I met Paul I didn't even know what that could be like. I think the reason this is so different is because we were friends for so long, and I never even thought about Paul as anything other than as a good mate."

"So how did it happen?"

"I hadn't seen him for a while, and then he phoned me for a contact for a story he was doing, and we arranged to meet up for a drink. I hardly bothered making an effort, I mean it was Paul, for heaven's sake, and then, when we met, we had the most brilliant evening and suddenly at the end there was all this weird chemistry, which blew my mind a bit."

"Did you sleep with him?"

Sal starts laughing. "You're joking! I didn't even kiss him, even though I wanted to, and I could tell he wanted to as well, but I found the whole thing really confusing."

"So what happened then?"

"He called me the next day to thank me for a really lovely evening, which, in itself, was weird, because in the past it had always been me phoning them to thank them for a lovely evening, which was actually just an excuse to phone them. And then he asked me out again, and that night something did happen, and that was that, really.

"And the weirdest thing of all is that it feels so right. I suppose it's true what they say, you never know it's right until it is, although I'm really scared of saying that out loud just in case he turns out to be a bastard, but somehow I don't think he will."

"And you know what?" she continues, as I shake my head. "I've never had anyone who looks after me before, and that's what I love. In the past I've always been the one cooking for them, cleaning for them, probably doing way too much for them, whereas Paul's the one who wants to do everything for me."

"And do you love it?" I say, and grin wickedly.

Sal grins back. "I love it. So anyway, Libby, enough about me. What about you, you've always got this fantastically tempestuous love life. Who's the latest?"

"Well, actually," I'm just about to tell her, when I see the door open and Nick walks in. Sal sees me looking over her shoulder and turns round.

"Nick!" She stands up and waves, and he comes over to join us.

"My favorite redhead," he says, giving her a big hug as I sit there feeling incredibly awkward and wondering what the hell I should say. And then he looks at me and I can already feel the first stirrings of lust in my groin and he grins and says, "My favorite brunette." And he puts his arms round me and gives me a hug too, and then he goes off to the bar to get a fresh round.

"You don't mind me asking Nick, do you?" Sal whispers once he's gone. "It's just that we were on the phone this morning and I told him I was seeing you, and when he asked if he could join us I couldn't really say no."

I feel like jumping in the air with joy.

"That's fine," I say. "No problem."

"It's really weird," she whispers. "I used to fancy him so much, but I don't even think he's good-looking anymore, that must mean I'm in love."

"Yup," I say, because I can't think of anything else to say and thank God Nick chooses that moment to pull up a chair and sit down.

"So," says Sal. "We were just talking about Libby's love life."

"Oh, yes?" says Nick, visibly perking up. "What were you saying?"

"She was just going to fill me in on her latest man, and before you say anything I know you've got one, it's written all over your face. Yup, you're in love."

Oh fuck. I can't help it. I feel a bright red, hot flush spread up from my neck until my cheeks are flaming red.

"Now I know you're in love," she laughs, as I think, shut the fuck up.

"Now this"—Nick grins—"I've got to hear."

"I'm not in love," I say forcefully. "Definitely not."

"Go on," says Nick, shoving me gently and playing completely dumb. "Tell us. You know you want to."

"Nick's brilliant at sorting out people's love lives, aren't you, Nick?" says Sal, who, at this precise moment in time, only seems to be opening her mouth to shove her foot further in.

Nick just nods, but he's grinning, and I know he's enjoying this.

"So come on, Libby, it's not like you to be reticent."

"Sal, I haven't got anything to talk about."

"I don't believe you," says Nick, as I kick him under the table.

"Ouch," says Sal. "What was that for?"

"Oh God, sorry," I say, as Nick rocks back in his chair and starts roaring with laughter.

"What is going on?" Sal's now looking confused.

"Classic," groans Nick. "Okay. Sorry. It's just that Libby and I . . ." And he stops.

Go on, I think. What are we? Are we going out? Are we seeing each other? Are we sleeping together? What?

"Libby and I . . ." he repeats, and stops again.

"Libby and you what?" says Sal, who I'm convinced knows exactly what he's trying to say, she's just getting her revenge.

"You know, we're—" And he tilts his head and raises his eyebrows.

"No," she says. "You're what?" And then she can't help it, she starts laughing. "Oh my God," she says. "I feel like a total idiot."

"It's okay," I say. "I should have said something."

"Yes, you bloody should have," she says. "Why didn't you?"

"I didn't know how to," I say, but in truth I didn't really want to.

"So you really did get on the other night?" she says with a smile.

"Very well," drawls Nick, putting his arm round me and giving me a smacker on the cheek.

"Oh no. Don't start getting all lovey-dovey on me."

"Sorry," says Nick, drawing away. "I just can't seem to keep my hands off her."

I sit there and smile. And smile. And smile.

And the waitress comes over to tell us there's a table waiting for us in the restaurant, so the three of us get up and walk in. Sal goes first, then me and Nick, and Nick grabs my waist as we're walking in and nuzzles my neck, whispering, "You look gorgeous tonight," and I smile broadly and go to sit down.

And we turn out to have a really nice evening. I like being with Nick and Sal. I like this feeling of Nick getting on with my friends, even though Sal is as much his friend as mine, possibly even more so. And more than that I like the fact that he spends most of the evening holding my hand under the table, and that he finds everything I say absolutely fascinating, even when it's not, and that he's making me feel like the most special woman in here.

We talk a bit about work, and then about people we know, and then we start sharing stories. We start with drinking stories—who can outdo the others with tales of being the most drunk, and naturally Nick wins that one. Then we do drinking and driving stories, which progresses into police stories, which forces me to reveal that once upon a time I met a guy who asked me out and then turned up at my parents' house in full police uniform—I think I win that one.

We move from there to dates from hell. Sal has us screaming with laughter when she tells us about the time she answered a Lonely Hearts ad, and they swapped photographs and the moment she set eyes on his 6' 2" hunky frame she decided she was in love, and then they met and he was 5' 2", fat and bald.

"I think he thought I wouldn't notice," she splutters, as Nick and I separately think of stories to beat it.

Nick has a superb stalking story. A statuesque blonde (she

bloody would be, wouldn't she) he picked up in a bar. He took her out a few times then decided she really wasn't very interesting, in fact, she was probably the prototype for your standard dumb blonde model, and he dumped her. She then bombarded him with phone calls, appeared at his flat every day, wrote him letters in which she told him of their wedding day plans, and eventually turned up with a kitchen knife saying if she couldn't have him, no one could.

Sal and I sit there openmouthed.

"That's terrible!" I say. "What the hell did you do?"

"I tried to wrestle the gun off her but I couldn't, and eventually a policeman showed up, and she held him hostage as well. He ended up getting shot, and the house was surrounded. She was put in a mental institution." He nods his head sadly.

"Hang on," I say. "You said she had a knife, not a gun."

"Did I? Oh shit." He shrugs. "You've got to admit, it was a good story, though."

"You mean you made it up?" Sal's confused.

"Not exactly," he said. "It did happen. It just happened to Mick in Brookside."

"Oh Nick," I say, as I start laughing. "You're hopeless."

And when we've finished our coffees and Sal starts yawning, we get the bill and leave, and I don't bother saying anything to Nick about him staying the night because both of us know he's going to, and when Sal asks Nick if he wants a lift to the tube he just says no, and Sal gets all embarrassed again.

So we say goodbye and go back to my flat, and when I walk in there's a slight moment of awkwardness when Nick notices the flashing red light on my answering machine that tells me there've been four messages.

I could listen to them now, but I don't, and before you get the wrong idea it's not because there may be other men who are calling me, it's because of Jules. I know what Jules is like. She's probably left a message saying, "Where are you? I hope you're not out shagging," or "Hope you're managing to walk properly after last night," or "How's the big love of your life going?", and I would die, just die, if Nick heard that.

"You've got messages," he says, sitting down.

"Yeah," I say nonchalantly. "Probably my mum or Jules. Anyway, whoever it is it's too late to call them. I'll listen to them tomorrow."

He jumps up and starts kissing my neck. "Not calls from tall dark handsome strangers, I hope?"

"As if!" I laugh, and then I get quite serious. "Nick," I say, and he can tell from the tone of my voice that I have something to say, so he pulls back and says, "Uh-oh, have I been a naughty boy? I've done something wrong haven't I? What have I done?"

"No," I laugh. "It's just that I want you to know that while I'm sleeping with you I wouldn't sleep with anyone else."

He nods seriously, taking it in. "I accept that," he says, "and I feel the same way. I know this isn't serious between us, but I agree that as long as we're sleeping together we won't be sleeping with anyone else. And the only thing I'd add to that is that if either of us is tempted, or meets someone else, we'll talk about it, be honest with each other."

"Perfect," I say, as I kiss him, but even as I say the word I'm hoping that he doesn't ever tell me that, that if anyone meets someone else, or is, as he put it, "tempted," it's me. I don't think that's too much to ask.

How can I turn down Jules's invitation to a dinner party, when Nick's sitting next to me in my flat, and can hear every word? And I can tell he can hear because he's grinning like an idiot and nodding, and it's not that I don't want to go, it's that I'm really not sure how Nick will fit in with my friends, not after meeting his the other night.

Although it has to be said that my friends would be a damn sight more welcoming than his were. Jesus, I felt like I'd been put through the mill, and I didn't come out well, which was hardly my fault.

It was, to put it nicely, a bloody nightmare. Not my cup of tea at all. I thought it was going to be just Nick and I, and then, when we met, he said he'd arranged to meet some friends of his and did I mind, and I lied and said that no, it was fine. And part of me was curious about his friends, because, even though I know Sal, I don't know any of the others, and I wanted to know who they were, what they were like.

We joined them in a pub (surprise, surbloodyprise), and from the minute we turned up I knew, from the look of the pub, that this wasn't going to be my sort of evening, because there are pubs, and there are pubs. You don't know what I'm talking about? Okay. I don't like pubs, I think I already told you that, but on the rare occasions I do go to them, I like pubs that are either like country pubs in the middle of London (the Clifton springs to mind), pubs that are trying to be something else (the Lansdowne, which is more of a restaurant now), or pubs that have been completely redone and are clean, bright and smart (the Queens).

Pubs I never set foot in are real pubs. The old-fashioned variety. Dark, dingy, smoky places with bottle-blond barmaids and dodgy customers doing deals at the bar. I could mention some names, but I wouldn't want any contracts taken out on my life, and the kind of people who go to these pubs would know exactly how to deal with that sort of thing.

And this was that sort of pub, except it was even darker, dingier and smokier than the nasty pubs of my imagination, and through the haze of smoke I could see a group of people at one end—all of them stopped talking when we walked in, and they waved to Nick before giving me the once-over.

As far as I was concerned, I'd dressed down for the occasion, in my uniform of sneakers, jeans and sloppy sweater. And okay, so the sweater did come from Nicole Farhi, but so what? That's casual for me. And yes, I was wearing jewelry, but it was silver, and so what if it came from Dinny Hall? Surely only those in the know would recognize that.

These women may not have been in the know, but one look at me, one look at them, and you could see, instantly, we weren't going to get on. All the people crowded round the tiny table in the pub looked like overgrown students. Big time. At least, I thought sniffily, checking them out in much the same way they were checking me out, at least my jeans are clean. Not one of the women was wearing makeup, and even though I wasn't wearing much—well, maybe a bit, but applied so it looked as if I was hardly wearing any—I could see them linger on my lipstick, and I felt like running and hiding.

And the clothes! God, the clothes. The women looked like Identikit socialists—dirty jeans, DMs and loose, shapeless sweaters with holes in them, and yes, I'm serious, even a couple of stains here and there. And, thinking about it, the men were wearing pretty much the same thing.

Oh Christ, I thought, walking up, I know I'm going to hate them, but I decided I was going to be charming and polite and make them like me, because, after all, they're Nick's friends, and I had to make an effort.

"This is Joanna," said Nick, as a dirty blonde scowled at me.

"How do you do," I said, holding out my arm to shake her hand. She looked at her neighbor in amazement, and hesitated with a smirk on her face before finally putting an incredibly limp hand in mine and sort of moving it vaguely, then pulling away.

"This is Pete," and I did the same thing, except Pete didn't bother taking my hand, he just looked up from his pint and said, "Awright?"

"Yes, thank you," I said. "How are you?"

He didn't say anything. Just smirked.

"Rog, Sam, Chris, Moose."

"I'm sorry?"

"That's my name," said Moose. "Awright?"

Nick went off to the bar to get a fresh round of drinks, and I noticed, with more than a hint of distaste, that all the women were drinking pints, but that didn't mean I had to. No fucking way.

So I stood there awkwardly, waiting for one of the men to offer me a stool, but no one did, they just carried on talking about Tony Blair and "New Labour bastards," and I stood like an idiot, wishing I were anywhere else but here.

And eventually I went to the table next to them and asked if I could take a stool, and they nodded, so I perched next to Joanna and tried to be friendly.

"I love your sweater," I lied, thinking that the best way of making friends is to offer so many compliments they can't possibly dislike you. "Where did you get it?"

"Camden Lock," she said, before turning away in disgust.

"So you're Libby," said Rog, as I breathed a sigh of relief that someone was actually going to talk to me, to be nice to me. "We've 'eard a lot about you."

"Oh," I said, smiling politely. "Nice things, I hope?"

He shrugged.

"What do you do, Rog?" I ventured, careful to fit his name in the sentence because I read somewhere that when you use people's names a lot it always makes them warm to you.

He looked at me for a few seconds, then shrugged. "Nothing."

"Oh." I didn't quite know what to say next. "Well," I carried on, "what would you like to do?"

He shrugged again. "Nothing."

"You're a bloody liar," said Joanna, and she turned to me. "He's an artist."

"Really?" I said. "What do you paint?"

"Abstract." Jesus, this is a losing battle.

"You work in PR, don't you?" said Chris, not the male variety, the female variety.

I nodded gratefully.

"Don't you think it's a complete waste of time?" she asked aggressively. "I mean, you're not exactly helping anyone, are you, just pandering to these stupid fucking celebrities."

"Actually, I quite enjoy it." I bristled. "Why, what do you do?"

"I work for Greenpeace," she said. "I couldn't stand a job like yours. At least with mine I know I'm making a difference to the world."

"Why, have you been out rescuing whales?" I asked innocently.

She huffed. "Not personally, but I have organized it."

There was a silence as everyone looked into their drinks, but I'm sure I saw Chris look at Pete and raise her eyebrows, and I sat there miserably knowing that look was about me.

"Do you live locally?" said Joanna, the only one in the crowd who seemed to be okay. Note that I wouldn't go as far as saying nice, just okay.

I shook my head. "I live in Ladbroke Grove."

"Really?" she said. "I've got friends there. They've got this fantastic Housing Association flat, huge. Do you rent or what?"

"No, I bought it," I said proudly.

"Oh," she said. "How did you afford that?"

"I saved for ages for the down payment," I lied, knowing that if I told the truth, that my parents had helped me, they'd probably all start hissing and spitting.

"You must be loaded," she said, and the others all looked at me, waiting to hear what I was going to say.

"Hardly." I tried to laugh. "I just try to be careful with money."

"I wish I had enough money to be careful with," she said.

"Do you work?"

"Nah." She shook her head. "I'm on the dole."

And I was stuck, because I wasn't going to make the same mistake of asking what she would be doing if she wasn't on the dole.

"So," said Moose finally. "We were talking about New Labour. What do you reckon about them?"

"I think they're all a bunch of untrustworthy bastards," I said firmly.

"Do you?" said Moose. "Even Blair?"

Oh shit. What do I say now? I think Tony Blair's pretty damn nice, but somehow I suspected that wasn't the thing to say.

"Especially Blair," I said, and thank God, they started nodding, and I felt like I'd passed some sort of test. Except unfortunately I didn't pass it for very long, and I sat there quietly as they all started talking politics, praying they weren't going to ask me for another opinion.

Nick came back, put his arm round me and whispered, "Sorry, I had to wait for ages at the bar. Are you okay?"

What was I going to say? That I found his friends disgusting? That they were rude and nasty? That I'd rather be sitting at home watching paint dry than sitting in this revolting pub with these revolting people? I didn't have the nerve to say anything, so I just nodded, and Nick thought I was okay, and so we ended up staying, and I didn't say another word all night, which was really all right, because everyone ignored me anyway. Nick kept trying to bring me into the conversation, but it was too political for me anyway, so I sat there wondering what the fuck I was doing there.

And every time Nick asked me if I was okay, I said yes, even though I quite obviously wasn't because I was so quiet. That's the thing, you see. People think I'm hugely confident because when I'm with people I know, or people I feel comfortable with, I'm absolutely fine, but put me in a crowd of people like this, people who are hostile and unfriendly, and I just clam up.

Eventually, at around ten o'clock, I couldn't stand it anymore.

"Nick," I whispered. "I've got a bit of a headache. Do you mind if we go?" Nick looked at me in surprise, because he'd been taking center stage and was obviously having a great time.

"Sure," he said. "Why didn't you say something before?"

"I thought it might go away," I lied. I stood up. "Nice to meet you all," I lied again, and as soon as we were outside I breathed a huge sigh of relief.

"You hated them, didn't you?" said Nick.

"I'm really sorry," I said. "I'm sure they're really nice people, but they weren't exactly friendly to me, and I didn't feel comfortable at all."

"God, I'm sorry, Libby," he said, and put his arms around me. "I'm so stupid. I just kind of assume that everyone I like will get on, and I know they can be a bit funny with strangers, but I didn't expect them to be that bad. We should have left ages ago."

"Don't worry." I snuggled into his shoulder as we walked off down the road. "Can we stay at mine tonight?"

Nick nodded, and I didn't feel the need to explain that after feeling so bloody insecure all evening I needed to be at home, I needed to be surrounded by my things, in my bed, feeling safe and comfortable and secure.

And that's when Jules phones.

"Hey, babe," she says. "Jamie and I are having people over for dinner next week, so do you want to bring the infamous Nick?"

Oh God. Nick with a bunch of barristers would be as awkward as me with a bunch of hard-line socialists. I'm about to say no, but Nick starts nodding vigorously because Jules is speaking so loud he can hear every word.

"He's sitting next to me," I warn. "And he's nodding, so I guess that's a yes."

"Wednesday night, eight-thirty, casual."

"Okay," I say, as Nick beams, thrilled at the chance of meeting my friends.

"So I finally get to meet Jules," he says, when I've put down the phone. "What's she like? What's Jamie like? Who are their friends?"

And I start laughing because he always makes me laugh, and then he starts tickling me, the bastard, and I scream for him to stop even though by this time I'm more or less hysterical with laughter, and luckily he does stop because a few more seconds and I'd have wet myself, and then he gets all soppy and serious and we start kissing, and I've never made love on a sofa before but it's lovely, and I forgive him for such a shitty evening and for having such shitty friends. In fact, right now, I think I'd forgive him pretty much anything.

Casual, Jules said, which could mean anything, but I know what it doesn't mean is jeans and sneakers. Nick's never seen me dressed up and I don't know what he'll think, and, although I know I look good in smarter clothes, I don't want him to think that we come from two different worlds, therefore what would be the point in carrying on. Even though it's true.

I still know there's no future in this, but, and I feel sick admitting it, I also know that I'm starting to think about him a hell of a lot more than I used to, and I also know that I'm starting to look forward to seeing him a hell of a lot more than I used to, and I know, or at least, I think, that there's a very strong possibility that I may be slightly out of my depth here.

But I'm an adult, I can handle this, and so what if I'm starting to like him a little bit more than I'd planned, what does that mean? That I should end it because I like him? No. Exactly. I'll just carry on and maybe this is just a phase, maybe in a little while I'll go back to how I was—cool, calm, collected, free.

And I know I hated his friends, but I'm nervous as shit of him meeting mine because I so badly want him to like them, want them to like him. I suppose what I really want is approval all round, but then how could they not like him, when he's so natural, and funny, and sweet? Oh God. We'll just have to see.

. . .

So here I am, in my bedroom, and I've arranged to pick Nick up at the tube station, and there are clothes everywhere, and bearing in mind I've completely changed my look since meeting Nick, I don't know what goes with what anymore, and though I want to look smart-ish, I don't want to look middle-aged smart, if you know what I mean. I want to look smart, cool and trendy, and finally I think I've got it.

A camel-colored print dress, hip-hugging, almost see-through, with very high Prada strappy sandals, and I'm not sure about the shoes, they might be a bit over the top, but they make me feel beautiful and the one thing I need tonight more than anything else is a shot of confidence.

I put my makeup on carefully, only a tiny bit, just to accentuate my eyes, my lips, and when I'm ready I stand back, and I know it sounds bigheaded, but God, I look amazing, I'd forgotten I could look like this, and never mind the fact that I can hardly walk in these bloody shoes, I look beautiful.

"Goodbye, Liam," I shout triumphantly as I pick up my bag and run out of the flat, "hello, Patsy," and I climb into the car to go and pick up Nick.

And bless him, he's made an effort. He's not wearing his usual uniform of jeans and sneakers, he's wearing chinos and brown lace-up shoes and a soft blue shirt that completely brings out the color of his eyes, and he looks gorgeous, and God, what a difference clothes can make, because I suddenly fancy him more than ever before.

"You look amazing," I say, as soon as he gets in. "Where are all these clothes from?" And I practically fall out of the car with shock when I notice that not only is his shirt beautiful, it's got a very familiar polo player on the left-hand side.

"That's not Ralph Lauren!" I say, when I've finally recovered, and I know that sounds like a stupid question because it's quite obviously the Ralph Lauren symbol, but this must be a fake if Nick's wearing it.

"Yes," he says, "it is. So?"

"So where did you get it?"

"My mother bought me all these clothes last year, but I never wear them."

"I know," I laugh. "I've never seen you in them, but, Nick, you look gorgeous."

He also looks very uncomfortable. Jesus, I would marry Nick if he looked like this all the time. Well, no, I probably wouldn't. Don't get too excited, it's just a figure of speech.

And then he looks at me, and does a very slow and very sexy wolf whistle.

"Christ," he says, taking in the outfit. "You look unbeliev-able."

"Unbelievable good or unbelievable bad?"

"Unbelievable sexy," he says, shaking his head in disbelief, as my head threatens to swell so much it won't fit in the car. "Why don't we not go, and I'll take you home and ravish you in-stead."

And I laugh, but as I look at him I see he half means it.

"You're nervous!" I'm amazed.

"No, I'm not," he says. A little too quickly.

"You are. Nick, why are you nervous?"

"I'm not." And then he pauses. "Okay. Maybe a bit."

"Why?"

"It's the first time I'll be meeting your friends, and Jules is your best friend, and I want to make a good impression."

He is so sweet.

"You are so sweet."

"Don't say I'm sweet," he growls. "I hate that."

"Sorry," I say, and reach over and give him a kiss. "But you are."

Chapter 10

"I thought you said you were having people over for dinner," I say, pulling Jules aside and whispering to her furiously. "You didn't tell me you were having a bloody party."

"You know how it is," she laughs. "It was meant to be six of us, and then we invited a couple more, and then someone else phoned and asked if they could bring someone, so before we knew it there were sixteen people. Anyway, what's the problem?"

"Nothing," I mutter, and there isn't really a problem, I just wasn't prepared for this, and somehow I thought it would be easier to introduce Nick at a dinner party, more intimate, less pressure, but I suppose, thinking about it, perhaps this is better.

"So where is he?" she says, looking around the room.

"Nick!" I call out to where Nick's already chatting to Jamie. "Come and meet Jules."

Jamie's smiling, so I assume whatever it is they were talking about went well, and he comes over with Nick to kiss me hello.

"Jules, Nick. Nick, Jules." Nick holds his hand out very formally, and I have to stifle a laugh because this is not Nick's way at all, but Jules being Jules just laughs and gives him a kiss on the cheek. "Welcome to our party," she says. "It's so nice to finally meet you."

"And you," says Nick, relaxing. "I've heard so much about you."

"Not half as much," she says, winking at me, "as I've heard about you."

"I've heard about Tom," he says, scooping up the gray

Persian kitten who's winding his way around Nick's legs. "Hello," he says to Tom, stroking him under the chin as he starts purring like an engine. "You're gorgeous, aren't you?"

"Well, Nick," says Jules, "you're in. Any man who likes cats is all right by me."

"I've got two at home with my parents," he says. "I miss them desperately but it wouldn't be fair to have them here, I haven't got a garden."

I look at Nick in surprise, because he never struck me as a cat sort of bloke, but I think what surprises me most is how he keeps surprising me. First the clothes that his mother bought him, and now the cats. And what's more, how come his mother has such good taste? On the rare occasions my mother buys me clothes—generally when they've been on holiday—they're disgusting. Huge voluminous T-shirts saying things like, "My mum went to Majorca and all I got was this lousy T-shirt." I've got about ten of them shoved away in a cupboard somewhere. I always mean to sleep in them, but I can't seem to face looking at the bloody things, never mind putting them on. But Ralph Lauren! Jesus. My mum wouldn't know Ralph Lauren if he came up and personally introduced himself.

"Libby says you're a writer," says Jamie.

Nick nods. "But it doesn't seem to be getting me anywhere. Unfortunately."

"It's got to be a novel, then."

"Yup."

"I've always wanted to write a novel," says Jamie. "I find it amazing that you have the discipline to sit down and write every day."

"I know, everyone does, but it's getting to the stage where I might have to start looking for other work. Obviously this book is my first love, but I just don't know how much longer I can keep sending out letters only to be rejected."

"So what sort of work would you look for?" asks Jules, as my eyes light up, because this is the first time he's ever mentioned it.

"Maybe TV work, scriptwriting, something like that."

"You ought to meet Charles," she says, turning to Jamie. "Isn't he a drama producer for one of the TV companies?"

Jamie nods. "He's the boyfriend of a friend of ours, Mara. They should be here soon, so I'll introduce you."

"So who else is coming?" I ask.

Jules reels off a list of names, and sure enough, they're all couples, and I thank God that this time I didn't have to turn down the invitation because I didn't want to come on my own.

"Oh, and there's a surprise for you."

"For me?" I love surprises, even though I pretend to hate them.

"Yup." She checks her watch. "In fact," she says, going to the door to answer the doorbell that's just rung, "this could be it. Come with me." I follow her out of the room, and the minute we're in the hallway she grabs me and whispers, "He's gorgeous!"

"I know," I whisper back.

"But no, I mean he's really gorgeous. So handsome! And sweet!"

"I know." I grin happily, as the doorbell rings again.

"All right, all right," she grumbles, running down to the front door. "Coming!"

It's Ginny and Richard, a couple I've met before who seem very nice, but he's a bit intimidating in that barrister, legal-ish sort of way, although they've always been charming.

I stand back as they kiss Jules hello, then Richard gives me a big smile and reaches down to kiss the air on either side of my cheeks. "Libby!" he exclaims. "How lovely to see you again!"

Ginny does the same thing, then all four of us move into the living room, as Jamie says hello, then goes off to get drinks.

"Nick!" says Richard. "I don't believe it!" and I stand open-mouthed as Richard gives Nick a manly hug and clasps his hand in both of his. "What on earth are you doing here?"

"I'm here with Libby," says Nick.

"What? You and Libby?"

He nods.

"I don't believe it." Richard turns to me. "I haven't seen Nick in years. We were at school together."

At school together? But I thought Richard went to . . .

"Didn't you go to Stowe?" I look at Richard, bemused.

"Most certainly did." He nods. "Both of us."

"You never told me you went to Stowe," I say to Nick, and he shrugs.

"You never asked."

"What a small world," says Jules, obviously delighted that her guests are getting on so well, and then the doorbell rings again.

More couples file in, some I know, but all well-spoken, well dressed, and very much at home standing around drinking Kir Royales and making small talk.

And there I was worrying about Nick, I think, watching him and Richard roar with laughter as they reminisce about what they used to get up to at school.

And I'm so impressed that Nick went to Stowe I completely forget about my surprise, and then the doorbell rings, and a familiar face appears in the doorway, and I'm so excited I practically spill my drink, and Jules grins as I shriek, "Olly!" and my darling brother rushes in and scoops me up in his arms, giving me a massive hug.

"I wanted to surprise you," he says, and I'm so happy he's here, this is so unexpected.

"What are you doing here?" I say, breathless with excitement.

"I rang him," said Jules, "because no party of ours would be quite the same if Olly wasn't here."

"For God's sake, don't tell Mum," he says. "She'd kill me if she knew I was down and wasn't staying there."

"Where are you staying? Will you stay with me?"

"No." He shakes his head. "I'm staying with Carolyn," and then I notice the tall, tanned girl standing in the doorway.

"Carolyn." He beckons her over. "This is my sister, Libby."

I shake her hand and approve immediately of her warm smile, the fact that she's so naturally pretty without makeup, her adoring look at Olly, which tells me that she is definitely not just a good friend.

"I'm so pleased to meet you," she says. "Olly talks about you all the time."

"Do you work together?"

She nods. "I'm a researcher. That's how we met."

I look at Olly and, without Carolyn noticing, I give him an almost imperceptible nod that tells him I approve, and he grins at me.

"Oh God," I say. "Where's Nick?" I look around, but he's suddenly disappeared.

"Nick?" says Olly. "Who's Nick, then? Your latest squeeze?"

And then I see Nick walk in from the kitchen and I call him over to introduce him and it turns out—another amazing fact I didn't know—that Nick's as big a Man United fan as Olly, and within minutes the pair of them are talking animatedly as if they've known each other for years.

Jules introduces Carolyn to Ginny, and then sweeps me into the kitchen to help her get the food ready.

"Everyone seems to be getting on, don't they?" she says, and I know that she was nervous, that she's always nervous before bringing together new people, but that she's such a good host-ess her evenings always turn out to be fine, apart from the cou-pley ones I don't go to, and that's not to say they're not fine, that's just to say that I wouldn't know.

"I can't believe how Nick's fitting in."

"Can't you?" says Jules, opening the oven and pulling out something that smells delicious. "Why ever not?"

"God, Jules, if you'd have met his friends the other night, you would have known why not. His crowd is so completely dif-ferent to ours."

"But he's fitting in perfectly," she says. "He seems very com-fortable."

And it's true, he does, and I don't know why this should

surprise me so much, but if anything I'd say that Nick feels even more comfortable here than I do, and these are my best friends, for God's sake. But don't get me wrong, I like it. In fact, I'd say I more than like it. I love it.

"I don't know why you keep saying there's no future in it," says Jules, opening a cupboard door. "I think you're perfect together."

"But that's just your first impression, Jules. You don't know him."

"So what do I need to know? He's handsome, obviously bright, and you seem to get on really well. What's the problem?"

How can I explain what the problem is? How can I tell her that I couldn't marry Nick because how would we live? I'd never be able to give up work, and our children would have to go to the local comprehensive, where they'd probably get in with the wrong crowd and end up taking drugs and hanging out in gangs. How can I tell her that my idea of hell would be to end up a harassed mother who had to try and be the breadwinner as well as bringing up the kids? That I'd always look a complete mess because I wouldn't have the time or the money to make an effort. That designer clothes would be something I'd only wear if someone like Jules took pity on me and gave me some hand-me-downs. That I'd have to say goodbye to the designer restaurants and bars I love so much, and on the rare occasions we went out for dinner it would have to be somewhere cheap and cheerful.

Actually, a lot of it doesn't sound so bad, but I know I'm talking myself into believing it's not so bad because I'm growing to like Nick more and more, and I'm trying to compromise, to change my lifestyle to fit into his because I have no other choice.

In fact, I haven't even been to a bloody designer restaurant or bar since before I met Nick, and okay, it's true, I don't miss them that much, but I wouldn't want to spend the rest of my life knowing that I couldn't go to them because I couldn't afford it. I may not be going now, but that's through choice.

How can I explain this to Jules when I know she wouldn't understand, particularly given that she's met Nick on her territory, when he's dressed up in clothes he never normally wears to fit in, and yes, he does fit in, but if she saw him on his territory, with his friends, doing what he likes to do, I'm sure she'd take my point. She'd have to. Wouldn't she?

"It's too long to go into," I say. "But I'm telling you, it's just a fling."

"Bullshit." She turns to look at me. "You're my best friend, Libby, and I know you better than anyone else in the world. You may be able to get away with telling other people that you don't care about him, that it's just sex, but look at you, for God's sake. You're crazy about him."

"What makes you say that?"

She sighs. "It's the way you look at him, the way your face lights up every time he says something, the way you hang on his every word. Don't worry," she says, seeing the dismay on my face. "I don't think he knows, but I do."

"So what do you think he thinks of me?" I can't help it. My insecurity raises its ugly head.

She shrugs. "It's much harder to tell with men, but my guess is he probably feels the same way. The only thing that worries me is that he did say at the beginning that he wasn't looking for a relationship, and I just think you have to remember that, because you've definitely fallen for him. He may well have fallen for you too, but, if the timing's wrong, then you might get hurt."

Timing. Jules is a big believer in timing. She always says that Jamie and she met at exactly the right time, that had it been any earlier she wouldn't have been ready for a relationship, not even with the gorgeous Jamie.

She looks at me closely and can see that what she's said has upset me, and her voice softens as she says, "Look, Libby, I don't want to see you hurt, and I think he probably does feel the same way about you, but you have to be aware that when men say they're not ready for a relationship, nine times out of ten it means that they're not ready for a relationship, and even if you're the most wonderful woman in the world it's not going to change their minds.

"But," she adds, almost to herself, "there are always women who can change their minds, I suppose."

That's what I needed to hear, and as soon as she says the words I make a decision. I'm going to be the woman who changes his mind. Except I don't share this with Jules, it's going to be my own little secret.

Jules sighs as the phone starts to ring. "Now who the hell is calling us now?" she says, putting down the bowls and running to pick up the phone.

"Hello? Hello?" There's a pause. "Hello? Is anyone there?" She puts the phone down and turns to me, annoyed. "That's the fourth bloody time that's happened this week. Why do these people keep putting the phone down?"

Jamie comes rushing into the kitchen, looking startled. "Who was that?" he asks breathlessly.

"God knows," she says. "I told you someone keeps ringing and putting it down when I pick up."

"Oh," says Jamie, as Jules picks up the bowls and leaves the room, and if I didn't know better I could swear he turns a whiter shade of pale. But no. I must be imagining it.

I bring the rest of the food into the living room and carefully put it down on the trestle table covered with a white damask tablecloth that they've set up at one end of the room.

"Mmm, this looks delicious," says Ginny, as Jules laughs.

"This?" she says. "It was nothing," and I know for Jules it probably was nothing, but to anyone who didn't know it looks like a Bacchanalian feast: mounds of chicken in a curried cream sauce; a huge, whole salmon, decorated with the thinnest slices of cucumber I've ever seen; piles of couscous surrounded by ratatouille; warm potato salad sprinkled with parsley and chives; bowls of mixed leaf salads; dishes of avocado, plum tomatoes and buffalo mozzarella cheese with fresh basil sprinkled over the top.

"Wait till you see what's for dessert," she whispers to me, and I groan in anticipation and rub my stomach.

"Don't tell me—" I say.

"Yup." She nods. "Your favorite."

"What's that?" says Nick, laughing at the expression of rapture on my face.

"Tiramisu."

We all grab plates and tuck in, piling them high, and then small groups of people seem to gather together without thinking, so within minutes there are little clusters of people dotted around the room, friends naturally gravitating toward friends.

I sit down with Nick, Olly, Carolyn and Jamie. Jules shouts she'll join us, but she wants to check that everyone's okay for drinks, and she waves Jamie aside when he says he'll do it, because Jules likes to be in control.

And I sit and watch Carolyn, and I watch how Nick reacts to Carolyn, because she really is very, very pretty, and I know she's going out with Olly, but I can't help that old insecurity that says that maybe Nick will fancy her, and maybe he'll fancy her more than he fancies me, and I'm waiting for him to start flirting with her, but he doesn't.

What he does is put an arm round me and rub my back, and I grin and relax, because it's a territorial thing; he's making sure everyone knows I'm with him and he's with me, and other than being polite to Carolyn he hardly seems to notice her.

"So what's all this about the gourmet vegetarian?" I say to Olly, as Carolyn laughs.

"Ridiculous, isn't it?" she says. "Olly can't cook to save his life and here he is, producing a show about food."

"Thank you, girls," says Olly, in mock disgust. "But actually I can cook."

"Bollocks!" I say.

"I can, Libby. Tell them what I made you the other night." He looks at Carolyn.

"He made me Chinese," she says, trying to suppress a smile.

"Really?" Now I'm impressed. "How on earth did you do that?"

Carolyn answers for him, which instantly makes me realize that perhaps she's not as transient as all of the other women I've heard about, that perhaps this has gone on longer than I thought, that perhaps this is serious, or at least serious in Olly terms, because, let's face it, it's all a question of relativity.

"I chopped the vegetables," she says, winking at me, "and Olly opened the packet of oyster sauce."

"Ah," says Nick. "That's exactly how I like to do my cooking."

"Yeah," agrees Olly. "It's a guy thing."

"You've never cooked for me," says Nick. "Can you cook?"

" 'Course I can cook," I exclaim. "I'll make you dinner next week."

"Damn," says Olly. "I needed a laugh. What a shame I'll be back in Manchester."

I hit him.

"So how do you two know each other?" Olly gestures at Nick and I.

"We met through a friend, Sally," says Nick.

"You don't know her," I add.

"So how long's this been going on?"

Three months, three weeks and two days, is what I could say, but I don't, because I'm not supposed to be counting, so I don't say anything at all and I wait to hear what Nick says.

"A couple of months now?" He looks at me, and I nod.

"Serious, then?" laughs Olly.

Nick blanches slightly.

"Bit of a record for you," continues Olly, missing the look on Nick's face.

I stand up. "Time for seconds. Anyone coming?"

• • •

We kiss everyone goodbye, and Olly gives me a big hug and whispers, "He's great. I'll be back in the office tomorrow afternoon, call me," and I tell Carolyn it was nice to meet her, which it was, and, as nice a time as I've had, it's even nicer finally to have Nick to myself.

And as we walk out Nick turns to me and says, "They were so nice! I had such a nice time!"

"Well, what did you expect from friends of mine?"

"They're just so different from the kind of people I mix with." He looks at me. "I suppose I didn't need to tell you that, did I?"

"Hardly," I laugh.

"But even though they're all obviously successful, they're really down-to-earth."

"Success doesn't mean you have to be pompous," I say.

Nick walks along in silence for a while, and I can tell he's thinking about something, and I could annoy the hell out of him by saying something incredibly trite like, what are you thinking or penny for your thoughts, but I don't.

And after a while he says, "It's not that I felt out of place, not at all, it's just sort of made me think about my life, about what I'm doing with it, about what I could be doing with it. Particularly bumping into Richard after all these years."

I walk next to him wondering whether just to listen or to give practical advice. I mean, I've bloody read *Men Are from Mars, Women Are from Venus*, but this is the bit I always get confused about. I can't remember what I'm supposed to do, so I don't say anything at all, because I don't want to alienate him by doing the wrong thing.

"I don't know," he sighs. "I feel a bit confused at the moment."

"Do you want to talk about it?" I say.

"I don't really know what there is to talk about," he says, and after that he's very quiet. He's quiet all the way home, he's quiet when I make him a coffee, and we get into bed and cuddle before falling asleep. Or maybe I should say, before he falls asleep, because this worries me. Part of me thinks this is good, this is a progression, that it's not only about sex anymore, that we're becoming friends, settling in, but the other part thinks, why the hell doesn't he want to have sex with me, and I can't help it, despite him being absolutely lovely to me tonight, I've got this horrible suspicion that he might be going off me.

Chapter 11

"He's great," repeats Olly on the phone the next day. "I'm really surprised."

"Surprised? Why?"

"He's just so normal and down-to-earth," Olly says, in a strange echo of what Nick said about everyone last night. "And I think he's good for you."

"In what way?"

"You seem really relaxed, much more so than you ever were with that other bloke, what was his name?"

"Jon?"

"Was he the poncey one with the Mazda?"

"He wasn't poncey."

"Oh, come on, Libby, he was awful."

"No, he wasn't." Why the hell am I defending him? He was awful.

"Okay, he wasn't awful, but he didn't treat you well, and Nick seems much better for you."

"It's not serious, though."

"You can never tell whether it's serious or not," Olly says mysteriously.

"Oh, so it's serious with Carolyn, then?"

"Did you like her?"

"I thought she was lovely."

"Mmm. She is, isn't she?"

"Really. And Mum would love her."

"Don't say anything. It's still early days."

"How early?"

"About a month."

"You go, guy! That's pretty good for you."

"I know."

"So do you think Nick likes me?"

"Of course he likes you. He wouldn't be with you if he didn't like you."

"I'm a little worried because he was a bit funny with me after we left."

"Funny how?"

"It's just that every night we're together we always have, umm"—it feels a bit weird, saying this to Olly, but what the hell, I know he'll tell me what he really thinks so I may as well be honest—"umm, sex, and last night he was really quiet after we left and we just had cuddles and then he fell asleep, and maybe I'm being really stupid and insecure, but it seems a bit strange."

"Women kill me," says Olly. "They really do. All the women I've ever met expect all men to be up and ready for sex anytime, anyplace, anyhow."

"Well, aren't they?"

"No!" he practically shouts. "Jesus, no. Sometimes we're tired, sometimes we're stressed, sometimes we're not in the mood. Nick was under a hell of a lot of pressure last night, meeting all of us for the first time, and it's completely under- standable that he just wanted to sleep."

I breathe a sigh of relief for the first time that day. "You don't think he's going off me?"

"Don't be so ridiculous."

"Okay," I say happily, "I'm being ridiculous, then?"

"Yes, Libby, you're being ridiculous."

That's the thing, you see. I suppose what I do is associate sex with how much someone likes me, and if I think about it, which I don't want to do that much, every time I've broken up with someone the last night we've spent together, we haven't had sex. And okay, admittedly, there have been other problems, like they've been a bit off with me, a bit distant, but still it always comes completely out of the blue when they turn around and tell me it's over.

And every time I think, I should have known that night. I should have known when they rolled over and said they were tired or not in the mood, or stressed, but maybe Olly has a point, and I suppose it is unfair that we expect them to be up for it whenever we are.

And Nick was lovely in the morning. Okay, we didn't have sex again, but hey, it was a late night, and I know I'm being ridiculous, and insecure, and probably slightly paranoid, but Olly makes me feel better about it, so by the time Jules phones to do the postmortem I'm feeling so okay I don't even bother mentioning it.

And she basically repeats what she said last night about Nick, the good stuff I mean, the stuff about him being nice to me and us being good together, and I drink it in, and I feel fine, and it doesn't bother me that Nick doesn't call me all morning because why would he? He's busy getting on with his life, and I'm busy getting on with mine.

At lunchtime Jo buzzes me and asks what I'm doing.

"Nothing," I reply, looking with distaste at the smoked salmon bagel on my desk that I don't really have the stomach for.

"I want to go shopping," she says. "Fancy coming with me?"

"Where?" I ask, feeling that old familiar buzz at the prospect of spending some money, a feeling I haven't had in a while.

"I thought we could get a cab to St. John's Wood and hit the high street."

"St. John's Wood? What the hell's in St. John's Wood?"

"Joseph, for starters."

"I'm coming."

As a receptionist on a completely crap salary Jo really shouldn't be able to afford the clothes she wears every day, but luckily for her she has extremely wealthy parents who never seem to think twice about giving her money for her wardrobe, and although we know we should all hate her for it, she's so nice we can't help but adore her.

And what's more she pays for the taxi.

"I'll get the one on the way back," I say, feeling slightly guilty as she puts her Louis Vuitton wallet back in her Gucci bag.

"Whatever," she says, tripping off down the high street, and it is a bit of a revelation for me, like a mini Bond Street in North London.

"How did you discover this?" I say, itching to go into practically every shop we pass.

"My parents live round the corner," she says, "so I spend most of my life here. So much easier than going into town."

She obviously does spend most of her life here because as soon as we walk into Larizia, our first stop, the girl in there says, "Hi, Jo! How are you?" and you just know that she's probably their best customer.

On to a clothes shop a couple of doors down, where I follow her around, watching as she expertly pulls things off the racks and flings them at the sales assistant with a cheeky grin, and I perch on a chair outside the changing room, giving her the yes or the no, although to be honest pretty much everything looks fantastic on her as she's so tall and thin.

And we go into Joseph, which is a bit of a scary experience, because the woman in there looks me up and down and evidently decides I'm not good enough to bother saying hello to, so she sticks her nose up in the air and carries on ordering the sales assistant around, and I sort of want to disappear.

"Aren't you going to even look?" says Jo, and I shrug and halfheartedly look, but I can't really be bothered. I realize that it's because I haven't got anywhere to wear these clothes anymore, that there wouldn't be any point in buying that "fabulous" chiffon shirt or those "wicked" PVC trousers, because my life with Nick just doesn't need those sorts of things.

"This isn't like you," says Jo, pulling a gold Amex out of her purse and paying for a pile of tissue-wrapped clothes. "What's going on?"

I shrug again, and think of explaining it to her, but then decide not to because I know what Jo would do. She'd snort with derision and tell me that you don't dress for the men in your life, you dress for yourself, and anyway what the hell was I doing going out with someone who quite clearly didn't enjoy doing the same things as me?

She wouldn't understand.

"I'm just a bit strapped for cash at the moment." I know she won't be able to say anything after this because she feels ever so slightly guilty at having so much money from her parents, and sure enough, she nods and drops the subject.

And when we get back to the office there's a note on my desk saying Nick called, and my heart, even after three months, etc., etc., still skips a little beat and I call him back immediately, which I know you're not supposed to do, but as I think I may have already mentioned, I'm a bit crap at playing hard to get, and I love the sound of his voice when he picks up the phone, and all my insecurities are forgotten because he called, and he didn't just call, he called the next day.

I think you'll all agree this is a bit of a result.

"Hello, my darling," he says.

"Hello, my darling," I echo.

"I'm bored," he says.

"Why don't you write?"

"I'm not in the mood."

"Oh. What are you in the mood for?"

"You. On a silver platter. Preferably with nothing on. No, wait, with a pair of red lace crotchless knickers."

"God, you're such a bloke!" I laugh. "Red lace crotchless knickers? How tacky."

"I thought I was a girl . . ."

"You are, but when it comes to sex you're very much a bloke."

"I'm sorry about last night. I'm phoning to apologize for being so tired and for not, you know, not ravishing you like I usually do."

"That's okay," I say, hugging myself with happiness. "I know that most women think all men are up for sex anytime, any-place, anyhow, but I don't think that, I know what a pressure that is for men, and it's fine if you don't feel like it.

"I didn't feel like it either," I conclude. Lying.

"Blimey! Are you sure you're not a bloke?"

I laugh.

"I was just worried you'd get the wrong idea," he says.

"Don't be silly," I trill with laughter. "It was lovely just cud-dling."

"You're so damned nice," he says, sounding serious. "God, how can you be this nice?"

"What d'you mean? This is just the way I am."

"I know, but I've never met anyone like you. You're so un-derstanding all the time, and so nice!"

"Stop saying I'm nice." I'm grinning. I'm grinning so hard any second now I might tell him I love him. Ha! Got you. That was a joke. Of course I don't love him.

"Okay. Are you busy as well as nice?"

"No," I lie. "Not a lot on this afternoon." As I say it I survey the pile of numbers I've got to call on my desk.

"What are you doing tonight?"

"Nothing planned." Another lie. I said I'd go to the movies with Jo, but hey, it's only Jo, and it's only the movies. She'll un-derstand. "What about you?"

"I'm meeting Rog for a drink. I miss you, will you come with?"

Shit. Dilemma. I want to see Nick more than anything, but I honestly don't think I could stand another night with one of his vile friends.

"Umm." I stall for time.

"Go on," he says.

"I'd better not," I say. "I kind of said I might go to the movies with Jo."

"All right," he grumbles. "What about later, after the movies?"

"You're thinking about sex again, aren't you?"

"I'm a bloke, Libby. I think about sex every six seconds."

I laugh.

"Why don't you come over when the movie's finished?" he says.

"Tell you what. Why don't you come over to me?"

"You really hate my flat, don't you?"

"It's not that I hate it exactly, I just prefer mine."

"I know," he says. "That's the problem. So do I."

• • •

Five minutes later Jules phones.

"I've just eaten a ton of chicken left over from last night, a ton of couscous, a whole packet of kettle crisps—the big ones—and a Mars Bar."

"I'm still sitting here looking at a smoked salmon bagel."

"I'm fat. I'm huge. I'm disgusting."

"You're not fat. So you ate a lot, big deal. Anyway, it's not bad food, it's healthy."

"Since when was a Mars Bar healthy?"

"Okay, maybe not the Mars Bar, but have a salad tonight and you'll be fine."

"I don't think I can," she groans. "I haven't got any will-power. I'll have to have more chicken."

"So you'll be good tomorrow. It'll be fine. You won't put on weight after one day of eating a lot."

"Really?"

"Really."

"What are you having tonight?"

"Dunno. If it makes you feel better I'll have a Chinese take-away."

"It makes me feel a lot better. What will you have?"

"Mmm. Let me think. How does barbecued spareribs, chicken and cashew nuts in yellow bean sauce and rice sound to you?"

"Not nearly bad enough. What kind of rice?"

"Steamed?"

"No, make it egg fried."

"Okay. Happy now?"

"Not yet. You can't have Chinese without having seaweed."

"Okay. I'll have seaweed. Happy now?"

"Very happy. God, Libby, you're such a pig." And we both start laughing.

• • •

I don't go to the movies, Jo blows me out, but I do have my Chinese, although I cheat slightly, at least I hope I do, because we've just won a new account of these supposedly unbelievable fat pills that are all the rage in America and have just come over here.

God knows what's in them, some sort of shellfish I think, and what they're supposed to do is attract all the fat you eat so instead of absorbing it, it goes straight through you. We've had loads of bottles lying round the office, and I filched a couple before I left, and I know the instructions say to take two to four with a large glass of water immediately before eating, but I decide to take six just to be on the safe side.

"Bloody hell!" I look in the mirror at my potbelly, and check the packet. How bloody long does it take for these damn things to work anyway? I sit and watch TV and wait for the chance to, er, expel the fat from my body, but no, not only is having a poo the last thing my body seems to want to do, my stomach's not going down either. Shit. It's too late. Nick will just have to put up with it.

Hmm. Maybe sit-ups would work. I hook my legs under the bed, wondering why on earth I don't exercise more often, because this is easy. And one. And two. And three. And four. And five. And, Jesus, why am I puffing already? And six. And seven. And eight. And nine. And I don't think I can go on any longer.

I stand up and look in the mirror, and my face is bright red and I look seriously unfit and oh, what the hell, I think I'll have another cigarette, and just when I've lit it the doorbell rings and oh my God! Look at me! I'm a complete state.

"What have you been up to?" says Nick, kissing me hello and smoothing back my hair.

"You wouldn't want to know."

"I think I would."

"Exercise."

"Urgh. Don't talk to me about exercise. I'm allergic to the bloody stuff."

"You don't need to do it," I say, rubbing his deliciously firm washboard stomach. "But look at this." I push my stomach out, figuring it's better to be up-front about it.

Nick recoils in horror. "What. Is. That?"

"I know," I say. "It's awful, isn't it?"

Nick moves closer, gets down on his knees and presses one ear against my stomach. "Yup." He nods sagely. "I know exactly what that is. It's a food baby."

I start laughing.

"In fact," he says, tapping my stomach in a doctor-ish sort of way, "I'd say it was a Chinese food baby."

How the hell did he know?

"How the hell do you know?"

Nick stands up and shrugs nonchalantly. "I'm paid to know."

I turn around and see the evidence in the kitchen. Foil cartons and white cardboard lids, which I meant to clear up because I wouldn't actually want any man in my life to know I exist almost solely on Chinese takeaways, I'd want him to think I eat ladylike things like lettuce and smoked salmon, but it's too damn late.

"Seeing as we might just about be in time to catch last orders," says Nick, "I thought maybe we could go out for a drink."

"Sure!" I say enthusiastically, sitting down and pulling my sneakers on. "Where d'you fancy?"

"How about the Westbourne?"

"Great." So it's off to the Westbourne we go, and funnily enough the Westbourne is about the first place I've been to with Nick where we both feel at home. Enough of a pub to make him relax, and trendy enough—i.e., filled with Notting

Hill Trustafarians—to make me relax, so all in all a bloody good choice, I think to myself.

It's a warm night, so we sit outside at a wooden table, and just as I think we're having a really nice time, Nick starts sighing again.

"What is it now?"

He sighs.

"Come on, Nick. There's something wrong, isn't there?"

He sighs again. And then he looks at me.

"I really like you, Libby," he says, and my heart sinks, because I know what's coming next. What's coming next is a But.

"No, I mean I really like you. But . . ." And he stops.

"I really like you too," I offer lamely.

"I know," he says. "That's what worries me."

Oh shit. Jules got it wrong. He does know, and true to form, he's backing off. Oh God, why didn't I play harder to get, why didn't I pretend to be cool?

"I just don't know what to do."

"I don't understand."

"I like you more than I've liked anyone for ages. I mean, over the last year there have been several women I could have got involved with, but I didn't because I wasn't ready for a relationship, and I wasn't ready to get involved with you, but I like you so much I sort of couldn't help it."

"Nick," I say slowly. "You're being very heavy about this, and this isn't what we're about. We're not having a relationship, we're just having fun, so what's wrong with that?"

"But we are having a relationship, you know that."

There's no point in denying it because he's right.

"And what scares me is that I know you need more. I know that at some point in the not too distant future you're going to want more commitment from me, and I know, quite categorically, that I won't be able to give it to you, even though I want to, more than anything else in the world, but I'm just not ready."

What can I say? He's right again.

He sighs.

"And I like you far too much to hurt you, and I know that inevitably I will."

"Maybe not." I bristle. "Maybe I'm not as involved as you think I am."

"Aren't you?"

I shrug. "I don't know."

"Look." He takes my hand. "You are the best person I've met in years, and if I'd met you in a year's time, or maybe even a few months, I know we could be happy together, but I can't give you what you need." He sighs again. "I haven't got my life together, and I can't deal with a relationship until I have. I do want to get my novel published, but I also know that I need some money, some stability, and I can't keep doing this forever. If I had a publishing deal, or a job, then it would be different, but I need to concentrate on that right now, and it's simply not the right time for me to have a relationship."

I think I'm going to start crying, but somehow I manage not to. I think about telling him that I don't mind, that it doesn't bother me that he doesn't have money, that I'm prepared to wait, but I know, deep down, that his mind is made up, and it really wouldn't make any difference.

"Is this it, then?" I say, in a very small voice, thinking, I knew it. I knew it when we didn't have sex.

"No," he sighs. "I don't know. I don't want to stop seeing you."

"So do we carry on?" Hope. Light at the end of the tunnel.

"I don't know. I don't think we can. But I don't want to lose you."

"You can't have it both ways," I say, amazed at where this resolve comes from, but praying that if I tell him I'll never see him again as a friend, he'll somehow find a way to work through this, to stay with me. "I can't be your friend," I continue. "I'm sorry, but I just can't."

"I don't know what to do. What do you think?"

"I think . . ." I stop, and suddenly I feel very grown-up. "I think it's late. I think we had a late night last night and that we're both tired, and that everything seems so much worse when you're tired. I think we should go home, sleep on it, and see how things are in the morning."

I think I said the right thing, because Nick relaxes and says, "Maybe you're right. Okay. Shall we go?" And we do.

So we go home, and we make love, and it really is making love, it's not just sex, because it's impossibly tender and throughout it all we gaze into each other's eyes and if I didn't know better I'd say that a couple of times Nick's were swimming with tears, but it was truly beautiful, and afterward I thought, how could he give this up? How could he say goodbye to me when we are so damn good together?

And we fall asleep cuddled up, and normally when we do that I move away after about twenty minutes because I can't stand sleeping that close to someone, I need space to sleep properly, but the next time I open my eyes his arms are still wrapped around me and it's ten to eight in the morning and I kiss him awake, thinking that last night must have been a bad dream.

We go to the tube together, but somehow it is different, even though we don't talk about last night. As we kiss goodbye Nick says to me, "Are you okay?" and I nod.

"Are you?" I say.

"I'm still confused," he says. "Even more so," and he gives me a hug, and I'm not sure I like this hug because it's so tight, so clingy, if I didn't know better I'd almost think it was the last one, but we stand there for ages, and eventually I break away and he says, "I'll call you," and I'm not sure what the hell is going on, but neither of us has actually said it's over, so maybe it's not, but if it isn't, then why do I feel like shit?

I feel like shit all day. I don't start crying, but I feel as if I'm on the brink every second, and it's a bit like having a nightmare case of PMS, when you know that the tiniest thing will push you over the edge, and you're literally clinging on to sanity by your fingertips.

Of course Jules is the first person I call when I get to the office, and she listens quietly while I relay what happened, and eventually she says, "It doesn't look good."

"I know it doesn't bloody look good, Jules. But what's happening?"

"What do you think?"

I don't think. I know. "I think it's over."

"I think you're probably right, in that it's over for now, but somehow I don't think it is finally over."

"What do you mean?"

"I think he really is confused, and that you'll need to give him space, and I could be wrong, but I think he'll come back."

But I don't want to give him space, I want to see him, be with him, convince him that I'm right for him.

"But you can't forget what you've always said," she continues softly, trying to ease my pain. "You never thought he'd be The One, so maybe this is a good thing."

"I know," I sigh. "But maybe I was wrong. I know it started as just a fling, but you can't sleep with someone on a regular basis that you really like and not get emotionally involved."

Jules laughs. "That's what I've been saying since the beginning."

"But I really thought I could," I groan. "I've done it before, why can't I do it now?"

"Because things are different in your early twenties. Apart from anything else you can afford it, you've got time, but, as I said before, after about twenty-five, you can't really do it because there are other things at stake, and unfortunately every man you meet becomes a potential husband, whether you admit it to yourself or not."

"You're right, you're right. I know you're right. But that doesn't stop it hurting."

"I know, my darling. And it will hurt for a while, but you have to get on with your life. What are you doing tonight?"

"Nothing."

"Right. I'm coming to pick you up at eight o'clock, and I want you in your best designer togs. We're going to Mezzo for a drink."

"I'm really not in the mood, Jules."

"I don't care. We're going to go out and get drunk and have some fun."

"Can't we do it another time?"

"No way. You are not moping by yourself. Just remember who you are, Libby. Three months ago and you would have jumped at the chance to dress up and meet rich men."

But I don't want rich men anymore, I think. I want Nick, but there's no getting out of it, so I say yes and miserably put down the phone, only for it to ring again two seconds later.

"Libby? It's Sal."

"Hi! How are you!" Just the person I need to speak to, because she knows Nick, maybe she'll have a better idea of what's going on.

"Nick just called me," she says. "Are you okay?"

Shit. That means he told her it was over.

"Did he tell you it was over?"

"No. Not exactly. He just said he was confused and he didn't think it was fair to you to keep going. I don't understand."

"Neither do I."

"Because he said he really likes you, and if he does, then why doesn't he get his shit together?"

"Exactly."

"God, I despair of him sometimes. He's done this too many bloody times."

"What?"

"Every time he gets close to having a relationship he goes into panic mode and runs away."

"You mean he's done this a lot?"

"Libby," she says gently. "You don't look the way Nick does and lead a life of celibacy, but, trust me, you're better off out of it. He's a lovely guy, but a complete fuck-up when it comes to commitment. You deserve better. We all do."

I can't believe I'm hearing this, not that I blame Sal for telling me, but I never knew. I suppose I never stopped to think about him doing this to anyone else, and okay, so he mentioned he'd met a few women that he could have got involved with but didn't, but I never thought he was a serial fucking commita-phobe. Or a womanizer, when it comes to that. And I start to feel sick, sick, sick.

This is really not what I need, and I can't bloody believe that it's happened again. That once again I've been unceremoni-ously dumped when I thought I was in control, I thought I had a handle on things, I thought that I wouldn't get hurt. What is wrong with me? I mean, I'm a good person, I'm nice to people, and animals, and I try to treat people with respect, and what happens?

I get bloody dumped.

Over and over and over again.

"Libby?" Sal's obviously wondering whether I've deserted her because I've been so busy thinking about this I forget to say anything.

"Sorry," I say. "I've just had enough, Sal."

"Libby, it's not your problem, it's his."

"Yeah, yeah, that's what I'm always told."

"I'm serious, Libby."

"Libby?" Jo's shouting from reception.

"Hang on a sec," I say to Sal. "Yeah?"

"Nick's on the line."

"Oh shit. Sal, it's Nick. I've gotta go."

"Okay, and listen, I'm here if you need me, okay?"

Christ, get off the bloody phone.

"Hi." My voice is strained when I say hello to Nick.

"Hi. I just wanted to phone to check you were okay."

"I'm okay. Sal just phoned."

"You don't mind me telling her?"

"Not really. Is this it, then?"

He sighs. "I don't know. But you know, it's not you. It's me."

I almost laugh.

"I think I might have to go into therapy or something," he sighs.

"Good idea." And hell, maybe I should do the same thing. Maybe if I went to see someone they'd help me understand why I keep attracting the bastards. Not that Nick's a bastard, it's just that none of the men I meet seem to be available. They're either physically unavailable, in other words they're never interested in me, or they're emotionally unavailable, see Nick.

"I'd really like it if we could stay friends," he says. "You're incredibly important to me, Libby."

Well, that's it, then, isn't it? He may as well have said it's over, he just didn't have the balls.

"I've got enough friends," I say. "Thanks."

His voice sounds sad. "Can I phone you?"

"If you want." Now it's my turn to be harsh.

"Listen, take care."

"Yup. Bye." I put down the phone and give in. I start crying. Fuck it. I don't care that I'm at work or that everyone's looking at me, and as I sit there with my shoulders heaving, a sob escapes my throat and that's it, moments later I'm crying like a baby and I get up and run to the loo, where I lock myself in a stall and just let go.

I hear the door open, but I don't stop. I can't stop.

"Libby? Are you okay?" It's Jo.

I try to answer her but the words don't come out, just great big hiccups and sobs.

"It's Nick, isn't it? Let me in." She starts banging on the cubicle door, so I get up and unlock it, then sit back down on the toilet seat (closed).

"They're all bastards," she says vehemently. "He's not worth it." She waits for a bit while I try to regain a bit of composure, which is hard when you've got snot running down your face and your eyes look remarkably like those of Dracula's daughter.

"I" hiccup "know" hiccup "it's just" hiccup "I" hiccup, hiccup, sob, sob.

"It's okay." She puts an arm round me, which is pretty damn difficult in the confines of the cubicle, but she manages it somehow and rubs my back and I can't help it—someone being this nice, this sympathetic, sets me off all over again.

"It's okay," she keeps saying softly. "It's okay."

But it's not okay, I think. It's not okay because I've got used to having Nick around, because I love having him around. Because for the first time in ages I wasn't some sad lonely person who either had to stay in on Saturday nights, or go out on the pull with the girls because there was nothing better to do.

It's not okay because I love, loved, having sex with Nick. Because there was nothing better than waking up and rolling over only to discover that you're not on your own.

It's not okay because he made me laugh. Because I didn't have to pretend to be anything other than who I am when I was with him. Because I don't believe that stuff about finding your other half, but because I do believe that what you look for is someone who makes you a better person when you're with them, who changes you for the better, who makes you the best person you can possibly be, and because I thought I had found that in Nick.

Even though I don't think I ever quite realized it until now.

And yes, maybe you're right, maybe I'm being overdramatic, maybe I'm blowing this up into something much bigger than it is because I'm feeling sorry for myself, but why the hell not, huh? Why the hell can't I feel like this, and whether it's true or not, it certainly feels true right now. And it feels like shit.

And oh my God, I'm never going to wake up next to him again. And oh my God, I'm never going to look in his eyes as we're making love, and oh my God, he's going to be doing that with someone else, and probably very soon, and me? I'm going to be on my own for the rest of my bloody life.

I start sobbing again.

There's a knock on the door. It's Lisa, another PR, who sits at the desk next to mine. Jo opens the door and I hear Lisa whisper, "Is Libby okay?"

"She's fine," says Jo, even though I'm quite patently not.

"Is there anything I can do?" says Lisa, and I know what that means. What that means is she'd kill to know what's going on, what's happened to me, and I'm sure that already a buzz has gone round the office and they're doubtless already laying bets on what it is that's made me cry, and they probably think I've got the sack.

And I hate myself for losing it at the office. That's the thing. When you set yourself up, as I've done, as this strong independent career woman, always in control, people get very nervous when you lose it, they don't quite know how to react, and sure enough, when half an hour's passed and I've finally managed to get a grip (mostly thanks to Jo and her Murine eye drops and waterproof mascara), I walk back in with head held high and everyone stops talking and starts pretending to be very busy.

A couple of minutes after I've sat down at my desk Lisa comes over and puts a cup of tea in front of me, which I suppose is very sweet, and then she looks at me with these big concerned eyes and says, "Are you okay?" and I nod.

"Do you want to talk about it?" she says, and I catch Jo's eye and Jo makes a face and I almost laugh, because I know, I just know, that Lisa is dying to know what it's all about.

"Thanks, Lisa," I say. "But there's really nothing to talk about."

"Oh," she says, the disappointment written all over her face, and then she leans forward conspiratorially, "It's not the job, is it?"

"No," I say sweetly, "it's not the job," and she can see she's not going to get anything more out of me, so she wanders off.

Somehow I manage to get things done today, although my voice keeps breaking in the middle of phone conversations with journalists, and I have to pretend I've got a stinking cold to explain my blocked-up nose.

Eventually I set off home, and perhaps because I've immersed myself in work, by the time I actually leave the building I really am starting to feel a lot better, and when Jules arrives I've been so busy reading I haven't even had time to get dressed, and the first thing we do after pouring ourselves a glass of wine is sit down and make a list. Yup, that list. The list I showed you when we first met.

And you know, looking at the list I start to feel one hell of a lot better, because yes, maybe he was nice, and yes, maybe he was sweet to me, but really, how could I ever have even thought of getting seriously involved? And Jesus, the thought of spending even one more night with his revolting friends in a revolting pub turns my stomach.

I leave Jules sitting in the living room as I go and get dressed, and fuck it, I'm going to make an effort. So I pull out a Joseph dress from last season and team it with my gorgeous Prada shoes, and I put on lots and lots of makeup, and I sweep my hair up into a big beehivey-type thing, and when I walk out Jules does a wolf whistle and claps her hands.

"Hooray!" she shouts, as she leaps up and grabs me, dancing round the living room. "We've got the old Libby back, the Libby we know and love."

"Was I really that bad?"

"Worse!" she laughs. "Now where are those smelly old sneakers?" She looks around the room.

"They're not smelly. Why?"

"They're going in the bin."

I panic. "No," I say, because the sneakers remind me of Nick, and I'm not quite ready to let go of the memories. "They're perfect for work," I say. "I want to keep them."

She looks at me in horror. "Are you serious?"

I nod.

"Have it your way." She shrugs. "But you look gorgeous, Libby, just like your old self." Bless her. She doesn't mention the fact that my eyes, despite a ton of mascara and cleverly applied eye shadow, look like pissholes in the snow.

And off we go, to Mezzo, and it's packed with City boys and glamorous girls, and we haven't been there five minutes before a group of chinless wonders send over some champagne, and okay, so they're not my type, but it's really quite nice to be in this sort of environment again, and I realize that, even though I thought I didn't miss it, I now think I did.

"So how come someone as gorgeous as you hasn't got a boyfriend?" says Ed, who is not my type at all. Tall, and stocky with a mustache, and I hate mustaches. No, actually, I despise mustaches, and he's also very, very straight.

And yes, he's probably rolling in money, and yes, I know that I'm looking for a rich man, but I don't want him to be straight, I want him to be just as comfortable at the opera as he would be at, say, an Oasis gig, and there aren't too many men around like that. In fact, it may well be that Jules nabbed the last of a dying breed, but I can still hope, can't I?

This guy Ed would probably be okay-looking without the mustache, but even if he shaved it off I just know he's too damn straight for me, but what the hell, I flick my hair around a bit and smile coyly as I say, "How do you know I haven't got a boyfriend?"

"Oh, umm. Er. Have you?" Inspired or what?

I shake my head and suddenly feel incredibly sad. Jules sees it and grabs me.

"Excuse us, boys. We'll be back in a sec."

We leave them moaning about why women always go off to the loo in pairs, and once we're in there she asks if I'm okay.

"I am. Really. I'm having quite a nice time. I don't know. It's just that I miss Nick."

"What about Ed?"

"What about him?"

"Might be worth a date. He's definitely interested."

"Nah," I say. "Not my type. Too straight."

"How d'you know? Sometimes people can surprise you."

"Okay. I'll show you." And we go back to join them.

"So," I say to Ed. "Been to any good gigs lately?"

"Gigs?" He looks completely bewildered. "Oh, ah. Gigs. Oh yes," and he starts laughing. "Hilarious," he says over and over, as I look at Jules and raise one eyebrow.

"You're very funny, Libby," he says, although I haven't quite got the joke. "I'd love to take you out for dinner."

"Okay." I shrug, not really giving a damn whether he does or not.

"May I have your number?"

Jesus, is this guy formal or what? I scrabble around in my bag for a pen, but no, once again I'm carrying a magic bag that eats pens, keys and lipsticks, and there's no pen to be found. Ed stops a passing waitress and asks for her pen, and he writes my number down carefully in a black leather wallet thing that holds small sheets of white paper and looks desperately expensive.

"I shall call you," he says. "And we shall go somewhere wonderful."

I literally have to force myself not to shrug and say, "Whatever." Instead I smile and say, "Lovely."

And when we leave, which is shortly afterward because all the emotion of this morning is starting to make me extremely tired, Ed shakes my hand and says, "It's been an absolute pleasure meeting you. I'll ring you about dinner." And that's it. We jump in a taxi and head home.

"I can't believe you pulled," says Jules. "You pulled someone on your first night as a single girl!"

"Oh, come on, Jules, he's not exactly a good pull."

"You're blind, Libby. He was lovely, and obviously smitten with you. Are you going to have dinner with him?"

"Dunno."

"Anyway, at least now you know there are other men out there, that it's not the end of the world."

I know she's right, it's just that I don't want any other men at the moment, I just want Nick.

"And," she continues, "he'll probably take you somewhere fantastic, he's obviously loaded."

"How can you tell?"

She looks at me in dismay. "Libby, everything I know I learned from you. Don't tell me you didn't notice the Rolex?"

I shake my head.

"The Hermès tie?"

I shake my head.

"The Porsche key ring?"

I shake my head.

"Maybe I will go out for dinner with him," I say, suddenly quite liking the idea of being driven around in a Porsche. "But just dinner. That's all."

Jules sits there and smiles to herself, and I give her a look.

"I know you so well," she chuckles, and I can't help it, I start laughing too.

The good mood lasts precisely as long as it takes me to get back to the flat. I open the front door and turn on the lights, kick off my shoes, and as I walk around I start fighting off the memories of Nick that seem to be everywhere I look.

The sofa where we curled, that first night, when he came back after Sal's get-together. The bath where he sat in that ridiculous bath hat. The bed. Oh my God. The bed.

I sink to the floor, tears streaming down my face, and I curl up, hugging my knees to my chest, crying like a baby.

Why did this have to happen to me? Why can't this work? I try to remember what Nick said, why it's ended, because it doesn't make sense. How can you like someone, I mean really like them, and still want to end it? He said it might have worked if we'd met in a few months' time, so maybe it could work now, maybe I could change his mind.

I stop thinking properly. I stand up, wipe the tears from my eyes and grab my car keys. The only thing that will make this better is seeing Nick. I have to see him. Talk to him. Make him see that this can work, that I don't care about his job, his money, because suddenly I don't. All that matters to me right now is being with him, working things out, and the only way I can do this is to go to him.

I climb in the car, filled with resolve, so intent on making this work that I forget to cry, I concentrate on maneuvering the car through London's streets, until eventually I pull up outside Nick's flat in Highgate.

I sit for a while in the car, suddenly unsure about ringing his bell, about actually confronting him, but I'm here now, and this is the only way, and I know that I don't believe it's over, I won't believe it's over, until I can talk to him face-to-face, and if he sees me, if he sees what he's doing to me, he'll change his mind. He has to.

Nick takes forever to answer the door. At one point I start turning back, feeling absolutely sick at what I'm doing, rethinking the whole thing, but just as I turn I hear a door upstairs, and then the soft clump of footsteps coming down the stairs.

The door opens and there he is. His hair mussed up, his eyes half closed with sleep, and he is obviously shocked to see me standing there.

We look at each other while I try to find the words, the words that will bring him back, but nothing comes out, and I try to blink back the tear that squeezes itself out of the corner of my right eye.

"Libby," he whispers, as he puts his arms around me, and I can't help it. I break down, sobbing my heart out because as he stands there with his arms around me, gently rubbing my back, I know that this is pointless, that I am making a fool of myself, that nothing will change his mind.

"You'd better come upstairs," he says eventually, gently disengaging himself and leading me upstairs by the hand, while I try to wipe my face.

We sit in silence for a while, me on the armchair, Nick on the futon, and all I want to do is climb into the futon with him and cuddle him, make everything okay, turn the clock back to how it was the other night. I can't believe things can change so quickly. I can't believe that I am no longer allowed to do this because it's over, and as I start to think about it the tears roll down my face again.

"God, Libby," Nick whispers. "I am so sorry. I never meant to hurt you."

"I don't understand," I blurt out. "You said if we met in a few months it would be okay, we could be together, so I don't understand why we can't just carry on."

Nick doesn't say anything. "I don't care about the money," I

sniffle, my voice becoming louder, almost as if he will understand me better if I shout. "I don't give a damn about you not
having a job. We're so good together, Nick, why do you have to
do this? Why can't we just carry on?"

"This is why," he says gently. "Because neither of us was
supposed to get emotionally involved. I never wanted to cause
you any pain, and it's killing me to see you like this."

"So why are you causing me this much pain?" I look up at
him, not caring that the tears are now flowing freely down my
face. "Why are you doing this to me?"

"Libby," he says, coming over and crouching down so that his
face is level with mine. "I told you from the beginning I wasn't
ready for a relationship. I knew you were getting more involved,
but I tried to deny it because I knew I couldn't give you, I can't
give you, what you want. I'm just not ready. I am so sorry."

"Okay," I snuffle, regaining some small measure of composure. "So you can't give me what I want. So what? So now I
know. Let's carry on anyway. You can't hurt me more than you
already have, and now I know exactly where I stand, so I don't
see why we can't keep seeing each other, not when we get on so
well, when things are so good between us." I am trying to bring
him closer, to draw him in through talking to him, but it seems
that the more I talk, the more distance there is between us.

"No, Libby." He shakes his head sadly. "I want to, but I can't
put you through this again, and it will happen again, because I
can't commit to anyone right now. And even though you say that
it doesn't matter, I know that that's what you're looking for, and
it couldn't work. Believe me," he says softly, touching my cheek,
"if I were to commit to anyone it would be to you, but I'm just
not ready."

The tears dry up as I realize that I cannot persuade him.
That his mind is made up. That now there is no doubt that it really is over. I stand up and go to the door, trying to regain some
self-respect, although even I know it's a little late for that.

"I'll call you," Nick says, walking down the stairs behind me
as I head for the front door, feeling like nothing is real, like this

is all a horrific nightmare. I don't bother saying anything. I just walk out and somehow manage to make it home.

• • •

"What did you do this time?" My mother's looking at me, and it's all I can do not to jump up and scream at her because this is absolutely typical, it's always my bloody fault. My mother would never stop to think that perhaps there was something wrong with these men, oh no. It's always that I've put them off.

"Did you come on too strong?" she says, and I wish, oh how I bloody wish, I'd never mentioned anything. I wasn't planning to, really I wasn't, but then my mother seems to have some sort of psychic sixth sense, and she could see something was wrong, and before I knew it, it just came out. That I'd split up with Nick. Although I omitted the part about turning up at his flat. That's something I'm trying hard to forget.

And yes, I regret it. I regret it because I allowed him to see me at my most vulnerable. I laid all my cards on the table and he swept them away without a second glance. In the few days since it happened, I've tried not to think about it, because the only thing I feel when I remember laying myself open in the way that I did is shame. Pure and absolute shame.

"No," I say viciously. "I did not come on too strong. He just doesn't want a relationship, okay?"

"What do you mean, he doesn't want a relationship? Since when does any man want a relationship?" She snorts with laughter at her little joke, and I look at her, wondering when in hell my mother became such an expert at relationships? I mean, she's only ever been with my dad, for God's sake. No one else would have her.

"You know you have to play hard to get, Libby. None of this jumping into bed on the first night and being there whenever they want you."

How the fuck would she know?

"You nineties women, I don't know." She shakes her head. "You all think that everything's equal now, but, when it comes to matters of the heart, it most certainly isn't. Men haven't changed: they love the thrill of the chase, and if you hand yourself over on a plate they'll lose interest. Simple as that."

"It's not like that, Mum," I say through gritted teeth. "It had nothing to do with that."

"I know you think I'm just your mum and I don't know anything, but let me tell you, I watch Vanessa, and Ricki, and Oprah, and you girls all say the same thing, and the answer's as clear to me as anything. You have to play hard to get, it's the answer to all your problems."

"Mum, you really don't know what you're talking about. Watching a few daytime telly shows does not make you an expert on relationships."

"That's what you think," she says firmly. "And anyway I'm not saying I'm an expert, all I'm saying is that I can see what you're doing wrong."

That's it. I've had enough. Again. "Why is it always me who's doing something wrong?" I practically shout. "Have you ever considered the fact that it might be men who have the problem? No, no, how stupid of me, of course it's my fault. It's always my bloody fault."

"No need for that sort of language," my mum says. "But have you ever considered why you're still single at twenty-seven?"

"It's only twenty-seven, for God's sake! I'm not exactly forty, I've got years."

My mum shakes her head sadly. "No, Libby, you haven't, not if you want to get married and have children, and I think it's high time you stopped and had a good long look at yourself and how you are with these boyfriends."

"You're amazing." I shake my head in disbelief. "Most girls my age would kill to have my life. I've got a flat, a great job, a car and plenty of disposable income. I've got a busy social life, hundreds of friends, and I meet celebrities every day."

"Fine," says my mother. "Fine. But I don't see any of these celebrities proposing to you, do you?"

"Can you not see that having a man is really not that important these days? That I'm far happier being a . . . a Singleton."

"A what?"

"Someone who's happier being single with no attachments."

"Libby, dear," she says patronizingly. "You know that's not true and I know that's not true."

Why does she always have to have the last bloody word? And what's more, the nasty old cow is right. Well, right about me not liking being single, I really don't know about the rest of that stuff, and even if she were right, I certainly wouldn't tell her.

"Mum, let's just drop it," I say, getting up to go.

"Oh, you can't go," she says. "You've only just got here. And I'm concerned about you, Libby, you look as if you've put on a bit of weight."

Jesus Christ. Talk about knowing where to hit the weak spot. And so what if I've put on a bit of weight, it's not like I'm huge or anything, but I've always strived to be seven pounds thinner, and trust my mother to notice that in the few days since that night at Nick's flat I've been eating like a pig, although I decided this morning that that was going to stop. Definitely.

"I haven't put on weight," I say, although I know from the scales that I'm four pounds heavier.

"Okay, okay," she sighs. "I simply don't want you to get fat, I'm only saying it for your own good."

"Look. I'm going."

"Not just yet." She stands up. "Tell you what, I've got some of your favorite caramel cakes here, why don't I just go and get them?"

"You just told me I'd put on weight!"

"One won't hurt you." And she bustles off.

Please tell me I'm not the only one with a completely mad, insensitive mother. Please say that all mothers are like this, that I'm not the only one who goes through hell every time she goes home to see her parents. I don't even know why I bloody go. Every weekend I'm expected for tea on Sunday, and every weekend I turn up, behave like a pissed-off teenager and run away as fast as I can.

Maybe I should do what Olly did. Maybe I should move to Manchester.

She comes back and puts a plate of caramel cakes on the table, and to piss her off I refuse them and tell her I'm on a diet.

"Have just the one," she says. "Look, I'll share one with you," and she picks one up and takes a bite, handing me the other half.

"I. Don't. Want. It," I say through gritted teeth. "Okay?"

"Libby, I wish you wouldn't always take offense when I try to help." She sighs and looks at me with those mournful eyes, and if I didn't know better I'd start feeling sorry for her. Fortunately, I know better.

"I'm your mother and I want what's best for you, and I'm only saying these things because I've got the benefit of experience and I can see things from a different perspective, that's all. And there's nothing I'd love more than to see you happy and with a good man."

I huff a bit but I don't say anything, and after a while she sighs again and evidently decides to give up on this particular line of conversation.

"Spoken to Olly recently?" she asks after a long silence.

Hmm. Now this would really get to her, if I told her that yes, actually, I had just spoken to him, I'd seen him, and not only that, I'd met his girlfriend, Carolyn. What, Mum? You didn't know he had a girlfriend? You didn't know he was in London? Gosh. I am surprised.

But no, I couldn't do that. Much as it would satisfy me to upset Mum right now, I couldn't do it to Olly, so I just nod and say we had a chat the other day.

"Did he mention anything to you about a girlfriend?" she says, trying to sound as if she doesn't care either way, and this is a bit odd because I'm sure Olly wouldn't have told her.

"Why?" I say carefully, not wishing to be drawn into a trap.

"Oh, no reason," she says lightly. "Only he mentioned he

was going away for the weekend and wouldn't tell me who with, so I wondered if he might have some special lady friend."

"If he has he hasn't told me," I lie, knowing that Olly would do his damnedest to keep Carolyn away from Mum, because, as far as Mum's concerned, no one's good enough for her darling son. Not that she'd ever say it out loud, she'd just come out with the odd well-aimed dart, something like, "It's a very interesting accent, darling. Whereabouts in London did you say she came from?" or "I'm sure it's all the rage now, but honestly, darling, her skirt was so short you could practically see her undies."

Believe me, I'm not making it up, she has actually said these things, and Olly does his best to ignore them, but somehow once she's said something he starts noticing it too, and Sara went out the window not long after Mum implied she was common, and Vicky? Well, even I had to admit that Vicky was a bit provocative. Dad loved her, though. Needless to say.

"I hope if he is with someone she's the right kind of girl."

"What on earth are you talking about?"

"Olly's a good boy, he deserves someone very special, not like those other girlfriends he's paraded through here over the years."

Bloody typical.

"Mum," I say, standing up and giving her the obligatory peck on the cheek. "I really am going now." And finally, thankfully, I manage to get away.

* * *

"Right," says Jules, curling up on my sofa, pen poised in hand. "You have to be completely honest, and I mean completely. I want to hear everything that you're looking for."

"But I'm not looking, Jules, I want some time out from relationships, I just want to be on my own for a bit."

"Okay, so in that case just tell me what your dream man is like."

I shrug. "He's tall, about six-one, and he's got light brown, no, make that dark brown hair."

"Eyes?"

"Green."

"Would he look like anyone famous? Mel Gibson?"

He'd look like Nick, I think sadly, pushing that thought away almost as quickly as it appears. "Eugh, no. No. Let me think. Who do I like? I know!" I shout. "Tom Berenger."

"Who's Tom Berenger?"

"The actor, *Platoon*? *Someone to Watch Over Me*?"

Jules shakes her head, but writes his name down anyway.

"Okay," she says. "What else?"

"He's got to be rich, seriously rich. He'd live in one of those huge stucco houses in Holland Park, but not a flat, it would be a whole house, and he'd rattle around in it waiting for his wife and her interior designer best friend to come and redo it all."

"Mmm," laughs Jules. "Now that I like the sound of."

"He'd probably be a businessman, he'd have his own business, God knows at what, and he'd drive a Ferrari."

"Bit flash, isn't it?"

"Okay. A Mercedes SLK."

Jules nods and writes it down. "Just the one car, then?"

"Good point. No, he'd have the Merc, and a Range Rover for weekends at his country pad, and he'd buy me that new BMW, you know, the sporty one, what is it, an F3 or a Z3 or something?"

"He would have to wear beautiful navy suits for work, but then when he's at home he'd be in really faded 501s and polo shirts, oh, and leather trousers because he'd have a motorbike as well."

"What kind of motorbike? A Harley?"

"Nah, way too common. An Indian."

"Okay." She keeps scribbling, and I hug my knees to my chest, wondering what else I can say about my dream man, because I love playing these fantasy games.

"I can't think of what else to say." I sit and think for a while.

"Er, Libby?" Jules looks up.

"Mmm?"

"Haven't you forgotten something?"

"What?"

"His personality?"

Well, what can you say about a personality, for heaven's sake? I mean, let's face it, we all want pretty much the same thing when it comes to personality. We want someone who's intelligent. We'd quite like him to be creative, although that's not a prerequisite if you're not into that kind of stuff. We'd like someone kind. Sensitive. Oh, and how could we forget, a good sense of humor, although that's a bit of a difficult one, because, as Carrie Fisher once said in a film, everyone thinks they have good taste and a sense of humor.

We'd like someone who likes going out for dinner and going to the movies. We'd like someone who's also very happy going on a long walk in the country, then curling up by a fire, and even though I'd never dream of actually going for a long walk in the country, it's a nice thought, and I'd definitely want someone who would, at the very least, appreciate that thought.

And before you think I'm completely superficial, I have to say in my defense that I honestly never gave the personality a second thought, because it's kind of an unspoken thing. Of course you assume he's going to have a personality you like, otherwise you wouldn't bother in the first place.

So, finally, we end up with a list that's two pages long. A page and a half of what he looks like, where he lives, how he lives, and a few hastily scribbled lines of the personality stuff, and when we've finished Jules tucks it into my bag and says, "I think you may have to compromise somewhat on the material side, but it always helps to write down what you think you're looking for. Now the next step is wardrobe."

Jules goes into the kitchen, opens the fridge, and pulls a black bin liner off a roll that's nestling there, and only Jules knows me well enough to know that due to the lack of space in my kitchen the vegetable drawer in the fridge is also home to various cleaning items that I rarely get around to using.

"What's that for?" I look at her suspiciously.

"This is for Nick memorabilia."

"But I don't have any memorabilia." Why do I still feel a pang of sadness when his name is mentioned unexpectedly?

"What, nothing? No photos? No letters? No sweatshirts that you borrowed and accidentally on purpose forgot to give back?"

I shake my head, and then I remember. "Wait!" I run into the bedroom and pull a T-shirt out of the dirty linen basket, and I can't help it. I'm completely ashamed to admit that I bury my nose in it to smell Nick, since he was the last person wearing it, but try as I might I can't smell him. All I can smell is the musty odor of dirty linen.

I go back into the living room, holding the T-shirt, and gingerly hand it to Jules, who, it has to be said, accepts it even more gingerly before stuffing it in the bag.

"Are you sure that's it?" I know she doesn't believe me, but I nod.

"So this is the last reminder?"

I nod again.

She ties the bin bag tightly and takes it out the front door, putting it with the rubbish.

"I thought you liked him," I moan, because I can't believe she's being so ruthless.

"I did like him," she says. "But the only way you're going to get over him properly is to remove all the evidence, and by going out with other men. Speaking of which, has that guy called?"

"Which guy?"

"Ed."

He has called. He called the day after I met him and left a rather nervous-sounding message on my machine, which was a bit peculiar because he was so self-assured when we met. "Hello, Libby," he said. "Er, it's, er, Ed here. We met last night at Mezzo. I was just wondering whether perhaps you'd, er, like to come out for dinner with me. It was lovely to meet you, and I wondered whether you might give me a call back."

Maybe he's just one of those blokes who hate answering

machines. Anyway, he left his home number, his work number and his mobile number, and he said he'd be in all day and at home that evening.

I didn't call back.

I mean, I know I said I'd have dinner with him, but I'm really not that bothered, and what would be the point? I don't fancy him, there's no stomach-churning lovely lustful feeling like I had with Nick when we first got together, like I still have when I think about Nick, and I'm sure he's a nice guy but I really can't see me getting involved with anyone right now, even if he does drive a Porsche. I just feel weary. Exhausted. That whole Nick thing has done me in, and right at this moment if I can't have him I don't want anyone.

Plus, this Ed character might not drive a Porsche anyway. He might be one of those wanky types who has a Porsche key ring to impress women he's trying to pick up in Mezzo.

"No," I lie, shaking my head. "He hasn't called."

"Really?" Jules looks surprised. "I can't believe he hasn't called, he seemed so smitten. Well, he will."

"I really don't care."

"I know," she says. "But it would do you good. He'll probably take you somewhere incredibly swanky and treat you like a princess and you'll have a good time. No one says you have to sleep with him, or even see him again for that matter, but you never know what his friends are like. You might meet the man of your dreams by being friends with him."

"Oh, shut up, Jules, you sound just like my mother."

• • •

And I know I will be fine, it's not like the other times I've broken up with boyfriends, when I've been so heartbroken I've cried solidly for about three weeks and not wanted to go anywhere or do anything. Okay, I had that one night from hell, but since then I've been really okay, and at least I know there's no point living on false hope. At least I know it really is over so I can move on. But I have to say that this time I feel a bit numb, still in a state of shock, really, although I don't feel that my world has ended, not completely. I suppose that the light at the end of the tunnel, though not very bright, is at least there.

They say that it never hurts as much after the first time, and I suppose there's an element of truth in that, but they also say that every time you get hurt the barriers go up a little bit higher, and you end up being hard and cynical, and not giving anything to anyone.

God, that that were true.

I wish that I could be hard and cynical. That I could take things slowly, not give too much of myself, because I'd be so frightened of getting hurt that there wouldn't be any other way. But no. Every time I meet someone I dive in headfirst, showering them with love and attention, and hoping that this time they're going to turn out to be different.

Chance would be a fine bloody thing.

I don't see the point in pretending to be something other than what you are, because if you do, at some point, you're going to have to reveal your true self, and if it's completely different, they're going to run off screaming.

But perhaps I'm learning to hold back a little bit, perhaps that's why this isn't hurting so much, or perhaps it's because Nick wasn't, isn't, The One, and although I was starting to like him more and more, I suppose deep down I knew I couldn't live his life, and that's why I'm really feeling okay.

But okay isn't great, and so what if I go through my CD collection once Jules has gone and pull out all the songs that I know are guaranteed to make me cry. So what if I start with R.E.M. and "Everybody Hurts," and sob like a baby. So what if I continue with Janis Ian's "At Seventeen," and start feeling like the biggest reject in the world. And yeah, so I stick on Everything but the Girl singing "I Don't Want to Talk About It," but Jesus, everyone's allowed to feel a bit sorry for themselves sometimes, aren't they?

So I sit, and keep putting on CDs, and cry and cry and cry, until I'm hiccuping madly and I've got a pounding headache, and the phone rings but I don't answer it because I'm not sure whether I can disguise the fact I've been crying this time, and I really don't want to have to explain myself to anyone right now.

The machine clicks on, I hear my message, and then I hear a voice. "Oh hello, er, Libby. It's Ed, we met the other night at Mezzo. I left you a message the other day but I thought perhaps you didn't get it, so I'm leaving you another one because I'd really love to see you."

Once again he leaves all his numbers, and I know this sounds bizarre, but it cheers me up a bit, the fact that someone likes me enough to leave two messages, and even though it doesn't cheer me up enough to actually pick up the phone, soon after he's finished speaking I decide that I might just call him back after all.

Chapter 14

Today is the day I'm going to phone Ed. Definitely. I thought about it last night, and Jules is absolutely right, I should be going out with other men, and I know he's not really my type, but what the hell. I am, as my mother reminded me, twenty-seven years old and I suppose what it's all about is a numbers game: go out with enough men and one of them's bound to be Mr. Right.

But in the meantime I've got my hands completely full at work. I'm trying to organize the launch for this TV series, and I've just finished the press release inviting all the journalists and photographers, when who should call up but Amanda Baker.

Not what I need right now at all.

"Hi, darling," she says, which throws me ever so slightly, because she's not the sort of person I'd ever darling, and she's never done this to me before, but I suppose since her recent radio appearances she's forgiven me my apparent lack of work on her behalf, and now she's treating me as if we're best friends.

"I thought we could go out for lunch," she says. "You know, a girls' lunch. You and me."

I'm so flummoxed I don't know what to say, so I stammer for a while, wondering what on earth is going on.

"Are you free today?" she says. "It's just that I'm so busy at the moment, but I'd love to see you and I thought we might go to Quo Vadis."

Now that's done it for me, because needless to say I haven't been to Quo Vadis yet, and it's one of those restaurants that you really ought to go to at least once, if only to say that you've been there.

"I'd love to," I say. "Shall I meet you there?"

"Perfect," she says. "Book the table for one-fifteen. All right, darling, see you later." And she's gone, leaving me sitting there looking at the receiver in my hand and wondering why on earth I'm supposed to book the table when she invited me.

So I'm walking round the office in a bemused fashion, asking if anyone's got the number for Quo Vadis, when Joe Cooper walks out of his office and says, "That's very posh. How come you're going to Quo Vadis?"

"This is really odd, Joe," I say. "Amanda Baker just phoned and invited me out for lunch, which is completely peculiar in itself because up until pretty damn recently I was her worst enemy, and I suddenly seem to have become her best friend, and then she asked me to book the table. All a bit weird."

Joe throws back his head with laughter. "Libby," he says. "This is Amanda's trick, she's done this with every PR she's ever worked with. She starts off mistrusting you and the minute you actually get her some coverage she decides you're her best friend. Don't worry about it, look at it this way, at least it will make your life easier."

I shrug. "S'pose so." And I scribble down the number on a yellow Post-it note and go to call the restaurant.

• • •

It's half past one, and I'm sitting at a window table trying to see out the stained glass and wondering what they do when it gets really hot in here, because there aren't any window latches so they can't open the windows. I'm trying to look very cool, as if I'm someone famous, because it seems that almost everybody else in here is. I've already spotted three television presenters, two pop stars, and the people at the table next to me are talking about their latest film, and since I don't recognize them I presume they're behind the camera, as it were. And no, I'm not trying to earwig, it's just that it's bloody difficult when you're sitting on your own not to hear what the table next door is talking about when they're so close to you they're practically sitting in your lap, and where the hell is Amanda anyway?

I ask for another Kir and puff away on my fourth cigarette, when I suddenly hear a familiar "Darling!" and look up and see Amanda kiss her way through the restaurant, greeting all the minor celebrities as if she's known them forever, and to my immense surprise they do all know her, and I suddenly feel quite pleased that she's meeting me, and I'm even more pleased when she sweeps up to the table and gives me two air-kisses before sitting down.

"Darling," she says, evidently in a much more ebullient mood than when we last met. "You look fab."

"So do you," I say. "It's lovely to see you."

"I thought that we really ought to get to know each other a bit better," she says, glancing round the room as she speaks, presumably just in case she's missing anything.

She orders a sparkling mineral water from the waiter, and we sit and make small talk for a while, and then, once we've ordered—me from the set lunch menu at £15.95 and Amanda from the à la carte menu—the conversation turns, as it so often does with single women, to men.

"Well, you know"—she leans forward conspiratorially—"my last affair was with . . ." She leans even closer and whispers the name of a well-known TV anchorman in my ear, then sits back to note my admiration, because the anchorman in question is indeed gorgeous, and I would normally tell you, but somehow I don't think Amanda would want you to know, because as well as being gorgeous he's also very married, and it wouldn't do his image any good at all.

But trust me. It's great gossip.

"So what happened?"

"He came out with all the usual shit about loving his wife but not being in love with her, and how they slept in separate beds, and he was only with her because it was good for his profile, and that he was going to leave her, he'd had enough. But of course he didn't."

"Amazing, isn't it?" I say. "Whenever our friends get involved with married men we hear about what they say and it's always the same and we always tell our friends that he's never going to leave her, but the minute it happens to us, the minute we meet a married man and he says he loves his wife but he's not in love with her, we believe him."

"I know," she laughs, but there's a tinge of bitterness in her laugh. "I really thought I was more clever than that. I really thought that he was different, that he was going to leave."

"So what made you realize he wasn't?"

"When I opened the pages of *Hello!* and read how excited they both were that she was pregnant again, with their sixth child."

"Jesus." I exhale loudly and sit back. "That must have hurt."

"It was a killer," she says. "So now I'm back on the dating scene, which is hell, really, because even though I'm famous . . ."

I suppress a snort.

". . . I just don't seem to meet any decent men. To be honest I think they're all a bit intimidated by me."

"I can understand that," I say.

"Really?" she says. "Why do you think it is?"

"Oh, er. Well, because you're famous, and you're very bright, and very attractive." I see her face fall. "I mean, you're beautiful, and that scares a lot of men off."

"I know." She nods. "You're absolutely right."

"It's the same for me," I say, and wait for her to ask me about my own love life, but she doesn't, and then I think how stupid I am to think a celebrity, even one as minor as Amanda, would be interested in anyone other than themselves. But fuck it. I want to talk about this. I need to talk about this. And somehow, sitting right here with this woman who's more than a stranger but not quite a friend, I find myself telling her all about it, which I suspect throws her a bit, because she's far more used to talking about herself than to listening to other people, but I can't help it. It all comes out.

"So," I end, having spoken nonstop for the last twenty minutes, "now there's this guy Ed pursuing me and I really don't know whether to call him, because even though he's nice enough I just can't see a future in it and I guess I'm still hung up on Nick, even though I know there's no future in that either."

"Ed who?" Amanda asks, a flicker of interest in her eyes.

"I don't know," I say, and I laugh, because I'm so uninterested I haven't even bothered to look at his business card. "Hang on," I say, fishing around in my bag. "His card's here somewhere."

I find my diary and pull out the card, glancing at it briefly. "Ed McMann."

"You're joking!" Amanda's gasping across the table at me. "No." She shakes her head. "It can't be." She grabs the card and starts laughing as she reads it. "Oh my God, Libby! Ed McMann! Don't you know who he is?"

I shake my head.

"He's only one of the most eligible bachelors in Britain. I can't believe you pulled Ed McMann and you didn't even realize who he was!"

"Who is he, then?"

"He's a financial whiz kid who everyone's talking about, because he seemed to appear out of nowhere. He's single, hugely rich and supposedly unbelievably intelligent. I've never met him, but my friend Robert knows him really well. I've been begging him to fix me up with him, but Robert keeps saying we wouldn't get on."

"But Amanda," I say slowly, "have you seen him? He's not exactly an oil painting." I laugh, although suddenly I'm slightly more interested in Ed. Not a lot, just slightly.

"So?" she says. "With his kind of money, who cares?"

"How come, if he's so rich and so eligible, he hasn't got a girlfriend?"

"That's the odd thing," she says. "He doesn't seem to have much luck with women. Robert says it's because he's a bit eccentric, but I don't really know."

"Well," I say, "maybe I will call him, then."

"Call him?" Amanda snorts. "Marry him, more like."

· · ·

By the end of our lunch, and I swear, no one is more surprised by this than me, I've made two decisions. One is to call Ed Mc-Mann this afternoon, and the other is that I quite like Amanda Baker. Okay, she's not someone whom I'd normally consider being friends with, but after our bit of female bonding over lunch, I think she's quite sweet really, and as we leave I decide that I'm going to try to get her a bit more coverage, work a bit harder for her. Don't get me wrong, I'm not saying that she's my new best friend or anything, it's just that she's all right, she's one of us, if you know what I'm saying.

So I go back to the office and pull out Ed McMann's business card again, and I sit for a while looking at it, and then I pick up the phone and dial his number.

"Hello, is Ed McMann there, please?"

"Who may I say is calling?"

"Libby Mason."

"And will he know what it's in connection with?"

"Yes."

"May I tell him?"

"Tell him what?"

"What it's in connection with?"

"It's, umm. Don't worry. He'll know." What is this, for heaven's sake? The Spanish Inquisition?

And then there's a silence, and I sit and listen to piped music for a while, and finally, just when I'm about to give up, Ed comes on the phone.

"Libby?"

"Ed?"

"Libby! I'm so delighted you phoned. I was so worried you didn't get my messages."

"I'm sorry," I say, "I've been running around like a madwoman, I've been so busy."

"Never mind, never mind. You've phoned now! I was giving up hope! When are you free for dinner?"

"I'll just look in my diary," I say, looking in my diary. "When were you thinking of?"

"Tomorrow night?"

Naturally there's nothing in my diary for tomorrow night, but do I really want to see this man so soon? Nah, I don't think I do, I think I'd be much happier staying in and watching the box.

"I'm sorry," I say, sounding as if I mean it. "But this week's horrendous. How about next week, that's looking pretty clear."

"Oh, umm. Okay. Actually, what about the weekend? Saturday night?"

Now Saturday night's a big night. Saturday night is not a night to give up for just anyone, particularly a man I don't even fancy, but then again, he's bound to take me somewhere nice, and he may not be Nick, but he is one of the most eligible men in Britain, and I really ought to be a bit more excited about this than I am, so okay, I'm game on.

And Ed is so excited I can practically hear him jumping up and down. He takes my address and I laugh to myself, wondering what he'll make of my tiny little basement flat in grotty Ladbroke Grove, because he must live in some unbelievable mansion somewhere, but I don't really care what he thinks, and he says he'll pick me up at eight and book somewhere special.

I say goodbye and ring Jules without even putting down the phone.

"I have a date with one of the most eligible men in Britain on Saturday night!" I say, and I do add an unspoken exclamation mark at the end of my sentence, because actually I'm pretty damn pleased with myself.

"Who?"

"Ed McMann."

"Ed? Ed that we met?"

"Yup."

"What do you mean, one of the most eligible bachelors in Britain?"

I repeat, word for word, what Amanda told me over lunch.

"Jesus," she says. "That's a result. And he sounds much more you than that Nick."

See? Already Nick's become "that Nick"—not someone involved in my life, someone in my past, someone who never had a future.

"In what way?"

"Oh, come on, Libby, he'll probably take you to amazing places and buy you wonderful presents and you'll love every minute of it."

"Jules, I think you're jumping a bit ahead of yourself here. I mean, I hardly know the guy, and I certainly don't fancy him. At least, I didn't the other night."

"Fine," she laughs. "Let's just wait and see."

• • •

I wake up on Saturday and have to admit that, while I'm not exactly jumping with joy at the prospect of tonight's date with Ed, I do have slight butterflies, but I suspect that's more to do with having a date at all rather than who the date's with. And I still miss Nick.

I get all the boring chores done—dry cleaners; cleaning the flat; sorting out all the shit I don't have time for during the week—and then, after I've settled in front of the *Brookside* omnibus, I start planning what to wear.

A black suit, I decide. A suit that's smart, sophisticated, and always makes me feel fantastic. But I don't want to look too straight, even though, from what I remember, Ed would make Pall Mall look positively curvy, so I team it with very high-heeled black strappy sandals and a beautiful gray silk scarf tied softly at my neck.

And I look in the mirror and I smile to myself because I certainly look the part, even if I don't feel it inside, and I feel that I can hold my head up high and walk in anywhere feeling good.

Not that I know where Ed's planning to take me, but I'm sure it will be somewhere expensive and impressive, and whenever I go to places like that I like to feel well-armed, and the best way of feeling like that is to look fantastic, preferably in designer clothes.

And the flat looks perfect. Well, as perfect as it can look. I even bought armfuls of flowers this morning, and I have to say I'm quite proud of the place, even though I know Ed will probably never have seen anything this small. I've done away with the clutter. At least, I've swept it under the sofa and into closets, so it looks pristine. I've sprayed air freshener around, so it smells like a summer meadow, or so it says on the can, and okay, it wouldn't pass my mother's inspection, but I'm damn sure it would pass everyone else's.

The only thing I haven't bothered to do is change the sheets, or even shave my legs when it comes to that, because I'm absolutely sure that I will not be going to bed with Ed, or anyone else for that matter, for a while yet, and at the grand old age of twenty-seven I've realized that the best contraception of all is hairy legs.

So my outer perfection hides my lower layer of stubble and graying Marks & Spencer knickers, but it hardly matters tonight, and I don't believe all that rubbish about you feeling more sexy when you're wearing sexy underwear. It's crap. As far as I'm concerned you feel more sexy when you've lost weight and you're having a good hair day. Simple as that.

And tonight I have lost weight (I've been practically starving myself since my mother's comment), I'm back to my usual, and I'm having a good hair day, so, when the doorbell rings at eight on the dot, I walk confidently to the door and open it with a gracious smile.

Chapter 15

I don't actually see Ed for a while. All I can see, when I open the door, is the most enormous bouquet of long-stemmed creamy white roses that I've ever seen in my life, and they completely take my breath away.

No one's ever bought me flowers before, you see. I know that sounds daft, but none of my boyfriends have ever been the romantic type, and I've always longed for someone who would bring me flowers and chocolates.

I was given chocolates once by a very keen man who arrived to pick me up and handed me a box of Milk Tray. I had to give him ten out of ten for effort, but Milk Tray? They should have been Belgian chocolates, at the very least.

And Jon bought me flowers once, but it was only because I'd gone over to his flat and he'd obviously been out buying loads of flowers for himself, and I was so upset that he didn't buy me any that I threw a wobbly, and when we left the flat he stopped outside the flower shop and bought me a bunch of wilting chrysanthemums, which was hardly the point. What I remember most clearly about him doing that was his face. He was so proud of himself because he thought I'd be over the moon, but if anything it pissed me off even more.

And here, on my doorstep, is a bunch of flowers so big it hides the man standing behind, and as I take the flowers and see Ed, my first thought is that he isn't nearly as bad as I remember him. In fact, apart from the disgusting mustache, he looks rather nice, really, and we stand there and sort of grin at each other because I'm not sure whether to kiss him or whether that would be too forward, and in the end he leans forward and gives me a kiss on the cheek and says that I look lovely.

I twirl around and he hands me the flowers and of course I invite him in. He stands in the living room and looks around and doesn't actually say anything, doesn't say how lovely it is, how clean, how pristine, which is a bit strange because most people, when they come to your house for the first time, compliment it out of politeness, even if they hate it.

I take the flowers and dig out a jug, which is the only thing I've got left since I've used up my one vase for the flowers I bought myself earlier, and as I arrange them Ed stands there rather awkwardly, so I try to make small talk with him.

"Did you find it all right?" I say, for want of something better.

"I got a bit lost," he says. "It's not really my neck of the woods."

"Where do you live?"

"Regent's Park."

"Oh, really? Whereabouts?"

"Do you know the park?"

I nod.

"Hanover Terrace."

Jesus Christ! Hanover Terrace! That's one of those huge sweeping Regency Nash terraces that sweeps along the side of the park next to the mosque. I once met someone whose parents live there, and I know that the houses are enormous, and each has its own little mews house at the end of the garden. But maybe Ed has a flat there, maybe it's not as impressive as I think.

"Do you have a flat?"

"Er, no, actually. I have a house."

"So you've got one of those little mews houses too?"

"Yes," he laughs. "But I still haven't figured out quite what to do with it. So how come you live here, Libby?"

"What, in Ladbroke Grove?"

"Yes."

"It's the only place I can afford," I laugh, and wait for him to smile, but he doesn't. He looks horrified.

"But it's not very safe," he says finally. "I don't think I'd be happy living here."

"It's fine," I say. "You get used to it, and I quite like the fact that there's such a mixture of people, there's always something going on. And it's great place to score drugs." I can't help this last comment, it just sort of comes out and I don't know what it is but something about him being so straight makes me want to shock him.

It works.

"You take drugs?" Now he looks completely disgusted.

"I'm joking."

"Oh." And then, thankfully, he starts laughing. "Hilarious," he says. "You're ever so funny, Libby."

I shrug and smile, and then the flowers are in the jug and the jug is on my mantelpiece, and we're ready to go.

"Libby, I didn't say this before but you really are looking absolutely beautiful tonight."

"Thank you." And thank God I've learned to be gracious about receiving compliments. For years I'd say things like, "What? In this old thing?" but now I accept compliments like the sophisticated woman I'm trying so hard to be.

"And I particularly like the scarf," he says. "It's beautiful."

"What? This old thing?" I couldn't help it. It just came out.

"Is it silk?"

I nod.

"I thought so. Shall we go?"

So we walk out the front door and I can't help but grin when I see his Porsche—a midnight blue Porsche Carrera, which would have been a convertible had I had anything to do with it, but hell, cars can always be changed, and it's still a beautiful, wonderful, sexy car.

And not only that. Ed walks round to my side first, opens the door and waits until I get in before closing it gently, and I almost want to hug myself because I can't believe I'm sitting in a Porsche with one of the most eligible men in Britain, and Jesus, what the hell did I put up with Nick for when I could have had this all along?

"I've booked a table at the River Cafe," he says. "Is that all right?"

All right? All right? It's fantastic because I haven't been—it's far too expensive for my meager pockets—and I've heard all about it and it's the best possible choice he could have made. Plus, and this is important, it's not too straight or stuffy, in fact it's pretty damn trendy, and I think I would have been extremely upset if we'd ended up somewhere too grown-up.

"I really wanted to take you to Marco Pierre White's restaurant, but I couldn't get a table," he admits. "I tried begging, but they were fully booked."

"That's fine," I say. "The River Cafe is perfect. I haven't been and I really want to go."

"Oh, good." He smiles at me. "I was so worried you wouldn't like it. Shall I put some music on?"

"Definitely," I say approvingly, reaching for the CDs stacked in the glove compartment. "You can always tell what a man's like by the music he listens to and the books he reads."

Ed laughs. "So what can you tell about me?"

I pull out the CDs and flick through. Oh dear. Opera and classical music. Lots and lots of opera. Wagner. Donizetti. Offenbach. Bizet. Oh God. I rifle through, praying that there's something I know, I don't even mind if it's something I don't particularly like, something like, say, Elton John or Billy Joel, but no. Nothing. So I pretend his question was a rhetorical one.

"What would you like me to put on?" Ed says.

"Well, actually," I say, deciding to bite the bullet and be completely honest. "I'm not really that into classical music."

"Oh." There's a silence. "So what kind of music do you listen to?"

"Pretty much anything and everything," I laugh. "Except classical and opera."

"But why not?"

"I don't know. I suppose I never listened to it when I was young, so I never developed an ear for it."

"How about this one, then?" he says, reaching over and taking a CD out of my hand. *"L'elisir d'amore,"* he says, in a perfect Italian accent, the *r*'s rolling off his tongue. "I think you'll like this."

He puts it on and looks at me for approval, and what can I say? It's all right, really, quite melodic, but it's opera, for God's sake, but I can't tell him this, so I just smile and tell him he made a good choice and that I like it.

And then as we stop at some traffic lights I turn my head and notice that in the car next to us—an old Peugeot 106, just in case you're interested—are two girls my age, and they're both looking enviously at the Porsche and at me, and I smile to myself and sink a little deeper into the seat because I'm quite enjoying this. Despite the music.

So I decide that I'm going to make an effort with Ed, even though I suspect he really isn't my type, but surely he could grow to be my type? Surely if he brings me flowers I could grow to like him? Fancy him? Couldn't I? I sneak a peek at him driving and feel a wave of disappointment rush over me, because he's not half as gorgeous as Nick, but then Nick isn't here, and Ed is.

"Tell me about your job, Libby," he says, concentrating on the road, but trying to be polite.

"Not much to tell," I say. "I work in PR on people like Sean Moore."

"Who?"

I look at him in amazement. "Sean Moore. You must know who he is. He's the biggest heartthrob since, well, since Angus Deayton."

"Oh, ha ha. I know who Angus Deayton is! He's the chap on that program, isn't he? The news one."

"Have I Got News for You."

Ed nods vigorously. "Yes, that's the one. Very funny show. Always try and catch it if I'm in on a Friday night."

"And are you usually in on a Friday night?"

"Not usually," he laughs. "Most Friday nights I'm working late."

"Don't you ever take time off?"

"To be honest with you I suppose I throw myself into work because I haven't met the right woman yet."

Now this is a first. I can't believe he's telling me this on our first date. And I'm eager to hear more.

"You mean you want to settle down?"

"Definitely," he says. "Absolutely. That's why I bought the house in Hanover Terrace. I thought it would be a perfect home for a family and children, but at the moment I'm still rattling around in it all by myself."

This is getting better and better. The most eligible bachelor in Britain is desperate to get married and he's taking me out! He's with me! And I can't believe his honesty, the fact that he's willing to admit he wants to get married, the fact that for the first time in my life I'm on a date with a man who doesn't appear to be allergic to commitment.

Although to be honest, I'm not sure about this whole scared of commitment business. I think it's become too handy, a useful phrase that men can bandy about whenever they feel like being assholes. And sure, I do believe there are some men who are genuinely terrified of commitment, but there aren't that many, and for the most part I think it's that they haven't met the right woman yet. Because if a man, no matter how scared he professed to be, met the woman of his dreams, he wouldn't want to let her go, would he? And sure, he might not want to actually get married, but if he were madly in love and risked losing her, he'd do it, wouldn't he?

That's what I think, anyway.

And I'm so used to playing games with men, to pretending that I'm this hard, tough, career woman who's very happy being single and really doesn't mind, no, loves having relationships which involve seeing each other twice a week if you're lucky, that I'm not quite sure what to do with someone this honest.

I decide to ask more questions. To see whether he really is for real.

"So how come you haven't married?"

"I don't know. I thought I had met the right woman, but then it turned out I hadn't, she wasn't the right one. You see, I suppose I'm quite old-fashioned. I don't understand these career girls, and yes, I think it's fine for girls to have a bit of independence, but I'm really looking for a wife. Someone who'll look after me and our children."

"So you wouldn't want her to work once she got married?"

He shakes his head. "Do you think that's too much to ask?"

"No," I say firmly. "I absolutely agree."

"Do you?"

"Yes. I think it's appalling that women continue their careers once they've had children. A mother ought to be at home with the children. I know too many women whose kids are completely neglected because they seem to be more interested in working late at the office."

This last bit isn't completely true, but what the hell, I know I'm on the right track and Ed's so excited he can hardly contain himself.

"Libby," he says, taking his eyes off the road and turning to me. "I'm jolly glad I met you. Jolly glad." And his grin's so wide for a second I think it's going to burst off his face.

When we get to the River Cafe, Ed walks up to the girl standing behind the desk at the front and says, "Hello!" in such an effusive tone I figure he must know her, but she stands there smiling awkwardly at him, which makes me think that he's this overexuberant all the time. "Ed McMann!" he says. "Table for two!"

"Oh, yes," she says, scanning her list. "Follow me."

"I hope it's a good table!" he says to her. "I asked for the best table in the restaurant. Are we by the window?"

"I'm afraid not," she says. "But you're as close as we could get you." And she leads us to a table in the middle of the room.

"Oh, jolly good!" Ed says loudly in his public school accent, and I cringe slightly as I notice how other people in the restaurant are turning to look at where this voice is coming from. "Très bien!" he then says, in a very, very bad French accent, and I can't help it, I start giggling, because if nothing else he's certainly a character.

"Umm, you speak French?" I say, as we sit down.

"Mais bien sur!" he says, and it comes out, "May bienne soor," and I sit there and wish he'd shut up, and then I mentally slap myself for being so nasty, because he's just a bit eccentric, that's all, and it's quite endearing in a weird sort of way, it simply takes a bit of getting used to. That's all.

And you know what? I have a really nice time. Ed's quite funny. He tells me lots of stories about investment banking, and admittedly a large part of each story goes completely over my head because investment banking is not exactly a subject I know an awful lot about, but he giggles as he tells them, and it's quite cute, not to mention infectious, and I find myself giggling with him and I'm quite surprised at how well this evening's going.

But just because he's good company doesn't mean I fancy him, but then maybe fancying someone isn't what it's all about? Maybe I've been wrong in waiting for that sweep you off your feet feeling, the feeling I had with Nick. And, let's face it, it didn't exactly work with Nick, did it, so maybe I've been looking for the wrong thing.

Here I am sitting with a man who's rich, charming, honest and wants to get married. Most women would kill to be sitting where I am right now, and okay, so he's not really my type, but maybe that could grow?

And as I sit I allow myself to imagine what it would be like kissing him. I picture his face moving closer to mine, and then, yuck! Oh God! That mustache! Yuck yuck yuck!

"Do you cook?" I'm brought back to earth by the sound of

Ed's voice, and I try to push the thought of him kissing me out of my head. Unfortunately, I don't manage to, but it lodges somewhere near the back, which is okay for now.

"I love cooking," I say. "But only for other people. I can never be bothered to cook for myself, but my ideal evening would be cooking for my close friends."

"Gosh!" he says. "You can cook too! Libby, is there anything you're not good at?"

"Sex?"

"Oh ha ha!" He rocks back in his chair, gulping with laughter. "Hilarious!" And I sit and smile, wondering who on earth this man is, but not in a bad way, in more of an intrigued way, and the bill arrives, which is always a bit of an awkward time because I'm never too sure whether to offer, but this time I decide not to because, after all, Ed did say he was old-fashioned, and anyway with the amount of wine we've had to drink, plus the champagne he ordered at the beginning, I couldn't afford it even if I wanted to. So I sit back and watch as Ed pulls out a platinum American Express card—platinum! I've never met anyone with a platinum American Express card before!—and when the waitress takes it away I lean forward and thank him for a lovely evening.

"Libby," he says earnestly. "The pleasure was all mine. I think you're fantastic!" And I smile because it feels like a long time since anyone's thought that about me, and I'm not sure whether anyone's really felt that way about me, ever. I'm used to being the chaser, the one to fall head over heels in love. I'm the one who's usually sitting there thinking that they're fantastic, although I'd never dare say it for fear of scaring them off, and here's someone who not only thinks it, but has the balls to say it!

I think I could get used to this, and quite frankly if I can't have Nick, then perhaps I can settle for having someone who completely adores me. Even though he hardly even knows me.

We get back in his car and on the way back we have that

whole relationship talk where they ask you why you're single, when your last relationship was and what the longest relationship you've ever had has been, and I say we have that talk but actually that's slightly wrong—I'm so busy trying to think of how to avoid saying I'm a complete nightmare in relationships because I'm so needy, paranoid and insecure that I forget to ask him anything at all.

But he doesn't seem to mind. In fact, he doesn't say anything as I tell him that I haven't met the right man yet, that I drifted apart from all my previous boyfriends, and that my longest relationship has been a year (well, okay then, nine months, but he doesn't have to know that, does he?). I do mention Nick, but I brush over it, brush over the pain that it caused, is still causing, and I do my best to be lighthearted about it, to say it meant nothing.

Ed nods thoughtfully and if I didn't know better I'd say he was definitely sizing me up for wife material, but maybe that's a bit ridiculous of me because this is only our first date.

Do I ask him in for coffee? I'm not sure I want him to come in for coffee. I'm not entirely sure how to deal with this whole scenario, but luckily Ed pulls up outside my flat and doesn't switch the engine off so I assume he'll be whizzing home.

"Hang on," he says, leaping out of the car. "I'll come and get you out." And he runs around the car and opens the door for me, and against my better judgment perhaps, I wish my mother could see me now!

"May I see you again?" he says and, without even thinking about whether I really want to, I find myself saying yes.

"Are you free tomorrow?" he says eagerly.

"I'm afraid not," I say, because okay, I'm only going to my parents, but tomorrow feels a bit too soon, and I know that if I were completely crazy about him I'd say of course tomorrow would be fine, but I'm still not entirely sure how I feel about this. Physically he is so not my type that I decide to give myself a few days' breathing space to think about this one.

"I could do next week, though," I say. "Tuesday?"

"Marvelous!" he says, without looking at his diary. "I'll pick you up at eight, how does that sound?"

"Fine," I say. "And thank you, again, for a lovely evening."

Ed walks me to my front door, and I turn awkwardly as I put my key in the lock, wondering exactly how to say goodbye, and even as I turn he's leaning down to give me two kisses on each cheek.

"Again, Libby," he says, turning to walk back toward the car, "the pleasure was all mine."

Chapter 16

I don't mean to say anything, really I don't, but my mother is banging on about me being single again, and before I know it it just slips out that last night I had a date with Ed McMann, and my mother being my mother knows exactly who Ed McMann is, and she's so shocked all the color practically drains from her face.

"Not Ed McMann the finance person?"

"Yes, Mum," I say, and I can't help the hint of pride in my voice. "Ed McMann the finance person."

For one ghastly minute I think she's about to hug me, but thankfully she doesn't.

"How on earth did you meet him?" she says.

"I met him at Mezzo," I say. "And he took my number, and he's been calling ever since."

"Mezzo?" she says in awe, because my mother, despite never actually leaving suburbia, dreams of doing so on a regular basis, and consequently reads every style magazine on the shelves. She is what we in PR would call aspirational. "What's it like?"

"It's fine." I shrug. "Big."

"And you met Ed McMann there? Well, Libby, all I can say is this time don't blow it."

"I beg your pardon?"

"You heard me. Don't mess this one up. Ed McMann's very, very rich."

"God, Mum," I say in disgust, "is that all you ever think about?"

• • •

And the funny thing is that all day Sunday, when I think about my evening with Ed, I find myself smiling, and it's not a lustful, falling-head-over-heels type of smile, but an I-had-quite-a-nice-time-and-I'm-surprised kind of smile, and although I wouldn't go as far as saying I can't wait until Tuesday, I would say that I'm quite looking forward to it because the man's definitely got something, I'm simply not entirely sure what it is.

And I feel quite grown-up about this. Sure, the fact that Ed's in his late thirties means I have to be mature when I'm with him anyway, but I feel incredibly grown-up at being able to go out with someone like him, though I don't feel all those things that I did with Nick.

Even the way my mother already seems to be planning the wedding day doesn't rile me. In fact, I think it's quite funny, although I'm not planning on marrying Ed.

Obviously.

• • •

"So tell me what he's like?"

I have my mother's undivided attention.

"He's nice."

"What do you mean, he's nice? There must be something else you can say about him."

"Okay. He's nice, and . . ."—I watch her face closely—"he drives a Porsche."

She practically swoons before regaining her composure. "A Porsche? What was it like, being driven in a Porsche?"

"Comfortable, Mum. What do you think?"

"So where did he take you?"

"The River Cafe."

"Ooh. That's meant to be very expensive. What did you have?"

I tell her, and quite enjoy that she hangs on my every word, and for once I'm getting as much attention as Olly.

"And does he want to see you again?"

I nod. "We're going out on Tuesday."

"That's so exciting! What are you going to wear? For heaven's sake don't wear one of those awful trouser suits you always wear. Wear something feminine. Haven't you got any nice dresses?"

I knew it was too good to last. Here we go again, Libby can't do anything right.

"My trouser suits happen to be designer, actually," I say indignantly. "And there's nothing wrong with them. Everyone wears them."

"But men like feminine women," she says defiantly. "They like to see a nice pair of legs."

I shake my head in amazement. "If I didn't know better I'd say you were still living in the 1950s."

"That's as may be," she says with a sniff. "But I know what men like, and I know they don't like hard, masculine, career girls."

Before I get a chance to tell her how ridiculous she's being, the phone rings. Talk about being saved by the bell. "Olly!" she says. "Hello, darling. How are you?"

I stretch and put my feet on the coffee table as I flick on the TV.

"Hang on. Off!" she says to me, brushing my feet from the table, so just to piss her off I turn the volume up to drown her out.

"Libby!" she shouts. "Turn that down. It's your brother. From Manchester."

As if I didn't know, but I turn it down.

"How's my gorgeous boy, then?" she says, as I grimace at the TV set. "Oh, Dad and I are fine, but we're missing you. When are you coming down to see us? I see. No, no, don't worry, I know how busy you are. How's the series coming along? You are clever, Olly!"

"You are clever, Olly!" I mimic to myself in what I mean to be a whisper, except she hears and shoots me a filthy look.

"Your sister's here," she says. "Yes. Hang on. All right, my darling. I'll speak to you this week. Big kiss from Dad and I." And she passes the phone to me.

"Hey, Oll," I say distractedly, because I'm watching some disgusting outfits being paraded up and down a catwalk on *The Clothes Show*.

"Hey, big sis. How's it going?"

"Fine. You?"

"Yeah. Good."

"How are your friends?"

"What?"

"You know, Oll, your friends."

"Oh!" He starts laughing. "You mean Carolyn?"

"Mmm hmm."

"She's really nice. Can't quite believe it, I just really like being with her."

"That's great, Oll." I ignore my mum looking quizzically at me, doubtless trying to work out what we're talking about.

"How 'bout you? How's Nick?"

"Finished. Kaput. Over."

"Oh, Libby, I'm sorry. He seemed like a really nice bloke. What happened?"

I look at my mum, who's now pretending to be immersed in dusting the side tables, but I know her ears are fully alert.

"Tell you later."

He laughs. "Mum's in the room, then?"

"As ever."

"Anyone new on the scene?"

"Kind of. Had dinner with this guy last night, and he's nice, but I'm not sure he's my type."

My mother raises an eyebrow.

"Anyway," I continue, "we'll see."

"Okay. You should come up and stay here," he says. "Seriously, it would be so nice to spend some time with you. I haven't seen you properly, just you and me, for ages."

"Yeah." I nod. "That'd be great. I'll check my diary and let you know."

We say goodbye and I get up to go.

"What would be really nice?" My mother's pretending she's not really interested.

"I might go and stay with Olly," I say. "He just invited me."

"Oh, what a good idea!" she says, suddenly beaming. "Maybe Dad and I will come too, we could all get the train up there together. A proper family outing!"

"Hmph." I shrug. "Maybe."

• • •

On Monday morning Jo buzzes me from reception.

"Jesus Christ!" she says. "You'd better come out here."

"Why?"

"Just come out here! Now!"

I walk through the office to the reception desk, and there, on the counter, is a forest. Well, okay, not quite a forest, but an arrangement of flowers that's so big it's threatening to take over the room.

"Jesus Christ!" I echo. "These are for me?"

"They certainly are," she says, the grin stretching across her face. "Come on, come on. Open the card. Who are they from?"

I open the card with fingers that are shaking ever so slightly, and I suppose a part of me hopes they're from Nick, though I know they won't be, because flowers aren't Nick's style, plus he could never afford something like this. These must have cost a fortune.

" 'Dearest Libby,' " I read out loud. " 'Just wanted to thank you for a wonderful evening. Can't wait until Tuesday. With love, Ed.' "

"Who the fuck's Ed?"

"Just an admirer," I say breezily, skipping back into the office with the flowers and loving, loving the admiring glances I get on the way.

And I know this might sound a bit stupid, but I'd quite like to send him something in return, even though I know you're not really supposed to, and it's not because I desperately fancy him, but because he did a nice thing for me and I'd like to repay him somehow.

And I suppose if I did fancy him I wouldn't be able to do this, because I'd be far too busy playing games and playing hard to get. But number one, I don't really care if me sending something to him scares him off, and number two, I'm pretty damn sure it won't anyway. I suppose it's sod's law, isn't it? The ones that like you are never the ones you're interested in, and the ones you like are always the bastards. But Ed's different. I'm not really sure how I feel. I know that I'm not in lust with him, but I also know that I'd like to see him again. I'm just so fed up with being on my own, and Nick may not want me, but Ed certainly does, and that's a bloody nice feeling. So this is why I want to do something for him.

But what?

I go back out to Jo.

"Okay," I sigh. "You win. I'll tell you everything if you help me out," and I do.

"Got it!" she says when I've finally finished, although I didn't give her the long version, I kept it as short as I possibly could. "Send him a virtual food basket!"

"A what?"

"On the Internet! You can go to these places and send virtual flowers and food baskets, they're amazing. It's a seriously cool thing to do, and you'll probably blow his mind. Hang on. Does he have e-mail?"

"How the hell should I know?"

"Check his business card."

So I run back and get it, and sure enough, there at the bottom is his e-mail address.

"Okay," says Jo. "Let me just get someone to cover for me, then I'll show you how to do it."

●　●　●

Ten minutes later Jo's sitting in front of the computer, tapping away, and there it is! A site that shows you pictures of flowers and presents which you can send to people.

"Is this going to cost anything?"

"Nah. Don't be daft. They're virtual, aren't they? That means they're not real."

She clicks on a picture of a basket stuffed with crisps, cakes and biscuits, then over her shoulder says to me, "What do you want to say?"

"How about, Dear Ed, thank you for your beautiful flowers. I thought you might be hungry but save the Oreos for me. They're my favorite. . . . Looking forward to seeing you on Tuesday. Libby."

"Love, Libby?" Jo asks, typing in my message.

"Oh, all right then. Love, Libby. So what happens now?"

"You just send it, and they get a message on their e-mail saying they've had a virtual delivery and it gives instructions on where to go to pick up the present."

"That's amazing. Can I have a go?"

"What? More admirers?"

"Hmm." Jo stands up and I sit in her place as she wanders back to reception, and ten minutes later I've sent virtual food baskets to Jules, Jamie, Olly and Sal.

Unsurprisingly, Jules calls half an hour later, and she's laughing so hard I can hardly hear her. "That is fantastic!" she splutters. "How in the hell did you do that?"

"More to the point, Jules, what are you doing checking your e-mail in the middle of the day? Shouldn't you be interior designing or something?"

"Should be," she says. "I was just getting on the Internet to try and find some suppliers of this Spanish furniture I'm looking for. Someone said they had a site on the Web, and my e-mail told me I had a delivery. It's bloody inspired, Libby! I love it!"

I tell her about the flowers and about sending the same

basket to Ed, and I can hear her squealing and clapping her hands on the other end of the phone.

"Jesus, Libby!" she says. "He's going to fall head over heels in love with you! I bet he's never met anyone like you before!"

I bet he hasn't either.

At the end of the day, just before I leave, I check my e-mail, just in case, and sure enough there's a message from EMcMann@compuserve.com.

"Dearest Libby," it says. "I'm now absolutely stuffed! What a delightful surprise, and I'm so pleased you received the flowers. I must say, no one's ever done anything like that for me before. . . . Can hardly wait to see you again. Much love, Ed."

"Cor," says Jo, who's standing behind me, reading this over my shoulder. "Now. He. Is. Keen."

And I go home with a smile on my face.

● ● ●

I sneaked off early today, to have enough time to get ready, because I want to look good tonight and not necessarily for Ed, more for me, but I could really get used to these flowers and this general feeling of having met someone who could, possibly, adore me.

So it's face pack time, and deep conditioning hair stuff time, and new MAC lipstick time, and anyway, there's nothing wrong in trying to look the best you can possibly look, is there? Plus, Nick never appreciated the designer Libby, and it's bloody nice to dress up again, even though I'm still thinking about Nick, just not quite as often.

And again, tonight, I don't bother with the old razors, because, like Ed as I do, I can't get my head round anything physical happening between us, and even if it were to happen, there's no way it would happen tonight, so that's why, underneath my trousers (yup, trousers; my mother can go to hell), my legs are again as hairy as, well, as someone who hasn't shaved them for a week or so.

I'd like to run with this one, as it were. Not jump into bed, or jump into a relationship, but keep seeing him and see what happens. Whether I might grow to like him, whether he might turn out to be someone special, whether I could actually persuade him to shave off that bloody mustache.

And I'm pretty damned pleased with how I look tonight. A pale gray trouser suit with little pearl earrings that are really not my style at all, but they were a present from my mum a couple of birthdays ago, and flat cream suede shoes.

God. If my mother could see me now! I look like the epitome of a sophisticated young woman. Apart from the trousers, that is. I almost laugh at the sight of myself because I look more like a Sloane Ranger than Princess Diana in her early days, but this look fits with Ed, and it's quite good fun, dressing up. I sort of feel a bit like a child playing a big game. Let's pretend to be sophisticated, smart and mature. What fun! Hey ho! Jesus.

The phone rings just as I've finished applying a final coat of clear nail polish. Couldn't have gone for my beloved blues or greens—far too trendy for Ed.

"What have you eaten today?" Naturally, it's Jules.

"Nothing for breakfast. A milk chocolate Hobnob at about eleven o'clock, d'you know how many calories they are?"

"I think they're about seventy-eight."

"Oh shit. Anyway. A Caesar salad for lunch, and an apple halfway through the afternoon."

"That's good. You've been really good. The biscuit wasn't bad, not if you compare it to what I've had today."

"Go on."

"Okay. For breakfast I had a huge bowl of cornflakes. Huge. Really. Disgusting. Then at about ten o'clock I was hungry again, so I had three chocolate Bourbons. At lunch I went out with a client and had grilled vegetables swimming in olive oil to start with, then a huge plate of pasta in a creamy sauce, and then we shared a crème brûlée but she hardly ate anything, I had practically the whole thing."

Jules is such a bloody liar. I know exactly what she's like. She probably had a tiny bowl of cornflakes. No Bourbons. Plain vegetables. A couple of mouthfuls of pasta and a taste of the crème brûlée. There's no way Jules would be as slim as she is if she really ate what she says she does. I know there are times when she's telling the truth, but I also know that most of the time she's so bloody fat-conscious she only picks at food, doesn't really eat anything. She's more than a little obsessed, which is why we have so many food phone calls a day. I don't mind, really I don't, but I wish she'd stop thinking about it quite as much as she does.

Although I suppose I'm not that much better.

But she encourages me.

Not that I wouldn't think about it at all if we didn't talk about it.

But I wouldn't think about it as much . . .

"I'm not going to have any dinner," she says firmly. "That's it for today. And tomorrow I'm going on a diet."

"Oh, for God's sake, Jules!"

"What? What?"

"Never mind." There's no point in telling her she doesn't need to lose weight, if anything she needs to put it on, because she won't believe me. The number of times we've gone out and the first thing she says to me is, "Do I look fat?" and I look at her skinny, waiflike frame and say, "No! Don't be ridiculous," and she says, "Can't you see it on my face? There? Look." And she taps a nonexistent double chin and spends the rest of the day, or evening, smoothing this invisible double chin away.

God. What it is to be a woman.

"So what are you wearing?"

I tell her.

"Mmm. Very sophis."

"I know. It's not really me, but I couldn't turn up in something dead trendy or he'd faint."

"You know what you are?"

"What?"

"You're a chameleon girlfriend."

"A what?"

"I was reading an article about it. It's about women who change their image, their hobbies, pretty much everything, depending on the man they're with."

I wish I didn't have to say this, but as usual Jules is absolutely right, and I've always done it. I've tried to change myself depending on the man of the moment, and I know it's wrong, even as I'm doing it I know it's wrong, but I can't seem to help it.

Jules has never done it, she's never had to, and once we sat down and tried to figure out why I do it although we didn't have a name for it at the time—and the only reason we could come up with was low self-esteem.

Jules has decided that because Olly was the one who had all the glory, I never think that anyone's going to like me for myself, and that's why I always try and become someone else. If you're confused, trust me, no one's more confused about it than me.

"So tell me something else I didn't know," I say bitterly, because, much as I love Jules, I suppose I'm slightly envious of her confidence.

"Don't take it like that," she says, sounding wounded. "It's fine. I'm quite jealous of it, in fact. You can wake up in the morning and think, hmm, who am I going to be today?"

I can't help it. I laugh.

"I wish I could be more like you sometimes," she says, and I nearly fall off my chair.

"Jules! You're nuts! You'd like to be single with no self-esteem and a radar that warns off all decent men and only attracts the bastards?"

"Ed's not a bastard."

"Not yet. Anyway, he's not good-looking enough to be a bastard."

"And Jon was good-looking?"

"Okay, okay, so he wasn't your type. But I thought he was good-looking."

"Listen, Jamie's back, I gotta go. Have a fantastic evening, and call me first thing."

"Thanks, sweetie. Bye."

"Oh, Libby?"

I put the receiver back to my ear.

"Don't do anything I wouldn't do!" And, cackling, she puts down the phone.

. . .

Now this is getting ridiculous. The doorbell rings, I open the door, and once again Ed's standing on the doorstep holding a huge bouquet of roses.

"Ed," I say, loving this attention but not wanting to get too used to it, to take it for granted. "You must stop buying me flowers. It's beginning to look like a florist's in here. I'm running out of vases!"

"Oh. Er. Sorry, Libby." He looks crestfallen and I feel like a bitch.

"No, no, don't be silly. It's just that you're spoiling me, but they're beautiful. Thank you."

He comes in and stands in the living room, as I open lots of cabinet doors, hoping that there's a vase I've forgotten about. In the end I pull a milk bottle out of the fridge and empty the milk down the sink.

And although I have to cut down the stems by about a foot, the roses actually look pretty damn nice in a milk bottle. It must be the mix of the luxury and the everyday.

A bit like me and Ed, really.

Chapter 17

We go to the Ivy, and Ed seems to know an awful lot of people in there, and I'm really beginning to enjoy being with this man who's so sophisticated and yet so naive at the same time. Because he is naive. He's somehow slightly gauche, awkward, and it's probably his most endearing quality.

He orders champagne, and as we raise our glasses, I hear a familiar swooping voice.

"Libby! Darling!" And I turn around and there, resplendent in a tiny black dress, is Amanda. I give her the obligatory air-kisses, and then she just stands there, looking at me, then at Ed, and I introduce them.

And it's quite extraordinary, because Ed stands up to shake her hand, and Amanda starts simpering like an idiot, fluttering her eyelashes and being all coy, and I'm really quite embarrassed for her, and I breathe a sigh of relief when she finally leaves.

"Who was that?"

"Amanda Baker. She's a television presenter."

"I see. Is she famous?"

"Not as famous as she'd like to be."

"Ha ha! That's very good, Libby. How do you know her?"

"I do her PR."

"So you could make her famous, then?"

"It's sort of catch-22. You can't be famous without being written about, and nobody wants to write about someone who isn't famous. But I'm trying."

"I don't watch much television, that's probably why I didn't recognize her. I only ever seem to watch the news."

"What do you do if you're at home at night?"

"Work usually. Listen to music."

"So if I told you I was in love with Dr. Doug Ross it wouldn't mean anything to you?"

His face falls. "Who's Dr. Doug Ross?"

"Never mind," I laugh. "You wouldn't understand."

• • •

The food's delicious, the champagne's delicious, and I'm loving sitting here star-spotting, although every time I whisper that another celebrity has just walked in, Ed stares at them in confusion, and it's quite amazing that he really doesn't have a clue who these people are. I mean, for God's sake, some of the people that have walked in here tonight are the biggest stars of stage and screen, and Ed's never seen them before in his life!

"Libby," he says, when we're waiting for our coffees. "I think you're extraordinary. I've never met anyone like you."

"Thank you. Really? How?" I know you're not supposed to fish for compliments, but I can't help it, and after Nick I deserve to have my ego inflated a little bit.

"You're just so bright, and sparky, and full of life. I really enjoy being with you. And . . ." He pauses.

"And?" I prompt.

"Well, I'm not sure whether I should say this yet, and it probably sounds ridiculous, but I really like you."

"That doesn't sound ridiculous."

"No. I mean I really like you."

"I like you too."

"Good. And I think we might have something special here."

I smile. I mean, what could I say? The guy hardly knows me.

• • •

"I thought you might like to see my house," he says, on the way back.

"I'd love to!" Which is true, I want to know more about him, more about where he lives, how he lives. I want to nose around his home and look for clues about who he is, whether I could be happy with him.

Please don't think I'm sounding ridiculous. It's not that I've decided he's The One or anything, but I do have a worrying tendency to, how shall I put it, plan ahead. The number of times I've sat in bed dreaming of my marriage to someone I've had one date with. And although I don't fancy Ed, it's quite good fun dreaming about it anyway. To be honest, he wouldn't figure that strongly in this particular daydream. Nah, when I daydream about getting married I'm far more concerned about the dress, the location, the bridesmaids. The groom tends to be a faceless person, he's really not that important.

So while I'm not planning the wedding just yet, I'd still like to see his home.

• • •

We pull up outside a sweeping terrace, and the thing I find most strange about where he lives is not the size or the grandeur, but the fact that someone his age lives there at all. I know he said he bought it as a family home, but it seems crazy to live somewhere that feels so middle-aged when you're still relatively young. And anyway, if I got married I'd want to buy a new home together, start afresh; I wouldn't want to move into the place he already lived in.

The hallway floor is one of those black-and-white marble numbers, and I can see that Ed's incredibly proud of his house as he flings open the doors to the most spectacular drawing room I've ever seen. Huge, airy, with stunning original moldings on the walls and ceiling, it's completely empty.

"Umm, have you recently moved in?" I ask.

"No. I've lived here for two years!" he says.

"What about furniture?"

"I've never got around to buying any," he says, shrugging. "I suppose I'm waiting for my wife to come in and redecorate."

"But you could have got an interior designer to do it."

"I did!" he says indignantly, pointing at the swagged, pelmeted curtains.

"Oh. Right," I say.

He leads me upstairs to his bedroom. Immaculate and huge, it leads into an enormous dressing room, lined wall to wall with cabinets, and then through to an en suite bathroom.

Next door is his study, and upstairs there's a gym, a sauna and more empty bedrooms. And more. And more. They seem to stretch on forever, and I honestly feel as if I've stumbled into a ghost house, because it's quite clear that none of these rooms is ever used. There's no warmth in this house, it's a museum, a showpiece, and I start to feel increasingly uncomfortable here.

We go downstairs to the basement. A country-style kitchen, and I breathe a sigh of relief because next to the kitchen there are sofas, and french doors leading on to a garden. Judging by the amount of books and papers piled around the room, this is the place he lives in.

And it really is quite cozy. Not perhaps exactly as I'd do it. I'd get rid of those dried flowers hanging from the ceiling for starters, but it's not at all bad.

Ed goes into the kitchen to make some coffee, and I sit and look around the room, deciding what I'd change if I lived here. I'd have the sofas re-covered in a bright blue-and-yellow checkered fabric, I'd get rid of that revolting limed kitchen table and put in an old scrubbed pine one, I'd . . .

"Do you like it?" Ed interrupts my thoughts.

"Your house?"

He nods.

"I think it's spectacular," I say, because it undoubtedly is, but I decide against telling him it's a bit like a morgue. "But don't you get a bit lonely rattling around in this huge place by yourself?"

"Yes," he says, suddenly looking like a little boy lost. "At times I do."

And he looks so sweet I want to hug him.

He comes to sit next to me on the sofa, and the air suddenly feels a lot more oppressive, and I know he's going to kiss me, but I'm not sure I want him to. I try to avoid looking at him, keeping my eyes fixed firmly on my coffee, because I can feel he's staring at me, and I'm praying, Jesus how I'm praying, that he doesn't put his coffee cup down.

He puts his coffee cup down.

And he sneaks an arm around the back of the sofa, not yet touching me, and I want to run out of there screaming because at this moment I know as an absolute certainty that I don't want to kiss him.

This, it has to be said, is a bit of a new feeling for me. If I bother going out with someone again after a first date, then it's because I fancy them, and I spend the rest of the second date praying they'll kiss me and wondering how they'll do it.

I remember Jon didn't kiss me until date number six. On date number four I was convinced it was going to happen. We'd been to the cinema, he dropped me home, and even after he declined coffee—he said he had an early meeting—I sat in the car with my face raised expectantly. He just smiled and kissed me on each cheek.

Two dates later he cooked me dinner at his flat, and after dinner I was standing in the kitchen helping him wash up, wondering whether I'd completely misjudged the situation and thinking he was only interested in me as a friend, when suddenly he grabbed me and started kissing me, and minutes later we'd sunk to the kitchen floor in a frenzy of passion.

And I remember how desperate I was for him to kiss me, so why am I so desperate for Ed not to kiss me now?

And more to the point, what the hell am I supposed to do? Suddenly, and I'm not really sure how this happens, suddenly he's kissing me, and I wish to God I could tell you that it was lovely, that my stomach turned over with lust, that I suddenly started to fancy him . . .

It was revolting.

You know how you forget what bad kissers are like when you haven't encountered a bad kisser for years? I'd forgotten. This was like the snogs of my teenage years, with spotty boys who were trying to be grown men, who didn't have a clue.

And I wish I could pinpoint exactly what it was that was so revolting, but I can't. Too much tongue. Too much saliva. Too much mustache. Yuck. Not nice at all. So I pull away and resist the urge to wipe my mouth with my sleeve, and I think that nothing, nothing will make me kiss him again.

Not even the Porsche.

But I don't mind cuddling him, and he puts his arms round me and that's quite nice, at least it would be if I wasn't so tense at the prospect of him kissing me again.

"Libby," he says after nuzzling my neck for a while. "I think I'd better take you home."

What? What? He's supposed to ask me to stay the night and I'm supposed to turn him down. What is this? He's supposed to be dying of lust for me, every fiber in his body aching for me. He's not supposed to want to take me home.

I know, I know. Never mind the fact that I don't want him, he's still supposed to want me. But at least it means I won't have to kiss him again.

We get in the car, and this time Ed keeps a hand on my thigh all the way back, but the funny thing is it's not sexual somehow, more proprietorial, and although I wish he'd take it off, I'm not quite sure how to tell him, so I do an awful lot of shuffling around and crossing and uncrossing my legs, but the hand stays.

"When can I see you again?" he says, walking me to the front door of my flat and insisting on holding my hand.

"Well, I'm a bit busy this week," I say.

"Oh." His face falls. "Actually, I wanted to invite you to a ball."

"A ball? What kind of ball?" My mother's voice echoes in my

head: go out with him because you never know what his friends are like.

"Some friends of mine in the country are having their annual ball. I think you'd really like them, and I'd love you to come."

"When is it?"

He tells me it's the weekend after next, and I tell him that I'd love to come.

"Do you have anything to wear?"

"I'm sure I've got something."

"Look, I hope you don't think this too forward of me, but I'd really like to buy you something special. Would you allow me to?"

What am I, stupid? As if I'm going to turn this down.

"If you're sure," I say.

"Absolutely. Why don't we go shopping on Saturday?"

My brain starts ticking quickly. Shopping. Daytime. No public displays of affection, therefore no kissing.

"That sounds lovely."

"Great! I'll see you on Saturday." His arms encircle my waist and his head moves in again, so I give him a few pecks on the lips, which aren't too bad really, and then with a mysterious smile I move away and go into my flat.

Quite well handled, if I say so myself.

But once I'm home, back in the safety of my flat, I start thinking about that kiss, and then, I can't help it, I start thinking about Nick kissing me, about how it made me feel, and that leads to other memories of Nick, and before I know it I'm sitting on my sofa with tears streaming down my cheeks, and Jesus Christ, haven't there been enough tears recently to last me a lifetime?

I miss him. I can't help it. I just miss him. And Ed, nice as he is, isn't Nick and never will be.

But it's funny how sometimes a little cry makes you feel a whole hell of a lot better, and when I've finished I feel sort of resigned. I know that it's over with Nick, and I know that I don't feel the same about Ed, but maybe love doesn't have to be about lust, maybe I could learn to love Ed. Maybe.

. . .

"Nah. I don't think there's any point."

"But he's so nice, Jules! Maybe it could grow."

"Libby, when he kissed you, you felt sick. What could grow, exactly?"

"I don't know," I huff. "Maybe I need to get used to his kissing."

"Then go for it."

"God, you're no help at all."

"Well, what am I supposed to say? I tell you not to bother and you say he's really nice, so I tell you to keep seeing him and you tell me I'm not helping. I can't win with you."

"Sorry," I grumble, curling my feet up under me on the sofa in Jules's kitchen.

"So what's going on now?" Jamie walks in, bends down and gives me a kiss on the cheek before ruffling Jules's hair as he heads to put the kettle on, and something about this affectionate gesture suddenly makes me feel incredibly lonely.

I want this too. I want someone who will adore me so much that they cannot even walk past me without touching me in some way. I want someone who will worship me, even when— as Jules is now—I'm sitting around in fluffy slippers with no makeup on and hair scraped back.

I'm sick and tired of being on my own. Most of the time I'm fine. Some of the time I even quite enjoy it. But at this precise moment in time I'm fed up with it. I've had enough. I'm twenty-seven years old and I deserve to be with someone. I deserve to live in a beautiful house, not a grotty little flat in Ladbroke Grove. I deserve to be with someone who brings me flowers and buys me presents. I deserve to be in a couple, someone's other half.

"More man problems?" Jamie says from the other end of the kitchen.

"Naturally," I say. "Isn't it always?"

Jamie brings three mugs of coffee over and sits down. "Jules said you'd been out with Ed McMann. Bit of a catch, I'd say."

"I know," I moan. "But I don't fancy him."

"Ah," says Jamie. "That could be a problem. But he's meant to be a nice guy. Maybe you need to give it time."

"Tell him about the kissing." Jules prods me.

I tell him about the kissing. I even tell him about the tongues, saliva and mustache bit.

Jamie makes a face. "I've got to be honest, Libs, it doesn't sound good."

"And meanwhile," Jules interrupts, "he's taking her shopping for a ball gown on Saturday."

"Look on the bright side," Jamie says. "At least you'll get a designer outfit out of it."

. . .

On Friday afternoon another bouquet arrives. This is getting silly. And what's even more ridiculous is that I'm becoming so used to getting flowers from Ed that I'm beginning to take them a little bit for granted. And my flat's looking less like a florist's and more like Kew Gardens every day.

God, will you listen to me?

Sorry, sorry, sorry. It's typical, isn't it? For twenty-seven years I've wanted someone who adores me and now I've found that person I just can't seem to get excited. Why can't I fancy him? Why can't I make myself fancy him? Maybe I can. Let's just see what happens on Saturday.

In the meantime I'm not going to send him anything else because quite frankly I'm not entirely sure whether I should be encouraging him. Not until I'm a bit more clear about how I feel, anyway.

And then a very peculiar thing happens. Just after the flowers arrive the phone rings.

"Libby? It's Nick."

"Nick who?" I'm so distracted by the flowers I'm not quite thinking straight.

"What do you mean, Nick who? Thanks a lot. It wasn't that long ago, surely."

"Nick!" My heart starts pounding. Perhaps he's changed his mind. Perhaps he's ringing because he misses me so much he's realized he's made a terrible mistake. Perhaps it will all be okay.

"Libby!"

"Oh my God! I'm so sorry! I was distracted. Hi!" I'm fighting to sound as normal as possible, and it's a hard struggle, but I think I'm winning.

"Hello, my darling. I was just sitting here doing nothing and I was thinking about you so I thought I'd phone and see how you are."

He called me darling! He was thinking about me!

"I'm absolutely great," I say, with conviction, because of course, now that he's phoned, I am. "How are you?"

"Oh, you know. Usual. Trying to write but can't seem to concentrate. Plus, I'm still trying to get over the most mind-blowing hangover."

"Where did you go? Anywhere nice?" I feel a huge twinge of jealousy at the thought that Nick might have been with another woman, and I pray that he wasn't, that he was somewhere dull. My prayers, for once, are answered.

"Just down the pub with Moose and that lot."

Thank God. At least I know he couldn't have fancied any of those awful women. God. Moose. Those friends. I suddenly remember that awful night, and as I remember how awkward I felt, how out of place, I realize that even though I adored Nick, I couldn't have done it. I couldn't have continued with that lifestyle, and suddenly I feel like laughing, because for the first time I realize I won't ever have to go to a pub with Moose and that lot again. And not only that, I'll never have to sleep in that filthy bedsit again. And I realize that for the first time in my life I might actually be able to stay friends with an ex-lover, and that for the first time in my life I want to stay friends with an ex-lover. And I really don't want anything more from him. Honestly.

"A heavy session?" I laugh, thrilled at this feeling of being set free.

"A very heavy session," he groans. "But I'm paying for it now. So what have you been up to? I've been thinking about you."

"Have you? That's nice. I've been very busy, actually. Everything's going really well."

There's a short silence before Nick asks, "How's your love life?"

"Umm. Well . . ." Oh fuck it. Why not? "I've sort of met someone."

There's a long silence.

"That's great, Libby!" he says finally, but if I didn't know better I'd say he didn't think it was great at all. "Who is he?"

"Just a guy. I don't know whether it's anything serious," I say. "Really, nothing to write home about, but he's nice, he treats me well."

"What does he do?"

"Investment banker."

Nick groans. "So he can afford to take you to all the places I never could?"

"Yup!" I say, and laugh.

"I knew you hated me not having money," Nick says suddenly.

"No, I didn't, Nick. I just hated staying the night in your disgusting bedsit."

We both laugh.

"I suppose now you're staying the night in Buckingham Palace?"

"Hanover Terrace, actually." I don't bother mentioning the fact that I don't even like kissing my new man, let alone thinking about going to bed with him.

"Seriously, Libby," he says. "I'm really happy that you've found someone."

"Are you?"

"Well, okay then, not really. Well, sort of. I am happy, but I'm also really sorry that things didn't work out with us."

This conversation seems to be going in a very strange direction, but I think it's okay, I think that I'm over Nick, that we probably both have regrets but that it's time to move on.

"I know," I say. "So am I, but, let's face it, we weren't exactly a match made in heaven."

There's a silence.

"I mean," I continue, "I think you're lovely, and I'd love to have you as my friend, but in hindsight we should probably never have been together."

"You're probably right," he sighs. "And anyway, I couldn't handle a relationship right now."

"I know," I laugh. "That's what you said when you dumped me."

"I didn't dump you! We just . . . parted."

"A bit like the Red Sea?"

"Exactly."

"And what about you, Nick?" I don't really want to ask this question, I don't really want to know, but I can't help it. "How's your love life?"

"Terrible." Thank you, thank you, thank you, God.

"No women, then?"

"Nah. Not since you."

"You must be getting withdrawal symptoms."

"I'm fine. I'm being very introverted and doing lots of thinking about love and life and all that stuff."

"Come up with any conclusions yet?"

"Yes. I've concluded that I'm completely screwed up."

"So tell me something else I didn't know."

"Thanks!" Indignant tone.

"Pleasure!" Light and breezy tone.

"So are we friends now?" A cautious tone.

"Of course! I'd love to be friends with you."

"Does that mean we could get together for a drink some-time?"

"As long as it's not with your disgusting friends."

Nick laughs. "No. Just you and me."

"That would be lovely."

"Okay. Listen, I'll call you next week and we'll sort some-thing out."

"Fine. I've gotta go, Nick, there's another call for me."

"Okay. God, it's so nice to hear your voice, Libby. I've missed you."

"I've missed you too."

● ● ●

I ring Jules immediately to tell her that Nick called, but as soon as she picks up the phone I can hear there's something wrong. Her voice is sounding flat, she doesn't sound as bright as she normally does, and I mentally kick myself for not thinking of her first.

"Jules?" I venture. "Is everything okay?"

I hear a long sigh.

"What's the matter?"

"God, Libby," she sighs. "I'm really worried. About Jamie."

"Jamie? What on earth are you worried about with Jamie?"

"I know this sounds crazy, and I know he works all the time, but the last couple of weeks he's been working late in the office, and last night I called him and there was no reply. When he got home I casually asked him if he went out, but he said no, he'd been in his office all night."

"So? He'd probably gone to the loo or something."

"For three hours? And that's not everything. He's been a bit distant lately but I tried to ignore it and when I did ask him if there was something the matter he said his mind was on a case and he was really busy."

"Jules, you're not telling me you think he's having an affair, are you? You're crazy, Jamie would never do that."

"I thought I was going mad," Jules says slowly, "but suddenly I've started remembering that over the last few weeks the phone's rung a few times and it's been put down when I've answered."

"So? Probably a wrong number."

"I know something's wrong, Libby. I can't explain it, it's almost like a sixth sense. I feel him distancing himself, and I'm sure he's met someone else."

"Jules, you're being ridiculous. I saw you together just the other day and you're still the perfect couple, and he still obviously adores you. Are you sure you're not imagining it? Jamie's hardly the type to have an affair. Jesus, Jules. I don't know what to say. I mean, how could he possibly be having an affair? Are you sure you're not going through an early menopause or something?"

"I don't know. Look, I've got to go. I haven't decided what to do yet but I'll fill you in."

I put down the phone, wondering whether Jules is going mad, whether Jamie would be unfaithful, trying to imagine what she must feel like. There isn't anything I can do, other than help out with some amateur sleuthing if she asks, but Jules isn't the type to start following Jamie around in sunglasses and a wig. She isn't the type to tap his phone calls or to trick him into revealing the truth.

I would be riffling through his pockets, checking his credit card statements, but Jules, despite her suspicions, won't really want to know. She'll blind herself to it, hoping that it will go away. But Jesus Christ, how could Jamie, Jamie, be having an affair?

Over the next few days Jules tries to change the subject when I ask how things are. "Fine," she says guardedly, and I know that there's no point in pushing her to talk about it. That she'll talk about it when she's ready, and that the only thing I can do is be there for her when she decides to open up.

But I'll tell you this. If Jamie is having an affair I'll kill him. Even the thought of him causing Jules pain makes me so angry

I want to go storming into his chambers now and kick the living daylights out of him. How could he? How dare he?

It seems as if a weight has suddenly descended on to my shoulders, and if I feel like this, how in the hell must Jules be feeling?

Chapter 18

"So you're actually going out with him?"

Amanda and I are once again having lunch, this time at Daphne's, and she's still treating me like her best friend, and I can't figure out why we're having lunch again so soon after the last one, but she phoned up and suggested it and anything to get me out of the office for a while.

Not that I don't enjoy work. I love my job. But recently I've found myself dreaming more and more about not having to work. Leading a life of luxury. Lunching at Daphne's and shopping at Joseph every day. Heaven.

And of course it doesn't help actually having lunch in Daphne's, because we're surrounded by the proverbial ladies who lunch, all immaculate in their little designer suits with their Gucci bags and perfectly streaked blond hair. They all look as if they spend a large part of every day at the hairdresser's or the manicurist's, and I feel like an old trollop in my Episode suit that's trying very hard to be Armani, and my Pied a Terre shoes that would like to come back in another life as a pair of Stephane Kelians.

"I'm not sure I'd say that," I say. "We're just sort of seeing each other."

"I think he's really quite sexy," says Amanda in a dreamy sort of voice while I look at her in horror.

"What? That mustache? Sexy?"

"I don't mind mustaches," she says. "Not if they have that much money. But surely if you're seeing him you must find him sexy?"

I shrug, because I'm not sure I want to tell Amanda about him kissing me, I'm not sure I trust her.

"Libby?" she pushes.

"I don't really know," I say eventually. "I'm not sure how I feel about him, but he treats me well and he's taking me out on Saturday to buy me an outfit for this ball he's taking me to. To be honest, I'm just enjoying being spoiled, no one's ever done anything like this for me before."

"He's taking you shopping?" Her eyes are wide.

I nod.

"Where are you going to go?"

"I don't know. You're probably the best person to ask. Where will I find a black-tie type dress?"

"Unlimited budget?"

"Well, not quite," I laugh. "But something nice."

"Why don't you go to Harvey Nichols? They've got a decent evening wear department, and if you don't find anything you like there, then they've got all the designer concessions."

"Excellent idea. Harvey Nichols it is."

"And I have to tell you, Libby, if you decide you don't want him, I'll have him."

I laugh, but then I look up and realize that Amanda's not laughing with me. She has this sort of strange smile on her face, and Jesus Christ, she's not bloody joking. Oh well, if I decide I don't want him she can have him. With pleasure. And am I going mad or might the fact that she wants him be making me want him just a teeny bit more?

On the way back to the office—I get a cab, on expenses, naturally—I decide that I could quite like Ed. Maybe I could even fancy him, and maybe the fact that I'm not thinking about him that much when I'm not with him is a good thing, maybe it means this is a proper relationship, not just lust, or the equivalent to a teenage crush. Because quite frankly I'm sick of falling madly in love and spending twenty-four hours a day thinking about them and crying with misery when they don't phone. I'm sick of being the kind of girl who, when they say jump, asks how high. I'm sick of always, always being the one to fall in love and get hurt. And maybe this is how it should be, getting on with my life and not putting all my energies into a relationship.

So when Saturday arrives I'm feeling okay about this. So, fine. I'm not crazy about him, but I am sort of looking forward to seeing him, and I think maybe this could work, maybe he could grow on me, so what I've done, in the days that have passed since my lunch with Amanda, is try to picture Ed as being much worse than he actually is. I know that might sound a bit bizarre, but I've pictured him as really ugly, his mustache as really big, his laugh really braying, and that way I'm hoping that I won't be disappointed when I open the door, that I'll actually be pleasantly surprised.

And you know what? It bloody works! I open the door and Ed is far, far better than I remember him, and I grin as I take the flowers—lilies this time—and reach up and give him a kiss on the lips.

Not tongues, okay? I want to enjoy this feeling of appreciating him for a little while, and I'm not ready to take it further. Not just yet.

"I've really looked forward to seeing you," he says, putting his arms around me and giving me a hug.

"Good," I say, as I hug him back.

I break away and he says, "So have you thought where to go?"

"Does Harvey Nichols sound okay?"

"Fine, fine," he says. "I don't really know anything about women's clothes, but if that's the place to go, then we'll go there. Have you had breakfast?"

I shake my head.

"Why don't I take you out for breakfast first?"

"Fine."

We drive up to Knightsbridge, park the car, and Ed takes me for yummy scrambled eggs and freshly squeezed orange juice, and I sit there watching all the beautiful people, thinking, I'm okay, I fit, I'm part of a couple.

Because it's very obvious that Ed and I are together. He sits gazing at me as I eat, stroking my face, my hair, and I bask in this adoration because it's so completely new for me. He refuses to let me pay, and quite frankly I'm feeling a bit ridiculous offering, and when we leave he takes my hand and I follow meekly, loving this submissive role of being a wealthy-woman-who-lunches-in-waiting.

I think we actually look like a pretty good couple. Ed in his casual but still oh-so-smart polo shirt, crisp dark blue jeans and brown suede Gucci loafers (of course I bloody noticed them, what do you think I am, blind or something?), and me in my camel silk trousers, brown mock-croc loafers and white linen shirt. Unfortunately, I haven't yet acquired lots of chunky gold Italian-style jewelery to complete the look, but I know we look like a young wealthy couple out shopping, we look like we to-tally belong in Knightsbridge, we look like we do this every Sat-urday.

And it gets better! In the evening wear department in Har-vey Nichols, Ed walks around silently looking at clothes as the sales assistant—a middle-aged woman bustles around showing me dresses. "Would your husband like this one?" she says at one point, and Ed overhears while I almost faint in alarm, because you should never, ever, bring up the M word, you should never even allow the M word to be mentioned by anybody else when you're with your new boyfriend, but Ed just smiles at me, a very tender, affectionate smile, and I can't help it. I grin back.

"I can see my wife in something like this," Ed says, and my heart turns over, and then it stops completely when I see what he's picked out. It's a twinset taffeta suit. The jacket's navy, with a nipped in waist and a flared peplum skirt, and the skirt's prob-ably mid-calf length. It is absolutely disgusting. It's the sort of thing my mother would wear.

"Umm, I don't think that's quite me, actually," I say, turning away.

"Would you just try it on?" he says. "For me?"

"Okay." I shrug, and take the outfit into the changing room. Jesus Christ, I look like my mother, and I wouldn't be caught dead in anything like this. I poke my head round the curtain. "Ed, I don't think this is quite, er, me."

"Let me see. Come out here."

I walk out with shoulders stooped, stomach pressed out, trying to look as disgusting as the suit, hoping to put him off.

"You really hate it, don't you?" he laughs.

"I really hate it."

"I think it's rather nice."

"Ed . . ." I say in a warning tone.

"Okay, okay. If you don't like it, then we'll find something else."

Eight more disgusting taffeta numbers and I'm beginning to lose heart. This was supposed to be fun, but Ed keeps making me try on these revolting, middle-aged, nasty outfits, and I'm beginning to seriously rethink this whole thing.

And then finally we leave the evening wear department, and, just as we're walking through the designer section, Ed stops and walks over to Donna Karan. There, on a dummy, is the most beautiful shimmering black dress I've ever seen. Long-sleeved, it swoops at the front and sweeps down to the floor in the most gorgeous, slinky, sexy way.

We both stand there for a while, admiring this dress, and then Ed turns to the assistant, who's hovering behind us, a bright smile on her face.

"Do you have this in a twelve?" he says, bless him, because he's remembered my size.

"Certainly, sir," she says, and smiles at me as she goes to get the dress.

And finally I feel like a princess. Actually, make that a queen. I stand straight and proud, admiring the way the dress cleverly hugs, but not too tightly, my figure, how it makes me look slim and tall, elegant and sophisticated. I imagine how I'd look with my hair swept up in a chic chignon, with high strappy sandals tripping off my feet, with tiny little diamond studs sparkling in my ears, oops, jumping ahead of myself here. Where on earth would I get diamond studs from?

I walk out of the changing room, and both Ed and the sales assistant gasp.

"You look beautiful!" Ed whispers, as the salesgirl just nods in agreement, and it's not like those times when salesgirls say you look lovely and you know that they say it to everyone, no matter how shit they look; I can see from this girl's face that she's as thrilled as I am with how the dress looks, and Jesus Christ, this dress has to be mine.

"That's the dress!" Ed says, and I beam as I admire myself in the full-length mirror.

"I love it!" I say. "It's the most beautiful thing I've ever worn."

Ed turns to the sales assistant. "Do you take American Express?"

I go back into the changing room, and I can't help myself, when I finally tug the dress off I sneak a quick look at the price.

And I almost faint.

Fifteen hundred pounds.

Jesus Christ. What the hell should I do? I don't think Ed realizes how much it is, and I can't let him spend this money on me, that's absurd. That's the most ridiculous amount of money I've ever seen in my whole life.

The sales assistant pops her head round, smiles at me and takes the dress as I try to look confident, even though I'm standing there in my graying M&S bra and knickers, and then the dress has gone, and I figure that if Ed has a problem with it, he'll tell me, because he's going to find out soon enough how much it is.

I finish getting dressed and walk out of the changing room, and Ed's sitting in a chair with a big grin on his face. By his feet is a bag, floaty wisps of tissue paper peeking out from the top.

"There you are, my darling," he says, handing me the bag. "A beautiful dress for my beautiful Libby."

"But Ed," I say, flushing because I can't believe he's done this, and I start to say something about the price, but he stops me.

"I don't want to hear another word about it," he says, so I reach up and kiss him.

"Thank you," I say. "No one's ever bought me anything so wonderful before."

"It's my pleasure," he says. "Now. What about shoes? Do you have shoes?"

I nod firmly. "Yes," I say. "I've got the perfect shoes."

"So do you need anything else?" he says. "While we're here, what about stockings, or a cape?"

"Ed," I say. "It's fine. I don't need anything else."

"So do you have plans for the rest of the day?"

I know what he means. He means this evening. And you know what? Fuck it. I don't mind spending the rest of my Saturday with him, evening included. I mean, Jesus Christ, for £1,500 it's the very least I can do.

• • •

We go back to Ed's house, and you know this time, the second time, it doesn't seem quite so cold and forbidding. I'm beginning to feel quite at home: I even offer to make tea while Ed makes some business calls. While I'm pottering in the kitchen, opening cabinets to find out where everything is, I'm starting to think that I could live in a house like this. I could, in fact, live in this house.

Oh, for God's sake, Libby! Stop it!

But anyway, this feels very cozy. Very coupley. Unbelievable, bearing in mind I hardly know this guy, but I do feel very comfortable with him, surprisingly so, and whether this is because I'm not in love with him and he, I suspect, is crazy about me, I don't know, but it's a nice feeling, really. Bit of a new one for me.

Ed comes down when he's finished his calls and puts his arms around me in the kitchen, and this time I have to kiss him again, I really can't get out of it, and while I can't say it's exactly amazing, I think it's a bit better than last time. I'm sure it's a bit better than last time. Maybe it's just a question of getting used to it. Maybe it will get better and better.

"Mmm," Ed says, burying his face in my neck. "You're so delicious, I could eat you up."

"Speaking of eating," I say brightly, "have you got any biscuits?"

Ed looks crestfallen.

"Cakes?" I say hopefully. "Anything?"

"Oh dear," he says. "I'm really sorry, Libby, I don't have anything at all."

"Toast?"

"Nothing. Look, wait here, I'll be back in a jiffy."

In a jiffy? In a jiffy? Who the hell says in a jiffy? Before I have a chance to stop him, because I'm not really hungry, it was just a diversionary tactic, Ed's grabbed his keys and disappeared out the door.

So what do I do? In normal circumstances I'd do what every girl would do left alone in her new man's house and start riffling. I'd normally be shuffling papers around, looking for evidence of previous girlfriends, opening drawers, looking in briefcases, but somehow I just instinctively know that Ed's so honest he doesn't have anything to hide and I'd be half relieved and half disappointed at not finding anything, so what I do at this present moment is pick up the phone and ring Jules. But I lower my voice just in case he should come back, because I wouldn't want him to think I'd be so rude as to use his phone without asking.

"Jules, it's me."

"Hi, babe. Back home already? So? What d'you get? What d'you get?"

"No, I'm not at home, I'm at his."

"Oh. Is he there?"

"No, he's gone out to get something to eat."

"So?"

"Jules. You. Are. Not. Going. To. Believe. This."

"What? What? Tell me, what?"

"He has just spent . . ." I pause for a bit of dramatic buildup.

"What? What?" Jules is practically shouting.

"One. Thousand. Five. Hundred. Pounds."

"Aaaaaaaargh!" Jules screams and drops the phone, and I can hear her doing her little Indian warrior dance in the background.

She comes back to the phone while I sit there laughing. "Yesssss!" she says. "Yessssss!"

"He has bought me the most stunning dress you have ever seen in your entire life, and it's a Donna Karan and I love it and I can't believe he spent that much money on me and you've never seen anything like this dress, and can you believe how much it was, can you believe he spent that much on me!" I pause to take a breath.

"Fucking hell!" says Jules. "Donna Karan? Fucking hell."

"I know, I know. Unbelievable."

"So did you kiss him to thank him?"

"Yes, I did, as it happens."

"And?"

"And it wasn't so bad."

"Oh my God! This is it! You're going to fall madly in love with him and marry him and we're going to be your poverty-stricken friends who aren't good enough to be seen with you."

I know what I should say here. I should say that she's being ridiculous, that of course I'm not going to marry him, that I've only just met him, for heaven's sake, but instead I find myself saying that they're not poverty-stricken at all, and of course they're good enough to be seen with me.

"So you promise you won't forget me when you're living in Hanover Terrace with your maid and your butler and everything?"

"Jules!" I admonish with a laugh, and then, in what I have to say is a very gracious tone, "Stop being so silly."

"So what's Ed getting to eat?"

"Biscuits, I think."

"Hmm. I've just had four chocolate Hobnobs."

"Milk or plain?"

"Milk. But I think it's okay because I only had a small salad for lunch, so it sort of balances out."

"And is everything okay now with you and Jamie?"

She sighs. "I don't know. He's been better recently, but I still think that something's wrong, but maybe you were right. Maybe I was just imagining it. Anyway, he's been bringing me the most stunning flowers, so we'll just have to see."

"I told you!" I laugh. "Jamie would never hurt you," and before I can carry on I hear the front door slam, and I quickly whisper bye and put the phone down as quietly as I can.

Ed walks in holding a cardboard box in one hand, one of those boxes you get at upmarket patisseries for cakes and things, and in the other is a plastic bag.

"Ed? What have you been doing?"

"I didn't know what you like, so I bought loads of things I thought you might."

"Give me that box!" I snatch the box in a most unladylike fashion, and tear off the ribbon to reveal tiny little chocolate eclairs, marzipan animals, strawberry tarts, vanilla slices oozing crème anglaise.

"Ed! You've bought enough to feed an army!" But I'm licking my lips as I say it, and when I look up Ed seems very pleased with himself because he can see how excited I am at the prospect of overdosing on all this cream.

"I got these as well," he says, offering the bag, and inside are packets of chocolate chip cookies, Swiss butter biscuits and those fancy oatmeal and chocolate numbers that you find only in very smart supermarkets.

"Ed!" I start laughing. "I can't believe how much food you've bought."

"You do like cream?" he says, sounding worried.

"Like it? I love it. God, I'm going to get fat being with you."

"I wouldn't mind," he says, putting the bag down and clasping me round the waist. "I'd still think you were perfect."

Now surely this man is way too good to pass up?

Ed doesn't eat the cream cakes. Nor does he touch the biscuits. It's only when I've eaten so much I feel absolutely sick that I realize this, and when I ask him why he's not eating he tells me he's not hungry, and at that precise moment I know that this man would do anything in the world for me, and I understand what an incredibly powerful feeling that is. I hope I don't blow it by—sick cow that I sometimes am—pushing him to see exactly how much he will take.

But we have a nice evening. To be honest I would be happy staying in, but we're still in the getting-to-know-you stages, and we're not quite ready for cozy, coupley evenings in, and as far as I'm concerned those only happen once you've slept together, and lovely as I'm beginning to think Ed is, I'm still not ready to sleep with him. Not yet.

So instead of curling up on the sofa and watching a video, we jump in the car and whizz down to the Screen on Baker Street to watch a film, and Ed insists on buying me a huge bucket of popcorn, even though the very thought of food is enough to make me sick after all that sugar, but it's sweet of him to do it.

And the strangest thing of all is that he is so intent on making me happy, on making sure that I'm all right during every single second that I'm in his company, on really looking after me in a way that no other man has ever done before, that I start thinking that maybe he could be The One after all.

The strangest thing happens later that week. Ed rings me at work and before I know it I've agreed to schlepp up to the City to meet him for a quick drink after work.

I get the tube to Moorgate, busily trying to follow the directions he'd given me on the phone, because West London might be fine, but as far as the City's concerned I may as well be from Spain.

People are milling about, looking as if they all know exactly where they're going, all wearing a uniform of dark suits and umbrellas, and I feel as if I've stepped into an alien world, because even the streets here are a world away from Kilburn or Ladbroke Grove, and there's a palpable buzz in the air, you can almost smell the money.

Eventually I find Ed's office, and go through to a smart reception with the ubiquitous black leather sofas and huge glass bowls of lilies on a large polished beech desk.

"May I help you?" says the girl behind the desk.

"I'm here to see Ed McMann," I say.

"Your name?"

"Oh. Sorry. Libby."

She smiles and picks up the phone, and a few seconds later directs me through to Ed's office.

I walk down the corridors, past meeting rooms filled with people deep in concentration, and eventually walk into a huge, open-plan room, with desks and people everywhere. The noise is almost deafening, and everyone seems to be on the phone, which is a bit like being at Joe Cooper, but this is so much bigger.

I stand there for a few seconds, unsure where to go, and then a girl catches my eye, smiles and says, "You look lost."

"I am," I say, smiling back. "I'm looking for Ed McMann?"

She points me to the other end of the room, to three offices with closed doors, and I knock on the door with Ed's name on it and wait for a few seconds until he opens it.

He's on the phone. His jacket's off, his sleeves are rolled up, and he's evidently having an argument with someone. He doesn't smile, just gestures me in and points to a chair, still talking to the person on the other end of the phone.

I sit and watch him, and suddenly I realize what authority he must have. I had never before thought of Ed as a powerful man, but, listening to his voice, I understand why he has reached the heights he has reached, and why he deserves, at least from his associates, an air of deference.

Because they are deferential. As I'm sitting there, Ed puts down the phone, kisses me, then walks to the door and shouts for someone to come into his office.

A middle-aged man, smartly dressed, walks in, and you can see, instantly, that he is intimidated by Ed. Ed gives him instructions on a deal he is brokering, a deal which, thanks to that last phone call, now appears to be problematic, and the man—Peter—murmurs that he will get on to it immediately.

And I can't help it. I'm impressed. If you really must know, I'm damned impressed. And it is at precisely this moment that I decide that perhaps this isn't such a big mistake after all.

● ● ●

The phone's ringing as I walk in the door, but for a while I have no idea who it is, because all I can hear is sobbing.

"Hello? Hello? Who is this?"

"It's me," and between the hiccups and the sobs I recognize Jules's voice and my face drains of color as I slowly sit down.

"Jules? What's the matter?"

"I . . ." She can't speak.

"I'm coming over," I say, and bang down the phone, grab my keys and head out the door.

Jules looks terrible. Her eyes are so puffy they've almost disappeared, and what little I can see of them is red raw. I walk in and put my arms around her, and she leans her head on my shoulder and collapses into a fresh round of tears.

Eventually the tears dissipate into hiccups, and I lead Jules, her shoulders heaving, into the kitchen and sit down on the sofa with my arm around her. I don't say anything, I just wait for her to talk.

"I don't know what to do," she says eventually, her pain almost breaking my heart. "I don't know what to do."

"What's happened?" Gentle, soothing tone of voice.

"He's gone," she says, as the tears start flowing again. "I don't know what to do."

An hour later, after countless tears, I have the full story, and it makes me feel sick. Sick, frightened and angry. I had always thought Jules and Jamie were the perfect couple. They had the marriage I aspired to have, the life I had always wanted. They had fulfilled a dream, and now that dream was lying in shreds around our feet.

Jamie, it seems, had walked in last night and said that they needed to talk. Jules had sat there with pounding heart as he told her that he had a confession, that he wasn't going to tell her, but that it was only fair that she should know. He said that he loved her, that he would never do anything to hurt her, and that he didn't know what had come over him.

He said that he had been having an affair with Laura, a lawyer he had met, but that it wasn't meant to be an affair—they had only slept together three times and he had felt so guilty that it was now over.

He said he was telling her because it was over, and because if anything it had made him realize how important Jules was. He couldn't live with himself anymore, with the guilt, and he hoped she would forgive him, and it would never happen again.

And Jules, apparently, sat there speechless, too shocked to say anything, feeling as if he had walked in and physically kicked her in the stomach.

After the shock came anger, at which point Jules ran to their bedroom and ripped open the cupboard doors, throwing his clothes into a heap and screaming at him to get out.

Jamie had started crying, trying to put his arms around her and telling her that he loved her, that he couldn't live without her, but Jules kept screaming at him to go. She spent the night pacing round the flat, and now anger has been replaced by desolation, and this is why she does not know what to do.

"I hate him," she sobs, as she finishes. "I absolutely bloody hate him," and I feel helpless as I try to comfort her, try to ease her pain.

"Jules," I say eventually, as once again the crying subsides. "Are you sure this is over, between you two, I mean? Shouldn't you try and talk about things, give this time?"

There is a silence, and then: "I don't know. I don't know what to do."

"He said it was over with this Laura," and Jules winces at the mention of her name, but I continue nevertheless, "and he loves you, and is it really worth throwing away your marriage because of a mistake?"

"A huge bloody mistake," she says. "I don't know if I can forgive him, if I can ever trust him again." And I sit there as she lets out the anger, lets out the pain, and I think, if this marriage is over, then perhaps I can no longer believe in the dream at all.

• • •

"Oll! What are you doing here?" I fling my arms around Olly, and he scoops me off the ground and swings me round.

"Sorry, sis," he laughs. "I seem to have a nasty habit of surprising you at the moment."

"It's not nasty," I say. "It's lovely!" And it's just what I need to lift my spirits, because I've been feeling almost as emotionally wrecked as Jules. It sounds crass to say that her pain is my pain, but it's just so fucking awful watching her crumple, and I'm trying to be there for her, trying to look after her, and I'm not complaining, but God, it's tiring.

My mum stands in the living room watching Olly and I, her face beaming because her beloved son is back home this weekend.

"How long are you down for?"

"Just this weekend, but then I'm coming down soon for a couple of weeks because we're shooting a load of stuff in London, when I'll move the team to the London offices."

"He's going to stay here, aren't you, Olly?" says my mum proudly. "It'll be just like old times having you back here again."

"Only if you promise to make a fuss of me and spoil me," says Olly, with a cheeky grin.

"Oh, you," says my mother grinning, flicking a dishcloth at Olly's legs.

"I've only been here five minutes," he says to me, "and already she's trying to feed me up. I think Mum thinks I haven't eaten since the last time I walked out of this house."

"It's not that I think you haven't eaten," Mum says. "It's just what you've been eating that concerns me."

Olly and I catch each other's eye, and we both suppress a grin because there was no way Mum meant a double entendre, and it's probably just the way our sick minds work anyway, but I know we're both thinking the same very rude thing.

"All that junk food, Olly. You need some good old-fashioned home cooking."

"Mmmmmm," says Olly, rubbing his stomach. "Does that mean . . ." He looks at her hopefully.

"Roast beef and Yorkshire pudding tonight. Your favorite."

"Thanks, Mum! What's for dessert?"

"What do you think?"

"Not spotted dick?"

She nods and smiles a very self-satisfied smile, at least in my eyes, and Olly leaps up and gives her a hug.

"Mum, have I ever told you you're the best?"

"Oh, it's nice to see you, Olly."

I sit there and watch them and wonder how in the hell he does it. How he manages never to put a foot wrong in her eyes. How he teases her and she loves it. He never gets her back up, never upsets her. And part of me, I suppose, is slightly envious of that. Not that I'd want that sort of relationship with her— God no—but I do sometimes wish I had a mother with whom I did have that sort of relationship.

Like Jo, for instance, at work. I know that she and her mum get on like a house on fire. As far as Jo's concerned, her mum's a friend who just happens to have given birth to her. They go out shopping together, have dinner together, and whenever Jo has a problem the first person she'll turn to for help is her mother.

And I've seen Jo's mother. Tall, soigné, elegant, she's so warm and friendly she just makes everyone fall in love with her. I remember the first time she came into the office to meet Jo for lunch. All the men banged on about how gorgeous she was, and all the women sighed and said they wished they had a mother like that. Especially me.

I'd die if my mother came into the office. Seriously. I'd want the ground beneath me to open and swallow me up. She'd be an embarrassment. The suburban housewife from hell who wouldn't know what to say to my colleagues or how to say it.

I sigh as she bustles into the kitchen to make some tea, and I settle back into the sofa with Olly.

"So how's Carolyn?"

"She's fine," he says.

"Still going strong?"

"Yeah, I know. Amazing. It's still going strong."

"So what's her secret?"

"I don't know really . . ." Like a man would ever take the time to analyze, but then Olly surprises me. "I think the thing is that she doesn't make any demands on me. Usually after a few weeks women start expecting things from you. They want to see you more and more often, and then they get pissed off when you're out with the boys, stuff like that. But Carolyn's really laid-back. She's happy to get on with her own life, and it's just really comfortable and relaxed, because I know she doesn't expect to see me all the time."

"So how often are you seeing her?"

"Well, actually," he laughs, "I suppose I am seeing her a lot, but that's because she's so easy to be with. And when I'm not with her she's out with her friends."

"That's brilliant, Olly," I say, and I wonder whether I could ever be more like Carolyn, whether I could be laid-back, low maintenance, but then I suppose I am like that with Ed. I'm really not that bothered about where he is when he's not with me, so maybe I've become a Carolyn after all.

"And you really like her?"

"I really like her. So what about you, Libby? What's going on with men in your life? Any action?"

"Yes, there is. Remember I told you about that guy I had dinner with?"

"Yup."

"I'm still seeing him, and he's really nice."

"Tell me about him."

"His name's Ed, he's thirty-nine—"

"Thirty-nine? Isn't that a bit old for you?"

"Nah, I like older men." As it happens I've never liked older men before, but there's something quite sophisticated about being the sort of woman who likes older men, and if I'm ever going to get the lifestyle I want I'm going to have to go for older men, because no one my age would have enough money.

"So go on."

"He's an investment banker . . ."

Olly lets out a high whistle. "Shit. He must be loaded."

"He is," I say, smiling happily. "But more important he's really nice to me, he treats me like a queen."

"You really like him?"

"Ye-es," I say. "I do really like him. The only thing is I'm not sure how much I fancy him, but I think I'm beginning to, so that's okay."

Shit. My bloody mother overheard that last bit.

"You don't know whether you fancy him? Fancy him? I've never heard anything so ridiculous, Libby. Since when do you have to fancy someone? It's not about fancying someone, it's about liking them and getting on with them. None of that fancying stuff lasts anyway, and do you think in my day we married people because we fancied them? D'you think I fancied your father?"

Olly and I both grimace. Not a thought I particularly want to dwell on, I have to say.

"It's Ed McMann, Olly," my mother says. "He's very rich and very nice, and Libby's worried about whether she fancies him or not. Honestly. I just don't know what to do with you sometimes."

"How do you know he's very nice?" I taunt. "You've never met him, he could be a complete bastard for all you know." Like Jamie, I think. And much as I hate to admit it, I think that my mother may be right, because Jules fancied Jamie. Jules thought she'd have a happy ending. Maybe it's not about fancying after all.

"I won't have that language in my house, Libby, and I've heard he's very nice."

"Oh right. Of course. Because you do mix in the same social circles."

My mother harrumphs and walks back into the kitchen.

"What was all that about?" Olly's looking confused.

"You know Mum. She's decided that come hell or high water I'm going to marry Ed, because he's rich and because she can boast to all her friends."

"Uh-oh," he says. "Sounds like you're in trouble. So when am I going to meet this Ed?"

My mother's back in the room, evidently having forgotten my last sarcastic remark.

"Ooh, I'd love to meet him too," she says, eyes brightening at the thought, any sarcasm forgiven.

"I think it's a little bit early on to start introducing him to my parents," I say, feeling physically sick at the thought.

"I don't think so," she says. "If he's as nice as you say he is then he'd be delighted to meet us."

I know how her mind works. She wants to meet him so she can drop it into the conversation at one of her ghastly coffee mornings. I can hear her now. "Had a marvelous time last night with Libby's new boyfriend. Ed McMann. Yes, that Ed Mc-Mann. Oh well, he obviously adores Libby, I think," and I can hear her lowering her voice, "I think we might be making plans soon . . ."

"I don't think so, Mum," I say. "Look, Olly, I've got to go." Even the added attraction of Olly being there doesn't make me want to stay in this house a second longer than is absolutely necessary. "Why don't you come with me and we can have a drink?"

"Olly's staying here," my mum says firmly. "And where are you going that's so important?"

"To Ed's," I lie, knowing that this will be the one thing she won't try to stop.

"How lovely," she trills. "Ask him if he'd like to come over for dinner."

"Yeah, really," I mutter, kissing her goodbye.

• • •

And when I get home there's a long, rambly message on my machine from Ed, and I ring him back, and he's so pleased to hear from me it's really sweet. And he asks me about my day, and I tell him I've just got back from my parents. Ed says he'd love to meet my parents.

"You are joking?"

"Of course not. Why would I joke about something like that?"

"Oh. Funnily enough my mum was saying the same thing."

"Well, there you are, then. Why don't we all go out for dinner this week?"

"Ed," I say slowly, not quite knowing what to say next. "Let's just wait until after the ball, okay?"

"Fine, fine. But I would like to meet them."

"Umm, don't you think that, umm, it might be a little soon? I mean, we haven't been seeing each other very long."

"Libby," he says calmly. "When it's right, it's right." And in a flood of confusion I say goodbye.

What the fuck does that mean, when it's right, it's right? What was he saying? Was he saying that he loves me? Was he saying that I'm The One? Do I feel the same way about him?

Normally I'd talk this through with Jules, but the only thing we talk about now on the phone is Jamie, and what she's going to do. But I need to know if she's okay, so I put my life on hold for the time being and call her. Her machine picks up and I start talking, and then she picks up the phone.

"How are you feeling?" I venture, surprised and incredibly relieved that she sounds almost, almost, like her normal self.

"Not great," she says. "But better than I was."

"Have you spoken to him?"

"I've left the machine on and he's been leaving pleading messages. I can't face speaking to him just yet, I've still got a lot to think about."

"So you think you might give him another chance?"

"I don't know. I can't believe what he's done, I can't believe how much this hurts, but you were right the other night, I have to think about the marriage, think about whether it's worth throwing it all away and starting again."

"Jules, do you still love him?"

"Of course I still love him. That's the bloody problem."

• • •

Selfish as I may be, I still need to talk to someone about my life, so I phone Sal. And I know I've been remiss, I haven't really made an effort with her recently, but that's kind of what happens when men get in the way. You suddenly find that a few weeks, or sometimes months, have gone by, and you've been meaning to speak to your friends, but somehow you've been too busy trying to build a relationship.

"Libby!" she says. "What a surprise!"

"Hi, Sal. How are you?"

"Never mind about me, how are you?"

"Fine, fine."

"You're okay, then?"

"Umm." I'm missing something here. "Okay about what?"

"Well, Nick and all that."

"Oh God, yes. Actually I've met someone new. Sort of."

"You're kidding! That's fantastic! Tell me everything!"

So I start to tell her, except I give her the short version, and then I get to the bit about him saying when it's right, it's right, and I hear Sal audibly draw her breath in.

"Jesus!" she says, after a short silence.

"I know. But what d'you think it means?"

"I think it means he's in love with you! Libby, that's so exciting! Ed McMann's in love with you!"

"He hasn't actually said that."

"Yet . . ."

"Well, yes. Yet. And maybe he meant something else."

"Like what?" Sal splutters.

And truth to be told I can't actually think of anything else.

"Listen," she says eventually. "I know this may well not be your thing, and Nick's coming, but presumably if you're going out with Ed that won't bother you anymore, and it's just that a few of us are meeting up tonight at the Clifton, and I don't know why I didn't think of you earlier, but d'you want to come?"

I suddenly have an inspired thought. "Sal, my brother Olly's in London this weekend. If he's still here, can he come too?"

" 'Course he can."

"And it's fine with Nick. It will be really lovely to see him."

But after I put the phone down I'm not so sure. First of all I'm no longer the sort of woman who goes to pubs, although admittedly I would make an exception for the Clifton, being as it is one of the few truly country-style pubs in St. John's Wood, not to mention the whole of London. And I'm not too sure I do want to see Nick.

I mean, yes, it was lovely talking to him on the phone the other day, but seeing him's another matter entirely, and I really don't know how I'll feel about him. In fact, if I'm really honest with you, I really don't know whether I want to know. If you see what I mean.

Because as long as I don't see him I can pretend it's okay. I can settle for Ed, because I don't have to face physically what I may never have again. I know that one look into Nick's eyes, and it will bring all the pain back again, and I'm not sure I can deal with that.

But I suppose I'll have to deal with it sooner or later, and who knows? I may be pleasantly surprised and discover that my feelings for him are on the wane.

And pigs might fly.

Oh, what the hell, it's not as if I've got anything better to do. I ring Olly and yes, he's still in London, and yes, Mum's beginning to get on his nerves a bit, and yes, yes, yes, he'd love to come out for a drink tonight.

I give Olly the details and arrange to meet him there, and once I've put down the phone I look at myself in my jeans and sloppy sweater, and I decide that, as befits a woman of my recently acquired social standing, I will dress up. I will be smart casual. I will blow Nick's socks off.

Yeah, yeah, yeah, I know. It's that old story again. Nick said he didn't want me anymore, but if I look completely incredible maybe he'll change his mind, and even though I'm with Ed now, I want to show Nick what he's missing out on, what he could have had, what someone else is now getting.

Or not, as the case may be, but Nick doesn't need to know that.

What to wear, what to wear? I riffle through my clothes, and eventually pull out some wide-legged navy trousers, which I team with navy J. P. Tod's shoes and a thin cream cashmere sweater.

Oops, sorry, I forgot to mention that I went on a bit of a shopping spree recently. It's Ed, you see. I can hardly go out with him to the smartest restaurants in London in all my old clothes, so I've bitten the bullet, pushed my overdraft to the very back of my head, and been hitting Joseph in a major, major fashion. (And no, couldn't face the woman in the St. John's Wood store, so I went up to Brompton Cross. Much nicer. They treated me like a human being.)

And, er, I probably shouldn't admit this, but on the way back from Joseph I happened to pass Emporio Armani, well, it wasn't exactly on the way back, more of a slight detour, but that's beside the point—and went in just to look, and I came out with masses of stuff. Armfuls. Fortunes.

I felt slightly sick for a while, but I'm Ed McMann's girlfriend . . . almost. I have to look the part. And anyway, I justified to Jo when she sat there open-mouthed listening to how much I'd spent (and Jo spends money like it's going out of fashion, so imagine how much I had to spend to shock her), it's only money. I mean, for God's sake, we're only here for about ninety years if we're lucky, so nothing really matters very much, and certainly not money.

Yup. This is the outfit. Nick will have heart failure.

● ● ●

I walk in the pub, and it's a bit like déjà vu, because sitting at a table on the other side of the bar are Sal and Paul, the gorgeous Kathy with an equally gorgeous and evidently new man by her side called Jared, and Nick.

And when I see Nick my heart does begin to beat a little faster because—and I know it hasn't been that long—I really had forgotten quite how blue his eyes are, and just how gorgeous his smile is.

He stands up and gives me a huge bear hug, and there's something incredibly sweet and painful about hugging this body that up until recently I knew so well, and I can't help my-self, those old loins start stirring and I don't want to let go. Ever.

No! Stop it, Libby! Nick is not for you. Nick has no money. Remember Moose. Remember the bedsit. I remember, and my heart slows down. It slows down even more when I think of the Porsche and the house in Hanover Terrace.

Nick stands back and looks at me, giving me a wolf whistle and a cheeky grin.

"Cor," he says. "If I didn't know better I'd say I was having a drink with Tara Palmer-Tomkinson."

"Don't say that!" I slap him lightly. "I don't look anything like her!"

"You do tonight," he says. "You're all sophisticated and sexy. Verrrrrry nice."

"You like my new look, then?"

"Mmm," he says. "I could definitely get used to it."

I almost laugh when I think of how I only ever wore jeans and sneakers with Nick because I thought that's what he wanted. Almost, but not quite, because Jules's description of me as a chameleon girlfriend is still in my mind, and I don't want to think about the fact that I might be doing it again.

"Hi, sorry I'm late." Olly walks in, and I give him a kiss, then introduce him round the table. I can see Kathy's eyes light up as she shakes his hand, and bless Olly, he barely even seems to notice her. This is when I realize that it really must be serious with Carolyn, because, up until he met her, Kathy would have been just his type.

"Nick! Good to see you again!" Nick stands up and they give each other a really warm, claspy sort of handshake, the sort of handshake that men give each other when they really like each other—and for a fleeting moment I wonder whether Olly will have this sort of relationship with Ed.

God, why am I even worrying about it? I mean, Ed's a nice bloke. He's nice to me. What's not to like?

"I was just saying that Libby looks fantastic," says Nick.

"Yeah. You do look nice. Very smart." Olly seems to notice

what I'm wearing for the first time. "That looks expensive. Had a pay rise?"

Nick chuckles as I blush. "No. It's courtesy of my overdraft facility."

"Who wants what?" Olly goes off to the bar to get the drinks, and I start chatting to Sal and Paul.

But while I'm chatting to them I keep feeling Nick's eyes on me, and I can feel myself holding in my stomach, straightening my back, tossing my hair around as I laugh in what I hope is a sexy and mysterious way.

And then there's a break in the conversation and Nick leans over to me. "You must be happy with this bloke," he says. "You're glowing."

"Am I?"

"Yes. You look like you're going to explode soon, a sort of thermonuclear reaction."

"Is that supposed to be a compliment?"

"It is a compliment."

"Okay. Well, thanks."

"And no food babies tonight, then?" He looks at my stomach and I laugh, and suddenly I'm swept back to that night in my flat when Nick knelt down and rubbed my stomach, and I feel this incredible yearning, and I meet his eyes which are watching me curiously, and I suddenly think that this is exactly what he intended.

He wanted to remind me of what we had, what it was like, and I don't know why he's doing this because he was the one who said he didn't want me, and as far as I'm concerned Nick is now a closed chapter. Or closing, anyway.

I change the subject.

"So how's the book coming along?"

"Finished!" he says, thanking Olly for the pint that's just been placed in front of him. "I'm about to send the finished manuscript off to a load of literary agents. I've had it with publishers. I don't think they even bother to read the bloody thing, so I'm going the agent route."

"Good luck," I say, and I mean it. "What do you think will happen?"

"I don't know," he says. "But unless I win the lottery very soon, I'm going to have to do something about a job."

There, you see? He did it again. Brought up the lottery. Made me think instantly of the first night we got it together, when we talked about what we'd do if we won the lottery.

"So go on," he says. "Tell me everything you've bought in the last week."

"What?"

"You said you'd been shopping. I want to know exactly what you bought and where you got it from."

I start to laugh. "Jesus, Nick. I'd forgotten what a girl you are."

"It's not that I'm a girl," he says. "It's just that I know the way to a girl's heart."

Chapter 20

"Darling, I'm leaving now."

"Okay, I'll see you in a little while."

I put down the phone to Ed and ring Jules.

"I feel awful," she says, as soon as she picks up the phone. "I completely forgot about the ball. Are you excited?"

"Jules, my darling, I didn't expect you to remember, you've got far too much to think about."

"I'll be fine," she says. "It's just weird being in this huge flat on my own. I feel a bit lost, I don't know what to do with myself."

"Look, I can cancel tonight. Why don't I come over? We can do face packs and girly things."

"That's so sweet of you, but no. I'm a big girl now and I can cope, and anyway I wouldn't ruin your date. I'll make some supper and have an early night. God knows this is exhausting me. It feels like I haven't slept for years."

I want so desperately for her and Jamie to get back together. I know he's done an appalling thing, he's betrayed her utterly and completely, but I also know, or at least I think I know, that for men sex doesn't have to mean an emotional commitment. That for many men it's simply physical gratification, and that Jamie, despite having made a major fuck-up, has admitted it's over. And I wonder whether three fucks, to put it crudely, are worth a marriage, are worth throwing away a man who might not be perfect, but who loves her, despite everything, and who is a good husband, will be a good father.

And I want them to get back together because I want to regain the equilibrium in our friendship, selfish as that may be. You see Jules has always been the strong one. Jules has been the one to whom I turn in times of pain, and now that she is turning to me, I am not sure that I am strong enough, or wise enough, to give her the advice she needs.

And I miss the easy banter of our friendship, although I hate to say, despite sounding completely exhausted, the more we talk the more Jules sounds like her old self. Maybe she's just putting on a very good act, but things are almost like they used to be.

"So did you ask him?" she says.

"I couldn't. How could I ask him whether or not we would be staying the night?"

Because for the last few days I have been terrified of this. The ball is in a country house in Midhurst, and I phoned the AA, who said it was about an hour and a half's drive from London, so does that mean we'll be driving back, or does it mean we're staying there, and if we are staying are we staying in the same room, or will they have organized separate rooms for us, and I'm really not sure I'm ready for this yet.

"You are such a wimp!" says Jules. "What are you going to do?"

"I don't know. I've packed clean knickers and a toothbrush just in case, but I don't want to be forced into a situation where I have to have sex with him before I'm ready."

"Don't you mean, make lurrve," she shrieks, giggling.

"Oh, Jules! Be serious."

"Okay, okay. Sorry. Look, Libby, I doubt very much whether Ed will force you into anything, he's far too much of a gentleman, so I would assume that if you are staying the night you will definitely have separate bedrooms."

"You really think so?"

"I really think so. Anyway, have you got a nightie or what?"

"I couldn't spend any more money, Jesus, do you know how much I've spent recently?"

"Yup."

"So I'm just taking a T-shirt."

"I hope it covers your bum. You might have to get up in the

middle of the night and wander down dark, frosty corridors looking for the loo."

"Do you really think I hadn't thought of that?"

"You're going to have a brilliant time. Think of your gorgeous dress."

"Okay, okay. You're right. I will have a brilliant time. I'll ring you tomorrow, either way. Are you sure you're going to be okay tonight?"

"I'm sure," she says. "Slowly getting used to enjoying the single life again. It's reminding me how jealous I am of your life."

"Oh yeah, really—you'd just love to be living in my tiny flat, fending off the bastards, trying to find Mr. Right."

"First of all, I may well be single again. Secondly, my self-esteem's taken the biggest knocking it's ever had and I'm not sure I'll ever feel the same, and thirdly, I thought I had found a decent man. It looks like we are pretty damn similar after all."

Shit. Why did I have to say that? I've unwittingly brought the conversation back round to Jamie.

"I'm sorry," Jules says after a pause. "I didn't mean that. I still feel so hurt. Look, I'd better go. Have a wonderful time tonight, and let me know how it went tomorrow."

"Are you sure?"

"Sure that you should have a wonderful time or sure that you should let me know tomorrow? On both counts I'm sure."

"No, are you sure you don't want to carry on talking?"

"No, Libby. I'm tired of talking about Jamie. I need a break."

"Okay. Just look after yourself."

"What am I, an invalid?"

"You know what I mean."

"I do know, and I can't tell you how much easier this is, having you there. I couldn't go through this without you, Libby, I really couldn't."

"You know I love you." There are tears filling my eyes.

"I know. And I love you too. Oh, and by the way, give him one for me," she says, with a faint hint of laughter that brings a smile to my face, because at least I know we've ended the conversation on a good note.

I put the phone down and it rings again immediately. Who the hell is it now?

I might have guessed.

"Ringing to remind you, darling, that if it's a sit-down dinner you work your way in from the outside of the cutlery."

What the fuck does my mother think I am? Ten years old?

"I can't believe you're ringing to tell me that." I shake my head, trying to stifle the urge simply to tell her to fuck off.

"I'm only trying to help, Libby," she says indignantly. "I don't want you showing me up."

"You? You? What on earth has anything got to do with you? You're not coming."

"I know, but you're still your mother's daughter."

"Oh, for God's sake."

"And have you taken a hot-water bottle? You know how these country mansions can get very drafty at night."

Typical. In the past, if ever my mother has had an inkling of me sleeping with a boyfriend before at least six months, she's gone bananas, and now she's practically encouraging it, and it's been, what? Two weeks?

"No, Mum," I sigh wearily. "I'm sure they'll have central heating. Look, I really have to go."

"All right, darling. Have a wonderful time, and ring me to-morrow and tell me everything."

"Yeah, Mum. I will."

As if.

Thank God, no flowers this time. And Ed doesn't say I look beautiful, because I'm just in my everyday clothes, my Donna Karan special in a zipped-up hanging cover, and I know this may sound crazy, but Ed seems ever so slightly nervous, which I find odd in a man who's so wealthy and sophisticated.

"Are you nervous?" I venture, as we set off from Ladbroke Grove.

"A little." He turns to me and grins. "Are you?"

"A little. But why are you nervous?"

He shrugs. "I really want you to like my friends, that's all."

Thank God for that. For one horrible minute there I thought he was worried about his friends liking me, worried that they might see beyond my designer dress to the not-nearly-good-enough suburban girl lurking just beneath the surface.

I know my mother spent her whole life telling me this is what she was raising me for, but the truth is I'm not sure how comfortable I am around these people, and chameleon woman that I so evidently am, I've raised my accent a few notches just to make absolutely sure I fit in.

And for a second, as we drive through Putney, I think that actually I'd be much happier going to the pub with Nick, although I know that isn't strictly true.

I suppose, what I'd really like is a man who can fit into both worlds. Who's just as happy going to a smart ball as going to the local Italian pizza joint (not pubs, never pubs). But if I really have to make a choice, then I'd have to choose the ball.

Wouldn't I?

God, would you listen to me? My entire life I've dreamed of finding a man like Ed, and now I have I'm starting to think that maybe I don't want this after all. Which is ridiculous. Because I've always wanted this, and I will make this work. I bloody will.

After a while Ed puts some music on—classical, naturally, and we sit there in this comfortable silence, and it is comfortable, and this feels so much nicer than the times I've spent with men in the past, desperately trying to think of something to say to fill the silences.

And finally we take an exit off the A3 and wind our way down country roads, as Ed tells me about the ball they had last year, and how wonderful it was, except that he didn't have anyone to share it with then, and how happy he is that I'm with him now.

We pull off the road and eventually come to a halt outside a pair of tall, black iron gates, and Ed speaks into an intercom, the gates open, and we're on a magnificent sweeping driveway, and I'm so impressed, and suddenly so nervous I can hardly speak.

Ed gets out of the car and comes round to open the door for me, which is really rather stupid because it's not like I can't get out of the car myself, but Ed seems to think this is the way to treat women, and as I take his hand and step out of the car I feel somewhat princesslike, and we both turn as a couple come walking out of the huge, heavy oak front door.

"Ed!" says the petite, blond woman, who turns out to be Sarah, one half of Sarah and Charlie, and I'm quite surprised because she's not in designer togs at all. In fact, and I know it's only four o'clock, she looks a bit of a mess.

"Sarah!" he says, giving her a kiss on each cheek as she looks interestedly over his shoulder at me, standing there awkwardly smiling because I'm not sure what else to do.

He shakes hands with Charlie and turns to me.

"This is—"

"Libby," says Sarah warmly, coming over to shake my hand. "I am so delighted to meet you. We've heard all about you."

"We certainly have," echoes Charlie, coming over to give me a huge kiss on the cheek. "Let me take your bags."

Uh-oh. Here it is. That bedroom moment. And I don't know why, but I'm vaguely disappointed that there isn't a butler or someone to carry my bags. I mean, if you're going to live in a place this stately, you may as well do it properly.

Charlie and Ed lag behind as Sarah leads me up this, well, the only word for it would be magnificent, staircase, as I wonder what on earth I'm going to do.

"So how long have you known Ed?" She turns with a warm smile.

"Not long," I venture. "Only a few weeks."

"He seems to be completely smitten." She winks, stops and opens a door. "We thought you might like this bedroom."

I walk in, mouth wide open, because I can't believe how beautiful it is. There's a huge oak four-poster bed, and for a moment I'm so taken in with the splendor of the damn thing I forget to think, fuck! Double bed.

"We've put Ed next door," she whispers, as the men approach. "We weren't sure . . ." She tails off as I breathe a sigh of relief and grin.

"That's perfect," I say, feeling as though I want to hug her. "Thank you."

She puts a hand gently on my arm and squeezes it. "I completely understand," she says. "It must be terribly daunting for you, having to meet all these strange people."

"You're not strange," I say, smiling, and she laughs.

"Come down when you're ready," she says. "We'll have tea." She turns and goes, and Ed comes in and gives me a hug.

"She's lovely," I say into his shoulder.

"I know," he says. "I knew you'd like them."

And then, naturally, insecurity hits.

"Do you think they liked me?"

"Of course they liked you," he guffaws. "How could they not?"

Thankfully he doesn't then expect me to engage in a passionate embrace, he just lets me go and says, "Shall we go down for tea in fifteen minutes?"

"Sure," I say, nodding, and Ed leaves the room and closes the door behind him.

I bounce up and down on the bed a few times, because this is what they do in the films when they walk into a fabulously sumptuous bedroom, and then I wonder what it is I'm supposed to do for the next fifteen minutes. I hang my dress in the wardrobe and then touch up my makeup, and there are still ten minutes to go, and no television to pass the time.

But on the side table I discover a host of glossy women's magazines, and I'm leafing through them, about to read an article on how women know When It's Right, when I hear a soft knock on the door, and Ed and I walk down for tea.

I'm introduced first to a large blue and yellow parrot squawking in a cage in the corner of the living room. Charles, "the cynical parrot," as he's described, has apparently perfected his speech when it comes to insults, but the only thing he says as I bend down to cluck at him is "Have a cup of tea," and, relieved, I leave him to go and meet everyone else in the room.

I suppose I was half expecting to hate his friends. I knew they were all much older than me—and, judging by Sarah and Charlie, who must be in their forties, most of them are, but I also thought they'd be those really English county types, who would look down their noses and be incredibly snotty to someone like me, but I was completely wrong.

We walk into the room and I'm dreading it, but as Sarah introduces me as "Ed's friend," with, incidentally, no special emphasis on the "friend," everyone is just incredibly friendly, and no one is nearly as smart or as intimidating as I'd feared.

In fact, I'd go as far as saying they all seemed very down-to-earth, and the only thing I found strange was mixing with people who were almost old enough to be my parents, but I'm mature enough to handle that.

I don't want to embarrass myself by scarfing, so I settle into an old sofa (and, not wishing to sound like my mother, but haven't they heard of Dustbusters? Couldn't they have hoovered, somehow, the dog hairs off the sofa?) and nibble daintily at a cucumber sandwich as Julia (one half of Julia and David) sits next to me and makes small talk.

"It's lovely to see Ed with someone," she says finally, after we've discussed PR versus being a housewife, which is what she is, we've both agreed that the grass is always greener, how she'd kill for my "exciting, glamorous" lifestyle, and how I think hers sounds like complete bliss.

"We're so used to Ed turning up on his own to these annual balls, and he's such a good chap, we've always wondered why he's never found himself someone lovely," she continues. "But now, it seems, he has."

I laugh. "Well, I don't know about that. It's very new. We're really just, umm, friends, right now."

"But from what I hear Ed's quite serious about you."

Should she be quite so candid? I mean, she hardly knows me.

I smile again. "We shall see," I say mysteriously, because I don't know quite what else to say.

I notice that the men seem to be on one side of the room, presumably discussing business, because occasionally I hear the odd "equity," "made a mint," "gilt-edged securities," while the women sit on my side of the room talking about the best places to shop in "town." Town being London.

"You're ever so lucky, Libby," says Sarah, moving to sit closer to me. "Libby lives in London," she explains to the rest of the women. "We have to make a particular journey whenever we want to buy anything special."

"Where do you live?" says a youngish woman who, I think, is called Emily, but I can't quite remember.

"Ladbroke Grove," I say, wishing I could say Regent's Park, or Knightsbridge, or Chelsea, and at the same time wishing it didn't matter, wishing I didn't still feel I had to impress these people. Among my friends I'm pretty damn proud of living in Ladbroke Grove, because it's trendy, but here, with Ed's friends, I know it's not even nearly good enough.

"How lovely," says Julia. "That's bang next door to Notting Hill, isn't it, and there are so many wonderful places in Notting Hill. Tell me, do you go to the Sugar Club?"

"Yes," I say, my face lighting up because I have actually been there. Once. "I go there all the time."

"Lucky you," they all coo. "Having all those wonderful places right on your doorstep."

And then the talk disintegrates into schools that their children go to, so I put down my cup of tea and wander on to the terrace, and sitting on the low brick wall that looks out on to sweeping gardens I wonder what Nick would think if he could see me now.

I turn as a hand rubs my back, and Ed leans down and plants a kiss on my cheek, and what's really sweet about this is that it's in full view of all his friends, but he doesn't seem to mind, and I think about all the men who have warned me about public displays of affection, and I look at Ed and wonder whether, if he was a bastard to me like all the others, I might like him better.

Except the thing is that I'm feeling very comfortable here, with his friends, and I think I am growing to like him more, for obviously hinting that we would want separate bedrooms, for not having sex as the first and only thing on his mind, for introducing me to this incredible lifestyle, for treating me like a goddess.

"Do you want to go for a walk?" he says. "I could show you the grounds."

I nod and link my arm through his, and his face lights up at my spontaneous display of tenderness, and he strokes my hand through his elbow. "I don't want you to get cold," he says. "Shall I go and get your jacket?"

"Don't worry." I lean up and give him a kiss on the cheek. "I'll be fine."

At seven o'clock everyone disappears to their respective bedrooms to get ready, all having been given strict instructions to be downstairs at eight-thirty.

And so much for cold, drafty corridors and seeking bathrooms. My room is lovely and warm, and I have an en suite bathroom, which Sarah has filled with delicious smelling bubble baths and soft, thick towels.

I soak for ages, right up until the water is practically cold, and grin to myself as I think where I am, who I'm with, and when I start shivering I consider running some more hot water in the bath, but don't, because they probably won't have enough to go round, and I get out, carefully, so as not to soak the floor, and go into the bedroom to try and reposition the dressing table mirror to give me enough light to do my makeup perfectly.

And finally, at 8:30 P.M., when I've just clipped on the tiny diamante studs, which, I'm sure, if you didn't look that closely, you might mistake for the real thing, there's a knock on my door and Ed's standing there in a dinner jacket.

Neither of us says anything for a while. I'm just so impressed with the difference black tie can make on a man. He looks, well, the word that springs to mind is powerful. He looks like a real man, and that's when I realize that up until now I've only ever been out with boys, and something about him looking like a real man makes me feel incredibly feminine, and eventually Ed is the first to speak.

"You look beautiful," he whispers. "Absolutely beautiful. Stunning. You'll be the most beautiful woman at the party."

There. He said it, didn't he? Woman. Not girl.

"You look lovely yourself," I say, grinning. "All dark and sexy and mysterious." I don't mention that the mustache ruins the effect somewhat, because I think I might just about be getting used to it . . . as long as it doesn't get too close to me.

And we walk down the staircase, my hand resting gently on his arm, and maybe I'm imagining it, but I do seem to be wearing the most stunning dress here, and we walk down to meet all those upturned faces, doubtless wondering who this girl is with Ed, and I do feel, for perhaps the first time in my life, truly, truly, beautiful.

We have an incredible evening. And though I can safely say that the people are slightly older than those I would normally socialize with, they are all so warm and friendly that after a while I start to forget the age difference.

The champagne helps of course.

And God, the champagne. And the food. And the thousands of tiny white fairy lights sprinkled around the trees surrounding the terrace. And the music. And the fact that I am high on the champagne, on the glamour, on the excitement of being at a party that truly looks like something you would see in a Hollywood movie, or perhaps because of the British accents, in a Merchant Ivory film.

It feels like the kind of party that I would only ever go to once in my life, because it is all so magical, and so beautiful, and so special, it could never be re-created. Except, of course, with Ed there would be parties like this all the time.

And the more champagne I drink—which, let me tell you, is a hell of a lot, because every time my glass is half empty a waiter-type person appears at my side as quietly as a ghost and refills it—the more attractive Ed becomes.

And at around one o'clock in the morning I'm thinking, yes. Yes. Tonight's the night. I'm going to do it tonight. And I think that perhaps this whole sex thing has become such an issue because it's been hanging over my head, because I've been so worried about it, and that if we got it out of the way it would all be fine, because it's bound to be better than I expect. Isn't it?

Ed's trying to stifle a yawn, and I laugh and put my arms around him, kissing him on the forehead, saying, "It's past your bedtime, isn't it, old man?"

And he snuggles up to me, smiling sleepily. "I'm not old."

"Okay. Older-than-me man."

"That's better. I'm fine. You're not ready for bed. I'm really happy staying up a bit longer. Ce n'est pas un problème."

Oh shut up with the bloody French, Ed. You're about to ruin the moment. But of course I don't say this. I say: "You mean a minute longer, don't you?"

"You're right," he laughs. "I am pretty tired."

"Come on." I take him by the hand and pull him to his feet. "I'm putting you to bed."

Now I know I could have said I'm taking you to bed, but that would have been too obvious, wouldn't it? That would have made him realize tonight is the night, and then we would have both had to walk upstairs knowing that once we made it into the room we were about to, as Jules put it, make lurrve, and halfway up we probably would have started throwing up with nerves or something.

So we say good night to Sarah and Charlie, and wave apologetically to people like Julia, who we can just about make out over the sea of heads, and we walk upstairs, me leading Ed by the hand. My heart's pounding, I can't believe I'm about to do it, and part of me wants—and God oh God, please don't think I sound like a total prostitute for saying this—part of me wants to give him something, to thank him for all he's done for me.

Ed stops outside his bedroom door and puts his arms around me.

"You are the most beautiful woman I've ever seen," he says, pulling me close. "What are you doing with me?"

And the way he says it makes my heart open, and I reach up to kiss him on the lips, and when I pull back I smile and say, "Would you stay with me tonight?" And my voice is a bit shaky because Ed is so old-fashioned. I do suddenly think, once the words are out, that he might take me for a brazen hussy, and I'd have to say goodbye to my newfound lifestyle.

"Are you sure?" he whispers back. "I don't mind sleeping on my own. In fact, I wasn't expecting—"

And I cut him off with a kiss as I, rather spectacularly I have to admit, open my bedroom door with one hand and pull him gently in with the other.

Chapter 21

Sometimes I feel so angry that I think I'm going to scream. It's like a deep well of anger, resentment, fury, whatever, and I have to concentrate incredibly hard, because at any moment it's all going to come flooding out and I'm just going to completely lose control.

This is how I feel this morning. Ed's sitting next to me, we've just driven past Guildford on our way back home, and I want to kill him. He keeps giving me these worrying glances, and putting his hand on my leg with a reassuring squeeze, and every time he does it I want to hit him.

And I know I'm being a bitch. I know I'm behaving like a spoiled brat who hasn't got what she wanted, but the more disgusting I am to him, the more he looks at me with these sad puppy-dog eyes, the worse I become.

So what was his terrible crime?

The sex was crap.

A joke.

Make that a complete farce.

I mean, here's this guy who's supposed to be one of the most eligible bachelors in the country, who has, he says, been out with people, and all I can say is he hasn't got a damn clue.

Not a clue.

And I'm furious with him for it, which I know is completely unfair, but I can't help it.

So okay, you're probably now dying to hear just how bad it was, so fine. I'll tell you, but before you think I'm being a total cow, just put yourself in my position, and ask yourself whether you might not be feeling exactly the same way.

I pulled Ed into my room and started kissing him, and the

kiss wasn't brilliant, still way too much saliva if you must know, so I stopped kissing him on the mouth and started to plant tiny kisses over his cheek and down his neck, which is when I realized what it is about him that somehow turns me off.

It's his smell. Not BO, or anything like that, but just his natural body smell. It seems to be kind of sour, not massively pleasant, so I decided I'd better keep my tongue firmly in my mouth from there on in.

I know, I know. I should have stopped there. I should have realized that the sexual chemistry quite obviously hadn't grown, at least not for me, but I kept going, thinking that Julia Roberts admitted in *Pretty Woman* that she never kissed the men she slept with (up until Richard Gere, of course, and who could blame her?), therefore I could have sex with Ed without having to kiss him either.

And because I didn't want to taste his skin, Ed obviously thought that these strange birdlike pecks I was giving him were the way to turn me on, so he started doing the same thing to me, at which point I promptly stopped, because it didn't feel the least bit sensuous, or sexy, or anything other than bloody irritating.

And then he said, "Do you want to use the bathroom to get undressed?" which was a bit odd, because I thought in the heat of the moment he would just rip my clothes off, but I went into the bathroom anyway with my T-shirt. When I came out Ed was lying in bed with the duvet tucked up under his chin, and my first instinct was to run far, far away.

But, being the determined woman I am, I squashed that instinct flat, and gingerly climbed into bed beside him. He cuddled up to me and started kissing me again, and I thought, this will be okay, I can do this.

And after a while I moved my hand down and felt the very thing that I had been completely dreading.

Y-fronts.

So I prized them off as gently as I could, given the fact that he had an enormous erection, and Ed started squeezing—

actually, perhaps kneading would be a more accurate description—my breasts through my T-shirt, and he did it for so long that I figured I may as well take my T-shirt off myself, which I did, and then he carried on kneading, and I have to say I was about as turned on as a loaf of bread.

And then, before I knew it, Ed was on top of me, and, even though penetration was now the very last thing on my mind, I reached for a condom and put it on for him, because, although he tried, he didn't seem to know what to do with it. Then he was inside me, and there was a look of pure bliss on his face, and he started moving a bit, and then, I kid you not, about six seconds later he groaned very loudly and collapsed on top of me.

And I lay there fuming.

Absolutely fucking fuming.

And while I was staring at the ceiling with his huge weight on top of me and thinking that this, without doubt, was the worst sex I'd ever had, the worst sex it was possible to have, Ed moved his face above mine, grinning like a Cheshire cat, and said, "That was wonderful, darling."

And then he must have seen that my face was completely blank, and he kissed me and said, "Was that okay?"

Well no, actually, it wasn't bloody okay. It was abysmal, and maybe I should have been more ladylike about it, maybe I should have just nodded, rolled over and gone to sleep, but I couldn't, I was just too damn frustrated, and disappointed, and angry.

So that's what I said.

And Ed rolled off me, looking as if he were going to cry, and this in itself made me even more furious, because he's not exactly a child, and how could a man of his age be so completely pathetic in bed?

But he didn't say anything, so I just kept ranting about how sex is a two-way street, and did he really think I would get turned on by ten minutes kneading my breasts, and hadn't he ever heard of the clitoris, and premature ejaculation wasn't exactly enjoyable, especially given that I'd had no foreplay whatsoever, and come to that, did he even know what the word "foreplay" meant.

And the more I ranted—because by this time I was really getting into it—the more upset he looked. Eventually, when I finished, he tried to put his arms round me and say sorry, but I just stormed off and went into the bathroom.

I sat on the loo seat, wishing to Christ I could talk to Jules. After a while I got a bit cold, so I went back into the bedroom, and Ed was sitting on the edge of the bed with his head hung low. He looked up and sighed.

"I really am sorry," he started. "I feel awful, it's just that I suppose I'm not terribly experienced, but if you help me I can learn, you can show me what to do. I really do think that we can work this out if we're both willing."

I harrumphed a bit and said that I didn't want to be his teacher, but then I started to feel really nasty, so after a while I said okay, we could work through this, and I got back into bed and allowed Ed to cuddle me, and, I suppose, we both fell asleep.

But the thing is I thought I'd feel better about it this morning, but I don't. I feel worse. Because while I don't believe that sex is the most important thing in a relationship, it has to be, at least, okay. I mean, I know that sex with Nick was completely fantastic, but I also know that it's very rarely like that, and that as long as it's good, you can get by.

And Ed probably is right, I probably could teach him what to do, what I like, but the fact of the matter is he's awkward. Awkward about his body, awkward about my body. Just gauche, and even if, say, technically he learns the right moves, it's never going to be silkily smooth and sensual and delicious.

And this morning I start thinking about what sex was like with Nick, and of course the more I think about how good it was, the more I start to resent Ed, and this is why we're driving home in a thick, tense silence.

Not that Sarah and Charles would have been able to tell. At least, I hope not, because they were so charming and so hospitable. I think, this morning, when we all met up over break-fast, I managed to hide the fact that I'd had the night from hell. When we said goodbye and I thanked them for everything, Sarah gave me a big hug and said we'd have to come up again.

So we hardly say a word on the way back, and when we reach my flat Ed brings my bag inside and says, "Can I call you later?" and I shrug and say, "S'pose so," behaving like a six-year-old, and he just looks incredibly sad and gives me a kiss on the cheek.

And the minute he's gone I pick up the phone and ring, nat-urally, Jules, ignoring the three messages on my answering ma-chine from my mother begging me to ring her as soon as I get back.

"Uh-oh," she says, hearing how flat my voice is. "Start at the beginning."

"Just tell me first," I say. "Any news from Jamie?"

"Well, yes," she says slowly. "He called last night sounding absolutely miserable, so I said he could come over this evening and talk about it."

"You're kidding!" I gasp. "Are you going to forgive him?"

"I want to see what he has to say first," she says. "because I know that even if I may be able to forgive him, I'll never be able to forget, and I still don't know if I'll ever be able to trust him again, and if you don't have trust, what is there?"

"Love?" I venture softly.

"Yes," she sighs. "There is that. Anyway, enough about me. Tell me everything about last night."

I try and forget how pissed off I am, and start at the begin-ning, describing everything to her, in graphic detail, what the people were like, what they were wearing, the atmosphere, the music, the champagne.

And then I get to the bit about going to bed and I stop.

"Go on," she prompts. "You did it, didn't you?"

"In a manner of speaking."

"Please don't tell me it was awful," she groans. "I couldn't cope."

"It was awful," I shriek. "No. I take that back. It was worse than awful. The worst experience of my life." And I tell her, exactly as I told you, what happened, and when I've finished speaking there's a silence.

"Hello?" I say. "Are you still there?"

"Hang on. I'm thinking."

"What are you thinking? Don't say that lust can grow, because I honestly don't think I can go through that again."

"Okay," Jules sighs. "I don't think that lust can grow, but I do think that he's obviously inexperienced, and that can be resolved. But," she adds ominously, "I also think that you mustn't try to talk yourself round this one."

"What do you mean?"

"I mean, don't ignore this and just carry on living out your fantasy."

"So you think I should end it?"

"No, that's not what I'm saying. What I'm saying is just be aware of how you're feeling now, because I worry that sometimes you jump in and do things that you know aren't right, just because you really want them to be right. And I don't mean that this isn't right, I just mean don't try to whitewash over the things that aren't."

And as she talks I can see my fantastic fantasy life slipping away, and I don't want it to slip away, I want to marry a rich man, someone like Ed, I want to live in a house in Hanover Terrace, but I also see the point that Jules is making. Even if I don't like it much.

"So what should I do now?"

"You don't have to do anything. Just wait and see what happens. But Libby, you don't have to be with this man. You don't have to make a lifelong decision after three weeks, that's all I'm saying. If it doesn't work out, fine. You'll move on."

And I can see that she's absolutely right, except it's bloody hard to not think about the life you've always wanted when it's right there, at your fingertips. And okay, I have been spending rather a large amount of time recently thinking about how I'd redecorate Hanover Terrace, and maybe it isn't very healthy, but it's a damn sight better than thinking about how to avoid nights down at the pub drinking pints with your mates.

"But do you think it is going to work out?"

"What do you want me to say, Libby?"

I want her to say yes, everything's going to be fine. I want her to tell me that Jamie was a crap lover when she first met him and that he then became the best in the world. I want her to tell me that it is entirely possible that Ed will become as good, as perfect, as I once thought Jamie was. As I still think it is possible for a man to be. Just not Jamie. Which is all slightly ridiculous, really, given that this morning I was more than ready to dump Ed and never see him again.

"I just want you to say what you really think."

"God, you're high maintenance sometimes. I've already told you. Look, do you want to come over?"

"Nah. I'm going to stay in and watch the box." I pause. "Unless you want me to."

"No. Don't worry about it. I should get ready for Jamie coming over anyway. Mentally steel myself and all that. But don't worry about Ed, it will all work out."

"Okay, thanks. Isn't that what I'm supposed to be saying to you?"

At five o'clock, just as the movie I've been watching finishes, the phone rings . . . again. And again I don't pick up the phone because it's probably my mother, who hasn't stopped ringing all day, and even though she hasn't left any more messages, every time she puts the phone down I dial 1471 and it's her bloody number.

I just can't face talking to her right now. I wouldn't know what to say, and actually I'm grateful as hell that there's been good TV on all day, because I haven't had to think about Ed, or last night.

But this time it's Ed on the phone, and as I hear his little worried voice I start feeling really bad, so I pick up the phone, and before he has a chance to say anything I apologize.

"I can't believe those things I said to you," I say, more than a touch sheepishly. "I feel like a complete bitch, and especially after you took me to such a wonderful party and you've been so incredibly sweet to me." I pause for a while. "I completely understand if you don't want to see me again."

"Of course I want to see you again!" splutters Ed. "I was phoning to apologize myself because I know last night was awkward, and I was just phoning to tell you that I'm willing to do anything, anything to make this relationship work. And I know that the physical side is very important to you, and I feel so ashamed that I'm so inexperienced, but I promise you, Libby, I'll learn. I even went out today and bought *The Joy of Sex*."

How could I have been so nasty?

"Have you started reading it yet, or are you just looking at the pictures?"

"No, no, I'm reading it, and I think I can learn how to, umm, well, satisfy you."

"Oh, Ed," I say, amazed at the lengths to which this man will go to make me happy. "You do satisfy me, and last night I was just in a really bad mood, and I'm sure we'll be fine."

"I think so too," he says, and I can hear from the relief in his voice that he really does. "You probably want to be on your own tonight, don't you?"

"Why? What were you thinking?" Umm, hello? Libby? You did want to stay on your own tonight. God, why am I such a complete pushover?

"I just wondered, perhaps, whether you wanted to come over and have supper. It would just be nice to see you and, sort of, make up for last night."

"Okay," I find myself saying. "I'll come over at eight, how's that?"

"Do you want me to come and pick you up?"

"Don't worry," I say, thinking I'm going to organize my own transport because I definitely won't be staying the night. "I'll make my own way there."

Why am I going over there? I can't believe I'm about to go

back and spend the evening with the man I wanted to kill just a few hours ago. But I so badly want this to work, and I'm not angry anymore, and he obviously is trying, poor thing. He must have died, going up to a cash desk to pay for *The Joy of Sex*, but look at the effort he's making. I have to try as well, and I think he's right about every relationship needing work, and I'm willing to work at it. I really am.

A million things go through my mind. How much I wanted Jon to tell me he loved me, but he never did. How I've felt like saying it to so many men so many times in the past, but how I've never dared because I've known as an absolute certainty that should the L word come from my lips, they would have scarpered. How I have spent years looking for someone who treats me like a queen and tells me he loves me. Except I never thought it would happen with someone like Ed.

And in all my fantasies when the tall, dark, faceless but presumably handsome love of my life tells me he loves me, I melt into his arms, murmuring, "I love you too."

But I really don't know what to say.

"I know this might seem odd, Libby," Ed says, holding my hand across the table, "because I know we haven't known each other very long, but my mother always said when it's right, it's right, and I know that you are the right woman for me. And I know things haven't been great, but I also know that we can work them out, so you might not be able to say that you love me too, which is fine, because I know that you will."

"I love you too." What else can I say? And the fact of the matter is, I may not love him, but I love the idea of loving him, and I think, for the moment, that might be enough. And Ed looks so happy I think his smile may well burst off his face.

"I really do love you," he says again. "And you make me so happy."

How can I not spend the night after this?

I walk upstairs, knowing that I have to try everything in my power to make this work, especially when I take in, once again, the softness of the carpets, the size of the bedroom, the grandeur of the swagged curtains, because I want this. This is exactly what I have always dreamed of.

And this time Ed seems to discover that nipples are an erogenous zone. That the clitoris is not just a useless body part. That I quite like soft, sweeping strokes down my stomach.

Okay, it's not perfect. He's still slightly clumsy, awkward, and he keeps on saying, "Is this okay? What about this? Do you like this?" And I try to show him by moving his hand, nodding, whispering back to him because he keeps asking me in a very loud voice, and it seems to be destroying the atmosphere somewhat, but eventually he slightly seems to get the hang of it.

And well before there is any question of actually having full-blown sex, I find that if I close my eyes and concentrate very hard, it starts to feel nice, and although I wouldn't normally be so selfish as to just lie there and not do anything while someone is slowly stroking my clitoris and asking if it's okay, I do feel that after last night I deserve at least the chance of an orgasm, and after what seems like hours, I feel a familiar warmth as the tingling feeling spreads up through my body, and I have an orgasm. I actually have an orgasm.

I open my eyes and smile at Ed, who's looking half pleased with himself and half worried, and he says, "Did you, umm, well. Was that?"

And I nod, and he exhales loudly as I laugh, and plant a soft kiss on his lips.

"Thank goodness for that," he says, and that's when I think that maybe sex will get better, maybe it won't be so bad, and I pull him on top of me and guide him inside me, and okay, if the truth be known I still can't quite handle kissing him, or licking him, or burying my nose in his neck, but it's a hell of a lot better than last night.

I think we make it to twelve seconds. Not that it matters, because after my orgasm I can quite happily go to sleep, but I want to do this for him, because he is so sweet, because he is trying so hard.

We lie in bed afterward, talking softly, and I am so pleased I gave him another chance.

"How did you learn all that in a day?" I ask eventually.

"I speed-read *The Joy of Sex*," he chuckles.

"You mean you didn't do any work today?"

"Of course not. This is far more important. You're far more important."

And I snuggle into his shoulder, just loving this feeling of being loved so much.

"Libby?"

"Hmm?" I'm almost asleep.

"I think perhaps it's time I met your parents."

I'm now wide awake.

"Umm. Why? Don't you think it's a bit soon?"

"Not if we're serious about each other, and I'm certainly serious about you."

Jesus, the thought of my parents meeting Ed makes me feel sick. My mother would go into Hyacinth Bucket overdrive, and I'd want to die.

"Umm, well, er." I struggle, unsuccessfully, to think of an excuse.

"Don't you want them to meet me?"

"Of course!" I lie. And it's not them meeting him that's the problem, it's him meeting them. I don't want Ed to see who I really am, who I'm trying so hard to leave behind. "I just think it's a bit soon, that's all."

"I think it's a good idea," he says, with a mysterious smile, and suddenly I think, shit! He's going to ask me to marry him! But it's much too soon for that, and even Ed wouldn't jump in this early on, I mean for God's sake, he hardly knows me.

And this is something of a worry, because he really doesn't know me, and it has crossed my mind that perhaps Ed isn't really bothering to get to know me. That perhaps he thinks I will make a suitable wife, a good mother, that perhaps he's not really interested in the rest, because he's already pigeonholed me, but that's very cynical of me, and I'm sure that isn't the case. He loves me, for Christ's sake, he must really feel it.

"Okay. We'll sort something out," I say vaguely, praying he'll forget about it.

"Great," he says, reaching out for his diary on the bedside table. Fuck. "What about Wednesday?"

"I'll have to check with them," I say, already knowing that my parents will definitely be busy on Wednesday. At least if I have anything to do with it. "I'll let you know."

"They could come here for dinner," he says. "We could cook."

"But you can't cook."

"Okay. Well, you can cook and I can help you."

See what I mean? He's already got me cooking, already placed me in the role of wife. Maybe I'm being ridiculous. After all, it does make sense that I should cook. Not that I'm the best cook in the world, as you already know, but I can probably follow a recipe a damn sight better than Ed.

"Okay," I say. "Maybe."

"I love you, Libby Mason," he says, kissing me before closing his eyes.

"I love you too."

"Are you entirely sure you know what you're doing?"

"Not in the slightest," I groan. "In fact, I think this may well be a nightmare come true."

"I'm glad I'm not the only one having her nightmare come true," Jules sighs.

Jamie did go over to see Jules that night. She said she opened the door and her very first feeling was this overwhelming maternal urge, because Jamie looked terrible.

"He'd lost so much weight," she said. "He obviously hadn't been eating a thing."

He'd looked haggard, and miserable, and just completely downtrodden. Jules invited him in and took him into the kitchen, where she'd spent all day cooking his favorite meal, so the smell of oxtail stew would permeate the air and make him realize just what he had thrown away. Or not. She hadn't, at that point, decided.

Jamie naturally commented on the food, but Jules didn't offer him any. She offered him a cup of tea instead, knowing that he prefers coffee. He said he didn't want anything.

He sat there, on the sofa, with his head in his hands, and when he eventually raised his eyes he looked at her pleadingly and said, "I miss you so much, Jules. I love you so much. I don't want to be without you."

And somehow this seemed to empower Jules, who suddenly felt she was in control, who discovered this pool of strength lurking within, and, looking at him, decided that she would make him suffer.

She was still unsure as to whether she would take him back,

but the only certainty she had was that, whatever her decision, she was going to make him pay.

So she told him that he had hurt her beyond measure. That he had broken down every belief she had ever had about marriage. That he had destroyed every dream she had ever had about her future. Their future.

Jamie didn't say a word.

She said that it was still far too early for her to make a decision about whether he could move back in. Too early to decide even whether she wanted to see him at the moment.

And Jamie apologized, repeatedly, and hung his head in shame.

She said she needed more time, and Jamie nodded and silently left. He turned to kiss her just as he was walking out the door, and Jules moved her head so he ended up kissing air.

"But Jesus, Libby," she says, when she has finished telling me this, as we are pushing the trolley round Sainsbury's, me once again having crept out of work slightly earlier than usual, "it was so hard. So fucking hard. All I wanted to do was rewind the clock and make things okay."

"So do you think they will be okay?"

"Who knows? All I do know is I won't be ready to take him back until he's suffered nearly as much as I have." She pauses. "And I've got this bloody work do I've got to go to tonight, which Jamie was supposed to come to, and I'm dreading it."

"Do you have to go?"

"Unfortunately, yes. Too many good contacts to pass up. Anyway," she continues, sighing, and attempting to smile, "tell me again why you decided to go through with this."

"This" being Ed meeting my parents.

"Because, Jules," I say in a mock exasperated tone, "it's going to happen sooner or later, and I may as well get it out of the way now."

"But it's your parents." Jules knows my parents. My parents, in fact, love Jules. They think she is the perfect woman, and many's the time my mother has compared me to Jules, with me, naturally, falling short. And Jules likes my parents—how could she not when every time she's been to their house my mother's clucked around her like a mother hen, going on about how thin she is and how much she needs feeding up.

And I've tried to tell Jules how completely awful my mother is, but she still thinks she's nice, which I suppose I might do as well if she wasn't my mother. Well, maybe not, but I can see that parents always seem a hell of a lot better if they're not yours.

"You don't think Ed's going to take your father for a walk round the garden after dinner and ask for your hand in marriage, do you?" she jokes as I throw a bag of spinach in the basket.

Actually, that's exactly what I had been thinking, and I can't believe that Jules thought it too. I turn to her in amazement. "Do you think he might do that? Really?"

She shrugs. "Do you?"

"It had crossed my mind. Damn. I need chocolate for the chocolate mousse but I forgot what kind of chocolate."

"Bourneville," she says, throwing a couple of big bars in the basket. "So what would you say?"

And suddenly I know exactly what I would say. "I think I'd say yes."

She gasps and stops dead in her tracks. "Yes? Are you serious? You hardly know the guy."

"But as you've always said, Jules, when it's right, it's right."

"I never said that."

"Oh, well, okay. But someone did. And I really do think it's right."

"So, the sex is crap, him speaking French irritates you beyond belief, and you think you could spend the rest of your life with this man?"

"Jules!" I admonish firmly. "The sex isn't crap. Okay, it wasn't great the first time, but it's much better now," and incidentally, given that I've now stayed at Ed's every night since

Sunday, we've had plenty of time to practice, "and the French annoys me a bit, but not that much, and yes, I can imagine spending the rest of my life with this man."

As it happens, that's not strictly true, because my fantasies haven't yet reached beyond the wedding day, but what a wedding I've been planning! I've worked it all out, from my Bruce Oldfield dress, to my bridesmaids, to the admiring looks of all the people I've ever known, because this will be no small wedding, this will be the wedding of the century.

Jules shakes her head. "Listen, Libby, I know things don't appear to have worked out with Jamie, but at least I loved him. I mean I really really loved him. Are you sure you know what you're doing?"

"Jules, for God's sake. It's highly unlikely that he will actually propose tonight, so I think we're both jumping ahead of ourselves here, and anyway even if we did get engaged we'd definitely have a long engagement."

"How long? The chicken's down here." She wheels the trolley down aisle eight.

"A year."

"Promise?"

"Promise."

Jules drops me home so I can pick up my recipe books, and I ring Mum once she's gone, just to check she's got the right address. Her voice is all fluttery and excited on the phone.

"Are you sure my green suit will be all right?"

"Mum, it doesn't matter what you wear, we're only staying in."

"But, darling, I want to make a good impression."

"It really doesn't matter, Mum. Your green suit will be fine."

"Should Dad wear a tie?"

"No, Mum," I sigh. "He doesn't have to wear a tie."

"I thought perhaps you might like me to bring some salmon mousse to start with. I made it anyway for us this morning, and I thought maybe we could bring it with."

"You think I can't cook, don't you?"

"No, darling. I'm just trying to help."

"Forget it, Mum, I've got all the food sorted out."

"Are you sure?"

"Yes, Mum, I'm sure."

"It's no trouble—"

"Mum!" Why, oh why, did I ever decide to go ahead with this?

• • •

Did I mention that Ed gave me the spare keys yesterday and told me to keep them?

I let myself into his house, lugging the bags of shopping, and go down to the kitchen. There's something very eerie about being in a house this size all by myself, so I turn on the lights and retune his radio to Virgin (it was, unsurprisingly, tuned to Radio 3), and rearrange a few things to make it a bit more cozy.

I must talk to him about getting the sofas re-covered.

I open the recipe books to the pages I've bookmarked and start to read. I went through them last night and picked out a Jules special which I'd scribbled down on the corner of a page for the main course, and a Delia special for dessert. I had a bit of a panic about starters, but Jules said I should try bruschetta, so I've got the ciabatta, garlic and tomatoes, and she says all I have to do is toast the bread, rub it with garlic and olive oil, and arrange tomatoes, olives and fresh basil on top, and the bonus is it's completely idiot-proof.

So there I am, boiling the spinach, seasoning the chicken breasts, making a total mess of the kitchen but trying my damndest to clear up as I go, because that, they say, is the mark of a true cook, when the phone rings.

Now there's something very weird about being in your boyfriend's house on your own and having the phone ring, and for a minute my heart stops, because what if it were another woman leaving a sultry, sexy message?

But then I remember I'm at Ed's, and Ed completely adores me, and the very last thing on earth I have to worry about is other women. And the machine picks up while I stop everything to hear who it is.

"Libby? Are you there? Pick up the phone."

It's Ed.

"Hi, darling. I'm here cooking."

"Yummy. What are you making?"

"It's a surprise."

"Have you got everything you need?"

"Yup. I went shopping with Jules."

"Which reminds me. I must meet Jules again properly. We ought to all go out for dinner sometime."

"That would be great," I say, not saying anything more about the separation, or about Jamie, because Ed doesn't need to know, although dinner is a brilliant idea, and I would love Jules to get to know Ed, even though now isn't the right time. But I need her approval more than anyone else's, and even though Jules was there the night we met, she didn't exactly talk to him, and I really want her to see how right for me he is. I'm just praying they get back together, so things can get back to normal. For all of us.

"I've got some things to do in the office and then I'll be home. Gosh, I must tell you, it's very nice indeed having someone to come home to. I'll be walking through the door to all sorts of nice cooking smells. We must do this more often."

"You mean get me round to cook a meal for when you get home?" I laugh, because I'm joking.

"Exactly," he says. "Nothing like a home-cooked meal."

"I'll have you know I had to leave work early to get this done. This won't be a regular occurrence or I'll get the sack."

"I'd look after you," he says. "You wouldn't need to work."

"Now that," I say, unable to believe my luck, "is exactly what a girl like me needs to hear."

I'm not entirely sure how to squeeze all the water out of the spinach, plus, what the hell does blanching mean anyway? I boiled it for fifteen minutes, and I stuck it through a colander and put it in the dish with the chicken breasts on top. Jules's recipe says use four large chilies, and I forgot the chilies in Sainsbury's so had to stop at a corner shop and sod's law they didn't have any big chilies, only the tiny ones, so I figured four small chilies would equal one big one, so I chop up the chilies and throw them in the sauce.

But the chocolate mousse is easy. I whip the egg whites until my arm is so stiff it's painful, and, although I haven't got a clue what a bain-marie is, I melt the chocolate, butter and sugar in a saucepan, and stir it into the egg whites. (What exactly is folding?)

Jules said make the bruschetta just before they arrive. Ed isn't home yet, and it's quarter to eight, which means my parents will be here any minute, so I stick the bread under the grill and start piling all the used dishes into the sink to wash.

The doorbell goes. I check my watch and it's ten to. Trust my parents to be early. I go to the door and here they are, Mum and Dad, standing on the doorstep. Mum grins expectantly, and Dad looks ever so uncomfortable in a suit and tie. Yes, she obviously forced him to wear a tie.

"Where's Ed," Mum says in a stage whisper.

"He'll be home any minute. He's stuck in the office. Come in." I kiss them both on the cheek, and step aside as they walk in, my mother, apparently, struck speechless for the first time in her life by the size of the hallway, while I smugly lead the way down to the kitchen.

"It's wonderful," she whispers. "Look, Dad," she says, nudging my father, "he's got real marble tops in the kitchen. This must have cost a fortune!"

"Do you want the guided tour?" I can't help myself, I want to feel smug for a little while longer. "Come on, take your coats off and I'll show you round."

"Do you think we ought?" says my mother. "Shouldn't we wait until Ed gets home?"

"Don't worry. It's fine," I say, as I hang the coats in the

cloakroom, which, incidentally, is about the size of my parents' bedroom.

And I lead them around the house, while they ooh and aah over the rooms, and even my father, a man not exactly known for his conversational skills, admits it's beautiful.

"It's not beautiful," admonishes my mother. "It's a palace." And then she turns to me, and you're not going to believe it but she actually has tears in her eyes. "Oh, Libby," she says, clasping her hands together as a tear threatens to trickle down her cheek. "I'm so happy for you."

"I'm not married to the guy, Mum," I say.

"Not yet," offers my dad, whose grin now matches my mother's.

"You'd better not mess this one up," says my mum, opening Ed's closet doors and inspecting his clothes. "You'll have me to answer to if you do."

"Mum, can't you give it a rest just for tonight?"

"Yes, dear," echoes my father as I look at him in amazement. "Don't give her a hard time."

My mother looks at both of us as if she doesn't know what we're talking about, then shakes her head and goes to look at the curtains. "Fully lined," she mutters to herself. "Must have cost a fortune with all these fancy swags."

"Shall we go downstairs?" The last thing I want is for Ed to catch us snooping round his bedroom, so we troop downstairs and I make them both gin and tonics while we sit and attempt to make small talk.

"I must say you seem very at home here," my mum sniffs. "You know where everything is."

I decide not to answer.

"But I'm not sure I like these sofas," she continues, because she has to find fault in something. "I think I'd have them recovered."

"I like them," I say firmly. "I wouldn't touch them."

"Oh well," she sighs. "Takes all sorts. So what are we having for dinner?"

"Bruschetta followed by, shit! shit! shit! shit!"

I leap up as my mother sniffs again. "Is that burning I smell, Libby?"

Fuck. Fuck, shit, and fuck again. I open the oven door to reveal eight lumps of charcoal steaming away, and I groan because I know exactly what my mother's going to say. I don't even have to go back into the dining area to hear her say it, because there she is, right behind me.

"I knew I should have brought the salmon mousse," she says.

And saved by the bell, or key turning in the lock in this case. We all freeze as Ed comes bounding down the stairs calling, "Helloooo? Hellooo? Anyone home?"

He sniffs as he walks into the kitchen but obviously decides to refrain from commenting—so much, I think, for coming home to good old-fashioned home cooking and immediately shakes hands with my mother and father.

"Thank you so much for coming," he says, his public school accent suddenly sounding ridiculously loud and affected next to my parents' suburban-but-trying-hard-to-escape accents, but he doesn't seem to notice, so I decide not to make an issue out of it.

Besides, I know they drive me up the wall but they are my parents, and I suppose, if I'm pushed, I'd have to admit that I do love them.

"Thank you so much for having us," says my mother, and I can't say I'm exactly surprised to notice that her accent has also gone up a few notches. Not in my estimation, I have to add.

"No, no, it's nothing. Think nothing of it. Can I give you a top-up?"

"Why thank you," says my mother, patting, yes, actually patting her hair as she holds out her glass. "That would be splendid."

Splendid? Splendid? Since when has the word "splendid" been a part of my mother's vocabulary? Even my dad looks slightly taken aback, and as I catch his eye he does his customary eye roll to the ceiling and I have to stifle the giggles.

"Did you find the house all right?" says Ed. "Did you drive?"

"We didn't have any problems, did we, Da—" She stops, having just realized that it's not quite the done thing to refer to Dad as Dad in the company of someone like Ed. "Alan?"

For a second there I wonder who she's talking about, because I don't think I've ever heard her call my dad anything but Dad.

"No, Jean," says my dad, putting a tiny emphasis on the word "Jean," because he seems to think it's as odd as I do. "No worries."

My mother gives my father a curt shake of the head, which my father and I understand to mean, don't say phrases like that, but Ed doesn't notice, and just hands them back their glasses.

"Da—Alan, don't have another one. You're driving."

"Oh, what a shame," says Ed. "I've got a lovely wine for dinner. I thought, as this was a special occasion, I'd open the 1961 Mouton Rothschild for dinner. You'll have some, won't you, Mrs. Mason?"

"Oh, call me Jean," my mother giggles. "Everyone else does."

"Mais bien sur," chuckles Ed along with my mother. "Jean." And I want to kill him, except my mother seems enormously impressed with these three words of craply accented French.

"Ooh," she exclaims. "You speak French?"

"Juste un peu," Ed laughs. "Et vous?"

"Moi?" My mother thinks this is the funniest thing she's ever said, and I go back to the stove to avoid watching any longer. Christ. Why oh why did I ever agree to this?

"Would you like to sit down at the table?" I say, in my most gracious hostess manner, because I figure the sooner I serve, the sooner we'll be finished, and the sooner they can go.

And obviously the bruschetta is a bit of a non-starter, as it were, so I bring the chicken to the table with rice and vegetables, and everyone holds their plate up as I serve them and Ed goes to bring the wine up from the cellar.

"He's absolutely charming," whispers my mother hurriedly, the minute he's left the room, still speaking in her "posh" voice. "And perfect for you."

And, despite myself, I breathe a sigh of relief, because finally someone, albeit only my mother, whose opinion I take as much notice of as Ross Perots, someone has given me their seal of approval, has told me exactly what I wanted to hear. That Ed is perfect for me.

And Ed comes back, opens the wine, and my mum and dad sit there watching us, waiting for one of us to start before picking up their knife and fork. Eventually I pick up my fork, so my mother picks up hers and takes the first mouthful.

I swear, I've seen cartoons where people go bright red and smoke starts pouring from their ears when they've eaten something hot, but I never thought it actually happened in real life.

Everyone stops, forks halfway to their mouths, and we all just stare at my mother as she drops her fork and sits there gasping, flapping her hands around.

"Here, here," says my father, holding up the wineglass because that's the only liquid on the table, and my mother gulps the whole thing down in one. "What's the matter?" says my father. "Did it go down the wrong way?"

Now there are tears streaming down my mother's face, and for God's sake, isn't she just overreacting a little bit? She's trying to speak but can't seem to get the words out, so she points to the food, furiously shaking her head.

"Mrs. Mason?" Ed's jumped up and gone over to her, terribly concerned, and I wonder how it is my mother always manages to make herself the center of attention. "Jean?" he continues. "Can I get you anything? Is it the food?"

My mother nods.

"Perhaps I'd better taste it," says Ed, going back to his plate and gingerly taking a tiny amount on his fork while I feel more and more of a failure. He tastes it, sits for precisely two seconds while it hits his tastebuds, then jumps up and runs to the kitchen, and the next thing I hear is the sound of the tap running.

"What is the problem?" I practically shriek, taking a forkful of food. "My cooking isn't that bad," and while my father's still comforting my mother and Ed's still in the kitchen, I take a mouthful.

Aaaaaaaaargh!!!!!!!

I run into the kitchen, shove Ed out of the way and lean under the sink, sticking my entire mouth under the water. It feels like my mouth is about to burn off, and I stay there for about three minutes, and the only good thing is that right at this moment I'm not thinking about the embarrassment, I'm far too busy thinking about cooling down my mouth.

Eventually, when I'm fairly certain there's no permanent damage and I think I can talk again, I walk back to face the music.

"What did you put in that?" My mother's face is puce.

"I only put four chilies in."

"That's not four chilies," she says. "What kind of chilies?"

"Well the recipe said four large ones, but I couldn't get them so I put sixteen small ones in."

"Sixteen?" Ed looks at me in horror as my father starts giggling.

"What? What? What's the problem? Four small chilies equals one large one."

My mother's looking at me as if she can't believe I'm her daughter.

"Libby," she says, after nudging my father, who quickly stops laughing and tries to make his face serious, "small chilies are four times the strength of large ones."

"Oh goodness," says Ed, looking slightly disconcerted. "I thought you said you could cook?"

"I can cook!" I say. "But how was I to know that about chilies?"

"I'm sorry, darling," he says, kissing me on the forehead,

which seems to perk my mother up no end. "I know you can cook. What about dessert?"

I fling my napkin on the table and go to fetch the chocolate mousse, and the minute I open the fridge door I know it's a complete disaster. It's basically just a big glass bowl of chocolate-colored slop, and I don't even bother bringing it to the table. I just tip the bowl so the whole lot slides into the dustbin.

"Umm," I say, coming back to the table. "There's been a bit of a problem with pudding."

"You know what I really fancy?" says Ed. "I'd really like a Chinese takeaway," and my parents both say what a brilliant idea, as I sit there too embarrassed to say anything.

And half an hour later there we sit, my parents in their smartest clothes, at the table that I've beautifully laid with table mats, Irish linen napkins and even flowers in the center, surrounded by tinfoil tubs of Chinese food, and it really isn't so bad, although I know my mother will never let me live this one down.

Ed seems to keep the evening going by telling my parents all about his investment banking, and my parents look completely riveted, although I'm sitting there half proud of him for making sure there are no uncomfortable silences and half bored to tears.

But my parents don't seem to mind. Actually, make that my mother doesn't seem to mind. My mother's sitting there listening to every word, smiling encouragingly and making all the right noises in all the right places, while my father just looks slightly uncomfortable, but then I suppose my father doesn't say much at the best of times.

And finally Ed and I see them to the door, while my mother makes big eyes at me, and I know she's simply dying to get me on the phone to do the postmortem, and presumably to have a go at me about the chilies, and Ed is as charming as he always is and walks them to their car, and thank God it's over.

"I'm really not that interested," Jules says, getting up to make another cup of tea.

"But Jules!" I make a face. "You said he's tall, handsome, sexy and funny. How can you not be interested?"

She turns and faces me. "Libby, I still love Jamie. I don't know what's going to happen with us, but the one thing I do know is that I don't want anyone to confuse the issue further."

"But it's only one night, for God's sake. And you don't have to do anything. Anyway, you did give him your number."

She sighs and runs her fingers through her hair. "I know," she moans. "I didn't know what else to say when he asked. Jesus. You go to a work party expecting to stay for twenty minutes, and some bloody bloke comes along who would have been exactly your type if you weren't married, and . . . I don't know. I'm not interested in going out on a date with him. I just didn't know what else to say."

"One date isn't going to hurt you. And if you and Jamie don't get back together, at least you'll know there are other men out there."

"But I'm not sure I want other men."

"You did say that, what was his name? Paul?" She nods. "Paul was the first man you'd met since you'd been married that you'd found attractive."

"But that doesn't mean I want to sleep with him."

"Who said anything about sleeping with him?"

"Go out with him, then."

"Oh, why did he have to bloody phone," she moans, bringing a fresh pot of tea over to the sofa. "Why couldn't he have been like all those men you used to meet who'd take your number and never phone?"

"Because he's not a bastard," I say, smirking. "And anyway. You never know. You might have a nice time."

• • •

"I've just finished the interview with the *Mail*, and I was passing so I thought I'd pop in and see if you wanted to have a coffee?"

Amanda, as usual, looks a vision of B-list loveliness, in a hot-pink trouser suit with chunky gold earrings, and a huge pair of Jackie O sunglasses, and evidently she's enjoying her newfound fame. Well, fame-ish, because Amanda has been "stepping out" with one of television's brightest actors thanks to me, and suddenly the papers are taking a huge interest in her.

There's no question of there being any romance, because once the actor in question is away from the cameras he's as camp as Amanda's suit, but naturally he's spent his whole life in the closet, and the news that he's gay wouldn't exactly help his status as a heartthrob.

So I organized that Amanda should accompany him to a film premiere, and the cameras flashed away, and Amanda even stopped to tell a journalist that they had no comment to make on their relationship, which was as good as telling them they were shagging, and it made page 3 the next day in several of the tabloids.

And she, of course, is over the moon. They've now been written about as TV's most glamorous couple, her haircut has been analyzed over and over again by the women's pages, and his macho masculine image has been more than confirmed in the public eye.

The *Telegraph* even phoned me last week and asked if they could do a feature on Amanda, which, as far as she's concerned, is the mark of true fame, and now I really do seem to have become her best friend.

I have to speak to her every day because the calls requesting interviews, photo shoots, sound bites, have been coming in thick and fast, and I really am starting to like her more, even though I know our friendship is a transient one, and I still have to slightly watch my guard.

"I'm so busy setting up your interviews," I laugh, extending my cheek for her to air-kiss. "I'm not sure."

"Amanda! Darling!" Joe Cooper walks out of his office and gives Amanda a huge kiss. "What do you think of all the coverage our Libby is getting for you?"

"It's wonderful!" she gushes. "You're doing the most amazing job. I came in to see if Libby would go for a coffee with me." She tells Joe that the *Telegraph* interview went fantastically, and Joe says of course I can go, so off we trot, Amanda still in her sunglasses, despite the weather being distinctly overcast.

And on our way to the Italian caff round the corner, which is the only place around here, a woman stops dead in her tracks when she sees us. She walks over and taps Amanda on the arm.

"Excuse me?" she says. "But aren't you Amanda Baker?"

Amanda nods graciously.

"Oh, I love you on TV. I watch you every morning."

"Why thank you," says Amanda, fishing around in her bag. "Would you like a signed picture?" And while I look on in amazement Amanda draws out a large glossy black-and-white photograph of herself as the woman stares in delight.

"To?" says Amanda, pausing regally as she looks at the woman.

"Jackie," she says. "Oh, I can't wait to tell my friends I've met you, and you're much more beautiful in the flesh."

"Thank you," says Amanda, scribbling away as the woman thanks her profusely and scuttles off.

"Jesus," I say. "Does that happen a lot?"

"All the time," she sighs. "It drives me mad."

But of course it doesn't drive her mad. She loves every minute of it. This is exactly what she's been waiting for, and she knows that, now she's got it, the mark of true stardom is to complain about it.

We order cappuccinos at the bar and sit down by the window, and Amanda finally takes her sunglasses off, and checks the room just to see if anyone's looking at her, but of course the Italian waiters are here all day, and don't have a chance to watch breakfast television.

"So," she says, running her fingers through her perfectly coiffed hair. "How are you?"

"Really well," I say. "Actually, I'm extremely well."

"Oh? How are things going with Mr. McMann?"

And I find myself telling her that he met my parents, and that everything's almost perfect, and that I think I may well have found myself Mr. Right.

"You'd better hang on to him," she says, when I've finished. "Because there are plenty of women who'd love to get their hands on Ed McMann."

She doesn't say she's one of those women, but then I suppose she doesn't have to. It's written all over her face, and the fact that she would so obviously love to have a shot at him makes me even more determined to make this work. To be Mrs. Ed McMann.

Oh? Did you think I might keep my name? Don't be ridiculous. There's no cachet in ringing up Nobu to book a table under the name Libby Mason, but there's a hell of a lot of cachet in booking a table as Ed McMann's wife. It's like those tests they do every few months on newsmagazine shows. Mr. and Mrs. Joe Bloggs ring up the ten top restaurants in town and ask for a table for two that night, only to be told they're fully booked for the next three months. And then one of the researchers rings up, saying that Jennifer Aniston and Brad Pitt are flying in, and they know it's short notice but could these same restaurants possibly squeeze them in, and naturally the restaurants fall over themselves to accommodate them, and say of course, whatever time would suit them.

Not that I'm suggesting that Ed McMann is in the same league as Elizabeth and Hugh, but anyone worth their salt ought to know who he is. And Jules did ask me whether I'd feel the same way if he were, say, Ed McMann, welder, but I got out of that one by saying that what he does is part and parcel of who he is, so I honestly couldn't answer that one.

Although I think you know what the answer is.

And when I get back to the office there's a message from Jules and a message from my mother. I ring Mum first, who can hardly contain her excitement, and spends twenty minutes telling me how wonderful he is, and how he's the best catch I'll ever have, and how she can see he adores me, and thank God she doesn't mention the cooking.

Just as I'm about to pick up the phone to ring the *Telegraph* to check they're happy with the interview and sort out the photo shoot, my phone rings again (trust me, the life of a PR is all about phone calls, personal or otherwise), and it's my father.

"What's wrong, Dad?" My father never, ever calls me. In fact, it took me a while to recognize his voice, so rarely does he actually speak.

"I just thought I'd phone to thank you for last night."

"Oh! Well, Mum already phoned. Did you enjoy it?"

"Yes. It was very nice. Are you happy with him, Libby?"

What is this? First my father phones me at work, and then he asks me about the state of my relationship. I need to get to the bottom of this.

"Why, Dad?"

"I know that your mother's over the moon because he's obviously very wealthy and very keen on you, but I just wondered whether you were very serious."

"You didn't like him, did you, Dad?" My heart sinks.

"Do you want me to be honest?"

"Yes." No.

"I think he's obviously smitten with you. In material terms he could probably give you everything you needed. But . . ." And he stops.

"Go on, Dad."

"Well, it's just that I'm not entirely sure he's for you."

"Why not?"

He sighs. "Nothing that I can exactly put my finger on, but I wanted to make sure you were happy, because I want what's best for you."

"And you don't think he is?" I have a feeling my dad wants to say more, but he doesn't, and I don't push him.

"If you're happy, Libby, then I'm happy."

"I'm happy, Dad. Honestly."

"Good. All right, darling, that's all. We'll see you on Sunday?"

"See you then. Bye, Dad."

"Bye."

What was all that about? Well, I knew my dad didn't feel comfortable last night, and I knew that he was falling asleep during all Ed's stories, and I'll even go so far as to admit that even I find Ed boring sometimes, but he does have other redeeming qualities, and nobody can keep you amused all the time. Can they?

I've already spoken to Jules twice today, but I want to know what she thinks of this strange conversation with my dad, plus she'd better have returned Paul's call, so I ring her mobile because I know she's on her way to a client.

"My dad hates him."

"You're joking!" she gasps. "Did he say that?"

"Well, no. Not exactly. But he didn't have to." And I tell her what he did say.

"Hmm. Could just be parental concern. I mean, Ed is quite a lot older than your other boyfriends, so maybe he's just worried about you."

"What's Ed being older got to do with anything?"

"Okay. Point taken. I'd tell you what I thought of Ed, and you know I'd be entirely honest. In fact, I've just had a brilliant idea. You know that guy Paul? Why don't the four of us go out for dinner? I couldn't face seeing him on my own, it's too like a date, but I could cope if you were there too, and then I could suss out Ed as well."

"Fantastic!" I say, and it is, even though it will feel completely weird without Jamie, but at least this way Jules will definitely see this guy again. I'm trying to fight Jamie's corner, but I don't think there's any harm in lining up a reserve, just in case. "When can you make it?"

"Friday night?"

"Perfect."

"Libby? Delivery again for you." It's Jo on the internal phone.

"Don't tell me yet more flowers."

"Nah. This one's more mysterious. Come and see."

I go to reception, where there's a large plastic Gucci carrier bag, and my heart, I swear, misses a beat, because we don't handle Gucci's PR (chance would be a fine bloody thing), so why is there a bag from Gucci with my name on it?

Jo rubs her hands together squealing, "Open it, open it," so I do, but first I pull out the card and read out loud: " 'To my darling Libby, for making such an effort last night. I love you. Ed.' "

"Oh my God," Jo squeals. "What's in the bloody bag?"

I slowly tear off the tissue paper, and open a drawstring fabric bag with Gucci printed on it, and pull out a chocolate brown leather Gucci bag. The one with bamboo handles. The one I've always wanted.

"You. Are. So. Fucking. Lucky," says Jo.

"You've got one of these!" I say, stroking the leather that's as soft as butter.

"Yeah, but I had to pay for it. Three ten."

"You're joking!" Now it's my turn to squeal.

"I can't believe your boyfriend bought you a Gucci bag!"

"Jesus Christ. Neither can I!"

Naturally, I have to phone Jules again, and, although she is excited, there's something about her voice, something slightly reserved, that makes me question her until she tells me what she's really thinking.

"I'm worried that it's almost like he's buying you."

"Don't be ridiculous," I snort, still stroking my gorgeous

new acquisition. "Three hundred quid for him is like three quid for the rest of us."

"Still," she says. "Lavishing presents on you would make it very difficult for you to leave."

"But I'm not going to leave," and for the first time I'm beginning to get slightly pissed off with Jules, which never, ever happens.

"God, I'm sorry," she says. "I'm being a complete killjoy. It's fantastic and I'm jealous, that's all."

"It is gorgeous," I say, smiling. "You really will be jealous when you see it."

"It's the one in *Tatler* this month, isn't it? The one that all the It Girls are supposed to have."

"Yup. That's the one."

"You lucky cow. 'Course I'm jealous, and I can't wait to meet him on Friday."

"Good. And I can't wait to meet Paul. Oh, and just in case you don't recognize me I'll be the one with the Gucci bag."

• • •

We get to Sartoria first, having found a parking space almost immediately, which is a bit of a miracle in the West End, and I order a Kir, which is what I've taken to ordering these days because it fits my new image as the smart, sophisticated partner of Ed McMann.

And in case you're wondering, I'm wearing a brown leather skirt that I picked up yesterday, because, much as I love my trousers, Ed has now grudgingly admitted that he completely adores women in skirts, so it's the least I can do to please him, and it does happen to look rather spectacular with my new Gucci bag. (Okay, okay, I'll stop now, I just had to mention it one more time.)

Ed sits next to me and holds my hand under the table, and every few minutes he kisses me on the lips, which, nice as it is to be so adored, is beginning to irritate me ever so slightly. I did try and extract my hand, but then he got that sad puppy-dog look on his face again, and I felt guilty, so I placed my hand back in his and gave him a reassuring squeeze.

And then Jules and Paul arrive (it sounds so wrong, Jules and Paul), and Ed stands up to shake their hands and say how lovely it is to see Jules again, while Paul stands there awkwardly waiting to be introduced to me.

Paul seems . . . he seems nice, which I know is pretty nondescript, but, despite being everything that Jules described, he's just not Jamie, and I really don't know whether I could get used to this man.

We sit and make small talk about how wonderful the restaurant is, and how we've all heard how marvelous the food is, and when the waiter comes to take our order Ed can't decide and he asks me to choose for him, which I do and which I love—this gesture of trust and intimacy.

And Ed is at his most charming, asking lots of questions, not, thank God, telling his bloody investment banking stories, and I'm praying and praying that Jules loves him.

I do get slightly exasperated when most of Ed's hors d'oeuvre ends up on his mustache, because this happened the other night as well, and I had to nudge him while I thought my parents weren't looking and gesture to wipe the food off. Tonight I'm feeling more confident, and I want Jules to see how close we are, so I pick up my napkin, raise my eyes to the ceiling and wipe the food off, and while Ed looks a bit sheepish, he's also delighted that I'm looking after him so well.

There is a moment when Jules is talking about someone she works with who's driving her mad by constantly changing her mind, and whom she describes as "mercurial."

"Umm, excuse me?" Ed interrupts her.

"Yes?" She stops in mid-flow.

"I don't think 'mercurial' is the word you mean."

Jules stopped dead in her tracks. "Umm. I think it is," she says slowly.

"I don't think it is. What did you mean?"

Jules looks at him as if he's mad, which I have to say, I think he is rather, because even I'm wary of challenging Jules when she's on a roll.

"Flighty. Constantly changing," she says. "A person who suffers from mood swings."

"As far as I'm aware, mercurial means of mercury, i.e., liquid, flowing."

"I think you'll find it can also mean constantly changing," she says, and from the tone of her voice I pray that Ed backs down.

"Please don't think me rude, but I think you'll find the Oxford English Dictionary defines it as 'of or containing mercury,'" Ed persists, while I want to die with embarrassment.

"Actually," says Paul, jumping in to save the day, "I think you'll find you're both right. As far as I can remember, mercurial means both of or containing mercury, and volatile."

"And Paul's a surgeon," I say, trying to break the ice, "therefore frighteningly clever, so I think we'll all have to agree with him."

Thank God, it does break the ice somewhat, but from there on in the atmosphere is slightly less convivial than it has been, and every now and then I see Jules shooting him daggers when she thinks neither of us is looking.

"Well, I must say," Ed exclaims as we're about to order coffee, evidently having completely missed the implication of his near-argument with Jules. "It's lovely to meet Libby's closest friend."

"Thank you," says Jules. "And it's lovely to meet you." This bit was said through gritted teeth. "Has Libby met your closest friends?"

And that's when I realize that apart from Sarah and Charlie and the people at the party in the country, not only have I not met any of Ed's friends, I haven't even heard about any. Everyone he talks about seems to be a colleague through work, and isn't this a bit strange? I look at Ed to see what he says.

"Ha, ha," he laughs. Umm, was there a joke? "I don't really have many friends."

"I can't think why not," mutters Jules, as I kick her under the table. "But you must have a few," she pushes, in a light tone of voice.

"Oh, yes. Yes. Charlie and Sarah of course. Libby's met them. And, umm. Well. I suppose I work so hard I haven't really had time to make that many friends."

I can see that Ed's slightly flummoxed, so I interject with: "Charlie and Sarah were lovely. I told you all about them, remember?"

Jules nods. "I just wondered what you did socially before you met Libby."

"I'm not a hugely social creature, ha ha," says Ed. "I'm either in the office or at home."

"You must be delighted you've met Libby, then," says Paul with a smile.

"Oh, I am," he says, beaming at me with relief at being let off the hook. "I am." And he leans over and kisses me on the lips.

"I'm just going to the ladies' room. Jules?"

"I'll come," she says, putting her napkin on the chair as we stand up and walk down to the loo.

"Well? What d'you think?" The words are out of her mouth before the door is even shut.

"He's lovely," I say. "A really nice guy."

"I know," she sighs, reapplying some lipstick. "But it's not the same, is it?"

"Well, no. I suppose it's not."

"Oh gawd," she says. "What am I going to do?"

"Are you planning on doing anything?" I look at her in amazement.

"I don't want to," she says. "But, and I know this sounds weird, but I kind of feel that if I were to be unfaithful as well, then we'd be equal, and then I could forgive him."

"Are you sure that's what you want to do?"

"No. I don't really want to do it. But I think it's the only way. Anyway, enough about me. Ed. He obviously adores you."

"I know that! But what do you think of him?"

"Do you want me to be completely honest?"

Suddenly I'm not so sure, because I don't want to fall out with Jules, not with my best friend, but I know it's not going to be good news, and I don't think I could stand to argue with her.

I shrug.

"Look," she says, calming down. "We haven't exactly got off to a great start. I didn't appreciate that whole mercurial business, so right at this moment I can't think of a great many positive things to say, but I can see that he's treating you incredibly well, and for that I'm grateful."

"You really don't like him?"

"I don't know. I'd need to spend more time with him. But the main thing is that you're happy."

"You will like him, you know," I say. "He's really a sweetheart once you get past all the pompous shit."

"You mean you can get past the pompous shit?"

"Oh, Jules!" I give her a hug. "Please be happy for me. He's treating me better than anyone I've ever met."

"That's what I'm scared of," she says into my shoulder. "I'm just scared that you've fallen for the way he's treating you, rather than for the man himself."

We disengage and it's my turn to reapply some lipstick. "I don't think that's the case," I say, painting on my top lip. "I really don't."

"Okay," she says, smiling at me in the mirror. "If you say so, then I believe you."

• • •

"Did you like them?"

"Yes," says Ed slowly, on the way back to his place.

"Did you like Jules?"

"She's certainly feisty," he says.

"You didn't like her, did you?"

"Of course I did," he says, reaching over to give me a kiss as we stop at a red light. "She's your best friend, so I have to like her."

I'm not sure that's entirely what I wanted to hear, plus I don't really believe him, but I'm sure they'll both get over it. I'm sure everything will be fine. It has to be.

We park the car and get out, and just as we're walking to the front door Ed suddenly turns and grabs me, enveloping me in a huge hug.

"I was going to wait," he says, "and do this properly. But I think I should probably ask you now. Will you marry me?"

These are the words I've waited my whole life to hear, so why isn't my heart soaring into the night sky? Why am I not dancing up the street with joy? Why do I feel so completely and utterly normal?

"Okay," I say eventually, watching Ed's expression turn from worried into rapturous.

"You will?"

"I will."

"You'll be my wife?"

"Yes."

"Oh goodness. I think we need to celebrate this with champagne."

So we go inside and as I sit on the sofa watching Ed open the champagne I wonder why this feels like the biggest anticlimax of my life. And even when he brings me the glass and sits next to me to cuddle me, I still don't feel ecstatically happy, but then maybe no one feels like this? Maybe the whole thing is a bit like a Hollywood film, the passionate love thing, the feeling of ecstasy when you're proposed to? Maybe none of it really exists, and, even if it did, this feeling of being grounded is so much safer, in some ways more real, and I definitely prefer being the loved rather than the lover, I'm much more in control.

And after we've celebrated for a while I pick up the phone and wake up my parents to tell them the good news.

My mother screams. Literally. Screams.

"She's getting married," she then shrieks at my father. "Oh, Libby, I don't know what to say I'm so excited and I can't believe it you're getting married and oh my good Lord I never thought I'd see the day and you're marrying Ed McMann and he's so eligible and you've got him . . ." I swear I'm not making this up, she doesn't take a breath.

Nor does she add, "Wait until I tell the neighbors," but I know that's what she's thinking.

And Dad comes on the phone and just says, "Congratulations, darling. I'm very happy for you," and then I pass the phone to Ed and I can hear my mother shrieking delight at Ed, and finally we put the phone down and I think about calling Jules, because, after my parents, she should be the first person in the world to know, but somehow I'm not so sure I want to tell her when I'm with Ed, I think I'd rather tell her when I'm on my own, so I leave that call until tomorrow morning and we go to bed.

Chapter 24

I didn't sleep all that well last night. Ed and I "made lurrve," and, although it's getting better, in some ways it's getting worse. His technique has improved immeasurably, but I now know exactly what he's going to be doing—I did try telling him that perhaps he ought to vary the routine a little bit, and then he got upset and said it felt like I was criticizing him. I tried to explain that even though he read up on sex in a textbook, the act itself shouldn't feel like a textbook, and it wasn't a criticism, it would just sometimes be nice if he surprised me, rather than going through exactly the same motions every time.

Ed apologized, and then I felt guilty, especially because this was the night we got engaged, so I apologized. Within minutes he was asleep, while I lay awake in his bed for hours, trying to get a grip on the situation. And yes, I was happy, but I lay there thinking that it all still felt a bit like a dream, and I couldn't quite get used to the fact that this was for life. That this man sleeping beside me would be the only man ever to sleep beside me for the rest of my life.

But Ed looked so sweet when he was fast asleep. I watched him for ages, and suddenly, at about three in the morning, I felt it. A huge burst of joy that spread up through my body, and that was when it hit me. I'm getting married! Me! Libby Mason! I'm going to be a wife! I'm never going to have to worry about being sad, lonely and single again!

I crept out of bed and walked around the house, opening all the doors and going into all the empty rooms, standing in them and grinning, knowing that all this was officially mine. And then I went into the gym and started leaping around a bit, until I realized that the whole house was shaking and I might wake Ed, and I didn't want to wake Ed. This was my moment. Oh my God! I'm getting married!

I went downstairs and made myself a cup of tea, and sat curled up on the sofa, still grinning manically at the prospect of living in this spectacular house. Of never having to shop in high street chains again. Of showing off my huge house to Jules. And Sally. And Nick.

Jesus Christ! What will Nick say? I'd like him to be happy for me, but I'd also like him to be just a little bit jealous. I want him to have a few regrets, to help my ego, I suppose.

I sat for a while thinking of all the people I'd want to know, and then I decided to make a bit of an engagement party list, except I couldn't find any paper and I was getting kind of sleepy by then anyway, so eventually I went back up and climbed into bed beside Ed, and finally, at 5:45 A.M., just as the birds were singing, I drifted off to sleep with a smile still on my face.

• • •

"I couldn't do it!" says Jules, when I ring her the next morning. "Paul came back here for coffee, and it was awful, Libby. It was so weird, sitting here drinking it and knowing that he was going to make a pass, and I was completely dreading it, so I kept getting up for biscuits, and sugar, and things, and it was awful."

"Well? Did you do it?"

"No!" she practically screams. "He tried to kiss me and I panicked! I started blabbing about how I hadn't been separated for very long and I wasn't sure I was ready and I couldn't do this. Oh, Libby. I feel such a total failure."

"What did he say?"

"What could he say? He was really sweet, and kissed me on the cheek and said he'd call me again but that he understood and he wasn't in any hurry."

"Do you still think that you'll be sleeping with him to get back at Jamie?"

"Oh shit. I don't know. I know that last night I couldn't, but now, this morning, I just don't know."

"Jules, do you really think it's going to help, getting back at Jamie?"

"At least we'll be equal, but I don't know if I can go through with it."

"So are you going to see Paul again?"

"He probably won't phone me now anyway. What do you think? Do you think he'll call?"

"Of course he will, and by the way I'm getting married."

"But what should I do when he calls?"

"Jules? Did you hear what I just said?"

"No. What?"

"I'm getting married!"

There's a long silence.

"Jules?"

"Oh my God!"

"I know! Can you believe it? Ed proposed when we got home last night."

"And you didn't call me? You cow! Why didn't you call me?"

"I wanted to tell you when I was alone. So. Aren't you going to congratulate me?"

"I can't believe it," she says. "When? When are you actually going to do it?"

"We never got round to talking about it. But don't worry, I do want to be engaged for about a year."

"Promise?"

"Promise. Jules, aren't you happy for me?"

"God, Libby. I'm over the moon. Are you with Ed tonight?"

"Nah. I'm having a night off. Just want to chill out on my own tonight."

"You mean I can't tempt you with a Marks & Sparks dinner and a selection of bridal magazines from which to choose your dress?"

"You've kept your bridal magazines?"

"Libby, I keep everything. I've got stacks and stacks of them, plus loads of info on hotels for the reception and everything."

"You've got me. I'm coming. Shall I come straight from work?"

"Yup. I'll get the champagne on ice. Damn. I wish Jamie were here."

Thank God. That's the first time she's given any indication that she misses him. "I know," I say. "Me too."

By lunchtime I think I've told the world, and though personal calls are normally frowned upon at work (not that you'd know it, the number of times I speak to Jules), Joe said it was fine to make a few this morning, and he sent Jo out to buy champagne so we could have a mini office celebration.

That's what I love about this job: everyone here is so laid-back that they'll jump on any excuse to have a knees-up. Joe is genuinely delighted for me, although, and I know this is paranoia striking, I hope it's not because he wants to get rid of me.

"Will we be saying goodbye to you?" he says, pouring some more champagne into my glass.

"You can't get rid of me that easily," I laugh. "I'll be here for at least another year."

"We'll be doing your PR next," he says, grinning. "Setting up features on the glamorous charity-supporting wife of Ed McMann."

I laugh. Although it's not a bad idea. And charity work would be a good thing to do, because other than shop, meet friends for lunch and eventually look after our children, how will I fill my days?

What bliss. I mean, I may well carry on working for a bit, maybe until I have children, but it won't be serious slogging work for peanut money. Maybe I'll work here part time, say, two days a week, and maybe I'll join some snazzy charity committee and organize fashion lunches and things. God. I'm almost tempted to leave now.

Everyone at work keeps congratulating me, and the champagne's going straight to my head, when Jo—who's been rushing back and forth to pick up the phone in between swigging champagne and chatting away shouts, "Libby, Nick's on the phone. D'you want to call him back?"

"No, I'll take it." I run to my desk, away from the hubbub, and pick up the phone.

"Hi, Nick!"

"Congratulations. Sal just told me."

Is it my imagination or does, ha ha, his voice sound just a teensy bit flat? Not that it bothers me anymore, talking to Nick, not now that I've got Ed.

"I know. Thanks. Can you believe it, me, getting married?"

"Well, no. Not really. It seems like only yesterday that we were going out."

Oh. I see. Now, all of a sudden, we were "going out." Before, we were just sort of seeing each other.

"As my mother always says, when it's right, it's right."

"And he's right?"

"Yup."

"I'm really happy for you, Libby. I hope he knows how lucky he is."

"Oh, he does," I laugh, because it's clear that Nick does have at least some regrets, which is always nice to hear when you were the one that was, to put it unceremoniously, dumped.

"Good. Listen, I can't stay on. I just wanted to say congratulations. I really hope you'll be happy, Libby. You deserve to be."

"Nick! This isn't like you. What's all this stuff about how lucky Ed is and how I deserve to be happy?" I can't help it. The champagne seems to have loosened my tongue.

Nick laughs. "I'm sorry. I've been thinking about you recently, and I suppose part of me kind of regrets things not working out."

"Aha!" I say. "I'll always be the one that got away."

"Yes," he says seriously. "I suspect you will. Anyway, I really must go, but we should get together soon. Maybe you and I could celebrate, for old times' sake."

"As long as you promise not to make a pass."

"That's going to be a hard one," he says, and I can hear from his voice that he's smiling. "But I can promise I won't make more than one."

"Perfect," I say. "One pass will do wonders for the ego," as indeed will this entire conversation, although naturally I keep that thought to myself. "I'll call you when things have settled down a bit, how's that?"

"That would be lovely. Oh, and give my love to Jules and Jamie."

Yet another one who doesn't know about Jamie. I put down the phone, thinking it was a shame it didn't work out with Nick. He seemed to fit in so well, so much better than Ed in some ways, and God knows there was certainly passion there. But Nick could never have given me the life I wanted, and anyway it's not lust that's important. It's not even whether someone fits in with my friends that matters. It's whether someone fits in with me, and Ed does.

I know Jules has loads of magazines, but I can't help myself. I have to sneak out midafternoon and buy three more, because Jules got married ages ago and fashions change, even in wedding dresses, and I want to know exactly what's in now.

And although I make all the calls I have to make and speak to all the people I have to speak to, those magazines perch in a plastic bag on the corner of my desk just whispering my name all afternoon. In the end I take them into the loo and sit on the closed seat, leafing through quickly, but dying to study every page, every dress.

And when I come back from the loo I idly doodle a few designs on my pad, dreaming about walking down the aisle while all my friends gasp at my incredible beauty and tiny waist, because in my fantasies I will have lost fourteen pounds by my wedding day, and I will of course be the most beautiful bride they've ever seen.

And then I think about engagement rings, and I go round the office to all the women who are married or engaged, and insist upon trying on their rings to see what sort suits my hand. Deborah has a beautiful antique emerald-cut emerald surrounded by tiny pavé diamonds, which looks incredible except I wouldn't have an emerald, I'd have to have a huge fuck-off diamond, and those pavé diamonds surrounding it are far too small, and, as I joke to Deborah while I inspect the ring on the third finger of my left hand, I can still move my hand around far too easily.

Becs has a pear-shaped diamond, which is more like it, and I quite like it being pear-shaped, although maybe I'd have one pear-shaped and two round ones on either side.

"Where are you thinking of getting it?" Becs says, laughing at me as I parade around the office with my hand splayed in front of me.

"Give me a chance!" I laugh. "I only got engaged a few hours ago! Isn't there some sort of rule on how much a man should spend on an engagement ring? Isn't it something like six months' salary or something?"

"Six months!" she shrieks. "In your dreams, love! It's one month, which still means your ring will cost a bloody fortune, given that you're marrying Ed McMann."

Jesus. I'm marrying Ed McMann! It hits me again and I whoop round the office telling everyone again that I'm marrying Ed McMann, until they're all completely sick of me and Joe tells me to shut up or go home, and I would have gone home, except I think I've been going home early a bit too often lately, so I skulk back to my desk and do a few more weddingy doodles until it actually is time to leave.

• • •

Jules staggers down the stairs under the weight of two cardboard boxes.

"They're in there," she announces as she drops them on the floor in the kitchen. "But first—" and she beckons me toward the door with her finger and grabs my hand.

"Where are we going?"

She's pulling me upstairs, and we end up in the spare room,

where she clambers on a chair and opens a cabinet at the top, pulling out a large white box.

I gasp. "It's your wedding dress, isn't it?"

"Yup," she says, lifting off the lid and carefully unwrapping the layers of tissue paper. "I thought you might like to try it on."

"Are you sure?"

"Go on. Let's see what kind of a bride you'll make."

I whip off my clothes and Jules helps me into the dress. It's not exactly a perfect fit—in fact, we don't even bother attempting to do up the tiny row of buttons at the back—but it gives me the bride effect, and we both stand there giggling as she shows me how to do those tiny measured steps down the aisle.

"Let me practice the stairs," I say, walking regally on to the landing, shoulders back, head held high, staring at myself in awe as I pass the mirror.

And eventually we kick off our shoes (don't worry, the wedding dress has been safely packed away again) and curl up on the sofas to work our way through the magazines.

"You can't have that one," Jules says in horror, as I show her this fairy-tale meringue dress with layers and layers of stiff tulle shooting out from a tiny boned waist. "You'll look like a huge cream puff."

"Oh, thanks a lot. Are you trying to tell me I'm fat?"

"Yeah, really." She raises her eyes to the ceiling. "You? Fat? Hardly. I'm just saying that those dresses are really unflattering. I think you should go for something much more simple. Remember my motto—"

"Yeah, yeah, yeah. Less is more."

"Exactly. I can see you in something really elegant and sophisticated. Here. What about something like this?" She slides her magazine over to my lap and points to a stunning ivory sheath.

"Mmm," I say, trying to imagine my head superimposed on to the model's. "That is gorgeous."

"Very sophis," she says.

"Mmm. But what about bridesmaids?"

"You could do something similar but on a smaller scale. Maybe knee length or something, in a different color."

"Oh God. Colors. What color?"

Two hours later we're groaning after a major pig-out, and at our feet are piles of pages I've torn out for ideas.

"You really are going to marry him, aren't you?" Jules says suddenly.

"What? Did you think this was all a joke?"

"Not a joke, but I just . . ."

"Jules, I really am going to marry him."

"Okay, but let me ask you one question. Are you in love with him?"

I pause. "Yes. Well. I love him."

"That's not what I asked," she says. "Are you in love with him?

"Jules," I say slowly, as if I'm talking to a child because I really want her to understand what I'm about to say. "You were incredibly lucky with Jamie, or at least, we all thought so at the time. You seemed to have found someone who was gorgeous, bright, funny, who adored you, who was your best friend and whom you completely fancied. You thought you'd found the perfect man, and it didn't work out."

"Thanks," she says bitterly. "Rub it in, why don't you."

"I didn't mean it like that," I say. "All I'm trying to say is that you thought you'd found the recipe for a lifetime of happiness, and it still didn't work out. Maybe what I have with Ed would work out. And maybe the fact that it isn't the same as it was with you and Jamie isn't such a bad thing, because at least I'm going into this with my eyes open."

"You mean you're having to compromise."

"Well, yes, but I do sort of think you have to compromise. Not on everything, but I think the most important thing is to look for a good man. A man who will look after you, who will be a good husband, a good father to your children. Someone who can be your best friend, who will see you through the ups and downs."

"But you have to fancy them."

"Of course you have to fancy them," I say. "But that's not nearly as important as the other things, because the fancying thing, the lust thing, always goes, and once it does you're left with nothing. But if you've chosen someone you're really compatible with, then you'll always be friends, and friendship is the most important thing."

"So you don't fancy Ed, but you like him as a friend?"

I sigh. "No. That's not what I'm saying. I do fancy Ed, but it's not that out-of-control feeling of frenzied lust that I felt about, say, Jon. Even with Nick I started to feel out of control toward the end . . ."

"That was because you really fell for him."

"But don't you see that this is really what I want? That I prefer being in control? That I've found someone who will always adore me, and whom I will always be friends with. And although I fancy him, the sex isn't the most important thing."

"That's because it's crap."

"It bloody is not crap."

"That's what you said."

"That was at the beginning," I grumble. "It's much better now."

"But it's not as good as Nick."

"But that's my whole point," I sigh in exasperation. "Nick wasn't for me. Sex isn't everything, and yes, the sex with Nick was amazing, but nothing else was."

"Yes it was. You got on fantastically."

"Well, okay, we did. But why are we talking about Nick? This isn't about Nick, it's got nothing to do with him. This is about what we look for in a partner."

"I'm just worried that you might be compromising a little too much, and I could understand it if you were thirty-seven or something, but you're twenty-seven, and it just seems a bit young to be making these sorts of compromises."

"Jules, I do love him, and I know he's very good for me, and it doesn't feel like a compromise to me. I can see how you'd think that, but I promise you, it's not. He's everything I've ever wanted."

"In terms of wealth," she says with a sniff.

"No. Not only that. I can really see us together."

"I'm sorry, I just don't want to see you making a big mistake. Marriage is such a huge step, you have to be completely sure."

"I am completely sure. I know that, because being involved with men I'm completely crazy about has only ever made me miserable."

"You'll never know now, will you?"

"Know what?"

"Whether you'd find someone whom you could fall completely in love with without being miserable; someone who'd feel the same way about you. This is it, Libby. No more men. No more adventures. No more getting excited over dates with someone you really like."

"Yes, and no more tears. No more feeling like a piece of shit when you've been dumped yet again. No more sitting at home crying while you're waiting for the phone to ring. No more being on that bloody awful dating scene. Jules, I promise you this is right. Ed is exactly what I've always looked for and I know I'll be happy. Anyway, I can't see why you're getting so uptight. It's not like we're walking down the aisle next week. I've already told you that we're going to be engaged for about a year."

"Okay, okay. I'm sorry. I really am happy for you, Libby, I simply want to be absolutely sure that you know what you're doing. You're going to be spending the rest of your life with Ed."

"I know," I say happily. "Let's get back to the wedding. So what colors do you think the bridesmaids' dresses should be?"

Chapter 25

"Where's Ed?" My mother's bright smile is disappearing as she stands on the doorstep looking over my shoulder.

"He had to work. Sorry," I say, pushing past her into the house, which isn't strictly true—I couldn't face another Ed and my family scenario.

"Jesus, Mum. What's all this?"

The dining table has been laid with my mother's best china that only ever seems to see the light of day once a year, and, peering through the clingfilm that covers the dishes, I can see my mother's completely gone to town.

"Obviously it's a waste of time," she says, reaching down and tightening the Saran Wrap covering a plate of finger sandwiches in the center of the table. "I thought Ed would be with you and I didn't want him to think we didn't know how to provide a nice tea."

"Mum, tea is tea, with maybe a cake or some scones or something. This is enough to feed an army. What have you got here?" I pull back some more clingfilm to find piles of tiny Danish pastries, and more to reveal a huge chocolate cake. Thank God Ed isn't here. Thank God he can't see my mother in all her suburban glory.

"Oh well," I say, taking a pastry. "I'm starving."

My mother sighs. "I was so looking forward to seeing Ed again. I thought we could all celebrate together."

The doorbell rings and I look up. "Who's that?"

"What am I going to tell Elaine and Phil?" she says, walking to the door as I sink into the sofa in disbelief. My mother's invited her bloody bridge partners, presumably to show off her new wealthy son-in-law-to-be.

"Hello, Libby," says Elaine, walking over at the same time as looking round the room. "Congratulations. Where's the lucky man?"

"Working," I say ungraciously, as she leans down to kiss my cheek.

"That's a pity," booms Phil, walking into the living room. "We were looking forward to meeting the famous Ed McMann. Well-done, girl. You've struck lucky there."

I force a pained smile on to my face as I nod.

"Where's Alan?" says Phil. "In the garden?"

My mother raises her eyes to the ceiling and nods. "With his rosebushes, as usual," and Elaine gives a thinkling laugh.

"At least your Alan does the gardening," says Elaine. "My Phil wouldn't know what a rosebush looks like."

"Thank you, Elaine," says Phil. "And who does all the DIY, then, I'd like to know?"

"I know, dear. You are wonderful with a drill, I'll give you that."

Phil's chest puffs out like a pigeon. "I'll go and see if Alan needs a hand," he says as he leaves the room.

And the doorbell rings again. I look at my mother with raised eyebrows, as she goes to answer it.

"Diane! Ken!" I hear her exclaim, and then I have to strain my ears to hear her voice, which drops down to what my mother thinks is a whisper. "Ed's not here. I'm so sorry, he had to work. You know how it is, being such a successful financier. Never mind." And her voice goes back to its normal booming self. "We've got a lovely tea."

"Libby!" says Ken, as if he's surprised to see me there. "Ay ay." He nudges me and winks. "What's all this about being a millionaire's wife, then?"

"Ken," warns Diane. "Leave the poor girl alone. She's probably fed up with all these people going on about it." I give her a grateful smile.

"We've heard all about him." She then, unbelievably, continues, taking off her tweed Country Casuals jacket, "Jean told us all about the house. He sounds wonderful. Aren't you a lucky girl?"

Why do I feel like a six-year-old around my parents' friends?

My mother comes over to me and prods me with her elbow.

"Yes," I say, smiling. "I'm a very lucky girl."

"Lovely bag," Diane then twitters, as she turns and sees my beloved Gucci, which is dumped next to the sofa. "That's not yours, Jean, is it?"

"No. It's Libby's," says my mum, who turns to me. "Looks expensive?" Said as a question.

"Yes. It's very expensive. Ed bought it for me."

"Not one of those Pucci ones, is it?" Diane says, walking over and—can you believe this—actually opening my bag to look at the label. "Oh!" she giggles. "I meant Gucci."

"Ed bought you a Gucci bag?" Now my mother's seriously impressed. I nod. "That Tara whatsername's got one of those."

"Tara?" Diane stands racking her brains for a neighbor/member of the bridge club called Tara.

"You know, Diane, that girl in all the papers. Tara Thompson-Parker."

"It's Tara Palmer-Tomkinson, actually," I say through gritted teeth.

"That's the one," Elaine says brightly from the dining table, where she's looking at all the goodies. "Goodness, Jean, look at this spread. You must have worked so hard."

"It was nothing," says my mum proudly. "No trouble."

"Oooh, look at that cake." Elaine removes some tinfoil for a peek. "Did you do that yourself?"

"Of course. I'd never serve a store-bought cake," says my mother. "You know how much I love baking."

Christ. I wish Olly were here. My mother on her own is bad

enough, but with her ridiculous, twittering friends it's just a total nightmare.

"You'll have to start cooking for your fiancé now," Elaine says, smiling at me, while my mother snorts merrily away. "What?" says Elaine, looking at my mother. "She'll have to get used to entertaining all his friends."

"Unfortunately for Libby, she didn't inherit my cooking skills," says my mother, who then proceeds to describe the food the other night, in great detail, while Elaine and Diane tut-tut and give me disbelieving looks and I want to kill them. All of them. And in my mother's case I'd make it particularly tortuous.

"I hear there are some wonderful cooking courses around," Diane says innocently, when they've finished laughing at me. "Maybe you should try that Pru Leith school. They're meant to be very good."

Oh please shut up. All of you.

"Maybe," I find myself saying.

"What a pity your Ed isn't here," Elaine says, after the awkward silence that followed. "We were so looking forward to meeting him."

"I know," I say, and then, I can't help it, it just comes out in a massively sarcastic tone: "He would have loved you."

My mother looks at me in horror. "Libby!"

"I'm really sorry," I say, and I am, I honestly didn't mean to say that. "I didn't mean that to come out the way it did."

Elaine does a perfect impersonation of my mother's sniff, while Diane pats my knee and smiles. "Don't worry," she says. "You must be under a lot of pressure, marrying someone like Ed."

"Mum," I mumble. "Mum, can I use the phone?"

"Go on," she sighs. "Take it upstairs." And I think even she is grateful to see the back of me for a few minutes.

"Jules. This is hell. I am going through living hell."

"Where are you?"

"At my bloody parents with their bloody friends, who are all taking the piss out of my cooking."

"Do you have to stay?"

I sigh. "For about an hour. Listen, what do you think about an engagement party?"

"Hmm. What about an engagement dinner?"

"What, instead of a party?"

"Well, you can always have a party later, but, seeing as Ed doesn't have that many friends, why don't you have a small dinner somewhere and introduce him to everyone? Otherwise you're going to have to go out with everyone separately, and this way you can get all the introductions out of the way."

"Yeah. Good idea. So have like an introductory dinner, and then have the party?"

"Yup, because it will be a bit weird to have the party when no one's met him."

"When should I do it?"

"Sooner the better."

"Should I just ring everyone and see when they're free?"

"Yeah. We could do next week if you want. Any night except Tuesday."

"Wednesday?"

"Fine. Who else will you ask?"

"Sally and Paul. Olly and Carolyn."

"He's still with her, then?"

"Mmm hmm."

"Oh good. I really liked her. Who else?"

"Well, how many do you think? Should it be everyone or just the inner circle?"

"Just the inner circle, I think. What about Nick?"

Is that really a good idea? "Do you think he'll come?"

"Yes. Plus you're always saying you're still friends."

"But then I need a woman for him. I know! Jo from work! They'd get on." Actually, I'm not sure that they would, which is why I'll ask her. Jo, like me, would never demean herself by going out with someone with no money whatsoever.

"Okay. Then you can ask those friends of Ed," says Jules. "What were their names?"

"Charlie and Sarah. Hmm. Don't know. Maybe not. They were really nice but they're quite a bit older, I'm not sure they'd fit in."

"Fine. Well have one dinner for your friends and another for Ed's." And then she stops and sighs.

"What's the matter, Jules?"

"Oh, I don't know," she says. "It's just that . . . well, it's just that it's going to be so weird celebrating this without Jamie. You know, being with all these people I know and being on my own."

"You could ask him," I say hesitantly.

"No way," she says firmly. "I'm not going to let him turn up and pretend to everyone that everything's fine."

"Are you sure?"

"No." She attempts a laugh. "But I'm still not going to ask him."

"Libby!" My mum's standing at the bottom of the stairs shouting for me.

"Shit, gotta go. The dragon's screaming."

"Call me later."

"Yup."

"So when will you have the engagement party?" Elaine's got a smudge of egg mayonnaise on her chin, and I'm quite enjoying the fact that no one's noticed, or if they have, they haven't bothered to say anything.

"We haven't really discussed it and by the way you seem to have left half your sandwich on your chin."

Her eyes widen as she hurriedly wipes her chin with a paper napkin.

"Sorry," I say cheerfully, enjoying her embarrassment, "but I always think you should tell people things like that."

"Yes. Er. Thank you."

"So what sort of party will it be?" says Diane loudly, over the sound of the football, which Phil insisted on turning on, so Phil,

Ken and my dad are huddled by the TV while "the girls"—as Phil called us—are on the sofa on the other side of the room.

"I don't know, but I think we'll probably have it at home."

"Hanover Terrace," my mum adds smugly.

"I know, dear," says Diane. "You already told me."

"I just can't believe my daughter's going to be living in Hanover Terrace," she says, almost crying with the sheer joy of it. "It's not a house, it's a mansion."

"I hope he's got good security." Elaine obviously feels left out. "Those sorts of houses are forever getting burgled."

"There wouldn't be anything to take," jokes my mother, "the house is practically empty."

"So you'll be redecorating, then?" says Elaine, as I nod. "How exciting. I noticed they had some lovely sofas in John Lewis the other day."

"Libby won't be buying anything in John Lewis," says my mother, as I look at her, wondering what on earth she's on about. "She'll be doing her shopping at Harrods, thank you very much."

Diane and Elaine look impressed.

"Actually," I say, "I think Harrods is a bit old-fashioned for me. I'm planning on going to the Conran Shop."

"The Conran Shop?" say Diane and Elaine in unison.

"You can't buy those modern newfangled things in the Conran Shop!" explains my mother. "They might look nice but I'll tell you this, Libby, they're not comfortable."

"And when was the last time you went to the Conran Shop?" I offer.

"Two days ago," shouts my father. It's halftime. "She decided she ought to learn a bit more about how the other half live."

Elaine and Diane giggle politely, while my mother pretends to smile at the same time as shooting daggers at my father.

"We just happened to be passing," she says, "so we thought we'd have a look and see what all the fuss was about."

"Passing?" I say, an evil smile on my lips. "Was that before or after lunch at Daphne's?"

She gives me a stony look.

"I think I'll just use the phone again." I stand up and make a move to go upstairs, and as my mother's about to protest, I add: "I'm calling Ed. Is that okay?"

"Oh yes," she simpers. "Of course. Do give him our love."

"Right." I walk on up to their room and sit on their bed to make the call.

"Hello, sweetieloveydarling!" Ed exclaims. "I miss you."

"What are you doing?"

"Working, but I've nearly finished. Are you coming over later?"

"I'll leave here in a minute, then I'll come."

"How are your parents?"

"A pain. As usual."

"Libby! Don't say that about them. They're your parents."

"Sorry," I grumble. "It's just that they've got their friends round, and it's all a bit much for me. What are we doing tonight?" I'm hoping that we'll be going out somewhere swish, because I haven't worn my new designer outfit for nothing.

"Sundays are always a bit difficult. I thought maybe we could go to the cinema? Or perhaps we could rent a video and watch it at home."

"Oh. I thought we were going out for dinner."

"Not on a Sunday, I think. Is that all right? Do you want to go out? I could always book somewhere."

"Don't worry," I say. "I'm happy staying in."

"I'll make sure everything's magnifique," he booms. "What would you like to eat? I'll go shopping now before you get here."

"I don't mind, Ed. Anything. I'm pretty full after tea here."

"Smoked salmon? Scrambled eggs? Pasta?"

"Anything, Ed. Really. I don't mind."

"All right, my darling. I can't wait to see you and I love you very very much."

"I know," I sigh. "I love you too."

I walk back into the living room and everyone turns to look at me.

"Well?" says my mother.

"Well what?" I positively sneer.

"Well what did he have to say?"

"Oh. He said he was really sorry he couldn't be here, and he was particularly sorry he missed the finger sandwiches and he can't wait to see you soon."

My mother sighs and turns, smiling, to Elaine and Diane. "I can't tell you how lovely it is to have such a charming son-in-law."

"He's not your son-in-law yet," I mutter.

"Speaking of which," my mother says, grabbing the opportunity, "when are you thinking of actually setting a date?"

"We haven't talked about it, but don't worry, I'm sure you'll be the first to know."

"I always think summer weddings are lovely," says Elaine.

"I'll bear it in mind. I'm sorry, everyone, but I must go. Ed's waiting for me."

I walk round the room and perfunctorily kiss all the guests goodbye, and my mother sees me to the door.

"You could have been a bit nicer to our guests," she hisses on the doorstep.

"You could have made it a bit less obvious that you'd invited them round to show off your daughter's boyfriend."

"Not boyfriend. Fiancé", she says. "And anyway. I didn't invite them round to show Ed off to them. I owed them, and I completely forgot you and Ed were supposed to be coming round."

"Which is why they were all so upset when he wasn't here."

My mother folds her arms and looks at me. "Honestly, Libby. Most girls would be over the moon to be engaged to Ed McMann, but you just seem to be in a permanent bad mood. I can't think what's the matter with you. Anyone would think you didn't want to be engaged to one of the most eligible men in the country."

• • •

"What are you wearing?" I've just disengaged from one of Ed's smothering hugs, and I look down to see these worn-out shabby old carpet slippers that are exactly like the worn-out shabby old carpet slippers my grandfather used to wear.

"My slippers," he says in a bemused tone. "They're my favorite slippers. Don't you like them?"

"Ed! They're old-man slippers. They're awful!"

Once again he gets that sad puppy-dog expression on his face, and this time it just irritates the fuck out of me.

"Ed, sometimes I think you're a sixty-year-old trapped in a younger man's body."

"What do you mean?"

"It's only that sometimes you seem so middle-aged." Shit, I think I've pushed this one a bit too far. "I'm sorry," I say, putting my arms around him and kissing him, which, thank God, removes the expression. "It's just that you aren't old and sometimes you behave a bit like an old fuddy-duddy."

"I'll throw them away," he says, kicking off the offensive slippers and carrying them to the dustbin. "There!" He closes the lid of the bin. "All gone. Happy now?"

"Yes," I snort, although it's not just about the slippers, and I do genuinely worry that Ed lives in another world. That he doesn't really have a clue what's going on, that I really am forcing myself to be compatible with someone who's too damn straight for me.

Would you listen to me?

"I'm in a bit of a bad mood. I'm sorry, darling. My parents seem to have that effect on me."

"I don't like Libby when she's grumpy," he says, sitting next to me on the sofa and pursing his lips for a kiss. I dutifully kiss him and he grins at me. "I like Libby when she's happy."

"I'll try to be happy," I say, and smile.

"That's better," he says, kissing me again and then kissing my neck and stroking my hair, and I know what this means. Yup. Move number two is hand up to my breast.

"Mmm," he says into my hair. "Libby smells sexy."

And then move number three is hand under the sweater, hand under the bra, bra strap undone (amidst much fumbling, I'll have you know).

"Shall we go to bed?" Ed says as he's pulling off my sweater.

"Why? What's wrong with the sofa?" I say.

"Oh no!" He looks horrified. "If we're going to play bouncy castles we have to do it in bed."

"Right. Bouncy castles. In bed. Okay." And I pick up my sweater and walk up the stairs, wondering how I'm supposed to be turned on by the words "bouncy castles." Wondering whether sex is ever going to improve with a man who refers to a fuck as "playing bouncy castles." Whether "bouncy castles" is as dirty as it's ever going to get.

And for a second there I do think about Nick. Well, okay. A few seconds, actually. I think about how sexy he was, how it was fucking, how it wasn't playing anything other than very dirty indeed, how incredibly turned on I was by the fact that we fucked our way all over his flat and all over mine.

Oh, and did I mention that once we did it in the car? Bit embarrassing, that one. It was at King's Cross. We'd stopped off to get the late-night papers one Saturday night, and both of us started feeling really horny once we got back in the car. An hour later there was a knock on the steamed-up window, and I rolled it down breathlessly to find a policeman standing there.

"Everything all right, madam?" he said, smirking.

"Oh yes. Fine."

"It's just that you've been here for an hour and this isn't the safest place, you know. All sorts of strange people here."

"Oh. Er. Sorry."

"Kissing your boyfriend good night, were you?" The smirk got bigger. Bloody cheek.

But no. Enough about Nick. Where was I? Oh yes. Playing "bouncy castles" with Ed. In bed. Which is fine. Not great. Not even good. Just okay. And for your information I do have an orgasm, but I suppose if someone, anyone, rubs long enough in the right place it's bound to happen, isn't it?

I try to do something different. I think it might be quite nice to go on top for a change, and as I clamber on top and guide him inside me, Ed looks completely baffled.

"What are you doing?" he booms.

"Just trying something new," I whisper back.

"Are you sure about this, darling?"

"Ed, shut up. You're destroying the moment."

"Sorry," he booms again. I give him a look.

I move on top of him for about a minute, and then he starts shaking his head and pulls me off him. "Sorry, darling," he says. "I don't think I like that at all," and then he gets back into his favored missionary position and starts pounding away, while I look at the ceiling and try to picture my wedding dress.

"That was gorgeous," he says, when he's finished.

"Mmm? Good," I murmur, halfway down the aisle once again.

"Libby? Was it, umm, good for you?"

"Yes, Ed. It was lovely," I lie, turning to kiss him as he gives me a grateful smile.

Ed gets up to go to the bathroom, and when he comes back I tell him about my idea for an introductory pre-engagement-party dinner. I do say it was mine, because I'm not entirely sure what reaction I'd get if he knew Jules came up with the idea.

"Excellent idea," he says. "I'll take everyone out for dinner."

"Don't be silly," I say. "Everyone will pay for themselves."

He looks at me in horror. "Libby, you can't invite people out for dinner and then expect them to pay. That's very bad form."

"Are you sure?"

"I wouldn't have it any other way."

"Okay," I say, shrugging. "If you don't mind." I tell him who I think we should invite and he says fine. And what's more, he doesn't even ask who Nick is.

Much as I hate to admit that my mother's ever right about anything, I can see that she does seem to have a point, that bit about me being in a bad mood, but the problem is the only time I'm really in a bad mood, other than when I'm at my parents' of course, is when I'm with Ed.

I just don't understand why all of a sudden he seems to irritate me, and there seems to be a bit of a pattern developing which is beginning to worry me. Ed constantly smothers me with affection, attention and love, and the more he smothers me the more claustrophobic I find it. Eventually I snap at him, and then he gets that look, and then I have a bit of breathing space, until I feel so guilty at hurting him I apologize and then he starts smothering me all over again.

You would think, given that I am one of the most self-aware people I know, that there would have been a book written about this syndrome, but I've flicked through all the usual ones, and I can't find anything that pertains to this particular problem.

And the thing is, maybe it isn't a problem. Maybe deep down I don't believe I deserve to be happy, so now that I have found a really good man who treats me well, I'm deliberately trying to sabotage it because I don't think I deserve someone who treats me well.

Or maybe he just irritates me.

But I don't want to consider that as an option because it's just too damn easy. It's too damn easy to say that I am irritated with Ed because he is an irritating person. And if I admitted that, then I couldn't marry him, and I so badly want to marry him, I so badly want this to work.

I suppose I've never had anyone treat me like this before, worship me in the way Ed does, want to do anything to make me happy, and I suspect I just don't know how to deal with it. Sometimes I feel as if I'm almost testing Ed. The more loving and giving he is to me, the more it pisses me off, the more I push him away. Sometimes I think I'm just seeing how far I can push him, because when, eventually, he dumps me, as he'd have to if I continued treating him the way I have been, then I can turn around and say, "See? I told you so?" Because everyone else has always dumped me eventually, and maybe part of me expects that, so in a sick sort of way I'm trying to create that situation.

I know it sounds complicated, but it makes sense to me. I ran it by Jules the other night, and she nodded in all the right places, but then didn't say anything at the end, so I just went into overdrive explaining why I was so convinced this was the case.

"Are you absolutely sure you should be engaged to him?" was all she said.

"Absolutely," I said, as I tried to explain that the only way out of this one, as far as I could see, was to work through it, and work through it with him. There would be no point in breaking off the engagement, being single again and then trying to deal with it. I have to be in it, experiencing it right now if I'm ever going to come through and learn how to really love.

Although I suspect learning how to really love isn't an issue for me. I've always felt that I've had masses of love to give. Before Ed I was always the one doing the smothering. I'd do whatever I could to make myself indispensable to whoever was the current man in my life. And I was always the one who drove them away. I suppose it's a bit like that old Groucho Marx saying—I wouldn't want to join any club that would have me as a member.

Perhaps the main issue, for me now, is actually learning how to be loved. All the men with whom I've been involved before Ed treated me appallingly, and the worse they treated me, the more I wanted to make them change, the more I'd shower love, affection and attention on them.

Much like Ed is doing to me.

God. I feel like I'm having a breakthrough. That's exactly what's happening. The roles have been reversed, and I'm doing to Ed exactly what has always been done to me. I remember Jon growing more and more distant. I remember him turning round at the end of the evening and saying, "I'm sorry, do you mind if you don't stay the night, I'd just really like to be on my own." I remember covering Jon with kisses as he became less and less affectionate.

Thank God I've realized this now. Before it's too late. Because I will work this one through, and I will walk down that aisle if it's the last thing I ever do.

. . .

"So come on, then, sis. Tell me all about him."

"Olly, you're going to be meeting him in about six hours. You'll see for yourself."

"He's definitely a big hit with Mum, but I'm never sure if that's a good sign or not."

"Tell me about it. Has Dad said anything to you?"

Is it my imagination or does Olly suddenly sound slightly shifty? "Nah," he says. "You know what Dad's like. Conversation isn't exactly his bag."

I laugh.

"Wait until they meet Carolyn," I say. "Then you'll know just what I've been going through."

"I know," he sighs. "I think I'm going to have to get it over with. I've told them about her, so now Mum's driving me mad."

"Ha ha! Good. Shit, someone needs me. Listen, I've gotta go, but you'll be there on time, won't you?"

"Yup. I'll see you then."

"All right, darling. Bye." I put the phone down and turn to Jo, who's been making worried faces at me while I've been chatting. "What's the matter, Jo?"

"You're going to kill me," she says. "I'm really, really sorry."

"Please don't tell me you can't come," I say slowly.

"I'm really sorry," she says, wincing. "My friend Jill called to check I was coming to her birthday party, and I completely forgot, and she went bananas when I said I couldn't make it, I'm so sorry."

"Don't worry," I sigh, completely pissed off but not enough to shout about it, because I probably would have done the same thing. It's what single women do. We'll make arrangements, and then if something better comes up, i.e., some event where we're more likely to meet Mr. Right, we'll cancel our first arrangements without even thinking about whether we're upsetting anyone.

And I'm not upset, it's just that the numbers are now uneven, and who the hell will I put with Nick? Thankfully, my phone rings, so Jo takes the opportunity to slink back to reception while I sigh a "hello" into the receiver.

"Darling! It's me." Now "me" could be any number of me's, but in this case I know, instantly, it's Amanda Baker, and a lightbulb in my head switches on.

"Amanda! I was just going to call you! I know this is incredibly short notice, but basically, umm"—time for a little white lie here—"Ed and I decided to get together with a few friends this evening and I know how horribly busy you are, but I really want you to come. I can't believe you called, I was literally, just this second, picking up the phone to call you."

"How lovely!" she exclaims, as I wait with bated breath. "Actually, I'm not doing anything tonight. I was going to have a bath and give myself lots of face packs and things, but I'd love to come out for dinner with Ed McMann. And you."

"Wonderful!" I exclaim, mustering up some enthusiasm from somewhere. "That's great!"

"Just tell me," she interrupts, "is it going to be couple hell?"

I laugh. "Sort of. But there is a single man there, although I don't think he's your type."

"That's okay, as long as I'm not the only single person there."

"Nope. Don't worry," and, as I tell her where to be and at what time, I breathe a sigh of relief because I never have to be ashamed of being single again.

I remember clearly all those times I'd turn down invitations to dinner parties because I'd always be the only person on my own, and those times I'd turn up to find I'd been fixed up with someone awful, and how inferior I felt to those cozy couples, how I vowed I'd never go again until I had a partner.

And now I do, and I never have to ask those questions, and even though my friends said I was being ridiculous, how could I possibly feel inferior to them just because I was single, even though I believed them at the time, as I put down the phone to Amanda, I realize, and I know this is not exactly a nice thing to realize, but I realize that I do feel slightly superior to her. I've got a partner. A fiancé. I'm now, officially, a grown-up.

Jules says there are three things that make you a grown-up: an eight-piece set of matching dishes, gin, vodka and whisky in the house; and making your bed every morning. But I disagree with her. I think you're officially a grown-up when you've got another half. When you don't have to live in fear of other couples. When you don't have to feel you're not good enough.

I make sure that Ed and I are early, the first to arrive, and we order champagne as we sit down. Ed kisses me and tells me how beautiful I am. Just as the champagne arrives, so does Jules, followed swiftly by Olly and Carolyn.

Ed kisses Jules, and shakes hands with the others, telling Olly how delighted he is to meet him, having heard so much about him.

"We're all thrilled Libby's finally settling down," Olly says, winking at me. "We're just slightly surprised at how quick it's all been."

"Ha ha!" laughs Ed. "I'm surprised myself, but when it's right, it's right."

Right.

"So where's Jamie, then?" Olly asks, looking at Jules quizzically. "Got a big case on again, I suppose?"

Jules manages to pull off a shrug that looks genuine to everyone but me, but then again I'm the only one who knows the truth. "You know how it is," she says with a sad smile. "Bloody barristers."

"You could have asked him, you know," I whisper, sidling up to her and pulling her to one side.

"I know," she says. "And he phoned today, and I so nearly asked him, but he hasn't suffered enough. Not yet."

"So what did you say?"

"Well, I told him you were having an engagement do tonight, and I think he thought I was going to invite him, but I changed the subject."

"How do you feel?"

"Lonely as hell."

I put my arm around her shoulders and give her a squeeze, and then I hear, "Libby!" and Sal comes bustling through the restaurant. "I'm so excited for you!" she says, throwing her arms around me and giving me a huge hug. "Paul and Nick are parking the car. They'll be here any second." She looks at the others, who are now standing by the side of the table making small talk, and seems to do a double take when she sees Ed. "Is that him?" she says finally, sounding surprised.

"Yes. Why? You sound surprised."

She shakes her head. "Sorry. God, I'm really sorry, Libby. It's just that, he's, well, he's not really what I would have thought you'd go for."

"You mean he's not good-looking?"

She leans forward and whispers, "I thought you hated mustaches."

"I do," I whisper back. "I'm working on it."

"You must think I'm really rude. He looks lovely. It's just that I've only ever really seen you with—" and she stops, checking that no one hears as she mouths "Nick" at me.

"And?"

"And I suppose I assumed that was your type."

"Sal, I don't have a type. I never have had a type. And Ed's lovely. You'll see."

"Of course he is!" she says, squeezing my arm. "He's marrying you, so he has to be!"

"Ed?" I call over to get his attention. "Come and meet Sal."

Ed walks over, smiling, and extends a hand, looking a bit taken aback when Sal reaches up and gives him a hug. "Lovely to meet you," she says. "We've heard all about you, except I suppose you're sick of hearing that, aren't you?"

Ed chuckles. "Not at all. Not at all. And how do you know Libby?"

As Sal's explaining, I see Paul walk into the restaurant with Nick at his heels, and for a second my heart catches in my throat. He's in his old chinos with his DMs and a scruffy old raincoat, but he looks so familiar, so gorgeous, that for a second I think I'm going to start crying.

"Libby. You look lovely," he says, giving me a sedate kiss on each cheek. "Congratulations."

"I'm so pleased you're here, Nick," I say, and I am. "I was a bit worried about, well, you know."

"Don't be silly. We're friends, aren't we? I wouldn't miss this for anything. I'm dying to know what the infamous Ed's like." Nick turns and sees Ed talking to Sally.

"That's not him, is it? Please tell me that's not him."

"Nick! What do you mean? Why not?"

"Libby, he's old enough to be your grandfather."

"Crap," I laugh, suddenly remembering Nick's sense of humor. "He's only ten years older than me."

"Nice 'tache," Nick says. "Hmm, I've always fancied one of those."

"Oh shut up." I slap him. "Anyway, hopefully he won't have it for much longer."

"If I were you I'd wait until he's asleep, then shave it off. The less painful the better."

"I might just do that," I laugh. "Come and meet him."

"Umm, is there a reason you've left an empty seat beside me?" Nick leans over the table to me. "Has my personal hygiene problem become that bad?"

I laugh. "No. Amanda Baker's coming. She's late, she should be here any minute."

"Amanda Baker?" Nick's eyes widen. "Here? Tonight? Sitting next to me? Phwooargh."

"I might have known you'd know who she is," I laugh. "You're the only person I know who watches daytime TV on a regular basis."

"When it comes to Amanda Baker," he drools, "the word salivate comes to mind. Is she my blind date, then?"

"No," I say sternly, suddenly feeling slightly nauseous, because what if they do get on? What if Amanda decides Nick's just her type? I'm not sure I could cope with that, seeing Nick and Amanda together. Oh shit. What have I done here?

"Speak of the devil," whispers Nick, as Amanda sashays toward the table.

"Libby!" she kisses me, then kisses Ed, moving back round the table to sit next to Nick. "I'm so sorry I'm late," she says. "I had to do another bloody interview." She waits for someone to comment on the fact that she's famous, but no one does, until Nick steps in to fill the void.

"I watch you all the time on TV," he says. "I never realized you were a friend of Libby's."

"Yes. Do you like the show?" Her face lights up, happy at being given the opportunity to talk about herself.

Jules rolls her eyes at me as I suppress a giggle, but I watch Amanda very carefully, and although she's obviously delighted at having found a fan, I can't hear a glimmer of flirtation in her voice, or a flicker of interest. I look up to catch Jules watching me watching her, and Jules raises an eyebrow as I shrug and turn to Ed, who's got his hand on my knee.

"Are you enjoying yourself?" he asks, pursing up for a kiss. I kiss him and nod.

"Are you?"

He smiles. "Of course," and looks round the table. "Who would like some more champagne?"

"Yes, please," says Sal, proffering her glass. "I'll never say no to a bit of fizz."

Ed refills her glass, then says, "Do you know Amanda?"

"We haven't met," says Sal, as Amanda looks up at the mention of her name. "Hello. I'm Sally Cross."

"How do you do," says Amanda, a distracted look on her face. "Sally Cross. That's a familiar name. Have we met before?"

"No, I don't think so," says Sal.

"What do you do? Are you in TV?"

Sal explains her job, and Amanda's voice immediately warms up. A journalist! Another potential hit to get a feature written about herself! They start talking shop, and after a few minutes Amanda stops in mid-flow and taps Nick on the shoulder, "Sorry, but could we swap places for a bit, it's just that it's so rude talking across you."

Nick shrugs and stands up, and Amanda pushes past him to sit in his recently vacated seat, as she carries on talking about her career as a presenter.

"How's the book going?" Olly shouts over to Nick.

Nick taps the side of his nose mysteriously. "All sorts of things going on, but can't talk about them.

"Yet," he adds.

Olly laughs. "You mean that we're actually going to be able to read it soon?"

"Time will tell," says Nick, in his Mystic Meg voice.

"You're an author?" Ed, for the first time this evening, is showing an interest in Nick.

"Aspiring," Nick says with a smile.

"You're not published, then?"

"Not yet. But things are looking hopeful."

"What sort of a book have you written?"

"Oh, it was political but I wasn't getting anywhere so now I'm trying a thriller, cloak-and-dagger type stuff."

"So if you're not published you must do other work."

"Nope. The only other work I do is walk to the dole office and back."

"Oh ha ha! Very funny." Ed's laughing, and Nick looks at him peculiarly.

"Yes, well, I'm glad you think it's funny. Unfortunately, it's not a joke."

"Oh gosh!" Ed colors a deep red. "I'm terribly sorry. I thought, I assumed you were joking."

"I wouldn't joke about a thing like that."

"I've never met anyone on the dole before," says Ed, digging himself deeper and deeper as far as I'm concerned. Nick catches my eye, and I can't help it, I shrug and raise my eyes to the ceiling.

"Well, there are plenty of us about," Nick says, as I decide to step in and help the conversation change course.

"Come on, Nick, tell us what your book's about."

"You wouldn't be interested," he says.

"Yes, yes! We would." Jules joins in with me, and for the next ten minutes Nick holds center stage as he details the plot for us, while I sit there absolutely staggered, because it is brilliant! Seriously, it is one of the most original ideas I've heard for ages, and I wish I'd listened to him before. I can't believe that no one's already done it.

"That sounds fantastic!" says Olly, who by now is also listening in. "You shouldn't have any trouble getting that published."

"I agree," says Paul. "I'd buy it."

"I hope you will," laughs Nick, who's puffed up with pride at the positive reaction to his story. "I expect all of you to contribute to my royalty payments."

Amanda and Sal have finished their shop talk, and Amanda taps Ed on the shoulder. "Binky Donnell says hello," she says, smiling, "and congratulations."

"Binky Donnell!" exclaims Ed, his eyes lighting up. "There's a name I haven't heard in a while. How is the old rascal?"

Nick nudges me and mouths, "Rascal?" I kick him under the table, but I can see that even Jules has a smirk on her face.

"He's lovely," she says. "I had dinner with Binky and Bunny last week."

Nick nudges me again and this time I can't help myself, I start giggling, and I honestly can't believe I'm going to marry someone who has friends called Binky and Bunny.

"I can't believe you're going to marry someone who has friends called Binky and Bunny," Nick mutters, when he's finally recovered.

"Oh I see," I say, "and Moose is so much better?"

"At least Moose is cool," Nick says, mock indignantly. "Binky and Bunny don't exactly have much street cred."

"How do you know? For all you know Binky drives a vintage Harley, and Bunny's a blond bombshell rock chick."

"With long floppy ears?"

"Quite possibly," I snort, and we both collapse with laughter again, completely unnoticed by Ed and Amanda, who are now shrieking with delight at having so many people in common. More power to them, as far as I'm concerned.

Even Jules shoots me an odd look, and I just shrug, more than happy that Ed's found something in common with at least one of my friends, even if Amanda isn't exactly a friend.

Olly and Carolyn are chatting away to Sal and Paul, and as far as I can tell the evening's a success. Everyone's had a chance to meet Ed, they all seem to be getting on, and okay, so not everyone's really had a chance to talk to Ed, but then that's always the problem with large groups of people at dinner, isn't it? Olly, for example, has barely exchanged words with Ed, but at least they've met, and it's a starting point. On the other hand, maybe they should have a bit more of a chat.

When the coffee arrives I get up and go to see Olly at the other end of the table.

"Why don't you talk to Ed a bit? Get to know him?"

Olly sighs. "Libby, I'm not sure what I'd have to say to him."

"Olly! That's not very nice. This is the man I'm marrying. You could make an effort. How do you know you wouldn't have anything to say to him?"

"Okay, you're right. But I've heard him across the table and . . ." He pauses.

"And what?"

"Nothing." He sighs. "Anyway. He's deep in conversation with your friend Amanda. I don't want to interrupt."

"Okay," I say warily. "Maybe you and Carolyn will come over for dinner with us?"

"Maybe," he says distractedly. "Look, let's talk about this tomorrow, shall we?"

"God, Oll. Anyone would think you'd taken an instant dislike to him."

"Libby, we'll talk about it tomorrow."

"So what did you think?" We're driving back home, and much as I hate to admit it I'm actually far more worried about what my friends thought of Ed, but I won't be able to get the lowdown until tomorrow morning, so in the meantime I want to know if Ed liked them, if he approved, if he can see them fitting into our lives.

"It was a great success." He smiles indulgently at me.

"No, I meant what did you think of my friends?"

And it suddenly occurs to me that this is an important conversation. That before now I would quite happily have sacrificed my friends for a man, but that I would never dream of doing that now, and that Ed's opinion matters far more than I ever dreamed. And not because I want him to like them, but that whatever he says will be a reflection of who he is, and that if he doesn't get it right, if he fails to approve, I'm not sure I'll ever be able to see him in the same light again.

"Oh, they were great fun," he says finally. "Especially Amanda. I definitely approve of Amanda."

"It's not about approval, Ed," I say slowly. "It's about liking the people whom I love. And Amanda isn't exactly a friend, more of a work colleague, and the only reason you liked her was because you both know so many of the same people, and that's probably because Amanda's such a bloody networker."

"Libby! That's not nice."

"Sorry," I mutter. "But it's true. Anyway, what did you think of Olly?"

"I didn't really talk to him," Ed says truthfully, "so we'll have to have him over for dinner, I think. Soon."

"Yup, okay. But he's nice, isn't he? Is he what you expected?"

"I didn't expect anything, and he seems awfully nice."

"What about Sal and Paul? Did you like them?"

"Well," he pauses. "I'm not sure I'm that happy about you being friends with tabloid journalists."

"What? Are you serious?"

"Well, yes. I wouldn't mind if they were on the FT, but their paper's such rubbish. I don't think they're, well, suitable really."

I can feel an argument coming on.

"What do you mean, suitable?"

"Darling, I'm not sure I trust them, that's all."

"But you don't even bloody know them."

"Don't swear at me, Libby."

"Sorry. But they're two of the nicest people I know. I can't believe you're judging them by their jobs. And their paper isn't exactly sleazy, plus they don't do news, they don't doorstep people or anything like that."

"Still," he says, looking quickly at me. "Oh, maybe you're right. I'm just being a judgmental old fuddy-duddy, but I do have to say I was very surprised that you are friendly with someone like that Nick fellow. How on earth do you know him?"

"Nick. Not that Nick fellow." My voice is becoming more and more strained. "I know him through Sal. Why?"

"Ah." He nods. "That makes sense."

How dare he. How dare he. How dare he.

"What. Makes. Sense?" The words, if Ed bothered to listen, are dangerously slow coming out of my mouth.

"He's terribly scruffy. So unkempt. Not the sort of person I'd have thought you'd associate with at all."

"But you hardly said two words to him."

"But, Libby, please. Look at the chap, what does he think he looks like? Those shabby clothes, and as for that business about being on the dole . . . I think it's best if you don't see him again."

"I can't believe you're saying this. I can't believe you're sitting here"—incidentally, I'm now spluttering with rage—"I can't believe you're trashing my friends. And most of all, I cannot believe how incredibly superficial you're being. You have judged all my friends either by their appearance or by their jobs, and I would have thought that you are old enough to know better. Evidently unlike you"—this last bit said through gritted teeth—"I choose my friends because of who they are, and not because of how much money they have or which bloody public school they went to."

I run out of steam then and sit there shaking with anger, and we don't say a word to each other the whole way back.

There have been times, in the past, when I've introduced boyfriends to friends and my friends haven't liked them, and I've been furious with those friends, furious with them for not seeing what I see, for having the temerity to tell me the truth, and yes, I've fallen out with people over it. But this time I can't see a grain of truth in what Ed is saying. I cannot see that my friends are bad people because they don't have as much money as he would like, because they do not dress in immaculate designer clothing, because they do not socialize with Binky and Bunny fucking Donnell.

And as we get out of the car outside Ed's house, I wonder whether I'm being too hard. Whether perhaps Nick's clothes are a bit shabby, whether Sal and Paul are perhaps not altogether my cup of tea, whether it would be a huge hardship for me to cut them out of my life, and the truth is that I really don't know. I don't know whether to compromise on this and try to forget about it and accept that they are not the sort of people the wife of Ed McMann should be socializing with. I just don't know what to think anymore.

We get undressed in stony silence, and, after I have climbed into bed and turned my back to Ed, he says he's sorry.

I ignore him.

He touches my shoulder and I shrug off his hand, and he says, again, that he's sorry.

"I didn't mean to hurt you," he says. "And you're right. I was wrong. I've been far too judgmental. Libby, my darling, I really am sorry."

And I turn to him and there are tears in his eyes, and I can see that he is sorry, so when he starts stroking my leg I accept his apology, but I don't feel anything. Completely numb. And when he thinks he's done enough foreplay and is ready to enter me, I still don't feel anything. And then he's inside me, pounding away on top of me, and this time I don't think about walking down the aisle, I just lie there with a strange pain in my chest, and this pain moves higher and higher, and suddenly I'm crying.

Huge, great heaving sobs. Like a child. And I push Ed off and run into the bathroom, locking the door, and look at myself in the mirror for a long time.

I have never felt so lonely in my life.

• • •

Despite myself, as soon as I get to the office the next morning I pick up the phone and ring Sal.

"Well? What did you think?"

"He's lovely!" exclaims Sal, and I start to relax.

"Really? You liked him?"

"He's very charming. Of course. You two look good together."

"God, Sal. I am so pleased to hear that."

"Why? Did you think I wouldn't?"

"No." Yes. "It's just that it's important to me what my friends think."

"Did he like us, then?"

"Yes! He thought you were lovely!" And as I say it I recognize the insincerity. My voice has exactly the same inflection as Sally's.

• • •

"I'm ringing up to thank you for last night." Why do I suddenly feel that Nick is playing a larger and larger role in my life? I mean, it's over. Finished. I'm getting married to someone else, yet suddenly I seem to be speaking to Nick, or seeing him, far more often than ever before.

"Did you enjoy it?"

"It was lovely to see you," he says warmly. "Especially looking so glowing and happy."

"Am I?" I'm surprised. I never dreamed Ed had that effect on me.

"Very much so," he laughs. "You're really going through with this?"

What does that mean? "We haven't set the date yet," I say. "And it doesn't really feel real at the moment."

"I suppose you're waiting until you've got that rock on your finger for it all to sink in," he says in a strange tone, which can only mean one thing. He's jealous. But then it hits me, what he's just said. The ring.

Oh God. The ring. The diamond that will make it all true. The diamond that will mean there's no going back. Because suddenly I'm not so sure, and suddenly I remember Jules's words: that this isn't about falling in love with love, or wanting to get married for the sake of being married, or getting excited about walking down the aisle, or living in Hanover Terrace, or any of those things. This is about spending the rest of my life with Ed, and as I think that I remember last night, and how I felt looking in the mirror, and I feel an icy dagger of fear splinter my heart.

No. I'm not going to think about this. I wrap the dagger in a fantasy of ivory lace, and surround it with images of my vast designer wardrobe, and start to feel slightly better.

"Just how big do you think the rock should be?"

"At least five carats, Libby." Nick sounds exasperated but jokey, like he used to. "And that's just the one in the middle. It will basically have to be so big, no one will be able to look at your finger without wearing sunglasses."

I chuckle. "That sounds like the one for me."

"So you're really going to do it?" he says, sounding suddenly serious.

" 'Course!" I say indignantly. "I don't go around getting engaged to every man I meet."

"You're telling me," he laughs.

I want to ask Nick what he thought of Ed, but I have a horrible feeling that Nick will tell the truth, which is why he hasn't volunteered the information himself, and I don't want to know. As far as I'm concerned my doubts are just pre-wedding nerves, but even so I don't want anyone else to corroborate them.

It isn't as if I shouldn't be nervous. Surely every bride feels this way? Aren't there people who become completely terrified the night before the wedding, who, despite being madly in love, suddenly doubt that they're doing the right thing? That's all that these feelings are, I realize with relief. It is perfectly natural for me to be doubting this. Everything's going to be fine.

Jo runs in and tells me Sean Moore's here for the meeting, so I say goodbye to Nick and spend the rest of the morning talking to Sean Moore, his agent and Joe Cooper about his publicity campaign. I do well. I think they're all happy with the work I've been doing, and when we're finished there's a message from Jules.

I don't call her back. Not yet. I go out for lunch with Jo and try to forget about everything, because right at this moment I feel that it's all getting a bit much for me. So we go to the Italian café and order milky cappuccinos, and tuna salad on toasted baps, and we sit there and gossip about everyone at work, and by the time I step back into the office at half past two I feel human again.

So when Jules calls again midafternoon I'm in a good mood, and I'm totally unprepared for what she's about to say.

"Libby, you might hate me for saying this, but after last night I've just got to."

"Go on. What is it?"

"Look, I'm only saying this because I love you and I don't want to see you make a mistake."

"Get to the point, Jules."

"Okay, okay. The thing is, I'm just really concerned that you haven't thought this through. You've been swept up in a whirlwind of excitement, and I'm worried that you haven't actually thought about the reality of it."

"Jules, you've said all this to me before. I know what I'm doing."

"Okay, fine. But I'm going to say it again, and I really want you to listen to me. Marriage is for life. It's not just about having a spectacular wedding day, it's about spending the rest of your life with that person, for better or worse. You can't just turn around and decide you're not compatible and walk away. What about children? If you have children Ed will want to send them to Eton, and would you really want your children brought up away from you? There are so many other things to consider, and I'm just so frightened that you haven't thought this through."

I start to feel sick, and immediately jump on the defensive. "What about you, then? If marriage is for life, how come you keep saying that Jamie has to suffer and you don't know whether you'll take him back? If you really believe what you're saying, then you'll do anything to save your own marriage, and that includes forgiving Jamie."

There's a long silence, and then I hear a catch in her throat as she says softly, "I'm trying."

"What?"

"I do believe what I just said, and all I've been thinking about is that I have to find it in my heart to forgive him, because I love him, because he's my husband, and because I don't want to live without him."

"Thank God," I practically scream.

"That doesn't mean everything's fine," she says slowly. "It's not, and I don't know if it will ever be fine again, but I'm going to tell him to come home."

"Yes!" I punch the air. "Thank God you've seen sense."

"Libby," she says, "stop changing the subject. You need to know that marriage is not a fairy tale. This has been the most nightmarish fucking thing that's ever happened to me, but I'm willing to work at it.

"Look," she continues. "I'm not saying that Ed's not for you, or that you can't marry him, but all I'm saying is you have to have more time. Marriage isn't easy. God knows I know that now. Anything that's irritating you slightly now will magnify a thousandfold once you're married. I think you need to be very sure. You need some time out on your own to think about this, to think about spending. The. Rest. Of. Your. Life. With. Ed."

There's a silence while I digest what she's just said, because, even though she's said it before, it never hit home. I came up with arguments to refute it, but now I see that she's right. That this—marriage—means I'll never have another flirtation again. I'll never be with anyone else again. I'll be sleeping with Ed, and only Ed, for the rest of my life. And I remember last night again, and I exhale deeply.

"Libby? Are you still there?"

"Yes." My voice sounds small. "I think you're right."

"I'm not saying this isn't it," she says, sounding relieved. "I'm just saying you need to be one hundred percent sure."

"I know." My voice still sounds small. "So what do I do?"

Jules tells me to tell Ed I've got a pitch coming up, and that everyone will be expected to work late for the next few days, and that I'll miss him desperately but I need to prove myself with this one because since I've met Ed I've barely concentrated on work, and if I don't do this I'll be in big trouble.

And as she says it I know that even though it's going to be difficult to tell him—I can already see his sad puppy-dog expression—it's a vaguely credible excuse, and she's right, I don't need weeks to think about this, just a few days on my own.

"Jules? Thanks. Really."

"Don't be ridiculous. That's what best friends are for."

But I still feel nervous as hell as I'm driving over to Ed's that night. I have nothing with me. No set of clean underwear, no change of clothes for tomorrow, no makeup bag, and I can see that Ed notices this as soon as he opens the door.

"Darling? Where are your things?"

I can't lie, I can't tell him they're in the car, and even though

I hadn't planned on saying this quite so soon, I haven't got much choice, have I?

"I'm not staying tonight," I say, and, predictably enough, he looks crestfallen.

"Is something the matter?" I can already see the fear in his eyes, and a wave of sympathy sweeps over me.

"Don't be silly, darling. Nothing's the matter. But I'd love a cup of tea."

Anything to stall for time.

We go into the kitchen and as I sit at the counter in silence Ed turns to me and asks worriedly, "There is something wrong, isn't there?"

"I already told you. No. There's nothing wrong. It's just that I'm in big trouble at work, and we've got a pitch coming up and I'm going to be working really hard the next few days, so I don't think I'm going to be able to spend much time with you."

Ed is visibly relieved as he puts the tea in front of me. "Is that all, darling? Don't worry about work. I'll look after you anyway and you know I won't want you working once we're married, so why don't you just hand in your notice?"

"I love my job," I say indignantly, suddenly realizing that, at the moment, I do. "I don't want to give it up quite yet. Although," I add as an afterthought, "it's very sweet of you to offer. I feel that I need to prove myself with this. You do understand, don't you?" I sip the tea.

"I suppose so," he says sadly. "But I will see you, won't I?"

"God, I hope so," I lie, reaching up and giving him a kiss, then pulling away just as I feel Ed getting passionate, because the last thing I want is to have sex tonight. I look at my watch. "Jesus, I've got to get back. Everyone's working late tonight in a frenzy."

"You mean you're going back to the office now?"

"I'm so sorry, darling," I say, grabbing my bag. "But they'll sack me if I'm not there. You'd better not call because the switchboard will be closed, but if there's anything urgent I'll leave the mobile on. I'll call you tomorrow," and I give him another peck and run out the door.

I catch Marks & Sparks off the Edgware Road just as they're about to close, but the security man is taken in by my pleading looks and winning smile, and he lets me in with a shake of his head.

Freedom. I feel free. I can eat whatever I want tonight, and I'm going to be in my flat for the whole night and refuse to answer the phone. I'm going to do what I want, when I want, and already I feel as if a load has been lifted. For the next few days I am completely free.

I run down the aisles throwing things in a basket. Mini pita breads, taramasalata, hummus, olives. I chuck in a packet of smoked salmon and some mini chicken tikkas. Fuck it. I'm having a blow-out. I hesitate over some vegetables, then decide they're far too healthy, so it's back to the deli section via the party section, where I can't help but be tempted by some gorgeous looking canapés.

And I dash up to the one remaining till that's open, and while the girl adds up my stuff I grab a handful of chocolate bars and add them to the pile.

Then back in the car and on to Ladbroke Grove, but not before stopping at the video store. And while I'm in the video store trying to decide between *Sleepless in Seattle* and *Sleepers*, my mobile rings and Ed's number flashes up on the screen. I press the busy button on the phone, and poor Ed gets my voice mail, and I know it's mean, but I don't want to have to deal with him right now. I just want to be on my own.

I choose *Sleepers*. The last thing I need is to watch a slushy romantic love story where the hero is gorgeous (if you're into Tom Hanks, that is, which I happen to be), and I whiz off home via the off-license, where I treat myself to a very expensive (that means more than 4.99) bottle of claret.

Home. Wonderful, fantastic home. As I'm unloading the bags the phone rings, and I hear Ed's voice on my machine.

"Sweetieloveydarling, I tried your mobile but you're not answering. I just wanted to ring and say that I miss you and I love you and I can't wait for us to get married. Don't worry about work, and I'll call you tomorrow. I love you very, very much."

"Fuck off," I mutter, as I pop the chicken tikka in the microwave to heat it up.

And the phone rings again.

"Libby, darling. It's Mum." As if I didn't know. "You're obviously out, probably having a wonderful time with Ed. Dad and I were just saying we hadn't heard from you for a few days and wondered how you are. Perhaps you and Ed would like to come over for supper next week? Oh well, you know how I hate talking into these little machines. If you don't get back too late give me a ring. Well. Ah. If you come back. If not, call me in the morning. Bye, bye, darling."

"And you can fuck off too," I shout, my mouth full of pita bread, as I gather up my food and collapse on to the sofa.

Thank God. It's Saturday morning and I've managed to avoid Ed since Thursday night. Okay, I know it's only one day, but I told Jo to tell him I was in a meeting when he called, and then yesterday, at around three o'clock when I knew he'd be at work, I rang his answering machine at home and told him I missed him and that I was fine, but really busy, and I'd have to work on Saturday but I'd call him in the evening, and maybe we could get together on Sunday.

Not that I am missing him. That's what's so extraordinary. I've loved having two nights in at home by myself. I haven't picked up the phone once, I've just pottered around, watching TV, reading magazines. I even attempted a bit of DIY and hung some pictures that have been propped up on top of the radiator since I moved in.

I thought that these "days off," as Jules put them, would be a time of reflection. I thought I'd be sitting around analyzing every aspect of our relationship and trying to work out whether Ed is The One, whether I do want to spend the rest of my life with him, but actually I haven't even thought about him. I've been far too busy being happy by myself.

Which I suppose is slightly worrying in itself.

So when the phone rings on Saturday morning, again I leave it because I've assumed it's Ed, but of course I leave the volume up just in case it's someone important like, well, I suppose like Jules, because really she's the only person I feel like talking to at the moment, not to mention the only person who really needs me right now.

Jamie moved back in two days ago. Jules was trying to be

cold, trying to let him know that they couldn't simply pick up where they left off, but, as she admitted to me in a whisper while Jamie was downstairs, "God, Libby, it's so nice to have him home," and her coldness toward him is warming up by the minute. Make that the second.

And I know, she knows, it won't be forgotten about, and the strangest thing of all is that, hearing this, I started kind of re-thinking the whole marriage thing. Not that I don't want to get married, it's just that maybe it isn't the happy ending. Maybe the marriage is just the beginning. Maybe getting married isn't going to be the answer to my prayers after all.

I mean, Jesus, it wasn't exactly the answer to Jules's prayers now, was it?

It isn't Jules. It's Nick.

I trip over the rug and stub my toe on the coffee table as I'm rushing to the phone to pick it up before Nick rings off and I pick up the phone shouting, "Shit!"

"Is that any way to greet your second-favorite man? If I piss you off that much why bother picking up the phone at all?"

"Ouch," I say, rubbing my toe. "I just stubbed my toe."

"Have you looked out the window?"

"No. Why? Are you sitting on my railings?"

He chuckles. "Nope. But it's a beautiful day. Far too nice to be staying inside. What are you doing?"

Like I even have to think about it. "Nothing. Absolutely nothing."

"Not spending the day with your fiancé, then?"

"Nope. He thinks I'm spending the day in the office."

"Oops. Do I smell trouble on the West London front?"

"Nah, not really. I just needed a bit of space. Anyway, why are you asking?"

"Just wondered if you wanted to come out to play."

"What kind of play?"

"Not that kind of play," he laughs. "Although now you men-tion it—"

"What do you want to do?" I resist all temptation to flirt.

"I thought maybe we could go for a walk on the heath, then window shop in Hampstead, maybe have lunch or something."

"That sounds fantastic!" It does. "I'd love to." I would.

"Great! How about I'll meet you outside the cinema on South End Green."

"Okay. Give me an hour." I look at my watch. "I'll see you at twelve."

"See you then."

And for the first time in what feels like ages I don't have to worry about what to wear. I don't have to worry about "looking the part," or being accepted, or wearing designer gear. I sling on my jeans that haven't seen the light of day since I met Ed, pull on some sneakers and inch on a tight, white, V-necked T-shirt. If I were with Ed, I'd loop a cardigan stylishly around my shoulders, but, seeing as it's Nick, I tie it round my waist and to be honest it's far more comfortable that way, at least I don't have to worry about it falling off.

I slap on a bit of makeup—because even though this isn't a romantic assignation, I wouldn't be caught dead leaving the house without something on—toss my hair around a bit and that's it. I'm ready.

And when I reach the cinema at noon, Nick's already there, sitting on the steps outside reading the *Guardian,* occasionally looking up and closing his eyes as the sun bathes his face in warmth.

There's a girl leaning against a lamppost trying to look as if she's also basking in sunlight, but as I approach I watch her sneaking looks at Nick, who is looking, it has to be said, decidedly gorgeous.

"Libby!" He stands up and flings his arms around me, giving me a smacker on the cheek, and as we walk off down the road he keeps an arm casually around my shoulders, and maybe this should make me feel uncomfortable, but there's nothing sexual, nothing intimate, it's just the mark of a good friend, and I laugh as I put my arm around his waist and give him a squeeze, instantly remembering the hard contours of his body, the way he looks when he is naked.

But then I remember I am the property of another, and I move away from him slightly, just enough for him to remove his arm, and I link arms with him instead, which feels much safer.

"Come on, come on," he urges, marching next to me. "If I'd known you were such a snail I wouldn't have asked you to come for a walk."

"We can't go for a walk yet," I say in horror. "It's practically lunchtime and I haven't had any breakfast. I'm starving."

"Okay. Shall we hit the high street?"

"To the high street we shall go." And giggling together we march up Downshire Hill.

"God, this is beautiful," I say halfway up the hill, stopping to peer into the windows of a tiny, cottagey whitewashed house.

"Mmm," agrees Nick. "This is one of my favorite roads in the whole of London. If I had money I'd definitely buy a house here."

"Money?" I look at him with horror. "But, Nick! You're forgetting. You don't want money. In fact, if I remember correctly, you'd give it all to the bloody politicians."

"Ah," he says, nodding sagely. "Yes, that is correct. I did once say I would give my lottery win to the bloody politicians, but of course I'd save a few million for myself."

"You've changed your tune."

"Yes, well. As you keep saying, I'm really a girl, and isn't it a woman's prerogative to change her mind?"

I laugh. "Are you quite sure you're not gay?"

"Never!" he exclaims loudly in a Winston Churchill voice. "When there are so many gorgeous women around." He leers at me and tries to pinch my bum as I shriek with laughter and run off.

"Wait, wait," he calls, and I stop and grin at him as he lopes toward me. "I am sorry m'lady for insulting you by partaking of your bottom."

"You're forgiven," I say. "Just don't make a habit of it." And then I get this flashback of Nick kissing my breasts, down to my stomach, and I shiver, horrified that I'm still thinking about it, that the memory of it, in the presence of the man himself, is definitely turning me on. I shake my head to try and dislodge the memory, but of course Nick is here, with me, so it doesn't really go away, just moves to the back of my mind, which seems to be fairly safe for now.

We walk past the police station, past a café, and as we pass the furniture shop on the corner I stop Nick and drag him to the window.

"It's gorgeous," I sigh. "Can we have a look?"

"Yes. Let's go in and look at all the things we could never afford." And then his face falls. "I mean, me. Sorry. I keep forgetting that you can probably afford the whole shop. A thousand times over."

"Not yet, I can't. Come on." I drag him in by the hand. "Let's drool."

I sigh with delight over the ethnic furniture, and shriek with horror at the prices.

"They want 970 for that piece of Indian tat?" says Nick very loudly, as he looks at the price of a coffee table.

"Sssh. Keep your voice down," I whisper, noting that the sales assistant's eyes are following us around the shop. Just as we walk out, Nick says, loud enough for the entire shop to hear, "You know Simon bought the very same table in India for 3.20. And what's more, he thought he was ripped off."

"You are incorrigible," I laugh, as we step outside.

"But really," he insists. "Those prices are laughable. And they do probably buy it in India for nothing. Think of all those poor people struggling in India, and thinking they're getting a bargain by selling their handcrafted stuff for a fiver."

"Hmm." I can see he has a point. "Are you getting on your political high horse again? I just want to be warned."

"Nah," he says, "the weather's far too lovely to get on any horse. Much more fun walking."

We continue up the hill, idly chatting about this and that, and then I remember how mysterious he was the other night about the book, and what's happening with it, and I ask him again if he'll tell me.

"Can't." He shakes his head. "It's a secret."

"Oh, pleeeeeeeeeeaaaaaaase," I plead, looking up at him hopefully. "I'll be your best friend."

"Nope."

"What about if we exchange secrets?"

Now he looks interested. "You mean you tell me one, then I'll tell you?"

He stops walking and turns to look at me. Now he's interested. "Okay, I'll do a deal with you. You tell me a secret, and if I think it's good enough, I'll tell you. How's that?"

"Okay, deal." And I stand there desperately trying to think of a secret, but I can't think of any. I could tell him that I cried during sex the other night, but I don't want him to know that, it wouldn't be fair on Ed, and anyway it isn't really a secret. But I don't really have secrets. And then I think of something.

"I've got one, but you have to promise you'll never tell anyone."

"I promise."

"It's really stupid."

"Libby! Just tell me."

"Okay. When I'm driving in my car I talk to myself."

"So? Loads of people talk to themselves."

"But I do it in an American accent."

"You're kidding!"

I shake my head.

"Give me an example."

I shake my head again.

"Oh, go on, just give me an idea of what you say, what you talk about."

Reluctantly, it has to be said, I stand in the middle of Hampstead High Street and in a crap American accent I say, "Did you have a good time tonight? Yeah, it was rilly cool."

And Nick collapses with laughter.

"I can't believe that," he splutters, and I start laughing too. "You are seriously weird."

"I am not. I bet loads of people do that."

"Not in an American accent. Go on, do some more." He wipes the tears from his eyes.

So I do a little bit more, and soon the pair of us are clutching each other to stop from falling down, and I'm holding my stomach because I'm laughing so hard it's hurting.

And when we recover I say, "Your turn. Now tell me about the book."

"No way. Your secret wasn't big enough."

"What? You're joking! You loved my secret."

"Only because it demonstrates what a completely weird person you are. It isn't that big a secret."

"You bastard." I hit him.

"Wanna try again?"

"Nope. You're not getting any more secrets out of me. Now I really am starving, what about here?" We're standing outside a café with tables dotted on the pavement, and I watch a couple leave a tip, then stand up.

"Quick, quick." Nick grabs me by the hand. "We must have that table."

I order a salade niçoise, and Nick has an egg and bacon baguette, but by the end of the meal we're feeding each other our respective meals, making a huge mess, and giggling like children.

And Nick insists on paying, which I feel slightly guilty about, because he really doesn't have much money, but he won't hear of accepting anything from me, and then we leave and walk up, past Whitestone Pond, and on to the heath.

And the weather is beautiful. It's a hot, hazy, lazy summer's day, and everyone's smiling, and this is London at its best, it's why I wouldn't live anywhere else.

After a while, kicking through the long grass until we're on open spaces, Nick says why don't we sit down and sunbathe for a bit, and I put my bag down, kick off my shoes and fold my arms behind my head, just listening to the birds and watching the trees blow slowly in the soft, occasional breeze.

"So," I say eventually, when we've been lying there for a bit in silence. "What did you think of Ed?" I don't know why I ask this question, but I suppose I think he'll echo Sal and say he seemed like a nice guy. I'm certainly not expecting what comes next. If I had been, I would never have asked.

"Do you want the truth?" Nick says seriously, and I shrug.

"I think he's awful," Nick says slowly, while I look at him with a smile because he's obviously joking.

He's not joking.

"I think he is absolutely horrific," he says, and there isn't even the merest hint of a smile. "Not only is he far too old for you, he's also far too straight for you. He's pompous, arrogant, and he doesn't fit into any aspect of your life. He treats you like some sort of trophy girlfriend, sorry, fiancée, with patronizing comments and pats on the head, and he has completely ignored who you really are because he's just not interested. He probably cannot believe his luck that someone like you would even look at him.

"And to be honest," he continues, while I sit openmouthed in shock. "I can't believe you would even look at him. I think he is quite possibly one of the most awful men I have ever met, and all I can think is that you've had some sort of mental block, because you would have to be absolutely crazy to even look at him, let alone consider marrying him."

I'm about to scream at him, to shout "How dare you," to splutter with indignation, and fury, and rage, but I don't. Nick just looks at me, waiting for a reaction, and I feel my eyes well up, and suddenly I'm crying. Hiccuping huge sobs, and before I know it Nick has his arms around me, and he's rubbing my back in great big circular motions, and I'm soaking his shoulder with my tears.

"Sssh, sssh," he's saying. "It's okay. It's all going to be okay." And this makes me cry even more, because, even though I don't want to be influenced by what Nick has just said, I know he's right. He's absolutely fucking right.

And eventually I calm down, and pull away and try to smile through my tears, finally absolutely sure that I have to end this with Ed, that I cannot go through with it, and Nick smiles at my wobbly smile, and Christ only knows how this happens, but we're kissing.

It's not that I kiss Nick, or that he kisses me, it just happens. One minute I'm smiling at him and the next second I'm locked into his arms.

His lips are on mine, and they're soft, and warm, and then, before I even register what's happening, my tongue takes on a life of its own and slips into his mouth, and he pushes me back on the grass and a moan escapes me, from somewhere deep down, and I want his kiss to swallow me up.

We can't stop. Neither of us. Not even when a group of teenagers walks past and starts catcalling and shouting things. I am lost in this kiss, in Nick, and I want it to go on forever.

Does it sound cliched to say that everything disappears? That it's as if there is nothing else on this planet except me, and Nick, and the feelings that are churning up inside me, feelings that I had honestly forgotten I ever had? That if we had not been in a public place there is no question that we would have ended up having sex? That when Nick's hand disappeared up my T-shirt to gently rub my breasts I would have let him carry on forever had it not been for my sense of decorum?

But we have to stop. Eventually. And as we pull apart and look at each other, my hands fly up to my mouth. "Oh my God," I whisper. "What have I done."

I am not the sort of person who is unfaithful, and, before you argue with me, I consider kissing someone, when you are engaged, going out with, or married to someone else, un- faithful.

Many years ago I caught Matthew, an old boyfriend, with someone else. When I say caught, I don't mean that I walked in on them, interrupting coitus, as it were. I mean that I was in the wrong place at the wrong time (or perhaps you would argue the right place at the right time), and that Matthew had no idea I would be there, and that I saw him kissing someone else.

It was a crowded party, and yes, admittedly, I was far too young to be getting serious with anyone, let alone Matthew. I stood there and watched them, frozen with horror, and I thought that my heart was actually going to break. Many years ago Matthew argued that it was only a kiss, that she was no one, that they hadn't even petted, let alone slept together, so what was the big deal about. But I vowed, there and then, that I would never do that. I decided that if ever I were in a relationship that made me so unhappy I was looking for emotional or physical gratification outside that relationship, I would first discuss it with my partner, and together we would try and work it out.

Of course I now know, thanks to Jamie, that nothing is quite as easy as that. I have surprised myself with the way I seem to have forgiven Jamie committing what I have always considered to be the cardinal sin, but there again, as Jamie confessed, it was simply physical gratification, which, although I don't condone it, I can sort of understand.

But the thing that's worrying me now, the thing that I could never have predicted, is what on earth you are supposed to do when your feelings are unfaithful?

Chapter 29

I didn't expect to be quite so upset, but I cried all night. I cried for the loss of my fantasies, for the loss of my dreams. And I cried at the memory of what it is like to be alone.

Last night, drowning in tears, Nick rang, and this time I didn't pick up the answering machine. He left a message—in other circumstances I would say a very sweet message—saying that he'd had a lovely time, and that he was sorry for compromising me, and that he hoped he hadn't offended me, but if I wanted to call him he would be there.

But I don't want to call him. I don't want to confuse the issue any further, and the only issue that's important right now is Ed.

Ed. I called him. Last night. I managed to calm down enough to pretend there was nothing wrong, although the first thing he asked was whether I had a cold because I sounded sniffly. He told me he loves me very, very much, and he said he'd missed me desperately, and we arranged to meet this evening.

He wants to take me out for dinner, a romantic evening, just the two of us, and I nearly broke down when he said this, because he doesn't have a clue what I'm going to say to him tonight.

I could have told him on the phone, but even I'm not that much of a bitch. I have to be brave, I have to do this face-to-face, and I feel physically sick at the very thought.

And then, at the end of the conversation, he said, "Darling, I think it's time we went shopping for a ring," and I didn't say anything. I couldn't say anything, and when I said we'd talk about it tonight, he sounded worried.

I feel like I've been drugged. I suppose that crying all night does that to you. You move as if in slow motion, your head too thick and fuzzy to think clearly, and eventually I ring Jules, because I can't do this on my own. I need to tell her what happened yesterday, to describe my feelings.

She knows instantly that something's wrong, and orders me over there immediately. They have a lunch with friends, but she sends Jamie off by himself, not, however, before I have a chance to see them together, to see how they are post-trauma. Jamie is being extra affectionate toward her, and although I can see she is trying to resist, when he puts his arms around her to say goodbye she leans into him and the expression on her face is one of relief.

And when he leaves she sits me down and makes me milky sweet tea without saying anything, just waits for me to start.

Haltingly I start to tell her about Nick, and when I've finished she doesn't say anything for a while, so I start blabbering and everything comes out in a big rush.

"I can't marry him," I say, tears already filling my eyes. "I can't. He's not what I want, and more important I'm not what he wants. Nick's right. I've realized that all this time he's been trying to turn me into the investment banker's wife, and that's not me, it never will be, and I never laugh with Ed, and you were right about everything, about me falling for the fantasy, and even though I know it was an appalling thing to do with Nick I think something like that had to happen to jolt me back to reality, and the thing is I'm seeing Ed tonight, and he's not a bad person, and I do genuinely think he adores me, and I just don't know what to say to him or how to say it, because however I put it it's going to destroy him." I stop, taking a deep breath.

Jules still doesn't say anything, so I carry on. "And you know the worst thing is that I don't love him, I don't think I even like him that much, and I know I was wrong to get into that with

Nick, but you see kissing him, Nick I mean, has made me understand just how much is missing with Ed, I mean our sex life is crap. Really. Awful."

I never thought I'd be able to stay in a relationship where the sex was awful. I always assumed I was one of those women with a high sex drive who would disappear out the door if they were crap, but I suppose it's amazing what you'll talk yourself into when you want something so desperately. That's it. I can't believe how desperately I wanted to get married.

"I know it's hard," Jules says finally. "But you're doing the right thing. Everything I've said to you is finally sinking in, and yes, Ed is a lovely guy, but he's not for you, and thank God you've seen that now rather than a year into the marriage."

I nod sadly.

"Do you think you would have actually gone through with it?"

"I don't know." I shrug sadly. "I think I just wanted to get married, but I'm sure at some point, even if it hadn't been for Nick, I would have realized all this. I think I've probably known it for a while, but I didn't have the heart to admit it to myself because he's the first man who's wanted to marry me and on paper he has everything I've ever wanted."

"Does this mean you've finally understood that money isn't everything?" Jules grins, and I smile back.

"Not everything," I say. "But all this means is that I'll have to make it myself."

"Which is a far healthier attitude."

"Yeah. I know."

"So you're going to tell him tonight?"

"Oh God." I sink my face into my hands. "This is going to be the hardest thing I've ever done."

Jules looks worried. "But you have to," she says firmly. "You have to be very honest and say that you won't make him happy."

"So I put the blame on myself rather than on him?"

She nods. "Isn't that what men always do?"

I stay at Jules's all morning, and by lunchtime I'm starting to feel much better. Until, that is, three o'clock approaches and I know that I've got to face my parents for tea.

Jules gives me a hug at the door and wishes me luck, and says I must call her when it's done, and I drive straight to my parents, feeling this cloud of dread hanging over me, and wondering how on earth to tell my parents.

My mother, being the witch that she is, can see something's wrong as soon as I walk in.

"You look like you've been crying," she says, stepping in for a closer look. "I hope everything's all right with you and Ed. What's the matter?"

"Nothing," I mutter, going into the living room and moving aside the newspaper in front of my father's face so I can kiss him hello.

My mother follows me in. "I know something's wrong, dear," she says firmly. "You may as well tell us now, get it out of the way, but I must say that I do hope it's nothing to do with Ed."

"Uh-oh," says my father, shuffling his feet into his slippers. "Girl talk. I'll leave you two alone, shall I? I'll be out in the garden."

"Come on, then, out with it."

"Leave me alone, Mum. I don't want to talk about it."

"Have you two had a lovers' tiff? I shouldn't worry about that, it'll blow over."

I sit there with my arms crossed, staring at the mute television picture, and refuse to speak as my mother perches on the edge of the armchair and mimics my pose.

"I hope it's nothing serious," she says, and before she has a chance to say anything more I stand up and march outside. "I'm going to see what Dad's done in the garden," I shout over my shoulder as I step through the french windows.

My dad's deadheading the roses, and I stand next to him as he hands me the dead heads in silence. My dad and I have never exactly had long conversations, but I know that the only way to do this is to tell him first, yet I don't know how to tell him, I don't know which words to use.

"Is it Ed, then?" my dad says slowly, not looking at me, just reaching up to a particularly high branch.

"Yes."

"Is it over?"

"Yes. Well. Not yet. But it will be tonight."

My dad just nods and carries on.

"D'you think I'm doing the right thing?"

My dad stops and finally looks at me.

"I couldn't tell you this before. I couldn't even tell your mother, not when she was so excited about having a rich son-in-law, but he wasn't for you, Libby. He wouldn't have made you happy."

"You didn't like him, did you, Dad?"

"It wasn't that I didn't like him," my dad says slowly. "It was just that he lives in a completely different world, and I worried that he didn't really approve of you the way you are, that he was trying to change you into something else."

God, I never realized my dad was that perceptive.

"And I didn't think you loved him," he continues, walking over to the bench at the end of the garden and sitting down before I join him.

"You see, the thing is," he says after we've both sat for a while in the sunshine, "the thing is that love is really the most important thing. I know it's hard for you to see it now"—he chuckles quietly—"but when I first laid eyes on your mother I thought she was fantastic, and I've never stopped loving her, not for a second. Oh yes, we've had our rough patches, and she can be a bit of an old battle-ax at times, but I still love her. That in-love feeling at the beginning settles down into a different, familiar sort of love, but it has to be there right from the start, otherwise it just won't work."

He looks at me and smiles. "You didn't love Ed. I could see that, but I couldn't say anything as long as you thought he was making you happy." He sighs, stands up and stretches before saying, "Do you want me to tell your mother?"

An hour later I'm sitting at the kitchen table watching my mother still wiping the tears from her eyes.

"What am I going to tell everyone?" she sniffles. "How could you do this to me?"

I shrug, not bothering to reply.

"You know, Libby, you may not find another man who treats you like Ed treated you."

"But, Mum," I sigh. "I don't love him. I'm never going to love him."

"And since when was that important? As I've said to you before, Libby, it's far more important to find a good man, and Ed is definitely a good man."

"But you and Dad were in love when you met."

"Pfff." She rolls her eyes. "It was so long ago I can't remember, but I'm sure it was about the same as you and Ed."

"Dad told me when he first saw you he thought you were fantastic."

Her face lights up and she beams as she says, "Did he? Oh well, I suppose I was a bit of a looker in those days."

"And he said you were madly in love." Okay, artistic license here.

My mother practically simpers. "He was terribly handsome himself, your father. When he was young."

"You see?" I persist. "I've never thought Ed is terribly handsome, and I've never felt madly in love with him, but I tried to pretend that that was okay, that I didn't need more, but now I've realized that I do. And I'm really sorry that Ed won't be your son-in-law, but you should want what's best for me, and it isn't him. I'm sorry, but it just isn't."

My mother opens her mouth as if she's about to say something, but, wonder of wonders, she doesn't seem able to think of anything to say, anything to prove me wrong. For once in my life I think she sees my point, and I think it's rendered her completely speechless.

So finally, after my traumatic afternoon, I head home in preparation for an even more traumatic evening, and maybe this is slightly sick, but I make far more of an effort tonight. I wear a biscuit-colored sweater and taupe trousers, and I'm tempted to carry the Gucci bag, but I don't, just in case he asks for it back. I do my makeup very slowly, making sure everything's perfectly blended, making sure I look my absolute best.

I'm ready well before the appointed hour, and pour a stiff vodka to steel myself, to provide me with Dutch courage, and I phone Jules for some moral support.

"You'll be fine," she tells me. "You need to be strong and know that you are doing the right thing."

So when the doorbell goes at seven-thirty, I walk toward it feeling strong, feeling calm, in control, but as soon as I open the door and see Ed standing on the doorstep, already looking crestfallen, I know that this really is going to be, as I predicted, one of the hardest things I've ever had to do.

But I also know, looking at his face, that I have to do it. That there is no going back. That I will not be tempted, even for an instant, to take the easy route and stay in this relationship, not even for one more night.

Ed leans forward and gives me a kiss, and I turn my head so he catches the corner of my mouth, and I look away quickly, so I don't have to see the confused expression on his face.

"You look beautiful," he says. "I've missed you." And he tries to pull me in for a kiss but I breeze away to pick up my coat.

"Shall we go?" I say, and I see that he doesn't understand; that he knows he's missing something, only he's not entirely sure what it is.

We walk out to the car in silence, and as I climb into the passenger seat I try to remember all the details of this Porsche, because chances are this will be the last time I'm ever in one. Ed turns on the engine and as we drive he keeps shooting me these worried glances, and I seem to have forgotten the art of making conversation, because I just can't think of anything to say to him.

"Poor Libby," Ed says finally, as we pull up to some traffic lights. "I can see you're exhausted. They've obviously been working you far too hard."

And I should feel something other than pity, but in that instant I do pity him, and I am enormously irritated by the fact that he cannot see what is blindingly obvious: that there is something drastically wrong, and that it's about to get a hell of a lot worse.

"I'm fine," I say. "Really. There are just some things I need to talk about with you."

There! The sad puppy-dog expression! Just as I predicted. Ed finally seems to cotton on to the fact that this isn't just my problem, this somehow involves him as well, and for the rest of the car journey he doesn't say a word. He puts some music on, bloody opera at that, and after a while I lean forward and switch it off, muttering that I've got a headache.

We get out of the car and go into the restaurant, and I am constantly aware that Ed is gazing at me with that ridiculous bloody expression. We sit down and Ed orders me a Kir, and then looks at me, waiting for me to say the words I now think he knows he's going to hear, the words he's terrified of hearing.

I'm not hungry. Really. Food is the very last thing on my mind, but the waiter brings the menu, and I have to make a pretense of looking at it and admiring the dishes, and eventually I order a green salad to start with, and penne as a main course, although right now I do not have a clue how I will manage to pass any food between my lips at all.

We sit in awkward silence, Ed looking at me, me looking at the other diners in the restaurant, wondering how they can be so normal, so happy, so coupley, when I am about to break this man's world apart.

And eventually, after much sighing and spluttering, I manage to get the first sentence out.

"Ed, we need to talk."

He doesn't say anything. Still. Just looks at me.

I sigh a bit more, and lapse into silence for a few more seconds, moving a few bits of lettuce around my plate, then putting down my knife and fork. I pick them up again, sigh, and put them down, pushing my hair back with my hands.

"Ed," I say softly. "This isn't working."

And he looks at me. Silently.

"This. Us. I'm not happy. I don't think I'm what you're looking for."

And he looks at me. Silently.

Now I expected arguments. I expected Ed to tell me that nothing in life is easy, least of all relationships, and that things need to be worked at, and that he would be willing to do anything to save this relationship, and perhaps my voice would become louder as I tried to explain that there is no point in working at it because I have made up my mind.

But I wasn't expecting this. Silence.

"I think you're wonderful," I say, going to take his hand to reinforce the point, but Ed moves his hand away, which shocks me slightly. I sit back and try again. "You are an incredible man. You are loving, giving, you have so many wonderful qualities, but I'm not the right woman for you."

At least I didn't say I'm not ready for a relationship, which is what you're always supposed to say in these circumstances, isn't it? Not that it makes any difference. No matter what the words are, the sentiments are the same: I don't love you enough to stay with you.

"You will meet someone one day who is perfect for you," I say earnestly, although even as I'm saying these words they sound patronizing as hell, "and I wish it were me. I wish I could be the woman you want me to be, but I can't."

And he looks at me.

The waiter comes over and says, "Is everything okay?", and Ed ignores him, still looking at me, but I force a smile and tell him it's fine but we're not that hungry, and he raises an eyebrow, takes the plates away.

And from there on in it is quite possibly the most awkward, uncomfortable, desperately sad evening I have ever spent. We sit there, Ed and I, in silence, Ed still looking at me, and me still looking around the restaurant, and when the bill finally comes we stand in silence and walk outside and into his car.

"Umm, I think it's probably a good idea for me to come back now and get my stuff." It could have waited, but I want this over, I want to be out of this, I don't want anything of mine to remain entangled with Ed's life.

So we go back to his house and Ed waits downstairs while I throw my nightdress, toothbrush, the few bits and pieces I had left there, into a bag, and when I come downstairs I find Ed sitting in the kitchen staring into space.

He looks at me, stands up and walks outside to the car, and this time he doesn't even attempt to use music to fill the silence that is becoming more and more oppressive by the second. And when, finally, we pull up outside my house, I look at him sadly, and twist his key off my key ring. "You'd better have this back," I say, and he nods.

"Can I call you?" I say, not because I want to call him, but because I can't just climb out of the car and say goodbye. Because I have never been in this position before, and I have absolutely no idea how to end this cleanly, how to, in fact, end this at all. Ed shrugs, and then, evidently having thought about it, shakes his head, and we sit there for a while, both of us presumably feeling like shit, and then I reach over, kiss him on the cheek and get out of the car.

He still hasn't uttered a word.

And later that night, while I'm lying in bed crying, because I never realized how much it would hurt to cause that much pain to someone who loves you, it suddenly strikes me that the reason Ed didn't say anything at all, all evening, was because he was holding back the tears.

Chapter 30

I don't bother getting up the next day. I ring the office at half past nine and croakily tell Jo I think I've picked up some kind of bug, and then burrow back under the duvet and sleep for another hour.

At half ten I wrap myself up in the duvet and collapse on the sofa, and for the next hour and a half I watch crap daytime television to take my mind off the fact that I am on my own again, and that I have been a complete fool. Because how can you tell your friends that you were so desperate to get married you said yes to the first candidate who asked, even when you didn't feel anything for him other than mild irritation and occasional bursts of friendship?

How do you say that you have spent the past few months planning, in meticulous detail, your wedding day, without giving a second thought to what lies beyond?

How can they understand that, despite my independence and so-called career, I was swept away by a fantasy, seduced by a lifestyle, and that I am evidently far more shallow than even I ever dreamed?

The day passes in a bit of a blur. I try not to think about it too much, which is bloody difficult, because when I do I just feel enormously sad, and when Jo rings from the office and says I've had an urgent message to call Amanda, I think, fuck it, at least it will take my mind off things.

"Amanda? It's Libby."

"Darling!" she exclaims. "Poor you! They told me you were ill and I said it could wait, but your receptionist insisted on disturbing you at home."

A likely bloody story. Jo would never insist on something like that, and I know that Amanda would have demanded that they give her my number.

"I'm okay," I croak. "Just a bit under the weather."

"You'll be fine soon," she says breezily. "It's just that I had a message from *Cosmo* this morning about wanting to interview me, and I wondered whether you could ring them back and set it up."

She rang me at home for that? When she could quite easily have picked up the phone herself and called, but then again, I suppose Amanda has to pretend she's a megastar, and hence cannot talk to anyone personally.

"Sure," I sigh wearily. "I'll ring them tomorrow."

"Great!" she enthuses. "Oh, and by the way, I had such a lovely time the other night. You're so lucky, getting engaged! To Ed McMann!"

"Actually," I groan, knowing that if I don't tell her now she'll be furious when she eventually finds out, "actually it's all off."

I think she stops breathing.

"Amanda? Are you still there?"

"Yes. Sorry. It's just that you two seemed so perfect together."

"Well, we weren't."

"But you're still together, surely, just not getting married yet?"

"No. It's over. Finished."

"Oh my God, poor, poor you. No wonder you're not at work. Are you okay?"

"I'm fine, and anyway, it wasn't his decision, it was mine."

"You're kidding?" She's laughing.

"No. Why?"

"You dumped Ed McMann?" she splutters. "Are you completely mad?"

"Jesus, Amanda, if you think he's so great, why don't you go out with him?"

There's another silence.

"Sorry," I mumble. "I didn't mean to be rude. He's just not for me, that's all."

"Right. Right. I completely understand. Oh well, plenty more fish in the sea," and a few seconds later she tells me her call waiting's going and she'd better answer it, so we say good-bye.

For a few minutes after I put the phone down I feel pretty damn awful. I mean, what if this is the last opportunity I'm ever going to have to get married? Maybe I have done the wrong thing. But then I remember his sad expression, his mustache, his habit of speaking French, and I know that I could never have gone through with it. Not for all the money in the world.

Later that afternoon, when Jules has left the fourth message of the day, I pick up the phone and she says she's coming over to check I'm okay.

"You look terrible," she says, as I open the door, still in pajamas.

"Thanks," I mutter. "What did you expect?"

"Sorry, I just didn't think you'd be this upset. You look like you've been crying for weeks."

"That's how I feel."

"Come here," she says, giving me a big hug, and when we pull apart I put the kettle on and make some tea, and we sit down as I give her all the details.

"I can understand how hard this is for you, but now you've got to get on with your life, and look on the bright side. You'll never make the same mistake again."

"I know," I sigh. "It's just that he seemed so hurt, he seemed to be in so much pain, and I don't think I've ever caused anyone that much pain before, and that hurts me."

"You were, as the saying goes, cruel to be kind. Far better to have done it now, you know that."

"Yes. I do know that. Oh God, now I've got to start going to parties again and getting back into that bloody singles scene."

"It's the best way of getting over someone."

"But I really don't want anyone else. I just want to be alone for a while."

"What about Nick?"

I shake my head. "I'm not ready for anything. And Nick isn't what I'm looking for either. Although"—and for the first time in what feels like days, a glimmer of a smile crosses my face—"although it might be worth it again for the sex."

"Don't you dare!" admonishes Jules. "You're not getting into that whole just a fling business again."

"Jules?" I sink back into the sofa and start giggling, "You know what? Thank God I'll never have to sleep with Ed again."

Jules starts to laugh. "Was it really that bad?"

"No," I say. "It was worse."

We carry on talking about it, and Jules makes me cups of tea, and generally treats me like an invalid, but I start to feel better, and as we talk I realize that, however upset I am, my foremost feeling is one of relief.

And then suddenly, unexpectedly, the doorbell interrupts our conversation, and we both jump. Jules looks at me and whispers, "Are you expecting anyone?"

"No," I whisper back. "Shit, I hope it's not Ed."

"Do you want me to get it?" she says, as I nod and settle back into the sofa, knowing that whoever it is Jules will send them packing, and praying that it isn't Ed, come to change my mind.

She comes back into the living room and right behind her, literally on her heels, is the very last person I expect to see right now. Nick.

Fuck.

He looks embarrassed. I want to die. I look like shit. My hair hasn't seen a brush since sometime early yesterday evening, I have no makeup on, save smudges of mascara underneath my eyes, and my flannel pajamas are hardly the stuff you'd want anyone other than your best friend to see. Ever.

"Umm. Hi," he says, as I wonder what the hell he's doing here and what the hell right he has to look so gorgeous when I look so terrible, and why the hell I didn't make an effort today just in case.

But what is he doing here?

"What are you doing here?"

Before he has a chance to answer, Jules, grinning broadly, has slipped her coat on and is already inching out the door. "Gosh, is that the time?" she says. "Must be off. I'll call you later." And with that she's gone.

"So?" I persist. "What are you doing here?"

"I was in the neighborhood and just happened to be passing, so I thought I'd drop a note in to apologize for what I said."

"What were you doing in this neighborhood?"

"Umm." I can see him desperately trying to think of something, and I watch him as his eyes flick around the room, looking for help. "Umm, I was dropping a video back."

"You borrowed a video from Ladbroke Grove when you live in Highgate?"

"Oh, okay. So what? So I called your office and they said you were ill and I thought I'd come and see if you were okay, and I feel so guilty about all that stuff I said, and everything else, well. Umm. You know . . ."

"There was no need to lie about it."

"Nice pajamas," he says, as I flush with embarrassment and tuck my legs underneath me to hide the faded knees (I told you they were old).

"Oh shut up and leave me alone," I harrumph. "Are you going to sit down or what?"

He sits. "So," he says, drumming on his knees, "how are you? You don't look ill, but"—and he peers at me closely—"you do look a little bit awful."

"Did you come here specifically to insult me or was there another reason?" I say, forgetting quite how terrible I look because quite frankly I no longer give a damn.

"Sorry, sorry. Anyway. I bought you a present." He fishes around in the pocket of his overcoat and, with a flourish, brings out a jar of Nutella.

"Nick! That's my favorite!" I'm already salivating as I reach out and grab it from him.

"I didn't want to bring you flowers," he says, grinning sheepishly. "That would be far too predictable. Anyway, that's my apology for the other day. I really am sorry, I just couldn't help myself."

"S'okay," I say, already undoing the cap and digging my index finger into the Nutella, sucking it clean, making noises of ecstasy.

"That's disgusting," Nick says, watching me. "Can't you use a spoon or something?"

I hold the jar out to him. "Want some?" And he grins as he digs his index finger into the jar too.

"So," he says eventually, "everything okay with Ed?"

"What do you mean?" I ask slowly.

"Well, it's just . . . after Saturday . . . I . . . well. I just wondered if everything was okay."

I sit for a few seconds debating whether or not to tell him, but I know he'll find out sooner or later, so he may as well hear it from me.

I take a deep breath. "Actually, no. It's not."

Nick raises an eyebrow questioningly.

"It's over."

"Oh my God," he says, genuinely shocked. "Not because of me? Not because of what I said?"

"No, you arrogant bastard, not because of you. Well, maybe a bit because of you, because I realized that you were right. Everything you said was true. He isn't what I want and in the long term I don't think it would work out."

"Jesus, Libby. I'm really sorry."

"Yeah, you look it."

"No, really. I am. I don't know what to say."

"There's nothing to say. It's fine. I'm fine. It's just one of those things."

"Do you want to talk about it?"

"There's nothing really to say. I kind of got swept away in a fantasy without thinking about what the implications were, and luckily I realized in time."

"Is Ed okay?"

"I don't know. I told him last night and he didn't say anything."

"What? Nothing?"

"Nope. Just sat there not saying a word all evening."

"Jesus," Nick exhales loudly. "Poor bastard."

"I know. I feel like a total bitch."

"No, you're not a bitch, Libby. At the end of the day you were just being cruel to be kind."

"Funny, that's exactly what Jules said."

"But it's true, and he'll get over it, he'll find someone else. You will too, you know."

"Forget it." I shake my head vehemently. "That's it. I'm taking a vow of celibacy. The last thing in the world I need right now is men."

"Even me?" I look up, and even though Nick is gorgeous, even though I do fancy him, I'll probably always fancy him, I know that I can't deal with this right now, that the last thing I need is to get involved with Nick on the rebound, so I shake my head sadly as I look him in the eye and try to smile.

"No," I say softly. "Even you."

• • •

Olly phones the next day.

"I heard," he says. "Mum called me this morning to tell me how upset she is. Are you okay?"

"I'm fine, Oll," I say. "I still feel a bit bruised, but actually I'm starting to feel relief."

Olly starts laughing. "I didn't want to say anything at the time but he was awful, you know."

"What?"

"Oh, come on. I can say it now, but he was a pompous old fart."

I can't handle hearing this from someone else I love. Sorry, not that I love Nick, but this is all a bit much for me. "Oll! Don't be so nasty. He wasn't that bad. Jesus, we only broke up a few days ago."

"Libby, I've never said this about any of your boyfriends in the past, but if you'd have married him I think I would have disowned you."

I'm truly, truly shocked. "Did you really feel that strongly?"

"Sorry, Libby, but not only was he fuck ugly, he was arrogant too. His only saving grace, as far as I can see, is his money. Oh, and the fact that he adored you."

I wince as the reality hits home. "Do you think everyone felt the same way?"

"I wouldn't like to hazard a guess. Look, I'm sorry if you're upset by this, but it's over now, I didn't think you'd mind me being honest."

"No," I sigh. "I don't. I just feel really stupid, but you know, Oll, he really wasn't a bad guy."

"Okay, fine. But he wasn't for you."

"No. I know that now. So has Mum forgiven me yet?"

"Nah. You know Mum. It'll take her about ten years to stop blaming you for finishing with Ed McMann."

"God, she's annoying. You'd think she'd have a bit of sympathy."

"Well, if it's any consolation she did say that she understood how you felt."

"You're kidding!"

"I know. I was as surprised as you. I think she's dreading telling the neighbors, but from what she was saying, I think she knows that it wasn't really right. She started banging on about her and Dad, and how in love they were. The woman's finally gone completely round the bend."

"Oh, Oll," I laugh. "You will never know how relieved I am."

It's been a month, and I really feel fine now. I've rediscovered my career, and no one at work can believe quite how hard I've been working, or quite how much I've achieved, but Jesus, isn't that the best way of getting over being single again?

And okay, so my evenings are slightly harder. Not that I want to be with Ed, it's just that I find myself at a loss for things to do, although my friends have been fantastic, and everyone's been inviting me to everything, and the best thing about going out with my friends again is that I know there's absolutely no possibility of me bumping into Ed. Ever.

Because now that I'm single again I've realized that I was living a total fantasy with Ed. I was wearing clothes I never thought I'd wear, going to places I never thought I'd go, and generally behaving in a way that absolutely, one hundred percent, was not me. You see, although I always thought that was the lifestyle I wanted, now that I've had a taste I know that I never again want to pretend to be something I'm not.

It is, however, a bit weird having to readjust to being single. Having to plan my diary meticulously so I'm not sitting at home every night eating takeaways, but I'd much rather be making the effort than be with Ed.

Although I'm still slightly thrown when Amanda rings me at work one day and out of the blue asks me if I'd mind if she went out with Ed.

"No, no," I say, in a falsely enthusiastic voice. "That's fine."

"Are you sure you don't mind?" she says, and I know that, even if I did, it wouldn't make a blind bit of difference to her.

They're probably perfectly suited, and Amanda's a far better social climber than I'll ever be, although my social aspirations seem to have gone down a peg or five.

"I'm delighted," I say, wondering whether they've already gone out, but I don't have to wonder very long, because later that afternoon Jo runs in brandishing the *Daily Express* and the late edition of the *Standard*.

"Okay," she says, perching her long legs on the edge of my desk. "Take a deep breath. Are you ready?"

I nod, and Jo opens the *Express* first and places it on my desk in front of me, and there, in Features, is a piece on London's new It couples. And taking pride of place with a large color photograph are Amanda Baker and Ed McMann. The picture is obviously from a paparazzo, and I note with interest how Amanda has perfected the pissed-off look and the pose of holding her hand in front of her face to pretend she doesn't want to be photographed.

"Jesus," I gasp. "That was quick work."

"Wait," laughs Jo. "It gets better," and with that she flings the *Standard* on top of the *Express* and opens it to the front page of the Homes and Property section, and in the Homes Gossip section is another picture of Amanda.

" '*Breakfast Break* presenter Amanda Baker,' " Jo reads out loud, " 'is selling her interior designed one-bedroom flat in Primrose Hill, where near neighbors include Liam Gallagher and Patsy Kensit and Harry Enfield. The estate agent has revealed she is moving to Hanover Terrace to be with her new love, Ed McMann. The flat has a picturesque roof terrace, and a beautifully presented aspect, and is now on the market at 185,000 through agents blah blah blah.' " Jo stops and checks to see how I'm taking it.

"Fucking hell," I splutter. "When the fuck did all this happen?"

Jo shrugs. "Dunno, but thank God you got out of it when you did. I mean, please. Look at that picture of Ed. Look at that 'tache. How could you?" And I examine the picture in the *Ex-*

press again and start to laugh. "I know." I shrug my shoulders. "What the hell was I thinking?"

Joe Cooper comes out of his office and sees us laughing, and he walks over to see what all the fuss is about.

"Are you okay with this?" he says, looking at me intently. "If there's any problem I'll put someone else on her account."

"No," I laugh. "I'm fine. I'm just bloody relieved it's not me in there."

*   *   *

"What are you doing on Saturday night?" Sal sounds excited.

"Noth-ing," I say slowly, always wary of committing myself before I know what I'm committing myself to. "Why?"

"We're having a party and you must come. Paul and I were talking the other night about how nobody has house parties anymore, in fact nobody even has parties."

"You're right. Weird, isn't it."

"Yup, so we've decided to have one. The biggest, loudest, fuck-off party you've ever been to."

I can already feel my own excitement rising at the prospect of a proper party, something to dress up for, something to look forward to.

"Are you having it in your place?" I'm picturing Sal's house in Clapham, her double reception room, the french doors opening on to a large garden.

"Yup, of course. Paul spent last weekend building a barbecue, and we're going to have a bar with sea breezes and martinis, and I've got to go out this afternoon and buy a load of fairy lights to string up in the trees."

I squeal with excitement. "Who's coming? Who's coming?"

"Everyone!" she shrieks. "No, but wait. I haven't finished. Paul's got a friend who's a DJ, and he's coming and bringing his recordy deck thingy to do all the music properly."

"Not techno rubbish?"

"Nah, for us old things? Nope, he says it's serious funk with a strong seventies flavor."

"Excellent, my favorite. What time will it start?"

"We thought around eight, and most people probably won't turn up until later, but I definitely want the hard core of close friends there early. Seriously, Libby, there'll be so much food and drink, and so many people, we think we're on to a bit of a winner."

"How many people?"

"We've got about eighty on the list, but everyone wants to bring friends because they're all saying the same thing, that no one has parties anymore."

"Sal, I cannot even begin to tell you how excited I am." And it's true. I am.

On Saturday afternoon I do something I haven't done for ages: I start getting ready for the party at three in the afternoon, and even though it brings back shades of my teenage years, I'm loving every minute of it.

I wash my hair in the shower, then smear a hot wax treatment all over it, cover it in a hot towel and spend the next hour chatting to Jules while it does its stuff.

I use an apricot facial scrub, then three different face packs, all of which I leave on for twenty minutes, and by the time I've finished my face is so tight and shiny you can almost see your reflection in it.

I dash out to the newsagent's and return with an armful of glossy magazines, because, chameleon woman that Jules so rightly once said I am, I haven't yet decided who I'm going to be tonight. Am I going to be sophisticated, trendy, funky or aloof? Do I slick back my hair, wear it in a spiky ponytail or have it loose and tousled around my shoulders? Should I stagger in heels, glide in pumps or stomp in sneakers?

Flicking through the magazines, I have a wild impulse to pluck my eyebrows into perfect, sardonic arches, so, grabbing the tweezers, I do just that, marveling at the difference it makes to my face, and wondering what else I can do to achieve model perfection.

At last, at precisely half past seven, I'm done. I survey myself in the mirror, in my floaty chiffon floor-length dress covered in a dusky flower print, demure until I walk, when the front slit sweeps aside revealing my newly tanned legs (I bought the fake stuff this morning and much to my amazement it left me with smooth brown legs, and no orange stripes). Flat strappy sandals complete the look, and I scoop my hair up into a messy ponytail, figuring I can always loosen it later, should I find someone to loosen it for.

I'm tempted to drive, but I'm planning to really let my hair down this evening (excuse the pun), and call a minicab instead. I make him stop outside the off-license so I can run in and get beer. I would normally have brought wine, but Sal warned me off, saying they were stuffing three huge dustbins with ice, and beer would be more appropriate.

There are only a handful of other people there when I arrive, and no one I recognize, but there's a buzz of excitement in the air already, and we all grin at each other and shake hands, chattering about how wonderful the weather is, and what a beautiful evening to have a party.

And the garden looks spectacular. Paul waves to me from behind the barbecue, the coals still jet-black, and behind him are makeshift wooden shelves, lined with what I can only assume must be Jell-O shots.

The trees surrounding the garden are all covered with tiny white fairy lights, but as Sal says as she shows me what they've done, we won't get the full effect until later. I say hi to Jools, the DJ, a scarily trendy and rather gorgeous bloke who's testing his system, too caught up in his music to notice the guests, other than to wave hello.

"I can't believe what you've done," I say, after Sal and I have knocked back a delicious lime Jell-O shot together. "This is amazing."

"Do you think everyone will turn up?" She shoots me a worried glance before looking around the garden. "I mean, hardly anyone's here yet."

"Don't worry." I check my watch. "It's only eight forty-five. People will start rolling in any minute now."

And sure enough, as if by magic, people do start arriving, and within an hour the garden is heaving, literally heaving, and the nicest thing about it is that, even though I don't know more than a handful of people, everyone feels like my closest friend, and I'm having a whale of a time dancing with some guy called Dave who isn't really my type but who's a bloody good dancer, and I know that I haven't had this much fun in ages.

And then Sal runs in and switches on the lights, and Paul moves around the garden, lighting the torches that have been strategically placed in the flower beds around the edge, and the whole night seems to take on a magical quality, and it does feel like the kind of night when anything could happen.

Soon there are crowds of people dancing, and although we're outside there's no breeze, and it's so hot I can feel beads of perspiration dotted on my forehead, and eventually I shout to Dave that I'm going to get a drink, and he nods, grins and turns to dance with the girl behind him.

The only drink to quench my thirst right now is good old tap water, so I push through the partygoers until I'm in Sal's tiny kitchen, and, leaning panting against the sink, I reach for a glass and gulp it down in about two seconds.

"John Travolta has nothing on you." I jump and with my hand on my heart I turn to see Nick lounging in the doorway with a big grin on his face.

"I hope you're not still in insulting mode," I say suspiciously.

"No!" He looks aghast. "I was serious. I never realized you were such a good dancer."

I shrug, secretly flattered. "How long have you been here?"

"Not long. We got here about fifteen minutes ago. Just in time to see those hips move."

I laugh self-consciously before asking, "We?" And then I notice her. Tall, skinny, cropped dark hair in that perfect gamine cut that you can only have when you are tremendously beautiful and live in Notting Hill, and of course she is tremendously beautiful, and I hate her. Instantly. Not that I'm jealous, in fact I'm happy that Nick has found someone. Well, okay. Maybe happy would be a bit of an overexaggeration, and why does she have to be so bloody beautiful?

"Hi." She smiles, and fuck. Her teeth are perfect. If I didn't know better I'd think she stepped straight out of an American advert for toothpaste. "I'm Cat." Great. This gets better. I shake her hand warily, and trying to be polite ask, "Is that your real name?"

"No." She shakes her head and laughs. "My real name's Sophie, but everyone used to tell me I looked like a cat at school and the name stuck." As I take in her catlike almond-shaped eyes, I note that her voice is immaculately polished, that lazy insouciant tone that immediately marks her out as a member of the upper classes. Or, at the very least, upper middle. I don't feel good enough, and I can't believe a friend of Nick is making me feel inadequate. Not that she's unfriendly, but she's so gorgeous I feel like a dumpy fraud, and I wish, instantly, that I had worn something more like her, a plain tank with baggy combat trousers and sneakers.

Nick smiles at me, waiting to see what I'll say next, probably proud as punch that he can show off his new girlfriend and she can be that gorgeous. Well, fuck you, I think, smiling at him graciously as I say, "I mustn't leave Dave alone for too long." And with that I sweep past them, ignoring his odd look at me, and go back into the garden.

Dave's still dancing with the other girl, and I tap him on the shoulder and grin at him as he turns, holds my hips, and moves his body perfectly in tune with mine. Over his shoulder I see Nick and Cat walk into the garden, and I throw my head back with laughter to prove I'm having a fantastic time, because Nick's looking at me and quite frankly he can go screw himself. Or Cat. Which he probably will be doing later.

Fuck.

Why does this bother me so much? Why do I care? After all, I was the one who turned him down. This time. And I really, really don't want a relationship right now, and even if I did, the last person I'd be interested in would be Nick. So why can't I take my eyes off the two of them, giggling together in the corner? Why do I feel a stab of jealousy when I remember how he used to do that with me? Why is he making her laugh and not me?

I resolve that there's only one solution to this dilemma, and that is to get drunk. Very, very drunk. I down my next sea breeze in one, much to Paul's astonishment, and then instantly start on another one. That's it. Much better.

Nick who?

I lose track of time, but soon the world suddenly becomes slightly hazy, and I know that I've probably had enough. More, and I'd run the risk of getting into bed only to have an attack of the deadly spins or, worse, throw up at the party. This is just perfect: hazy, friendly, just enough to make me happy. Who cares. I've got no problems other than who to dance with next.

Nick who?

Sal comes up and grabs me. "Did you see her?"

"See who?"

"Cat?"

I nod.

"She's gorgeous, isn't she? Who would have thought it."

"Yeah, who would have bloody thought it." And I give Sal a drunken kiss on the cheek and go staggering off to the barbecue, not that I'm hungry, it's just that drinking on an empty stomach is not exactly clever, and I know that if I don't have something to eat, anything, I really won't be very well at all.

I tear at a chicken kebab, not really tasting it, and, as I throw the stick merrily over my shoulder, I see Nick standing by himself on the other side of the garden, and when I catch his eye he starts walking over to me, so I head off in the other direction and make myself very busy flirting with a group of men I've never seen before, who seem more than happy to make me feel welcome.

Ha! That will show him. Nick has skulked off, presumably to find his precious Cat.

The party's in full throttle at two in the morning, despite the neighbors' complaints, but gradually people have started disappearing, and I haven't seen Nick for ages and I'm slightly drunk and very tired and actually I'm now wondering how I'm going to get home.

I go inside, to the living room at the front of the house, which is pitch-black and empty and, bumping into the coffee table en route, I finally make it to the sofa and slump down.

"Fuck!"

"Fuck!" I jump back up to hear rustling, then footsteps, then the light's switched on.

"Libby? What are you doing?"

"What am I doing? What the hell are you doing? I'm looking at Nick suspiciously as he starts to laugh, and it sobers me up instantly.

"I was just lying down for a bit. In the dark. I know you still have a soft spot for me but did you really have to leap on top of me to prove it?"

"I didn't," I grumble, sitting down again. "I didn't know you were there. Anyway. Where's Cat?"

"Gone. She's off to some other party."

"Why didn't you go too?"

"Her friends are far too Notting Hill for me. You know, they're all those bloody awful Trustafarians and I can't stand them."

I look at him strangely. "So how do you . . . I mean, do you find it difficult . . . well . . ."

Now it's Nick's turn to look at me strangely. "What? What are you talking about? Libby, you're pissed."

"No, no." I shake my head to clear it. "I mean, if you don't like her friends, well, it's just that I can't see her getting on with yours, you know, Moose and that lot, and, well . . ." I stumble into silence.

"Libby, what the fuck are you on about, all this friends stuff? Cat's always had bloody awful friends. Apart from the old ones, that is. Some of her friends at school were completely gorgeous when they were fourteen."

I still don't understand, and then it slowly dawns on me. "Cat's not your . . ."

"Sister? Yes. Why? What did you think?" And then he sees exactly what I thought and he roars with laughter. "God, Libby. You are fantastic. Cat? My girlfriend?" and he snorts with laughter again.

"Well, how was I to know?" I go on the defensive because what else can I do?

"I don't know," Nick splutters, wiping the tears from his eyes. "I just, well. Even if she wasn't my sister she wouldn't be my type."

"No?" I resist the urge to ask him what would be his type.

"No. Look, how are you getting home? You're not driving, are you?"

"No."

"Thank Christ for that. If you get a cab I'll come with you to check you get home okay, then I'll take it on home."

"Okay." Actually, with a bit of a shock I realize that I'm not sure it is okay. I'm not sure that I want him to go back to his home, but maybe I'm just drunk.

Nick calls a cab, and when it arrives we hug Sal and Paul goodbye and stumble into the backseat, and I pretend to look out the window for a bit, but the only thing I'm concentrating on is keeping my breathing as normal as possible, because the fact that it's so dark in here, so quiet, and that there is a gorgeous, sexy man sitting inches away from me, is making it very, very difficult to pretend that the only thing on my mind right now is friendship.

"Nearly there," he says, as the cab turns from Holland Park into Ladbroke Grove, and I smile and lean my forehead against the window, and wonder how I can prolong this evening, how I can make him stay, without putting myself on the line by actually asking him.

And then we're outside my house, and we just sit and look at each other as the cab driver taps his fingers impatiently on the wheel.

"Shit," Nick says suddenly, slapping his palm on his forehead. "I knew there was something I forgot to tell you."

"What?"

"It's a long story."

The cab driver, who's listening, sighs, and I say, "Do you want to come in? You can always call another cab."

"Great!" he says, reaching into his pocket and pulling some money out. "I'll get this." And he follows me inside the door.

Nick closes the front door behind me, and stands in front of the light switch, so as I fumble to turn on the lights I don't feel anything. Except Nick's hand. He grabs my wrist and doesn't say anything, and we stand in the darkness, just listening to the sound of each other's breathing and is it my imagination or does the breathing become heavier, slower?

And then Nick takes my hand, and possibly the darkness makes it feel like it's happening in slow motion, and he places it on his cheek, and I can't help myself, I start stroking his cheek, and then I'm tracing his lips, unable to see anything, but knowing his face so well from memory, and then his lips are open and he's gently sucking my finger, fingers, into his mouth.

I gasp, and Nick pulls me very gently toward him, and our mouths find each other's in the darkness and Nick leans back against the wall, holding me tightly, kissing me slowly, sensually, until I think my legs are going to give way.

And then very gently he moves around and, holding one arm out to guide him, falls slowly on to the sofa, pulling me with him, and within seconds my dress is around my waist, and I am moaning softly as he gently teases me with his tongue.

And the only thing that's going through my mind is how did I do without this for so long, how could I have ever settled for anything less?

Nick's hand moves up my thigh, stroking, gliding, as I groan into his neck and softly bite the skin there, and I reach down for his belt buckle and listen as his belt clicks undone, and I unzip the zipper of his trousers and stroke the length of his hard-on, and he inhales sharply before kissing me again.

We move to the bedroom, and we make slow, languorous, passionate love, and as he enters me, just at that moment before he starts moving inside me, three words enter my head: I've come home. It's difficult to explain, but there is something so familiar, so comfortable, so right about this moment, it suddenly feels like I am exactly where I should be, at exactly the right time, with exactly the right person.

I'm far too busy losing myself in the moment to dwell on this any further, and after we have made love, after we have murmured to each other and are lying in bed, side by side, with Nick's arm around my shoulders, gently stroking my hair, I remember he had said he had something to tell me.

I lean over and kiss him gently on the nose. "So what was it you had to tell me, then?" I whisper.

Nick opens his eyes. "Actually, there are two things."

"And they are?"

Nick pulls his arm out from under me and sits up in bed, turning to look at me as he takes my hand. "Libby," he says seriously, while I start to get worried. "I know you're probably not ready to hear this, but the thing is, well . . ." He stops.

"Yes?" I prompt, not having a clue what he is going to say.

"Well, the thing is that I think I might be in love with you . . ." My mouth falls open, and he gulps before continuing. "I'm not entirely sure because I don't think I've ever been in love before and it's a bit of a new feeling for me, but it's just that I haven't been able to stop thinking about you, and I don't know whether it was just the timing last time, that I wasn't ready, but now I think I am, and you may not even want me, but I just had to say something, because every morning when I wake up you're the first thing on my mind, and every night before I go to sleep you're the last person I think of, and I have no idea what you are going to say but I wanted you to know."

And I sit there, my heart racing at hearing these words, at hearing them from Nick, at seeing the expression in his eyes, which are glistening with emotion, and I know he means it. I know that he is in love with me, and not the way that Ed loved me, not for my potential, or because I would make a good wife, or for any of those other superficial reasons, but for me. He loves me for who I am.

And suddenly I realize that although I've never thought about being in love with Nick before, all the right ingredients are there. I fancy him. I like him. He's my friend. He makes me laugh. I love being with him. And I start to feel all sort of warm and glowy, and screw the other stuff. Screw the stuff about him having no money, and living in a bedsit, and not being what I thought I wanted. I'm just going to go with this and see where it ends up. I mean, no one says I have to marry the guy, for God's sake.

And anyway. I no longer think that marriage is the be-all and end-all. Not by a long shot. Not after Jules and Jamie, and as she put it the other day: "It's a long hard struggle, but I think we'll get there." I'm not sure I'm ready for that struggle. Not yet.

"Nick," I say, leaning down to kiss him. "No one's ever said that to me before. If I'm being really honest, I don't know how I feel about you yet, I think it's still a little early for me to talk about love, but I know that I do love being with you, and I'd like to give it a shot. Just being together, I mean, and seeing where it goes."

Relief spreads over his face.

"So," I say curiously, after we've snuggled up and kissed for a few minutes. "What was the other thing?"

"Other thing?"

"You said you had two things to tell me."

"Oh yes. That. It's nothing major"—and he grins—"I've got a publishing deal!"